The Idea of Creativity

Philosophy of History and Culture

Editor

Michael Krausz

Bryn Mawr College

VOLUME 28

The Idea of Creativity

Edited by

Michael Krausz, Denis Dutton and Karen Bardsley

BRILL

LEIDEN • BOSTON
2009

This book is printed on acid-free paper.

Library of Congress Cataloging-in-Publication Data

The idea of creativity / edited by Michael Krausz, Denis Dutton, and Karen Bardsley.
   p. cm. -- (Philosophy of history and culture, ISSN 0922-6001 ; v. 28)
Includes index.
ISBN 978-90-04-17444-3 (hardback : alk. paper) 1. Creative ability. I. Krausz, Michael. II.
Dutton, Denis. III. Bardsley, Karen. IV. Title. V. Series.

BF408.I36 2009
153.3'5--dc22

2008055174

ISSN 0922-6001
ISBN 978 90 04 17444 3

CONTENTS

PART TWO

CREATIVITY, IMAGINATION, AND SELF

PART THREE

FORMS AND DOMAINS OF CREATIVITY

ACKNOWLEDGMENTS

The editors gratefully acknowledge Margaret Boden, John M. Carvalho, David Davies, Berys Gaut, Michael Krausz, Peter Lamarque, Tomas Leddy, Paisley Livingston, and Dean Keith Simonton, who wrote new works especially for this volume.

Eight of the essays appeared in an earlier volume, *The Idea of Creativity in Science and Art*, edited by Denis Dutton and Michael Krausz, published in 1981 by Martinus Nijhoff Publishers, The Hague (series editor, Harold Durfee). Those are the works by Larry Briskman, Rom Harré, Carl Hausman, Albert Hofstadter, I. C. Jarvie, Arthur Koestler, Michael Polanyi, and F. E. Sparshott. We thank Harold Durfee who, in the name of Martinus Nijhoff Publishers, granted the rights to reprint the Jarvie, Hofstadter, and Harré works. In addition, the following holders graciously granted copyright permissions as follows:

Briskman's work originally appeared as "Creative Product and Creative Process in Science and Art," *Inquiry* 23 (1980), 83–106. We wish to thank Taylor & Francis (UK) Journals for permission to reprint the work in this volume. Hausman's work originally appeared as "Criteria of Creativity," *Philosophy and Phenomenological Research* 40 (1979) 237–249. We extend thanks to Blackwell Publishing Company for permission to reprint the work. Koestler's work originally appeared as "Three Domains of Creativity," in *Challenges of Humanistic Psychology*, edited by F. T. Bugental (McGraw Hill, 1967), 30–40. No copyright is currently in force for this work. We express our appreciation to John Polanyi for his permission to reprint Michael Polanyi, "The Creative Imagination," which originally appeared in *Chemical and Engineering News* 44 (1966): 85–93. Sparshott's work originally appeared as, "Every Horse Has a Mouth: A Personal Poetics," *Philosophy and Literature 1* (1977). We thank Johns Hopkins University Press for the permission to reprint the work in this volume.

Finally, we could not have produced the volume without the tireless and expert assistance of Elizabeth D. Boepple. The editors and authors are extremely grateful to her.

CONTRIBUTORS

KAREN BARDSLEY took the PhD in Philosophy from McGill University in 2004. She is currently an Assistant Professor of Philosophy at Morehead State University in Kentucky. Her research interests include philosophy of film, philosophy of mind, aesthetics, and ethics. In aesthetics, she has written on the roles of illusion and imagination in cinematic experience, the role of perception in the interpretation of visual representations, and the value of real world beliefs to the assessment and categorization of fictional works. In ethics, she has written on the rationality of feelings of gratitude towards nature.

MARGARET BODEN is Research Professor of Cognitive Science in the School of Cognitive and Computing Sciences at the University of Sussex, UK, where she works on the philosophy and history of psychology and artificial intelligence, with a particular focus on the phenomena of purpose and creativity. Her notable works include *Artificial Intelligence and Natural Man* (1977/1987) and *The Creative Mind: Myths and Mechanisms* (1991/2004), which has been translated into many languages worldwide. In 2002, Boden received an OBE (Order of the British Empire) for services to cognitive science.

LARRY BRISKMAN (1947–2002) took the PhD from University of Edinburgh. He studied under Karl Popper, Imre Lakatos, and Paul Feyerabend. Popper remained the dominant intellectual influence on Briskman's philosophical outlook. Briskman's academic publications were mostly in the philosophy of science but included forays into the philosophy of logic and creativity in science and art. His most signal contribution to the Popperian tradition was his articulation and development of "the epistemological bootstrap." Briskman's last major publication was "Rationality, Science, and History" (1990).

JOHN M. CARVALHO took the PhD in Philosophy from Duquesne University in 1987. He is currently Associate Professor and Chair of the Philosophy Department at Villanova University, where he teaches courses on the philosophy of contemporary music, philosophy of film, history of philosophy, critical theory, post-structuralism, psychoanalysis, and aesthetics. Recent publications include, "Dance of Dionysus: The Body in Nietzsche's Philosophy of Music" (2003); "Fact and Fiction: Writing the Difference between Suicide and Death in the Life of Michel Foucault" (2006); and "Subtle Bodies and the Other Jouissance" (2008). A book of essays titled *Thinking with Images* is nearing completion.

DAVID DAVIES took the PhD in Philosophy from University of Western Ontario in 1987. He is currently Associate Professor in the Department of Philosophy at McGill University. He is the author of *Art as Performance* (2004) and *Aesthetics and Literature* (2007), and editor of *Terrence Malick: The Thin Red Line* (2008). Davies has published articles on philosophical issues in the philosophies of film, photography, literature, and the visual arts, as well as topics in metaphysics, philosophy of mind, philosophy of language, and philosophy of science. Davies is currently working on a book on the philosophical foundations of the performing arts.

DENIS DUTTON is currently Professor of Philosophy at the University of Canterbury, New Zealand. His areas of specialty include aesthetics and the philosophy of art. His recent research focuses on Darwinian applications in aesthetics: the manner in which human interests, pleasures, and tastes are shaped by the evolution of the human species. He edits the *Journal Philosophy and Literature* and the Internet webpage, *Arts & Letters Daily* (http://aldaily.com/). He is author of *The Art Instinct: Beauty, Pleasure, and Natural Selection* (2008).

BERYS GAUT took the PhD from Princeton University in 1991 and is currently a Senior Lecturer in Moral Philosophy at University of St. Andrews in Scotland. His research interests include aesthetics, especially its relation to ethics and to theories of creativity, philosophy of film and film theory, moral theory, and Kant's moral philosophy. He is author of *Art, Emotion, and Ethics* (2007) and is currently completing *A Philosophy of Cinematic Art* (forthcoming, 2009). Gaut is co-editor of *The Routledge Companion to Aesthetics*, and is Chairman of the Management Committee of *The Philosophical Quarterly*.

ROM HARRÉ taught philosophy of science at Oxford University during 1954–1994. He is currently Emeritus Fellow of Linacre College, Oxford. Harré has published widely on topics in the philosophy of physics and chemistry. Recently he has turned to studies in discursive psychology. Harré's publications include *Great Scientific Experiments: 20 Experiments that*

Changed Our View of the World (1981); *Personal Being: A Theory for Individual Psychology* (1984); *Motives and Mechanisms: An Introduction to the Psychology of Action* (with David D. Clarke and Nicola De Carlo, 1985); *Varieties of Realism* (1986); *The Discursive Mind* (1994); and *One Thousand Years of Philosophy: From Ramanuja to Wittgenstein* (2000). His most recent book is *Wittgenstein and Psychology: A Practical Guide* (with Michael A. Tissaw, 2005). In 1971, Harré, with Paul F. Secord, founded *The Journal for the Theory of Social Behaviour*, with which he is still associated. Currently, he teaches at Georgetown University in Washington, D.C. Harré is also the Director of the Centre for the Natural and Social Sciences at the London School of Economics.

CARL R. HAUSMAN took the PhD in philosophy at Northwestern University in 1960 and is Professor Emeritus at Pennsylvania State University. Hausman has published "The Role of Aesthetic Emotion in R. G. Collingwood's Conception of Creative Activity" (1992); "Charles S. Peirce's Evolutionary Philosophy" (1997); "Aaron Ridley's Defense of Collingwood Pursued" (1998); *Classical American Pragmatism: Its Contemporary Vitality* (1999); and "Charles Peirce's Evolutionary Realism as a Process" (2004).

ALBERT HOFSTADTER (1910–1989) took the PhD in Philosophy at Columbia University in 1936. He taught at Columbia during 1950–1967, University of California at Santa Cruz during 1967–1975, and at New School for Social Research in New York during 1976–1978. He published *Philosophies of Art and Beauty: Selected Readings in Aesthetics from Plato to Heidegger* (edited with Richard Francis Kuhns, 1964); *Truth and Art* (1965); *Agony and Epitaph: Man, His Art, and His Poetry* (1970); and "On the Interpretation of Works of Art" (1979). He also translated and wrote introductions for Martin Heidegger's *Poetry, Language, and Thought* (1971) and *The Basic Problem of Phenomenology* (1982).

I. C. JARVIE took the PhD in Philosophy from the University of London in 1961. He studied scientific method under Karl Popper, and the arts under the influence of Ernst Gombrich. His other great intellectual debt is to Ernest Gellner. These remain his intellectual compasses. A member of the Royal Society of Canada, Jarvie retired from full-time teaching at York University in 2003. He continues active contributions to scholarship, most notably as Managing Editor of the journal *Philosophy of the Social Sciences*. He is author of *Movies and Society* (1970), *Philosophy and the Film* (1987), and numerous other studies in sociology, philosophy, and film history. Most recently, with Joseph Agassi he co-authored *A Critical Rationalist Aesthetics* (2008).

ARTHUR KOESTLER (1905–1983) studied science and psychology at the University of Vienna and settled in Israel. He served as science editor for *Ullstein.* Koestler's publications include *Arrow in Blue* (1952); *The Invisible Writing* (1954); *The Yogi and the Commissar* (1945); *The Sleepwalkers* (1959); *The Lotus and the Robot* (1960); and *The Thirteenth Tribe* (1976). Among his many novels, Koestler's magnum opus was *Darkness at Noon* (1940). Koestler received the Sonning Prize from the University of Copenhagen and an honorary doctorate from Queen's University, Ontario, both in 1968. In 1972, Koestler received an OBE (Order of the British Empire), and in 1974, he was named a Companion of the Royal Society of Literature.

MICHAEL KRAUSZ took the PhD in Philosophy from the University of Toronto in 1969. He is currently the Milton C. Nahm Professor of Philosophy at Bryn Mawr College. Since 2002, he has also been on the Liberal Arts faculty of the Curtis Institute of Music in Philadelphia. Among Krausz's publications are *Rightness and Reasons: Interpretation in Cultural Practices* (1993); *Varieties of Relativism* (with Rom Harré, 1995); *Limits of Rightness* (2000); and *Interpretation and Transformation: Explorations in Art and the Self* (2007). He is editor and contributor to nine other volumes on such topics as relativism, rationality, cultural identity, metaphysics of culture, creativity, interpretation of music, and the philosophy of R. G. Collingwood. Andreea Ritivoi (2003) edited a volume dedicated to Krausz's philosophical work, *Interpretation and Its Objects: Studies in the Philosophy of Michael Krausz.* As a visual artist, Krausz has had twenty-one solo exhibitions in galleries in the United States, Scotland, and India. As a musician, he has been guest conductor of several professional symphony orchestras in Bulgaria. Since 2005, Krausz has been the Artistic Director and Conductor of The Great Hall Chamber Orchestra at Bryn Mawr.

PETER LAMARQUE is Professor of Philosophy at the University of York, UK. During 1995—2008, he was Editor of the *British Journal of Aesthetics.* He is the author of *Fictional Points of View* (1996) and *The Philosophy of Literature* (2008), and co-author, with Stein Haugom Olsen, of *Truth, Fiction, and Literature: A Philosophical Perspective* (1994). He also edited *Phi-*

losophy and Fiction (1983); *Concise Encyclopaedia of Philosophy of Language* (1997); and an anthology (with S. H. Olsen), *Aesthetics and the Philosophy of Art: The Analytic Tradition* (2003).

THOMAS LEDDY took the PhD in Philosophy from Boston University in 1983. He is currently Professor and Associate Chair of the Philosophy Department at San José State University in California, where he specializes in aesthetics and the philosophy of art. He has authored an article on John Dewey's aesthetics in the on-line Stanford Encyclopedia of Philosophy. Other publications include, "The Socratic Quest in Art and Philosophy" (1993) and "Everyday Surface Aesthetic Qualities: 'Neat,' 'Messy,' 'Clean,' 'Dirty'" (1995). He is a member of the American Society for Aesthetics and is an avid photographer. One of Leddy's works is displayed in the collection of the city of San José, California.

PAISLEY LIVINGSTON took his PhD at Johns Hopkins University in 1981. He is currently Professor and Chair of the Department of Philosophy at Lingnan University, Hong Kong. He is the author of *Ingmar Bergman and the Rituals of Arts* (1982); *Literature and Rationality: Ideas of Agency in Theory and Fiction* (1991); *Models of Desire: René Girard and the Psychology of Mimesis* (1992); *Art and Intention: A Philosophical Study* (2005); and *Art and Intention* (2005). He also co-edited (with Berys Gaut) *The Creation of Art: New Essays in Philosophical Aesthetics* (2003).

MICHAEL POLANYI (1891–1976) completed a medical degree in 1913 and his PhD in physical chemistry in 1917 at the University of Budapest. He moved to Berlin to a position at the Kaiser Wilhelm Institute for Fiber Chemistry in 1920, and in 1923, he became director of the chemical kinetics research group in Fritz Haber's Institute for Physical Chemistry and Electrochemistry. Polanyi's best-known work was in the field of chemical kinetics and dynamics. His philosophy of science argues that scientific knowledge is tacit in character: it cannot be spoken, only demonstrated and imitated. Among his many publications, his first group of philosophical essays appeared in 1946 under the title *Science, Faith, and* Society, followed by *Personal Knowledge: Towards a Post-Critical Philosophy* (1958); *The Tacit Dimension* (1966); and *Meaning* (1975).

DEAN KEITH SIMONTON took the PhD in Social Psychology from Harvard University in 1975. He is currently Distinguished Professor of Psychology at the University of California, Davis. His many publications examine various aspects of genius, creativity, leadership, talent, and aesthetics. Among his nine books are, *Genius, Creativity, and Leadership* (1984); *Psychology, Science, and History* (1990); *Greatness* (1994); *Origins of Genius* (1999); *Great Psychologists* (2002); *Creativity in Science* (2004); and *Genius 101* (forthcoming). His awards include the William James Book Award, the Sir Francis Galton Award for Outstanding Contributions to the Study of Creativity, the Rudolf Arnheim Award for Outstanding Contributions to Psychology and the Arts, the George A. Miller Outstanding Article Award, the Theoretical Innovation Prize in Personality and Social Psychology, the President's Award from the National Association for Gifted Children, the Mensa Award for Excellence in Research, and the Robert S. Daniel Award for Four-Year College/University Teaching.

F. E. SPARSHOTT was educated in Britain at King's School, Rochester, and Corpus Christi College, Oxford, where he took the MA in 1950. He taught philosophy at the University of Toronto during 1950–1991. He has been a member of the League of Canadian Poets since 1968, and was its president during 1977–1979. He was awarded the President's Medal for Best Single Poem by the University of Western Ontario (1958), and won the first prize for poetry in the CBC Radio Literary Competition (1981). He has been a Fellow of the Royal Society of Canada since 1977 and Doctor of Laws, honoris causa, University of Toronto since 2000. He has published nine books of academic prose, most recently, *The Future of Aesthetics* (1998), and twelve volumes of verse, most recently *Scoring in Injury Time* (2006). Other works include: *The Cave of Trophonius and Other Poems* (1983); *Storms and Screens* (1985); *Sculling to Byzantium* (1989); *Taking Life Seriously: A Study of the Nicomachean Ethics* (1994); *The Hanging Gardens of Etobicoke* (2nd ed., 1994); *Views from the Zucchini Gazebo* (1994); and *Home from the Air* (1997). Currently, Sparshott is University Professor Emeritus, University of Toronto, and Professor Emeritus of Philosophy, Victoria College of the University of Toronto.

INTRODUCTION

Michael Krausz

This volume collects seventeen essays that address the question, What is Creativity? This general question encompasses more specific ones that the authors address in the three parts of the volume. Here, then, are those specific questions along with abbreviated summaries of the essays that answer them.

Part One
Explaining Creativity: Persons, Processes, and Products

Part One addresses these questions: What are the criteria for creativity? Should we assign logical priority to creative persons, creative processes, or creative products? Is creativity essentially mysterious? Can creativity be explained? If creativity is explainable, can it be explained naturalistically? Is creativity unpredictable? Is creativity goal-directed? What role does skill play in creativity? How does a creative product relate to medium and work?

Carl Hausman offers the following four criteria of creativity. Created outcomes have intelligible structures that are irreducible; created outcomes are unpredictable; the structures of created outcomes are inherently and usually instrumentally valuable; and the acts that lead to created outcomes include an element of spontaneity. In emphasizing the idea that the intelligibility of a creative outcome is discernible in a structure that is unprecedented and unpredictable, Hausman resists a determinism that excludes novelty or newness of intelligibility.

Larry Briskman asserts that, in contrast to creative persons and creative processes, the creativity of the product is what has logical priority. We can only identify persons and processes as creative via our prior identification of products as creative. A scientific or artistic product, for example, is not creative because a creative person or a creative process produced it. Instead, we deem persons to be creative persons and their processes to be creative process only in light of the prior evaluation of the product as a creative product. We deem the person involved and the psychological process involved as being creative because they succeed in producing a product that we deem to be creative.

I. C. Jarvie holds that creativity is interesting precisely because and to the extent that it is uniquely mysterious. Only with repeatable events is explanatory progress made. Yet creative achievements are unique events. They are not repeatable. Hence, creativity has something inexplicable about it. Jarvie's view contrasts with the thought that nothing is mysterious, or inexplicable.

In contrast, Dean Simonton argues that we should bring the study of creativity into the scientific mainstream. Rather than representing some mysterious process, we should examine creativity from a naturalistic perspective. He suggests that creative processes function analogously to those that govern the evolution of species. Accordingly, Darwin's theory can be considered an implicit theory of creativity.

Berys Gaut affirms that an act is creative insofar as it produces something innovative and valuable. Further, as long as one merely follows a routine, one is not being creative. A brute, mechanical search does not require insight, imaginative leaps, or anything other than persistence. At the same time, we should allow a role for the skillful exploitation of chance. Gaut asserts that the creative process can but need not be goal-directed. He opposes anti-teleological models of creativity.

Peter Lamarque is concerned with the relation between medium and created work. He asks whether a literary work, for example, is identical to its text. Lamarque affirms that the work a maker undertakes to create involves the manipulation of a vehicular medium constrained by an artistic medium. Completed works possess intentional properties of an aesthetic, artistic, or representational kind. Further, the possession of those properties is possible only in an appropriate cultural context. Established practices must exist to make possible the existence of works, be they paintings, sculptures, or symphonies. In short, a work must be a cultural entity.

Part Two
Creativity, Imagination, and Self

Part Two addresses these questions: Is creativity essentially inspirational or rationalistic? How do intuition and awareness relate to creativity? What is the relation between creativity and habits of attention? How does creativity relate to self-transformation? How does creativity relate to our sense of place in the world? How does our knowledge of the circumstances of creativity effect our appreciation of its products?

Paisley Livingston explores the conceptual space defined by two extreme theses—the inspirationist idea that artistic creativity is a sudden, involuntary, and ultimately inexplicable event, and the rationalistic counterthesis, which characterizes artistic creation as a deliberate selection from amongst an array of previously known options. Livingston adduces Henri Poincaré's surmisal that while unconscious mental process blindly generates combinations, the aesthetic sensibility scans the results. That sensibility singles out those results that are especially pleasing, elegant, harmonious, or well proportioned. Livingston also suggests that in moments of incubation, when artists or scientists have set aside their work and have taken up some unrelated pastime, their minds are not idle.

Michael Polanyi calls all thoughts of things that are not yet present, acts of the imagination. In turn, intuition integrates those acts. The final sanction of discovery lies in the recognition of a coherence that intuition detects and accepts as real. Intuition informs the imagination, which in its turn releases the powers of intuition. Accordingly, Polanyi recognizes two kinds of awareness: awareness of the object at which we are looking, and awareness of innumerable clues that we integrate to the sight of the object. We have a subsidiary awareness of the clues that bear upon the object of our focus. Intuitive powers integrate the largely unspecifiable clues, and the process of integration is not fully definable.

Francis Sparshott suggests that poets develop a uniquely personal way of finding themes and ways of working them. Poets are known for their sustained habit of attention. As they scrutinize the world for themes, they look ceaselessly for ways of proceeding. Their style is a style of search, not a habit of acceptance. Their minds are restless scanners. Though poets cannot describe it fully, they know nothing better than their way of proceeding. They know what to do next. The style of truly original and creative poets determines their way of changing and developing. Innovators astonish us by the total development of their practice, not by each work taken singly.

Michael Krausz outlines the personal program that motivates his artistic production and self-transformation. His personal program values process over product, and accommodates nondualistic experiences as benchmarks of his creative life journey. He regards self-transformation as a creative product. This program resists any sharp distinction between creative process and creative product. Creative persons, processes, and products are not fundamentally independent. Krausz suggests, therefore, that we should substitute the idea of a creative work for the idea of a creative product. For the idea of work incorporates processes and products. 'Work' is a verb *and* a noun: a *doing* and that which *is done*. A work or a 'life-work' provides the normative context in which thingly products may have meaning and significance. Accordingly, a self and its transformation may be a creative work.

Albert Hofstadter holds that underlying the creative process is the passion to be free: to find selfhood in, and with, what is not self, to find self-recognition in the other. Hofstadter allies this suggestion to Martin Heidegger's phrase, 'gathered in the appropriation.' Hofstadter suggests that the creative artist—the photographer, for example—seeks a form-content unity to which he can give himself and which will give itself to him. The creative artist searches for a new reconciliation of oppositions in a living and non-mechanical unity.

David Davies argues that our knowledge of the history of the making of an artwork can bear upon our appreciation and evaluation of it. In that sense, such knowledge can be artistically relevant. Davies urges that an action or process is creative only if it manifests novelty that we view as valuable in the context of practice. It does so according to the intentional and imaginative agency of the individual concerned. Our characterization of the artist's engagement with the artistic medium will locate that activity in an artistic context to which various moves can be seen as responses. Creativity itself and ascriptions of creativity make sense only against the background of a tradition. So, creativity itself is a characteristic of the process, not of the product, despite its being only by virtue of merits of the product as embedded in its context of generation that the process is properly so viewed.

Part Three
Forms and Domains of Creativity

Part Three addresses these questions: What forms of creativity are there? How do forms of creativity relate to different domains of human activity? How do creative scientists make phenomena intelligible? Can a reader of a creative literary work, for example, also be a creator of it? Rather than adding something to the world, does creativity involve subtracting something from the world?

Margaret Boden distinguishes between historical creativity (H-creativity)—involving new ideas not already known by other people—from psychological or personal creativity (P-creativity)—involving ideas that are new for the individual concerned. An idea that is H-creative must also be P-creative, but not vice versa. Boden also distinguishes among three types of creativity: combinational, exploratory, and transformational. Combinational creativity involves the generation of unfamiliar combinations of familiar ideas. In exploratory creativity, the existing stylistic rules or conventions are used to generate novel structures. Transformational creativity involves an alternation in a style of thinking or conceptual space. Here structures can now be generated which could not be generated before. Transformationally creative thinkers may vary old rules, or they may drop or add new ones.

Arthur Koestler believes that all creative activity falls into one of three categories or some combination of them. These three categories of creativity are artistic originality, scientific discovery, and comic inspiration. Yet no sharp break separates them. The creative act is for the scientist, as it is for the artist, a leap into the dark, where both are equally dependent upon fallible intuitions. Conscious and unconscious processes enter into all three forms of creative activity. Conscious thinking generally plays only a subordinate part in the brief, decisive phase of the creative act itself. Significant elements of irrationality are embedded in the creative process. The creative act consists in combining previously unrelated structures such that the emergent whole contains more than its constituent parts. Scientific discovery and artistic inspiration share an underlying pattern, which is a temporary regression, culminating in the bisociative act that combines previously separate frames of perception or universes of discourse.

Rom Harré affirms that the intelligibility of scientific theory derives from the intelligibility of the novel entities and forms conceived in the creative scientific imagination. Science is produced by the existence of an organizing conception that is brought to the phenomena. The conception creates the possibility of perceiving similarities that bring the phenomena into the same class and supplies generalities. Harré emphasizes the explanatory power of a designating icon and its power to make our experience of the world intelligible. Creativity in science is found in the icons of the reality beyond yet productive of our experience. Our scientific icons are depictions of the processes that bring the patterns of phenomena into being. Further, a great scientist cites supporting evidence, not as premises or as evidence, but as anecdotes illustrative of the power of the theory to make certain widely selected phenomena intelligible.

Thomas Leddy claims that the many interpretations of a text are generated by the interaction of the text with its readers. Each reading of a text is a construction insofar as it creates an understanding of it. Leddy holds that creativity is a process that is continuous—from the initiation of the work through to its so-called completion, and then on into the work of different readers and critics. The reader does not replace the writer as the creative artist, yet the reader should not be excluded from the creative process. Rather, readers continue the creative process begun by the writer through their interpretation of the work. Leddy affirms further that when we interpret a literary work, we interpret our worlds and ourselves. Accordingly, the understanding of creativity in such cases requires these layers of dialectical confrontation: between originating writer and interpreting reader, between interpreting readers, and among various forces within the culture. Differing interpretations may reflect different and competing general attitudes and philosophies of life.

Guided by the works of French philosopher Gilles Deleuze, John Carvalho compares creativity in philosophy with creativity in art. Creativity in art cannot add something of interest to the world by merely repeating or modifying what is already in it. Rather, creativity in art should tear away what obscures something exceptional. Creativity in art strips away the distracting, reductive, and mundane elements that populate the Whole, toward a creation that stands out in its singularity. This singularity may appear new and original in our experience. Yet, while overlooked, it was always there. The same point applies to creativity in philosophy. For Deleuze, a 'universal thought flow' already exists and is replete with everything that has *been thought*. The creative philosopher extracts a concept from this universal thought flow by subtracting from it everything that is distracting, idle, and common. The philosopher subtracts the noise, babble, and nonsense in this flow and draws it toward a concept that opens onto what is singular, irregular, and different.

These abbreviated summaries serve as an invitation to reflect upon the challenging question, What is creativity? The essays discuss a range of interrelated issues. They propound differing views, urge contrasting emphases, and reflect diverse philosophical idioms. The aim of this collection will have been served if its reader gleans the rich and varied ways of understanding the idea of creativity.

PART ONE

EXPLAINING CREATIVITY:
PERSONS, PROCESSES, AND PRODUCTS

CHAPTER ONE

CRITERIA OF CREATIVITY[1]

Carl R. Hausman

I

In *The Courage to Create*,[2] Rollo May defines creativity, in its 'authentic'
form, as "the process of *bringing something new into being*."[3] In the course
of his discussion, he considers several kinds of experiences, which he
claims to be essential moments of the creative process: 'encounter,'
'courage,' and a 'drive toward form,' among others. Beyond this, there
is little attempt to explore the presuppositions and the complexities of
the concept of bringing something new into being.

I do not cite May's book in order to criticize it or to minimize its
potential value for the layman and perhaps for some psychologists and
psychiatrists. Without question, the book offers an interesting perspective on some of the problems connected with the creative process.
However, as in so much of the literature on the subject, the book displays a conspicuous lack of attention to the task of providing a conceptual framework within which creativity is to be discussed.

The purpose of the following remarks is to suggest what I believe
are the most obvious, basic expectations without which neither an
activity nor its outcome would be regarded as an example of creativity.
My account of these expectations attempts to specify criteria or necessary conditions of creativity based upon a characterization of newness.
These criteria should serve as the fundamental limits of a conceptual
framework, which must be presupposed in a discussion of creative
acts. But let me emphasize at the outset that I do not intend to write
'creatively' about creativity. Nor do I intend to rest my case on a series

---

[1] The following discussion is a version of a paper presented at a session of The
Society for the Philosophy of Creativity, Pacific Division, in conjunction with the
American Philosophical Association meetings, Berkeley, California, 26 March 1976.
Reprinted from *Philosophy and Phenomenological Research* 40 (1979): 237–249.
[2] Rollo May, *The Courage to Create* (New York: Norton, 1975).
[3] Ibid., 39.

of examples, which are assumed to be instances of creativity. To the contrary, what is needed at the beginning of a study of creativity is a sober, straightforward structural account—an account that avoids as much as possible metaphorically couched expressions of praise for what is creative, and which postpones claims to provide immediate 'insight' into the nature of creativity. Thus, in what follows, I shall attempt to lay out a bare conceptual skeleton, leaving for other discussions the attempt to fill out the flesh for the skeleton.[4] My approach is phenomenological in its basic orientation, but phenomenological primarily in the sense that I intend to focus on the most general, necessary ingredients in creative achievement.

An attempt to find criteria can be undertaken in one or more of three possible ways. We can proceed inductively with no preconceptions about which things are viewed as examples of creativity. Thus, we can simply begin with an enumeration and a description of processes that have been called 'creative' and outcomes that have been called 'creations.' Or, we can begin by stipulating which instances are to be included and which excluded. Finally, we can combine these approaches. If we were to proceed inductively and rely on the way the term 'creativity' has occurred in all its uses, we would have to include such examples as home-making, salesmanship, and beautiful scenes in nature, as well as the work of Giott, Shakespeare, Beethoven, and Albert Einstein. This approach, I think, includes too much and spreads the reference of creativity too thin. On the other hand, if we stipulate the exclusion of such things as creative salesmanship, nature, etc., the approach, unless justified, is open to the charge of arbitrariness. The third approach, which I have in fact adopted, is to proceed descriptively under the constraints of the premise that there is a select range of phenomena, which are most clearly and unquestionably examples of creative acts and of outcomes, that are creations. The examples of creativity, which will serve as a basis for the criteria, are selected from the most dramatic and renowned instances of those outcomes that have been called creations.

It will be noticed that I have referred here to the outcome of creative acts. The term 'outcome' is not used to refer to results or effects of necessary and sufficient conditions. This usage would belie my view

---

[4] I have tried to take a step in this direction in *A Discourse on Novelty and Creation* (The Hague: Martinus Nijhoff, 1975). This book also develops at greater length, but with different emphases, the criteria suggested in this paper.

that creativity is not fully amenable to rational explanation. Outcome here refers only to the terminus of an activity, to whatever an activity articulates and to what is publicly accessible. Attention is directed to such outcomes because I see no way to distinguish one act from another without reference to what the act manifests—to something discriminable in the form in which the act reaches completion. And the form in which an act reaches completion can be found only in the outcome.

The most striking or eminent outcomes are chosen because these should show most clearly and sharply what called creativity to our attention. It is these which have been and are exemplary for other less dramatic outcomes, such as the results of cooking, or gardening, that are sometimes called creations. If an inquirer wishes to find some degree of creativity in hobbies and do-it-yourself projects—in everyone's activity—then what he will look for as creative in these activities has been drawn from encounters with dramatic cases.

II

The criteria of creativity which I shall consider are telescoped in the following claim: creativity occurs on condition that a new and valuable intelligibility comes into being. We begin, then, with the basis for three criteria: newness, newness of intelligibility, and newness of valuable intelligibility. Discussion of the three key terms, 'new,' 'valuable,' and 'intelligibility' will serve as an account of these criteria. I shall begin with the term new. But it will be seen that examination of this term cannot be understood apart from the others. As criteria of creativity, these terms are interdependent.

The outcome of an act, which is considered creative, then, must seem to be new or novel. We might use other words to suggest this, such as 'original,' 'fresh,' or 'innovative.' These, however, depend on the acknowledgment of the fundamental and more common characteristic, newness or novelty. But what is newness?

A minimal condition or common denominator of newness is that it is present where something is different from its past. A thing that is new must at least be different from what preceded it. In this sense, every discriminable item is new, as a singular. It can be regarded as unique, as a discrete, specific item which is identifiably distinct with respect to all other items. It may be unique as a single instance of general, repeatable types or kinds. Each blade of grass, grain of sand,

and molecule is different from every other blade of grass, grain of sand, and molecule. Likewise, what is unique may be a general or universal. Angularity, the quality of hardness, or a law of nature—each has an identity that is different from all other generals as well as distinctly relative to its particular instances. And what is unique may be an actual experience or activity or consciousness, each of which is different from every other experience or act of consciousness.

The minimal condition of newness has been given priority, either explicitly or implicitly, by some writers who claim that the world is everywhere open to creative acts. Some philosophers—such as William James, or those who adopt one aspect of a Whiteheadian view—suggest that every activity or occasion is unique. Each experience, event, and object is new in the sense of being a unique actualized integration of components. As such, it is new in being different. And all things to this extent exemplify creativity. Creativity, then, pervades all things.

It seems to me that universalizing creativity in this way makes the meaning of creativity too broad. The price paid for this democratic application is that we have no way to distinguish among creations. With respect to uniqueness in the sense of being different, we do not have even degrees of creativity. A stone exemplifies creativity as much as a painting by Giotto. Except perhaps as a metaphysical category, this universal meaning of creativity does not advance our understanding. It does not help us understand what the creation of a more special or striking kind is. The point that some condition other than unique-ness in the sense of difference is needed can be seen if we notice that 'uniqueness' is a term that usually includes more than sheer difference. There must be some merit in being different, and the attribution of the term 'unique' implies that it is good to be different. However, the value of being different still is insufficient to justify regarding a valuable and different outcome of an act as a creation in any other sense than the universal, thin sense. For one thing, many of the acts and outcomes which, like all acts and outcomes which in this view are unique, are different in certain *ways* that make them unacceptable candidates as creative or as creations. If this were not so, then the distinction between creative acts and imitation, routine processes, or hackwork would be meaningless.

Now, the *way* singular is unique, which is to say, the way they are different and therefore valuable, is the key to a second and more radi-cal sense of newness. This point can be considered in terms of the way in which what is unique may be regarded as intelligible.

The most widely accepted view of intelligibility requires that what is intelligible be related to what is familiar. On this view, even if an outcome of a process is different as a singular, its difference is irrelevant to its intelligibility, since it is classified or identified with reference to other things. Thus insofar as it is knowable, the outcome is reducible. In addition, it may also be reducible if it is treated as an instance of regularities and is related to antecedent conditions so that predictions of it are possible. On either alternative, as classified or as an instance of regularity and as predictable, its difference is denied, overlooked, or at least construed as trivial for the purposes of knowledge. Its being different does not contribute to its intelligibility.

Now, according to those who admire uniqueness, the difference noticed in an outcome may be considered thus reducible. Yet, the differences are not denied, overlooked, or viewed as trivial. The outcome is regarded as an individual rather than a repeatable instance. Thus, even though the characteristics of the outcome may be found elsewhere, the outcome is nevertheless significantly different, for the identity of the outcome is said to resist exhaustive characterization. Something is left over. Of course, there are many variations of the interpretation of things as individuals. What is important here, however, is the question whether, on any such interpretation, the differences that mark the individual are peculiar to it so that these differences include or exclude intelligibility. Uniqueness, though not trivial, is regarded as unintelligible because, with respect to uniqueness, the thing is neither describable and sharable through discourse nor predictable, except to the extent of predicting that some individual exhibiting common traits and exemplifying regularities will occur if certain conditions prevail. With respect to what is intelligible, one example will do as well as another. Insofar as the unique thing is intelligible, its newness vanishes.

The minimal condition of newness—irreducible and unintelligible difference—however, is not the only order of newness. Nor is intelligibility exclusively dependent on familiarity. There is a radical and intelligible newness that appears in some outcomes. And it is this order of intelligible newness that is overlooked or left unexamined in so much of the literature on creativity. Failure to give this order of intelligible newness its due has led to too many views that either reduce creativity to natural events or treat creativity as wholly unintelligible and mysterious.

Sometimes there are features of an outcome that do not contribute to its intelligibility as a classifiable and predictable thing. Yet these features contribute to and comprise a complex that constitutes an irreducible intelligible identity. What is irreducible is not an unintelligible element of the outcome. Nor is what is irreducible the bare particularity or discreteness of an individual. What is irreducible is an identity without precedent, an identity not foreseeable in terms of repeatable data. The outcome is new in the sense of being different as an intelligibility. This kind of newness is what I have called 'Novelty Proper.' This is to say that the outcome is novel or new in the proper sense of newness, not in the sense of newness in its lowest common denominator, as a condition universally present in things, but in the sense that is expected when an outcome is regarded as a creation in the radical sense.

New intelligibility is intelligibility that occurs with an identity which appears as a sort of a 'Gestalt,' that is not reducible to its elements or conditions. The thing regarded as intelligible is an integration of elements, an ordered cluster or matrix whose identity is discernible in a complex of coherent, mutually relevant features. Such an identity appears in what may be called a 'structure.' The structure is distinctive, individual, and unique. And it is unfamiliar in that it is different from all prior structures. It is irreducible. Yet it is intelligible.

This suggestion, that order or coherence is necessary for unprecedented intelligibility, might be challenged on the ground that creations appear to be incoherent just to the extent that they violate established standards of coherence. Furthermore, many contemporary works of art which are creations seem to depend on incoherence for their import, for they explicitly violate an order that tends toward unity. They thrive on disunity or disintegration.

With respect to the first point, I must agree that creations are in crucial respects incoherent. But they are so in relation to their external contexts. They are in conflict with the standards of coherence in their pasts. However, what is at issue is a coherence that is internal, an order given within the inner context of the creation, within the boundary and focus that distinguish it from other things in the world. Admittedly, if this is new, it must contrast with what was coherent before it appeared.

With respect to the second part of the objection, it should be said that overlooking the order in the internal constitution of created outcomes and emphasizing the relation to their external contexts also lead to the claim that many creations are explicit expressions of disunity.

What is taken to be disunity and incoherence in works of art may well be dependent on the unfamiliarity of the creation. To be sure, the order of any outcome that is a creation is elusive. So was the work of Giotto or of Beethoven at one time. But these and all outcomes that call forth response and assessment of them as creations must be based on a recognition of some integrating interaction of their components. There must be at least some inner connections and recurrent components, even if they are only subtly manifest. Without this minimal order, there would be nothing to discriminate. There would be nothing sufficiently determinate to focus attention. Such discriminable focus is what I mean by 'coherence.'

A new intelligibility, then, is not an instance or example of a general or a universal. Rather, it is a type that is recognizable nowhere else, under no other conditions than those relevant to itself. Its individuality is one of contrast rather than sheer difference of singularity. It contrasts in intelligibility, or in its structural constitution, with all else that was intelligible before it came into being. Thus, the outcome constitutes its own context which contrasts with its outer context of the past. At the same time, the external context is essential to the recognition of newness, for if the outcome were isolated and not seen within a larger context, it would just be itself and not regarded as different, much less a creation.

I hope that my point can be illustrated briefly. Beethoven's *Ninth Symphony* exhibits a structure that contrasts with his own previously created symphonies. The introduction of the human voice into this orchestral form marks a break with the past. But this break would have been connected with an outcome that is unintelligible if the voice parts were not interwoven with orchestral parts, all contributing to a new focus that makes the qualities of the composition mutually relevant. A new biological species that evolves in nature exhibits a structure that contrasts with structures in its past. The features that sustain it interact with themselves as well as established features so that a different type is established. Over a period of time the new type passes on its structure to offspring and a new kind is established and functions in a continuing evolutionary process. But the initial occurrence of what becomes a species, even if this occurrence appears gradually, is an occurrence manifest in an outcome that exhibits a contrasting structure.

III

The reason for examining the term new in the initial characterization of creativity was to draw out and elaborate criteria of creativity. The first criterion of creativity thus far suggested is that an instance of creativity is found in an outcome that must exhibit a structure which is different from all precedent structures. This formulation of the main criterion has three consequences, consideration of which will indicate further criteria.

First, with respect to the outcome, we should notice that since its intelligibility is unprecedented, it is underived and is something that was not predicted. But also, its intelligibility is discernible in a structure that *could not have been* predicted. If the structure were predictable in principle, it would be wholly dependent on prior intelligibility for its own intelligibility. And the structure then would have precedence. It would be derived and prefigured, traceable to antecedents and classified as an instance of general and repeatable conceptualizable items. It would have been known, anticipated, and describable, if sufficient knowledge had been available. To interpret creations this way would be to presuppose some form of determinism, and a determinism which excludes Novelty Proper or newness of intelligibility from the intelligible world. A creation in the radical sense, then, must exhibit structure that is both unprecedented and unpredictable.

The second consequence of the requirement that a criterion must exhibit a structure which is not derived from prior structures was suggested earlier in the observation that those who find newness wherever there is uniqueness seem to include value in their conception of what it is to be unique. Uniqueness is considered good, good aesthetically, morally, or in some ontological or metaphysical sense. What has been said about the coherence that must be present in the ordering of components of the creation similarly suggests value: an epistemological value. Coherence contributes to making the creation recognizable and knowable. It contributes to intelligibility, since it is the basis for the definiteness required for recognizability.

However, the value of coherence pervades all intelligible things. Like the value of uniqueness, this value is too broad. Something more than epistemological value is at stake. If it were not, eccentricities would be admitted as creations. For these exemplify what I am calling Novelty Proper, possessing some coherence as recognizable structure. But as merely eccentric, they do not merit being considered creations. Being different as a different intelligibility is not sufficient. The outcome must be intelligible in some definite *respect* which is valuable. Its intelligibility must constitute the creation as a model, as an exemplary outcome. This value must initially be inherent. The outcome of a creation is valuable for its own sake. It must exhibit an intelligibility that is good in and for itself. Yet if it contributes to its future, it also has instrumental value. In this connection, it should be acknowledged that not all creations seem to contribute to their futures, at least directly. Bach culminated a tradition, for example. His creations were new structures which, though new, perfected their pasts. On the other hand, El Greco's work awaited a later time to serve the tradition of painting. Some of Picasso's experimental innovations appear to have terminated in strands within a tradition, which was not advanced by them. Finally, judgments about the presence of value change. When this happens, either outcomes that were not deemed creations come to be seen as creations, or formerly recognized creations are forgotten or denied status as examples of creativity. They no longer are viewed as contributing to traditions. Yet whenever an outcome is regarded as a creation, it must be regarded as manifesting at least inherent value. It must show itself to be intelligible, as exhibiting structure that is intelligible in some respect that is inherently valuable. Only then could it be exemplary and instrumentally valuable.

The third consequence of the first criterion pertains to the activity that leads to a creation—that is, the creative act. What has been said about outcomes or creations suggests that there is an element of serendipity in creative acts. Such activity is not governed by rules that require, or are required by, the end. As Kant says in *The Critique of Judgment*, the rules are given to art through the talent of the genius. If they were not, the creation would already be complete in principle. The design of the end would be prefigured. And a creative act would be comparable to the process by which an acorn grows into an oak. If one assumes some form of determinism, it might be claimed that creating is simply conforming to a pattern and an envisaged form or structure. Wolfgang Amadeus Mozart is said to have constructed whole musical compositions without working in any external medium. Thus, if we view the symphony as a mental thing, we might say that it is an envisaged end and that writing a score for it is an act of creation that conforms to its antecedently known structure. But if we say that creations are sometimes completed in the mind of the creator in this way, we do not thereby avoid acknowledging serendipity or the presence of spontaneity in the act. We have simply shifted its locus. We still have before us an act, now 'internal,' 'in the mind,' in which the rules constituting it were introduced for the first time and in which an unprecedented structure came to be envisaged by the creator.

The creative act, then, is a transforming act. It proceeds in accord with constraints that are given not only by the personality and environment of the creator and by the medium in which he works, but also in the spontaneity of the act itself. The requirements of the developing structure are themselves developed. The creator does not set out with a pre-envisaged target. The creative artist does not know till he has said it what he wants to say or how he will say it. He constitutes his target as he discovers how to aim at it. Thus, the creative act is discontinuous. It includes at one or more of its stages a break with the constraints that prior intelligibility imposed on the creator. Further, it includes a break in continuities connecting intelligibilities, or structures by which things are duplicable and known before creation takes place.

At the same time, the creative act is not wholly uncontrolled. If there is serendipity, it is not sheer accident. The creator must not only exercise critical judgment in deciding what to accept and reject when possibilities occur to him, but he must also form, refine, and integrate these, even though he knows only with a degree of imprecision what the final integration will be. And most important, he must assume responsibility for what he brings into being. Even automatic writers and the most romantic interpreters of their own creative acts must accept responsibility for the outcome that they believe has its source beyond them.

The responsibility indicates once more the role of value in the creation. For if creators bring their outcomes into being responsibly, they are offered as what ought to be. Moreover, the responsibility of forming an intelligibility which represents a repudiation of what was before acceptable is conducive to the anguish frequently reported by artists. It also confirms why writers like Rollo May speak of the need for courage to create.

With the initial statement of the criteria of creativity and these consequences in mind, the criteria can now be formulated: (1) a creation must manifest what I have termed Novelty Proper, or a structure that is different and un-derived from past structures and is thus unpredictable; (2) a creation must be inherently and often instrumentally valuable; (3) the act that leads to the creation includes spontaneity as well as directed control.

IV

The adequacy of the criteria I have offered is determined not only by the acceptability of the assumptions and observations that suggest them, but also by their application and their resistance to the challenge of counterexamples. It will be helpful to sketch briefly several applications and possible objections.

First, it might be asked how the criteria apply to Egyptian art. Examples of Egyptian art seem to be repetitive, stylized, and unchanging with respect to their forms. Their intelligibilities seem to be common throughout numerous examples. Does not Egyptian art, therefore, fall outside the criteria? I think it does not. When we regard Egyptian art as creative, we admire it as a general accomplishment seen from the perspective of whole periods. And with respect to a whole period, the form of its examples does contrast with earlier periods. Further, when examples are appreciated as individual works, there are superadded variations from one example to another, variations or contrasts within a common stylized way of depicting, but nevertheless contrasts that show the mark of Novelty Proper. Artists who work according to formulas are regarded as creative because they do not blindly conform to these. They vary the formulas in subtle ways for the sake of approximating or perfecting the formula.

A second application of the criteria suggests that they may be too broad. Consider the experience, for example, of a child learning the multiplication tables. Such learning is not ordinarily viewed as creative. Yet the child's knowledge certainly is new for him. His knowledge consists in apprehending identities for the first time. Is not the child's learning process therefore creative? It is true that in accord with the criteria, there is a sense in which the child might be regarded as creative, though in a very restricted way. He is creative insofar as the novelty in question is severely bounded and personal and insofar as there is directed, deliberate effort coupled with discovery. But the child is hardly creative in the way Poincaré or Newton was. And the criteria do account for this difference. For the child's learning does not introduce spontaneity, the origin of constraints and requirements within the activity of learning; nor does his learning issue in an unprecedented structure. The child's experience can be said to be unprecedented only in the sense of universal all-pervasive novelty according to which each experience can be construed in terms of its uniqueness. But this is not the radical newness or the mark of radical creativity which is at issue.

A third troublesome case for which the criteria are appropriate already has been mentioned. It concerns eccentricities or mere deviations, and acts which are undertaken with the aim of being different for the sake of different. Unfortunately, our admiration for creativity has provoked efforts to be different on the part of would-be creators. Such persons become obsessed, at best, with contributing to society or tradition in some field, or at worst, with enhancing their own self-images. They try deliberately to be different and they offer their eccentricities as creations. The outcomes of their activities may manifest Novelty Proper, insofar as they exhibit unprecedented and unpredictable structures—though they do so less often than their producers would like to think. However, eccentricities lack the criterion of value. They fail to serve as exemplary or as possible models for future work, and they fail to culminate a tradition. A producer of one of them might insist that our blindness prevents our seeing his work as valuable. He may be correct. Nevertheless, until the alleged values of the contrasting structures are recognized, his outcomes will not be deemed creations. But I think it is doubtful that they ever will be. It has been said that an artist sets out, not deliberately to make something beautiful, but rather to express himself. It should also be said that a creative artist sets out not with the intention expressed as 'I shall be creative,' but rather with the intention to articulate and give form to the elements of a medium. He does this more out of compulsion to work than from the desire to conform to a rule that his work be different. He envisages an outcome that will have determinateness, though it is not yet determined. He envisages an outcome that will be valuable, but not an outcome whose specific value is given. He acknowledges that something he will do ought to be, but he knows not how nor in what respect it ought to be.

There are other applications which further test the criteria of creativity. I do not have space or time to explore these here. However, before concluding, I do want to indicate several philosophical problems raised by acceptance of the criteria. These are problems which need to be dealt with in a theory of creativity that affirms the proposed criteria. First, there is an issue raised by the conception of intelligibility which I have adopted. If intelligibility depends upon the presence of identities, we may ask whether the identities that make things intelligible are immanent to those things. Are they identical with the totality of features relevant to the created outcome? It seems that they must be, since new identities have no prior being or status. If they are new, they must appear for the first time within those things which they make intelligible. This is where they are discovered and created. On the other hand, as identities, they must endure; they must have some constancy so that they are not exhaustively bound by an instant of time and a single place. They must be atemporal as well as temporal in their initial occurrences.

There is a second, related problem. The notion of Novelty Proper is paradoxical. Novelty Proper is exemplified in outcomes that are unfamiliar with respect to their intelligibility. Yet, as intelligible, they must appear *as if* they were familiar. Moreover, what is both intelligible and unfamiliar, though manifest as if it were familiar, is not convertible into something already identifiable that makes the new intelligibility predictable. If it were, newness would be denied in favor of deriving the unfamiliar from what is prefigured.

Now, it should be pointed out that the paradox here is not peculiar to the notion of Novelty Proper. The paradox is simply made evident most sharply and dramatically in the case of creative acts which are instances of Novelty Proper. All learning includes recognition of something not before familiar to the learner. One may insist that such learning is possible because what appears to be unfamiliar is learned because it is referred to the familiar, to a fund of experience that was gradually acquired. But this answer does not account for the first instance of learning, or the encounter with what begins the fund of experience. Something must initially be unfamiliar without a ready-made set of familiar experiences to which it can be traced. Furthermore, the initial recognition of the *connection* that holds between unfamiliar experience to be learned and what is already acquired is itself a recognition of a formerly unknown connection that must occur for the first time.

It should be noted, however, that creative experience is also like learning experience, in that it concerns something unfamiliar initially but which can grow familiar. Unless this was so, our vision of the intelligible world could not grow; what is intelligible could never change.

The third problem to be mentioned centers on the consequence that the criteria I have proposed seems to preclude the possibility of explaining creativity. Creative acts cannot be explained in accord with the traditional requirement that explanations show how things to be explained are predictable. If explanation of creative acts is possible, it must be of a different kind that meets different requirements.

The suggestion I have made elsewhere is that a different kind of explanation is appropriate to creativity. I would call this other kind 'an account' rather than 'explanation,' since the term account need not bring with it the standard criteria of explanation. The term account is looser in meaning and thus more consonant with what it may accomplish in applying to creative acts. The model for this kind of explanation includes the use of metaphorical expression. Metaphors are used by those who try to speak about creations. Indeed, they seem to be required in order to point us to new intelligibilities. However, more important, metaphors are themselves creations. Consequently, examination of their structure is suggestive of the general character of the structures exhibited in all creations. And if this is so, then metaphors will conform to the criteria of the phenomena for which they are intended to account. Since the purpose of this paper has been to propose criteria of creativity, I must resist embarking on the further task of exploring metaphorical expression.

In conclusion, then, let me reformulate these criteria. Creativity is expected wherever acts in which there is controlled serendipity issue in valuable Novelty Proper. Consequently, the criteria of creativity are: (1) created outcomes have intelligible structures that are irreducible; (2) the structures of created outcomes are unpredictable; (3) the structures of created outcomes are inherently and usually instrumentally valuable; (4) and the acts that lead to created outcomes include an element of spontaneity so that although they are directed and are controlled, they are discontinuous.

CHAPTER TWO

CREATIVE PRODUCT AND CREATIVE PROCESS IN SCIENCE AND ART[1]

Larry Briskman

I *Introduction*

In the past few decades, creativity has become rather like money: everyone seems to want more of it. Just as we are living in monetarily inflationary times, so too the notion of creativity has undergone a wholesale devaluation. Soon we shall not only be carting away our weekly salaries in wheelbarrows, but the very act of doing so shall come to be called a creative one. Yet however lax popular standards may become, there seems to me to be one aspect of creativity which will remain constant, and that is that creativity is something *valuable*, and that the notion of creativity is permeated with *evaluation*. To adjudge something to be 'creative,' in other words, is to bestow upon it an honorific title, to claim that it deserves to be highly valued for one reason or another.[2] Hence, without standards and values, creativity ceases to exist, just as morality ceases to exist. But as with morality, how high (or low) we set the standards is partially a matter for our decision. In this essay, then, I shall adopt a fairly restrictive standard, and in consequence limit the notion of creativity to Science and Art. I hope that by doing so I do not prejudge any important issues, except

[1] Revised and greatly expanded version of a paper first presented at seminars in the Universities of Edinburgh and Leeds. I want to thank the participants in those seminars, and especially Stanley Eveling, Leon Pompa, and Geoffrey Cantor, for their critical comments and suggestions. In addition, I owe special thanks to Michael Krausz for a series of stimulating discussions of issues related to this chapter. Reprinted from *Inquiry* 23 (1980): 83–106 and *The Concept of Creativity in Science and Art*, eds. D. Dutton and M. Krausz (The Hague, Boston, London: Martinus Nijhoff Publishers, 1981), 129–155, *all rights reserved*.
[2] A similar point has been made by Vincent Tomas in his article "Creativity in Art," reprinted in *Creativity in the Arts*, ed. V. Tomas (Englewood Cliffs: Prentice-Hall, 1964), 97–109.

one upon which I insist: namely, that creativity is something we value, and that the notion of creativity is an evaluative one.

II   *Creativity: Possibility or Necessity?*

For all our valuing of creativity, it appears to be, not least of all to creative scientists and artists themselves, a kind of mystery, a kind of miracle. Thus, Mozart writes of his best musical ideas: "*Whence* and *how* they come I know not; nor can I force them."[3] In a similar vein, Tchaikovsky writes that "the germ of a future composition comes suddenly and unexpectedly";[4] while Helmholtz reports that his ideas often "arrived suddenly, without any effort on my part, like an inspiration."[5] Equally, Gauss, in referring to an arithmetical theorem which he had for years tried unsuccessfully to prove, writes: "Finally, two days ago, I succeeded, not on account of my painful efforts, but by the grace of God. Like a sudden flash of lightning, the riddle happened to be solved."[6] Such quotations could, in fact, be multiplied almost indefinitely; so consider finally, and more lightly, Desmond Morris's recent report that a journalist once asked Picasso: What is creativity? Picasso answered, "I don't know, and if I did I wouldn't tell you."[7]

Now I certainly do not want to claim to know more about creativity than does Picasso, but it does seem to me that the mysteriousness and miraculousness of creativity is, in effect, an important datum about it. It is, I think, something from which we can learn, and which we should try to explain. Yet if we do assume that creativity is a mysterious miracle, then it becomes one of the most mysterious of all miracles—for it is (*pace* Hume) a repeatable miracle. How, then, can we make rational sense of this 'miracle'? How, in other words, is creativity possible?

---

[3] From a letter, reprinted in *Creativity: Selected Readings*, ed. P. E. Vernon (Harmondsworth: Penguin, 1970), 55 (Italics in the original).
[4] Ibid., 57.
[5] Quoted in R. S. Woodworth, *Experimental Psychology* (New York: Holt, 1938).
[6] Quoted in Jacques Hadamard, *The Psychology of Invention in the Mathematical Field* (Princeton: Princeton University Press, 1949), 15.
[7] In H. A. Krebs and J. H. Shelly, eds., *The Creative Process in Science and Medicine* (Amsterdam: Elsevier, 1975), 31. Morris also reports (58) that a journalist asked Picasso: "What do you think of chimpanzee painting?" and Picasso bit him!

It is, I believe, crucial to see that the problem is to explain the possibility of creativity, *not* its necessity. For if we were to actually succeed in explaining the necessity of creativity, or the necessity of specific creative achievements, then in a sense we would have explained *too much*. To see this, consider what would be involved in such an explanation: take some specific creative scientific or artistic achievement C, and assume that we had some general theory of creativity, or of the creative process, T according to which C was necessary. This would mean that given T, and a description of some relevant set of prior circumstances or initial conditions P, we could actually deduce the attainment of C. But this implies that anyone in possession of T, and given the description P, would have *ipso facto* been in a position to himself create C; and would, moreover be able in principle to simulate the actual creative process of the creator of C. Thus, a general theory of creativity, or of the creative process, along the lines of T would provide a kind of recipe for being creative; it would, in effect, provide a set of explicit instructions for attaining creative achievements.

This possibility would, I maintain, have a number of untoward consequences. First, T would rob the actual creator of C of any particular, or individual, claim to creativity, for on the assumption that P was publicly available, T would provide a publicly available, quasi-mechanical, means for creating C. Moreover, T would provide a means for reaching innumerable creative achievements $(C', C'', \ldots)$ effortlessly, since all we would have to do would be to enumerate, one after another, statements describing as yet unrealized sets of relevant initial conditions $(P', P'', \ldots)$ and then deduce what would be their resultant. By hypothesis, these resultants $(C', C'', \ldots)$ would *have to be* creative ones, for otherwise T would not be the type of general theory of the *creative* process (as opposed to some other kind of process) which we are here envisaging. In other words, T would make creativity both too easy and too cheap, since we could have creative achievements for the asking, and this would mean that there would no longer be much point in calling such achievements creative ones. Thirdly, T would turn every creative achievement into something to be expected, given the relevant prior conditions. But this means not only that there need be no surprises, subjectively speaking, but also that there would be *no objective novelty*. For the existence of T would entail that the achievement C was, so to speak, already 'contained within' the prior conditions P, and this means that relative to P, C was no novelty. Since, I take it, the novelty of C relative to what preceded it is at least a necessary condition of C's creativity, it follows that T, far from making creativity necessary, would actually make it *impossible*.[8] In essence, then, a theory such as T would eliminate all the mystery and miraculousness of creativity, but it would also eliminate creativity itself.

The above arguments, if correct, go some way towards clearing up what I take to be one of the main mysteries concerning creativity: namely, the mystery of why creativity itself seems to be a mystery. That is, the above arguments against the possibility of a general theory of creativity along the lines of T yield a kind of meta-expectation to the effect that creative achievements will seem mysterious and miraculous even to those who are themselves responsible for them, for in the absence of something like T, creative artists and scientists will be *themselves surprised* by their own creative achievements; even they could not have foreseen or expected them. Moreover, if a theory of creativity of type T is impossible, then there can be no complete explanation of, and hence no explicit set of instructions for, the attainment of creative achievements. But this means that the creative thinker will himself be unable to specify, even in a *post hoc* fashion, *precisely* how he reached his achievement. Hence, his own creativeness will remain a mystery to him in two ways: first, he could not have predicted it; second, he cannot explain afterwards *precisely* how he managed it. Small wonder then that creative thinkers appeal, at the crucial points in their description of their own creative processes, to inspirations, Divine Grace, and so on. Wolfgang Amadeus Mozart, for example, was thus a better philosopher than he knew when he reported that he did not know whence and how his best musical ideas came, and that he could not force them.

The problem then, as I see it, is emphatically *not* to remove all the miraculousness and mystery from creativity, for that would be to remove creativity itself. Rather, it is to try to explain how creativity is possible, without making it necessary. To adapt Jacques Monod's beautiful idea about the biosphere: we want a theory according to which creative scientific and artistic achievements have the *right* to exist, not one

---

[8] I should point out here that, strictly speaking, C would lack novelty relative not to P alone, but only relative to P together with T. But on the assumption either that what T *describes* existed prior to C, or that T *itself* existed prior to C, if follows that, since C is deducible from P plus T, C is no novelty relative to what preceded it, to what existed prior to it.

according to which they are under an *obligation* to exist.[9] Hence, how is creativity possible? *Not*, why is creativity necessary?

III   *Why the Interest?*

I turn, in this section, away from the main problem to a more prosaic aspect of creativity: namely, why have so many thinkers been interested in it? Undoubtedly, different thinkers have different motivations, different reasons for their interest. But it is, I think, instructive to investigate a few typical reasons for this interest, as this will help to bring to the surface some false hopes which, I believe, have been raised by research into creativity. It will emerge, not unexpectedly perhaps, that the philosophers have been on the side of the angels; while the social scientists, and especially the psychologists, have been the villains of the piece. Moreover, their very villainy will actually help us to zero in on our initial problem.

On the whole then, contemporary philosophers have been concerned with creativity as an aspect of the problem of human freedom. Popper, for example, has argued[10] that no scientific prediction (and hence, no scientific explanation) of the growth of scientific knowledge is possible, on the grounds that we cannot come to know today what we shall only come to know tomorrow. It follows that what Popper calls the world of 'objective mind' (or of 'theories, arguments, and problems-in-themselves') is an essentially *open* world, in that it cannot contain a theory which will predict the appearance in that world of all future theories. But for Popper this world of objective mind (his World 3) interacts both with the world of mental states (his World 2) and with the world of physical states (his World 1)—the latter interaction being mediated through the World 2.[11] It follows that both the mental world, and more importantly, the physical world, are also open; and this both rules out a purely physical determinism and, in turn, kicks open the door to the possibility of human freedom. In other

---

[9] See J. Monod, *Chance and Necessity* (New York: Knopf, 1971), especially chap. 2.

[10] In his "Indeterminism in Quantum Physics and in Classical Physics," *British Journal for the Philosophy of Science* 1 (1950), and elsewhere.

[11] For Popper's World 3 theory, see his *Objective Knowledge* (Oxford: Oxford University Press, 1972), especially chap. 3, 4, 6. I should say here that my approach in this chapter has been greatly influenced by Popper's "objectivist" epistemology.

words, for Popper, the creative potentiality of human thought, the possibility of genuinely creative, unpredictable additions to his World 3, opens up the door to human freedom.

As a second example, consider the existentialist philosophers. For them, the notion of human freedom is linked to Jean-Paul Sartre's idea of man's being a 'being-for-itself,' a being whose existence precedes its 'essence' and who is thus condemned to creating his own essence, rather than a 'being-in-itself,' a being whose essence is already defined for it. In this way, existentialists too connect the possibility of human freedom to the possibility of human creativity—man is free precisely because he both can and must create himself, because his existence precedes his essence. Thus, Sartre writes: "If existence really does precede essence, there is no explaining things away by reference to a fixed and given human nature. In other words, there is no determinism, man is free, man is freedom."[12]

Now although I would not wish to endorse a radical existentialist view, the point I do wish to stress is that contemporary philosophers have not, on the whole, seen creativity as something which can be controlled, manipulated, engineered, or predicted. Quite the contrary, they have seen in scientific and artistic creativity an essential element of unpredictability, an area of human thought and action in which men are capable of breaking out of their temporarily self-imposed (or externally imposed) 'prisons' into roomier and better prisons. And the man who can break out of his prison demonstrates his relative autonomy (or freedom) from it.[13]

In part, perhaps, these rather 'heroic' views of creativity may stem from the fact that philosophical interest in it has not been pragmatically oriented. The psychologist, however, has enjoyed no such luxury, for psychological interest in creativity has, since the early 1950s, been unabashedly pragmatic in orientation. J. P. Guilford, a highly influential

---

[12] From J. P. Sartre, *Existentialism*, trans. Bernard Frechtman (New York: The Philosophical Library, 1947).

[13] *A propos* of this, Popper writes, "At any moment we are prisoners caught in the framework of our theories; our expectations; our past experiences; our language. But we are prisoners in a Pickwickian sense: if we try, we can break out of our framework at any time" ("Normal Science and its Dangers," in *Criticism and the Growth of Knowledge*, eds. I. Lakatos and A. Musgrave (Cambridge: Cambridge University Press, 1970), 56. Popper does, I think, tend to underemphasize the *difficulty* of such "breakouts." In fact, I believe that were such breakouts easy to achieve, we would no longer see them as creative.

figure in the psychological creativity 'movement,' writes, "the most urgent reason [for studying creativity] is that we are in a mortal struggle for the survival of our way of life in the world."[14] N. E. Golovin, writing in 1959, warned that unless the United States either increased the number of scientists and engineers she was producing or else enhanced "the average level of creative capabilities of such scientists and engineers" she was bound to lose out in the struggle with the Soviet Union.[15] While the American psychologist T. A. Razik was even more explicit, saying, "In the presence of the Russian threat," he wrote:

> 'creativity' could no longer be left to the chance occurrences of the genius; neither could it be left in the realm of the wholly mysterious and the untouchable. Men *had* to be able to do something about it; creativity *had* to be a property in many men; it *had* to be something identifiable; it *had* to be subject to the effects of efforts to gain more of it.[16]

In other words, creativity could (at least in part) be controlled, manipulated, engineered, and predicted. In fact, it *had* to be.[17]

---

[14] J. P. Guilford, "Traits of Creativity," reprinted in *Creativity*, ed. P. E. Vernon, 167–188. Quote from 167.

[15] N. E. Golovin, "The Creative Person in Science," in C. W. Taylor and F. Barron, eds., *Scientific Creativity: Its Recognition and Development* (New York: Wiley, 1963), 7–23 (Quote on 8). This volume consists of selected papers from *three* conferences on "The Identification of Creative Scientific Talent" held at the University of Utah in 1954, 1957, and 1959, and supported by the U.S. National Science Foundation. This latter fact, together with the fact that Golovin himself served for a time on the White House staff, indicates both the degree of official U.S. support for the study of creativity and the extent to which American psychologists encouraged the belief in the great practical potentialities of their research.

[16] T. A. Razik, "Psychometric Measurement of Creativity," reprinted in *Creativity*, ed. 155–166. The quote, with italics in the original, is from 156.

[17] What, one wonders, is the reasoning behind such optimism? An instructive analogy can be drawn between many twentieth century students of creativity and seventeenth century students of methodology. For seventeenth century thinkers, like Bacon and Descartes, scientific progress was to be guaranteed by "the man of method" whose relentless application of the correct methodology would ensure continuous progress. But we now live in a post-Einsteinian age (in art, a post-Picasso age) and our idea of scientific (and artistic) progress is a more dramatic, revolutionary one. As a result, I conjecture, many twentieth century thinkers have come to see 'the man of creative imagination' as the new guarantor of scientific progress. Hence, the idea that creativity *had to be* something we could do something about; for otherwise scientific progress becomes a *contingent accident*, a matter of fortuitous happenstance. The lesson, I suspect, has yet to be learned that there is *no* guarantee of scientific progress, and that the fact that we have any knowledge worthy of the name *at all* is itself a miraculously improbable occurrence.

IV *Product, Process, or Person?*

Thus convinced of the potential practical utility, indeed urgency, of
research into creativity, psychometricians such as Guilford and Razik,
influenced by what could be called 'the cult of personality,' set out to
identify (through factor analysis) a set of personality traits which might
be thought to discriminate between creative and non-creative people.[18]
The idea behind this, one supposes, is that there is some unique concatenation of traits, which go to make up 'the creative personality' or
'the creative person.' Moreover, one assumes, this creative person will
initiate or carry out (or perhaps even 'undergo') some specifiable psychological process—'the creative process"—to reach some creative
outcome, "the creative product." This, then, suggests the basis for a
kind of psychological research program,[19] which offers us the hope that,
via an identification of the creative person and of the creative process,
we will be able to both explain and foster creativity and, at least in
part, predict both *who* is likely to produce creative products (creative
persons, who else?) and *when* they are so likely to produce them (when
they are initiating or undergoing a creative process, when else?).

And so it would be—if, that is, it were possible to identify creative
people or a creative process *independently* of the creative product. In
effect, it is just this possibility which I here wish to deny. Clearly, unless
we can identify a person as creative, or some special process as the
creative process, independently of the product, which is supposed to
be the outcome, we cannot predict the appearance of such a product
on the basis of theories of the creative personality or the creative process. My claim, then, is that creative people and creative processes can
only be identified via our prior identification of their scientific or artistic *products* as themselves creative. That is, the person is a creative one
and the process was a creative process only in the light of our prior

---

[18] The main methodological tools of such studies were the so-called open-ended
tests of creativity. As Liam Hudson has pointed out in his book *Contrary Imaginations*
(Harmondsworth: Penguin, 1967), 126: "Open-ended tests are known throughout the
United States as creativity tests. Yet... there is scarcely a shred of factual support for
this." For the severe problems involved in validating such tests (that is, in showing that
they are actually testing creativity!) see R. J. Shapiro's, "Criterion Problem," in *Creativity*, ed. P. E. Vernon, 257–269.

[19] The notion of a 'research program' is due largely to the writings of Popper,
Agassi, and especially Lakatos. For a discussion of psychology's dominant modern
metaphysical research program—behaviorism—and some suggested reasons for its
current demise, see my "Is a Kuhnian Analysis Applicable to Psychology?" *Science
Studies* 2 (1972): 87–97. For further reflections on behaviorism, see my "Skinnerism
and Pseudo-Science," *Philosophy of the Social Sciences* 9 (1979): 81–103.

evaluation of the product itself as a creative product. If this is correct, then it follows that a scientific or artistic product is not creative *because* it was produced by a creative person or a creative process, but rather that both the psychological process involved, and the person involved, are deemed to be creative *because* they succeed in producing a product deemed to be creative. It is the creativity of the product which has, so to speak, logical priority. It also follows that any attempted explanation of the creativity of the product on the basis of the creativity of the person, or of his (or her) psychological characteristics or processes, commits the fallacy of *post hoc, ergo propter hoc*. This implies that the psychological research program outlined earlier is an incoherent one.

Now the above account, if accepted, clearly raises a crucial question: for if we cannot identify or explain the creativity of a product by reference to the person who produced it, or the process of which it is the outcome, how *can* we identify and explain this creativity? The short answer, I believe, is that we can only identify and explain the creativity of a scientific or artistic product by reference to *prior* scientific or artistic products. That is, a work of art or a scientific theory does not, as it were, wear its creativity on its sleeve ("essentially," or non-relationally); but neither does it gain its creativity by being related, as outcome, to some specific psychological process. Rather, it possesses it in relation to previous artistic or scientific products; its creativity is to be understood and explained in terms of its relation to these prior products. Clearly, such an explanation can *never* have predictive import, for we shall have to be already acquainted with the product whose creativity we want to explain *before* we can explain why it is a creative product. Thus, *even if* we could predict, based on our knowledge of persons' psychology, that they will produce certain products, *even then* we would not have predicted, on that basis alone, that they will produce a *creative* product. For the creativity of the product resides not in its psychological origins, but in its objective relations to other, previous, products. And this, in effect, provides one possible clue to the answer to our initial question: How is creativity possible? For if the creativity of a product resides in its relations to prior products, then creativity might be possible through the critical interaction of the creator with those prior products themselves. And, as might be expected, that such a critical interaction will actually yield a creative product is indeterminate and cannot be predicted. In other words, creativity becomes possible, but not necessary.[20]

---

[20] At this point, it will be useful to clear up two possible misunderstandings: First, I am not here assuming that a critical interaction with prior products is the *only* way

V *Priority of the Product: An Argument*

The skeptic (in this instance, the psychologist) may still be unmoved, for I have yet to give an argument for the thesis that the creativity of the product has logical priority over the creativity of the person and his (or her) psychological characteristics or processes. Nor have I sufficiently argued the view that the creativity of the product cannot reside in its psychological origins, but only in its objective relation to prior products. Although these two theses seem to me to be almost obvious, those who still harbor the hope that creativity *must* be fundamentally a property of people and their psychology, and hence something which we can (at least in part) control, foster, and predict, will rightly demand an argument. I shall, therefore, have to oblige them.

A first, and crucial, argument seems to me to be this: in attempting to deal with creativity "scientifically," psychologists are obliged to assume that creativity has the status of a *fact*—that it exists purely naturalistically, in the way that gravity exists, or the moon exists. Only against such a background does it make sense to talk of the creative personality, or of creative "psychological processes," as objects of scientific investigation. Now even if there do exist, as facts, certain psychological processes and personality traits related to creativity, that these are *creative* psychological processes or traits of the *creative* personality is not itself a fact but an evaluation. That is, although we can study certain personality traits and certain psychological processes as facts, we cannot *identify* these personality traits or psychological processes *as creative ones* independently of our standards and values. The reason for this is simple. As I mentioned at the start of this essay, to adjudge some person, process, or product to be creative is to bestow upon it an honorific

---

in which creativity might be possible. My point, rather, is that *if* the creativity of a product resides in its relations to previous products, then the *least mysterious* way in which creativity might be possible is via an interaction of the creator with those prior products. Second, my point of view does *not* entail that whenever we adjudge a certain product *X* to be creative that we are *ipso facto* forced into judging the producer of *X* to be creative, or the process by which he created *X* to be a creative process. (Think of the monkey at his typewriter typing out *Hamlet* and you will see why we do not want to be so forced!) In other words, we may very well insist upon additional conditions which have to be met (additional, that is, to the production of a creative product) *before* we will call the producer, or his means of production, creative. In fact, I shall attempt to spell out some of these additional conditions in Sections V and VII. What my point of view does entail, however, is that we *cannot* call a person, or his processes, creative without reference to his products; not that we *must* call him, or his processes, creative given such reference.

title, to claim that it deserves to be highly prized, highly *valued*, for one reason or another. The question then is: *what* do we evaluate, *to what* do our standards apply, in the first instance? Do we initially evaluate people, processes, or products as creative?

As far as I can see, all we have to go on, initially, is a person's *output* (linguistic, scientific, artistic, etc.). For example, would we know anything of the musical "genius" of a Beethoven, or the scientific "creativity" of an Einstein, if both had been totally paralyzed, deaf, dumb mutes unable to externalize that genius in objective scientific or artistic products? Clearly not. What if Ludwig van Beethoven had written only uninspiring pastiche, or Einstein had never contributed more to science than a best selling high school physics textbook? Would they *still be* the creative giants we now consider them to be? Again, the answer, I think, is clearly not. In other words, what we evaluate as creative, that to which our standards apply in the first instance, are a person's products. But since *creative* psychological processes and traits of the *creative* personality do not exist as facts *per se*, but only as the result of an evaluation, and since our evaluation must, in the first instance, be applied to a person's products, it follows that we cannot identify, independently of such products, creative persons or creative psychological processes. Moreover, psychologists, insofar as they study such processes and personality traits as facts *per se*, independently of all evaluations (that is, insofar as they study them "scientifically"), simply are *not* studying creativity. In other words, a purely "scientific" study of creativity, and *a fortiori* a purely psychological (or even sociological) study of creativity, is impossible.[21]

It is, I think, important to be clear about the above argument. I do not deny (but nor, for that matter, do I assert) that there may be certain independently identifiable psychological processes or personality traits

---

[21] Incidentally, a similar argument can be used to show that a purely scientific psychology or sociology of *knowledge* is equally impossible. For 'knowledge,' like creativity, is a normative or evaluative notion, which applies, in the first instance, to the outcomes or products *of* research and not to the psychological processes or sociological conditions involved *in* research. Thus, we cannot identify as facts *per se* any sociological conditions of knowledge. In other words, far from replacing epistemology, there cannot even *be* a sociology or psychology of knowledge in the absence of epistemology. For in the absence of epistemology (or 'the criteriological science of knowledge,' to adopt Collingwood's terminology) there simply *is* no knowledge, and so clearly no psychology or sociology *of* it. *Pace* H. V. O. Quine, epistemology cannot be naturalized. For some rather disastrous consequences of ignoring the evaluative aspect of knowledge, and of blurring the fact/value distinction, see my "Toulmin's Evolutionary Epistemology," *Philosophical Quarterly* 24 (1974): 60–69.

related to creativity. Nor do I deny that these can be studied as facts, which is to say scientifically. What I *do* deny is that they exist qua *creative* psychological processes, or qua traits of the *creative* personality, simply as facts. Rather, that we are dealing with a *creative* psychological process, or a trait of the *creative* personality, is a question of our evaluation, of our standards. Since we can only apply these standards, in the first instance, to the generated products, it follows that we cannot identify the *creativity* of a psychological process, or of a personality trait, independently of the product and of our evaluation of it. In other words, (1) the creativity of the product has logical priority over (2) the creativity of persons and their psychological processes, for we cannot identify (2) independently of (1). This means that we equally cannot explain (1) by making reference to (2). So if we *do* want to explain the creativity of some scientific or artistic product *C*, we shall, it appears, have to make reference not to (2), but to *C*'s objective relation to prior scientific or artistic achievements. These two theses are those I set out to argue.

VI *Priority of the Product: A Further Argument*

It might, perhaps, be thought that the above argument is too abstract or conceptual to carry much conviction. In this section, I shall attempt to offer a more "concrete" indication of the priority of creative products over any purely psychological account of the creative process (leaving aside now any consideration of the creative person or traits of the creative personality). Basically, what I shall attempt to argue here is that we cannot even *describe*, let alone understand or explain, the creative process without reference to the products which are its outcome. In other words, even if we could, *per impossibile*, identify some psychological process as a creative one independently of our identification of its outcome (or product) as creative, even then we could not describe this process in the absence of reference to its products, and so could not conceptualize it as being *purely* psychological.

Consider, then, some creative artist (a painter, say) who wants to express some idea, some emotion, some vision; or who desires to solve some artistic problem (for example, the problem of "painting a dark object in the dark");[22] or who wants to give the illusion of reality. Con-

---

[22] The Japanese painter, Yasuo Kuniyoshi, reports (in *The Creative Process: A Symposium*, ed. B. Ghiselin [Berkeley: University of California Press, 1952], 55) that this was, in

sider, equally, a theoretical physicist trying to explain some recalcitrant experimental result; or an experimentalist attempting to devise some method for testing a theoretical prediction. It must, I think, be obvious that it would be highly unlikely for the artist to have the completed painting in his mind, all at once, right from the very start; or for the theoretician to have his complete final explanatory structure before him, in his mind's eye, at the very moment he began work on his problem. Rather, one would expect, the artist must build up his painting gradually, stroke by stroke; while the theoretician must build up his conjectural explanation bit by bit (even though he may have got his explanatory "core idea" in a flash). But if this is the case, then it is highly likely that the very thought processes of the artist or scientist will themselves be affected by the work done so far. In other words, the creator, in his very process of creation, is constantly interacting with his own prior products; and this interaction is one of genuine feedback, for the creator is as much influenced by his own initial creations as these were influenced by him. Thus, for example, the scientist's own subjective thinking is itself as much a product of his objective efforts as these are a product of his thinking. While with respect to art, the American painter Ben Shahn makes the same point forcefully: "Painting," he says, "is both creative and responsive. It is an intimately communicative affair between painter and his painting, a conversation back and forth, the painting telling the painter even as it receives its shape and form."[23]

If all this is correct, then it follows that we shall not be able to describe, let alone understand, the creative process unless we make reference to the "intermediary" products which function, so to speak, as "tools" in the creative process itself. In other words, it once again seems that we cannot think of the creative process as being a *purely* psychological process, for our account of that process shall have to make reference not only to the psychological processes of the creator but also to the (intermediary) products which are themselves helping

---

fact, an artistic problem which he tried to solve. The idea that the artist confronts objective problems is well known to any reader of Gombrich's brilliant *Art and Illusion* (Princeton: Princeton University Press, 1960). I should mention that in my view an artist's subjective desire to express some idea, emotion, or vision itself constitutes an *objective* artistic problem—namely, the problem of *how* to express it *given* the means at his disposal. Such a problem may only be soluble if the artist invents or discovers new means, not previously at his disposal. We might call this, paraphrasing Lakatos, a 'creative problem-shift.'

[23] Ben Shahn, "The Biography of a Painting," in *Creativity in the Arts*, ed. V. Tomas, 32.

to *shape* these psychological processes. To put it bluntly: not only are we unable to identify a psychological process as creative in the absence of an identification (or evaluation) of its resultant product as itself creative, but we are unable to identify *any purely psychological process at all as the creative process*. For any such process which we are likely to call creative will involve an ineliminable interaction between the creator's psychological states and his own products, with the latter having a genuine feedback upon, and thus themselves actually helping to create, the former. So once again we can see a kind of priority in the product; for although we can describe the creativity of the product without reference to any psychological process (i.e., we can describe it with reference to prior products), we *cannot* describe the creativity of some psychological process without reference to any products. And this is true for two reasons: first, because the process is a creative one *only if* it issues in a product deemed to be a creative one; and second, because any process worthy of the name creative will involve an ineliminable interaction with intermediary products which themselves help to create the psychological states of the creator.[24]

VII   *Aspects of Creative Products*

So far, I have been arguing for a non-psychological approach to the problem of creativity. It is, however, time to put a little more meat onto the anti-psychological bones, and to outline what I hope is a plausible solution to our main problem: namely, how is creativity possible? As I have already indicated, we cannot identify a process as creative until we have identified (or evaluated) its outcome or product to be creative. So we may say that the creativity of the product will set the *job specifi-*

---

[24] It might here be objected that the fact that creative people talk of 'inspiration,' 'Divine Grace,' 'sudden and unexpected ideas,' 'bisociation,' and so on when describing their own creative work invalidates my argument. I do not agree—such sudden flashes of 'illumination' are invariably preceded by the production of unsuccessful efforts which themselves help to shape the very illumination in question. Moreover, it might be said that examples such as Coleridge's composing of "Kubla Kahn" refutes my suggestion, in that it seems to have emerged full-blown from Coleridge's head without the benefit of any interaction with intermediary products. Again, I am not so sure—at the very least Coleridge had to critically interact with his 'finished' product before accepting it *as finished*, and this means that before this conscious acceptance the product can be thought of as an intermediary one even though it may be identical to the finished one!

cation for any process which we will deem to be creative. That is, until we have answered the question, "What aspects of artistic and scientific products lead us to evaluate them as creative ones?" we cannot answer the question "What kind of process could possibly result in such products?" and so cannot answer our primary question "How is creativity possible?" For creativity is only possible insofar as it is possible to produce creative products. In this section, then, I shall have to concentrate on the former question, and attempt to outline some aspects of creative products. Only afterwards will we be in a position to tackle our main question head on.

One of the most striking—and in way, paradoxical—features of great creative advances is how often they appear to be, with hindsight, almost obvious. Einstein puts the point nicely: "In the light of knowledge attained, the happy achievement seems almost a matter of course, and any intelligent student can grasp it without too much trouble. But the years of anxious searching in the dark, with their intense longing, their alternation of confidence and exhaustion, and the final emergence into the light—only those who have themselves experienced it can understand that."[25]

But if creative achievements often seem obvious, "a matter of course," in retrospect, why are they so difficult to achieve? The answer lies, naturally enough, in Einstein's telling phrase about "the years of anxious searching *in the dark*." That is, great creative advances tend to shed light where none has been shed before; one thus cannot approach one's target clearly, because until one has actually reached it, one cannot say precisely what it is (or even if it exists).[26] Popper makes substantially the same point when he compares the quest for new knowledge with the situation of "a blind man who searches in a dark room for a black hat which is—perhaps—not there."[27] Small wonder, then, that creative

---

[25] Quoted in Banesh Hoffmann and Helen Dukas, *Albert Einstein: Creator and Rebel* (New York: Viking, 1972), 124.

[26] This fact about creativity calls to mind what could be called 'Plato's Paradox': namely, that one cannot search for something unless one knows what one is searching for. But plausibly one cannot know what one is searching for until one has actually found it. Hence, one cannot search for something until one has found it. In other words, one cannot search for something! This argument is not simply a sophism, for it indicates that one must either have some *imprecise* idea of what one is looking for, or else some *recognitional criteria* for saying that one has found what one is looking for. The importance of such recognitional criteria for creative activity will be discussed in Section VII.

[27] Karl Popper, "Replies to my Critics," in *The Philosophy of Karl Popper*, ed. P. Schilpp (LaSalle: Open Court, 1974), vol. 2, 1061.

advances may be simultaneously difficult to make and yet, once made, appear obvious or a "matter of course." For after the advance, we are bathing in its reflected light, and some of that light may very well reflect back onto that very advance itself. Why, then, are creative advances in science or art the result of such an "anxious searching in the dark"? What features of the creative scientific, or artistic product are responsible for this? A first step on the way to an answer can, I think, be taken if we recognize that, as a minimum requirement, a creative product must be a *novel* product. Now the notion of novelty requires a background—what is novel against one background may not be novel relative to another background. In other words, the notion of *absolute* novelty is incoherent; we can only judge the novelty of a product by comparing it to those previous products which constitute the background against which it emerged. Thus, at the very least, a creative product must not be contained within, so to speak, the background of prior products; this partially accounts for the fact that the creator is "in the dark."

But the novelty of a product is clearly only a necessary condition of its creativity, not a sufficient condition: for the madman who, in Bertrand Russell's apt phrase, believes himself to be a poached egg may very well be uttering a novel thought, but few of us, I imagine, would want to say that he was producing a *creative* one. So if novelty is not enough, what ingredients need be added in order to get creativity? A second requirement, I maintain, is that the novelty must be put to some good purpose. It must achieve some desired or desirable result. In short, it must be *valuable* novelty. My suggestion is that a scientific or artistic product is valuable insofar as it constitutes or incorporates a *solution* to a *problem*; and the notion of a problem, like the notion of novelty, demands a background; what is problematic against one background may not be problematic against another. But this means that the notion of a solution to a problem must be relative to a background as well. Now a *genuine* problem is always one that cannot be solved simply with the available means, or on the basis of the background against which it *is* a problem. In other words, once we see creative products as solutions to problems, we can understand why they *must* be novel; for insofar as a genuine problem only emerges against a background, and cannot be solved on the basis of that background alone, a solution to such a problem *must* constitute a novel addition to that background. Moreover, it also follows that although the creative product is a novel one, a kind of "internal connection" must exist between this novel product and the background of prior products—namely, the internal connection of a solution to the problem it solves.[28]

We have thus far reached the following result: a creative scientific or artistic product constitutes or incorporates a novel solution to a problem, inherent in a background of prior products, but not soluble based on these prior products themselves. But this is not yet the whole story, for novel solutions to problem-solutions may be related to their background in at least two different ways. First, they may simply go beyond, or extend, the existing background. Second, and more interestingly, they may actually *conflict* with this existing background, or necessitate the *modification* of this background. That is, they may improve upon, and thus supplant, parts of this background. In fact, it seems to me that when we are thinking of really great creative achievements (especially in science, although similar considerations can, I think, be applied to certain aspects of art) we are in the main thinking of this latter case. For example, having inherited the problem of unifying terrestrial and celestial physics from the tradition of Galileo and Kepler, Isaac Newton actually solves the problem in such a way as to force the modification of that tradition. For his solution conflicts with, and improves upon, the theories of Galileo and Kepler; it supplants them while at the same time explaining them (as limiting cases). Equally, Einstein inherits the problem of reconciling Newtonian mechanics with Maxwellian electrodynamics, and the theory he puts forward solves the problem in such a way as to supersede and replace Newton's theory. In other words, really outstanding creative achievements have a habit of breaking, in important ways, with the tradition out of which they emerged. They, so to speak, *transcend* this tradition. Moreover, insofar as creative products actually conflict with the tradition out of which they emerge, insofar as they are prohibited by that tradition, creative thinking actually involves the thinking of *forbidden thoughts*.[29] No wonder then that

---

[28] Interestingly, the idea that a creative product is a novel problem-solution enables us to explain how even *old* ideas may qualify as creative products. For the required novelty is no longer sheer temporal novelty; rather it is the novelty of a solution relative to a problem. An old idea, invoked in a new problem-situation, could constitute a novel solution. We might, for example, construe Dalton's creativity in this light, for Dalton recognized in the old *physical* ideas of the atomists the potential solution to a pressing *chemical* problem (that of explaining the law of constant proportions) and thus built his 'new system of chemical philosophy' upon an atomistic basis. In other words, Dalton did not create the idea of atoms, but he used that idea *creatively*.

[29] I owe this way of seeing the thing to Stanley Eveling.

the creative process involves not only a searching in the dark but also, as Einstein put it, an "*anxious* searching in the dark."

We are now almost in a position to complete our characterization of the creative product. Only one important aspect remains—that of *evaluation*. For a creative product must not only incorporate a novel problem-solution conflicting with the tradition out of which it emerged, it must also be an acceptable problem-solution. That is, it must be evaluated favorably; it must meet certain standards or certain criteria of acceptability. Such standards will, of course, differ for different endeavors, and those applicable in science will quite reasonably diverge from those applicable to art (although there are, I think, more similarities here than are often imagined). Nevertheless, the point remains that before a novel problem-solution can be given the honorific title creative, it must be evaluated positively as meeting certain standards. Moreover, these standards will normally themselves be incorporated into the background of prior products, in the tradition, against which the problem-solution has emerged.[30] In other words, from the point of view of the background itself, the creative product surpasses that background in a positively evaluated way, in a way meeting certain stringent requirements or standards already inherent in that background.

To sum up this section: a creative scientific, or artistic, product has, I suggest, the following characteristics. First, relative to the background of prior products, it is a *novel* product. Second, it puts this novelty to a desirable purpose by *solving a problem*, such problems being themselves relative to this background and emerging from it. Third, it does so in such a way as to actually *conflict* with parts of this background, to necessitate its partial modification, and to supplant and improve upon parts of it. Finally, this novel, conflicting, problem-solution must be favorably evaluated; it must meet certain exacting standards which are themselves part of the background it partially supplants. I shall call any product,

---

[30] It might be thought that this entails that creative contributions to 'methodology' or 'criteriology' (i.e., the theory of rational standards) is impossible. This is a mistake: a novel methodological idea which solves an outstanding problem in our current methodological theories may actually constitute an improvement from the point of view of the *older* standards themselves. This, in effect, is how the rational improvement of rational standards is itself possible. Agassi has christened this view 'the bootstrap theory of rationality' and suggests that of a series of criteria of rationality each can constitute 'an improvement on its predecessor by its predecessor's own lights.' See Joseph Agassi, "Criteria for Plausible Arguments," *Mind* 83 (1974): 406–416. For further elaboration of, and suggested modifications to, Agassi's idea of bootstrap rationality, see my "Historicist Relativism and Bootstrap Rationality," *The Monist* 60 (1977): 509–539.

which meets all four of these demands a "transcendent product," for it may be said to transcend the background of prior products against which it emerged. In short, then, the thesis of this section can be simply stated: creative scientific or artistic products are transcendent products: they transcend the tradition out of which they sprang.[31]

VIII   *How Is Creativity Possible?*

A creative product, then, is a transcendent product. So the question "How is creativity possible?" can be significantly reformulated: How, after all, is it possible to produce transcendent products? In this section I shall have to canvass, all too briefly, I am afraid, a number of different possible answers to this question, and shall use the results of the previous section as the *desiderata* with which any successful theory or model of the creative process will have to cope. In other words, the transcendent nature of creative products shall constitute the *explicandum*, and an acceptable model of the creative process shall have to explain how it is possible for such products to exist.

As a first possibility, consider what could be called the *mechanistic* approach to the creative process. The mechanist tends to see all natural processes (and hence, for him, the creative process) as occurring according to law; he believes that if some thing (or state of affairs) S exists at time t_1 then there must have existed *prior* things (or states of affairs) at an earlier time t_0 which, together with these laws, are responsible for the appearance of S. The mechanist need not necessarily be a determinist (although he usually is), for some of his laws might be probabilistic only. But what he insists upon is that one be able to trace the existence of S back to earlier conditions out of which it arose according to law. Can such a model account for the appearance of a transcendent product C? The answer, I think, is pretty clearly "no."

---

[31] The notion of transcendence here developed is not an absolute one—it admits of *degrees*. For differing products may meet the four demands to a greater or lesser extent; or a product may meet only some of the demands and not others. For example, it might meet demands 1, 2, and 4, yet fail to meet demand 3 (i.e., it fails to necessitate any alterations in the background). Thus, from the point of view of this chapter, it is perfectly sensible to talk of *degrees of creativity* as well. This seems to me to be a crucially valuable result. In fact, I would say that any theory, which made creativity into an 'all-or-nothing' thing (as Koestler's 'bisociative' theory seems to do) should, for that very reason, be rejected.

First, the arguments presented in Sections I, IV, and V already militate against the mechanist. Second, it is difficult to see how such a model could make sense of the novelty of *C*, for insofar as it tries to explain the appearance of *C* based on prior conditions, it is trying to trace what is new back to that which is old. Moreover, what *are* the prior conditions against which a transcendent product appears? Seemingly these will consist, in the main, of the background of prior products and especially the problem, emerging out of them, which the transcendent product comes to solve. But this means that the mechanist must be conceiving of the laws governing the creative process, which transform the prior conditions into *C*, as a kind of problem-solving algorithm; that is, a kind of function which "maps" the prior conditions (including the problem) into a resultant outcome *C* (incorporating a solution). But if such a problem-solving algorithm actually exists, then there are in fact no genuinely *open* problems (except, perhaps, that of discovering the algorithm!), and so the very possibility of producing transcendent products disappears.[32] We thus reach a conclusion very much in the spirit of Section I: mechanism, far from making creativity possible, would actually rule it out.

Traditionally, at least since the eighteenth century, the only alternative that philosophers have attributed to mechanism is *randomness*, or pure chance. Moreover, as every geneticist knows, randomness can be a fertile source of novelty. In fact, it almost has to be, since, by definition, pure randomness can result in virtually *anything*, including novelty. So randomness, as a model of the creative process, at least has this in its favor: it can account for the possibility of novelty. But this is about all. For one of the most striking facts about transcendent products is their *appropriateness*, the internal connection which exists between these products and the background against which they emerge. This appropriateness is shown not only in such products constituting solutions to problems, but also in the fact that they meet certain exacting standards,

---

[32] One can, I think, go even further and *prove* that no such problem-solving algorithm (call it *F*) can exist. For *F* would map problems into solutions (i.e., Solution=*F* [Problem]). But problems are themselves functions of the background of prior products (i.e., Problem=*f* [Background]). Combining these two we get that Solution=*F*(*f* [Background]). But solutions often *contradict* this background. How can a function map an *x* into something inconsistent with *x*? Only, I suspect, by being itself inconsistent. So no *consistent* problem-solving algorithm of the type envisaged can exist and an inconsistent one would be of no use whatsoever, since out of it we could get anything as a solution to anything!

and it would, I think, be a bit *too* miraculous if products exhibiting these characteristics were the outcome of pure chance. Moreover, randomness would, in any case, have to be supplemented by something like recognition criteria, or selection criteria; otherwise the creator would either just go on generating products ad infinitum, or else he would stop by pure chance. So randomness is not enough; it cannot explain the appropriateness of transcendent products.

The failure of both mechanism and randomness to account for the possibility of creativity has actually led some philosophers to entertain a teleological model of the creative process: that is, the idea that somehow or other the creator is actually being "pulled" into the future by the transcendent product which he has not yet produced. Apart from the fact that I find this idea mildly incoherent, in that it insists upon "the control by the not-yet-there total situation over the present,"[33] it has other weaknesses as well. For in a sense, like mechanism, the teleological account seems to explain *too much*: for if the artist or scientist is being pulled into the future by his final creation, why does he ever *fail?* Why is the production of transcendent products so *difficult?* Why all the anxious searching in the dark? Moreover, and it seems to me that this is crucial, if the creator is being pulled into the future by his final product, how can he ever fail to recognize it once he has reached it? For he seemingly will no longer *feel* any pull. But there are some dramatic examples of creators actually hitting upon what ultimately turned out to be their final product, only to reject it. Thus Einstein, in 1913 or 1914, generated and considered the "actual field equations only to discard them for what at the time seemed compelling reasons."[34] If these field equations were themselves actually pulling Einstein towards them, his discarding of them is well nigh incomprehensible.

But the teleologist does have a point in his favor: the creator *is* being influenced by his products, only by the products he has managed to generate *so far* and not by some hypothetical product which is not yet there. Moreover, his activity *is* goal-directed, purposive, for he is trying to solve a problem. In addition, the creator will himself normally be aware of those very standards which his solution will have to meet if it is to be an acceptable one, and he can thus employ these standards as part of his solution-recognition apparatus. He can thus accept or

---

[33] E. Vivas, "Naturalism and Creativity," in *Creativity in the Arts*, ed. V. Tomas, 90.
[34] Banesh Hoffmann and Helen Dukas, 119.

reject aspects of what he has done so far on the basis of his knowledge of the problem he is trying to solve and of the standards which his solution must meet. In other words, we can say that the creator is under the "plastic" or "soft" control of his *job specification*—of the problem, and of the standards required of a solution.[35]

We are, I think, finally in a position to outline a plausible answer to our question. Basically, the answer rests upon the Darwinian idea of blind variation and selective retention. As should be obvious, Darwinism manages to transcend the limits of a strict mechanism (by recognizing the fertility of blind variation) while avoiding an out-and-out teleology (since these variations are selected rather than directed). This appears to be exactly what we are looking for—namely, a process combining "blindness" with "control." In other words, I am suggesting that we may plausibly view the creative process on a Darwinian model, as a case of the blind generation of variants coupled with the selective retention of "successful" variants, *all* under the plastic control of the creative job specification.[36]

To elaborate: we want a process which allows for the production of novelty but which is *not random*, for we want to be able to explain the *appropriateness* of the creative product. Moreover, we want a process in which the final product does not itself *direct* its very production—that is, we want a process which is *blind*. However, we also need a process in which the question of production has, in effect, been controlled (plastically) by those very factors which will enable the product to be a transcendent one—in other words, the process, cannot be *too* blind. The only way to satisfy all of these *desiderata* at once, I suggest, is to see the creator as (1) critically interacting with prior products, with a tradition, so as to put himself "in touch" with problems and standards for acceptable solutions; (2) generating *blindly, but not randomly*, a hopefully potential solution or fragments of such a solution—*blindly*, because these are generated without foreknowledge of success; *not randomly*,

---

[35] The notion of plastic control is due to Popper. The reason that the control of problems and standards is only plastic or soft (as opposed to 'cast-iron') is that these can themselves be modified by the very attempts to solve them or satisfy them.

[36] The psychologist Donald Campbell has already suggested a Darwinian model of the creative process in his paper, "Blind Variation and Selective Retention in Creative Thought as in Other Knowledge Processes," *Psychological Review* 67 (1960): 380–400. Where my account differs from his, however, is in seeing this Darwinian process as under the plastic control of the creative job specification. In a sense, from my point of view, Campbell's process is just a bit *too* blind.

because the generation is itself already under the plastic control of the relevant problem, the background of prior products, and the relevant standards; (3) critically interacting with this initial, fragmentary product so as to select or reject it, either in part or in its entirety, such a selection procedure being again under the plastic control of the problem, the background, and the relevant standards; (4) generating blindly, but not randomly, further hopefully potential solutions or fragments, this time under the plastic control not only of the initial problem, the background, and the relevant standards, but also under the plastic control of *what he has already done*, of his initial effort; (5) repeat step (3) (that is, critical selection); (6) repeat step (4) (that is, blind, but not random, generation); etc. *until*, hopefully, one has managed to generate or assemble a product which either meets the initial job specification or else meets some improved job specification—this improved job specification being itself the outcome of the above process.

It is essential to recognize that if the above schema is to work, the control which the problem, the relevant standards, and especially the background of prior products (the background "knowledge," so to speak) exercise over the creator *must* be a plastic control, not a "cast-iron" one. For the problem, standards, or background knowledge may themselves have to be modified during the very process itself. This becomes particularly clear if we remember that often the way to a solution to a problem is actually blocked by some of the background knowledge, even though the problem owes its very existence *to* this background knowledge. In this event, the creator will not be able to solve his problem unless he generates a potential solution that actually conflicts with this background knowledge; and this helps to explain why our third requirement on transcendent products sometimes *must be* fulfilled, if some of the other requirements are also to be fulfilled. Naturally, however, since the above process is blind—that is, since there is no foreknowledge of a solution—the creator cannot *know* (in advance) that his way *will be* blocked by a particular aspect of the background. But he might, through constant frustration, come to suspect that it is being so blocked, and thus loosen the control that he will allow this background to have over him; that is, he may be driven into becoming a potential revolutionary! Equally, however, his frustration might lead him to suspect that the very problem itself, which he is trying to solve, is in need of radical reformulation, and in *this* case he will loosen the control which his initial formulation has exercised over his generation and selection of variants. Clearly, if the control of either the background or the problem were cast-iron, it would be impossible for the creator to loosen their control over his generation and selection of variants. In other words, the *plasticity* of the control is crucial to the possibility of creativity, but so is the *control itself*. This is, perhaps, singularly paradoxical and mysterious; but then again, so is what we are trying to explain with its help.

The above account is, I fear, no more than the sketch of a theory, not a full-blown one. But it does, I believe, indicate how it might be possible to produce transcendent products, for it does help us to understand both the novelty and appropriateness of such products, as well as why they may come to conflict with the tradition out of which they sprang. Moreover, such a theory does *not* explain too much, for it clearly does not guarantee success. Nor does it turn creative achievements into something to be expected, or a matter of course. Just as evolutionary theory does not make *Homo Sapiens* into a necessary being, but does give him the right to exist, so too the theory of the creative process which I have presented gives transcendent products the right to exist, but no existential necessity. It thus leaves ample room for the mystery and miraculousness of great creative achievements; and for the inspiration, luck, or Divine Grace which great creators appeal to in their descriptions of their own creative processes.

IX *Conclusion: Transcendence and Self-Transcendence*

I have been arguing that creative products are what I have termed transcendent products—that they transcend the tradition out of which they spring. I have also been arguing that neither mechanism, nor pure randomness, nor teleology will ever be able to satisfactorily account for the emergence of such products, and so explain how creativity is possible. Rather, I have suggested, we must seek the explanation in a Darwinian process of variation and selection, which is itself under the plastic control, not of the yet-to-be realized transcendent product, but of the already realized *idea* of such products. But I cannot conclude without a brief mention of what I see to be the implications of all this for the creator himself; for the person who is, after all, ultimately responsible for the creative achievement he has produced.

It is well to remember that creative scientists and artists are as much the inheritors of tradition as they is the transcenders of tradition. In a sense, the scientist or artist is personally as much the *product* of a tradition as the producer of a product, which transcends that tradition. In other words, creative artists or scientists do not simply produce a transcendent product; in a sense, they actually transcend *themselves*. They produce something that they could not have willed, and which they could not know they had the ability to produce. As the bearer of tradition, they have not only gone beyond *it*, they have gone beyond *themselves*; they have transcended their Selves. One is reminded of the beautiful story about Haydn who, listening for the first time to his *Creation*, broke into tears and said: "I have not written this."[37]

---

[37] Reported in Popper's *Objective Knowledge*, 180. The idea of self-transcendence has been beautifully explored in Gombrich's paper, "Art and Self-Transcendence," in *The Palace of Value in a World of Facts*, eds. A. Tiselius and S. Nilsson (New York: Wiley Interscience Division, 1970) 125–133.

CHAPTER THREE

THE RATIONALITY OF CREATIVITY[1]

I. C. Jarvie

I *Introduction*

My title links two abstract nouns that are usually set over against each other, seen as contrasting, if not in opposition. The view that informs this paper is that what can usefully be said about creativity is very little, and rather trite; and that it is co-extensive with the rational element in creativity. There may or may not be other than rational elements in creativity; confronted with them, my inclination would be for the first time to invoke Wittgenstein: "whereof one cannot speak, thereof one should be silent." The little I think can be said about the rationality of creativity will be confined to section five. The preceding sections will offer a general critique of the literature, bringing out its poverty and its irrationality.

Much of the growing literature on creativity,[2] it seems to me, bypasses several quite decisive arguments. Properly understood, these arguments vitiate much of the debate in that literature. These arguments are the following: the problem to be solved by studying creativity is not clearly specified; creativity is treated as a psychological rather than a logical issue; that to explain creativity is to explain it away; and, when we create an explanation that explains creativity, it also, paradoxically, must explain itself. To each of these arguments I shall devote a section.

---

[1] Reprinted from *The Concept of Creativity in Science and Art*, eds. D. Dutton and M. Krausz (The Hague/Boston/London: Martinus Nijhoff Publishers, 1981), 109–128, *all rights reserved*.

[2] See J. P. Guilford, "Creativity," *American Psychologist* 5 (1950): 444–454; Arthur Koestler, *The Act of Creation* (London: Hutchinson, 1964); P. E. Vernon, *Creativity* (Harmondsworth: Penguin, 1970); J. W. Getzels and P. W. Jackson, *Creativity and Intelligence* (New York: Wiley, 1962); Anthony Storr, *The Dynamics of Creation* (New York: Atheneum, 1972); *Journal of Creative Behaviour* (1967).

II   *What Is the Problem?*

What problem is it intended that theories of creativity solve? This, to be sure, is a question rather than an argument. But the absence of a satisfactory answer to the question can be turned into an argument against the enterprise. Einstein remarked in several places that formulating the problem clearly constitutes the better part of the solution. Of course, different writers work on different problems. Were I to *set* problems concerning creativity for others to work on, I might instance the paradox that the originality of an original idea only becomes 'visible' against the background of an intellectual tradition, and those in an intellectual tradition can become trapped in it and blind to new ideas. I might ask whether ideas accumulate, or are reached in one jump. My self-imposed task is not, however, to set problems in this way; it is to express dissatisfaction with a body of literature.

J. P. Guilford,[3] in a paper often cited as initiating the modern literature on creativity, posed two questions for further research. (1) How can we discover creative promise in our children and youth? (2) How can we promote the development of creative personalities? Guilford was, at the time, President of the American Psychological Association, and his setting up of the problems for future research deserves close scrutiny. (1) tells us some children may be creatively promising. (2) implies that there are 'creative personalities' (creatively promising people?), whose development can be promoted. Creativity, then, is envisaged by Guilford as some sort of dependent variable, and the idea is to spot it and get to work on those factors, which affect it, in order to foster it.

But what is creativity that we should be interested in discovering it and promoting it? Presumably, it is something like the ability to produce new and original ideas, creations, inventions, and the like. But why should we want to discover thinkers, artists, and inventors, and promote their development? Is it because we want to increase the output of papers, works of art, and patents? Academics, art critics, and patent offices already complain loudly that they can scarcely keep up with the flood. And perhaps much of the flood are ideas, works of art, and inventions that are neither new, nor original, but merely dross. Output alone, then, I take it, cannot be the object of promoting creativity. Obviously, it is output of quality that is to be promoted.

---

[3] J. P. Guilford, "Creativity."

This aim is a rather complex one. Should there be an increase in the output of quality; or that plus a decrease in the output of trash; or merely a decrease in the output of trash? If the second or third, then an overall drop in output as such seems likely; if the first, I would suggest it is impossible—you get more quality only by getting more, and that includes more trash. At the moment, the rate of trash production seems to vary directly with the rate of production. Inverting the relationship might be very desirable. Its accomplishment strikes me as very unlikely, as I shall argue below, because part of the price of maximizing output is a great deal of waste.

Another possible answer to why we want to spot creativity is not because we want to increase it in general, but because we want urgently to foster it in particular cases. Think-tanks, brainstorm sessions, game theory, war games, contingency planning, futurology and economic model-builders all yearn to be creative in this sense; so do cancer researchers, unified field theorists, and governments faced with inflation. All these groups act as though a general theory of creativity might help them to achieve solutions to their problems, and might also help to achieve them sooner. These aims are at once absurdly over-ambitious and perfectly straightforward. It is absurd to imagine us ever being able to solve such pressing problems in a relatively straightforward or mechanical way. Our world does not seem to be made like that. If we routinize a type of problem, as we have in mathematics with tables, logarithms and calculators, that only transfers our ambition from what is now 'routine calculation,' to deeper and harder problems. The common sense side of the ambition to crack the pressing problems of humanity is heuristics and rules of thumb; general advice for analyzing problems, thinking about them, and so on. These have been forthcoming since intellectual endeavor began. An increase in them looks unlikely, on the face of it, to help with urgent problems.

So far, I have given two answers to the question of why we should want to discover and promote creativity. One is to increase quality output, the other is to facilitate the solution to urgent problems. Both answers are rather pragmatic; to do with practical social gains. Perhaps this is because we have implicitly equated creativity with cognition and technology, rather than with art. We rarely hear cries for an increase in the bulk quantity of art (even of quality art), unless it be from artists; artistic output is rarely acknowledged to be socially urgent (although a case can be made). But for miracle drugs, new sources of energy, even Polaroid movies, there is social urgency. As regards artistic creativity, then, neither output nor urgency constitutes a good reason for investigation. We need a third answer to the question 'why research into creativity at all,' an answer that is not pragmatic, and that takes account of works of art as well as cognition and technology. My suggestion would be: the simple desire to explain the creative achievement, to understand it better, to get at the truth about it. At the moment, creativity is in the *virtus dormativa* phase: 'creativity' is a property ascribed to certain artistic and intellectual achievements by certain creators who are said to possess the capacity to 'create,' as evidenced by the creativity of their work.

This is a parlous state of affairs indeed—provided only that an explanation of creativity is possible (my skepticism on this score will emerge presently). What, exactly, is in need of explanation; what is the problem? What fact or facts clash with what beliefs, theories, or expectations in the matter of creativity? I confess to not being sure. The obvious explanation of such uncertainty is that different writers have different problems, as we have already noted. There is, however, the possibility that the problems are connected, and hence can be set out in an orderly way. My suggestion for the status of most fundamental problem of all, from which the others branch off, is this. Creative achievements are unique events; explanatory progress is made only with repeatable events. Hence there is something inexplicable about creativity. Or, rather, to all new, interesting, novel, ingenious, pleasing, inventive, gifted: and other cognitive, technological: and artistic acts there is attributed a common property, something they all exemplify, something that can thus be studied and explained: this is called creativity. Thus the inaccessible uniqueness of creation is made to yield to the belief that nothing is mysterious, remote, inexplicable.

This fundamental problem is, I believe, absorbed during our elementary education. We are taught that artistic, cognitive, and technical achievements are unique events, miracles, strokes of luck (or genius) which we should mainly be concerned to welcome and study.[4] This fundamental epistemological pessimism seems to foreclose the problem: creativity just is an inexplicable 'gift.' Our rationality is signaled to the extent that we accept and make the best of this situation. That same education, however, also indicates an epistemological optimism:

---

[4] In the same way that chess masters record and study the grand masters and their great games. No one seems to be trying to find out what makes a great game great and thus deprive it of its mystique. Cf. Section III, below.

the achievements of science and technology suggest that all problems will sooner or later yield to human thought. We seem to have truth and beauty in such abundance that it is inconceivable that we cannot reach the truth about beauty, originality, etc. Although I claim this problem of inexplicable uniqueness to be the fundamental one behind the creativity literature, I do not claim it is soluble. I suspect that many who contribute to the literature mistakenly believe that because they have found a problem, or what looks like one, it must be soluble. Its insolubility, and indeed ultimate incoherence, in my view vitiates the entire literature.

Given, though, for the moment, that this is a soluble problem, let us continue discussing the attempt to explain creativity. Perhaps if we could explain creativity, specify the laws it obeys and the initial conditions productive of it, then the aims of increased output and/or urgent solutions would be facilitated. The problems of output and urgency would then clearly be subordinate to the problem of inexplicable uniqueness. Were that so, might it not have been better organization on my part to begin with explanation as an aim, and then to move on to increased output and urgent solutions as subordinate or by-product aims? The reason I did not proceed in this way is because of the possibility that an explanation of creativity would not solve the practical problems of output and urgency. Our understanding of earthquakes, continental drift, ice ages, red giants and black holes may make us feel better, emotionally and intellectually, but they do not give us any power over the processes in question. Is it not entirely possible that the concatenation of elements required for creativity obey laws such that human intervention is not possible? Maybe creativity is an outcome of trial and error, and obeys only the laws of chance. We can explain the roulette wheel without being about to gamble on it successfully.

For example, one strand in the literature, which undoubtedly can be traced back to Freud, is the idea that creativity is a manifestation of psychological disorder.[5] The most extreme recent case is Storr's argument that Einstein's genius was a by-product of a psychological condition, namely schizophrenia (could the schizophrenia not be a

---

[5] Storr, *The Dynamics of Creation*, 61ff. Jean Cocteau somewhere compares being creative to being pregnant. Salvador Dali expresses similar ideas in *The Secret Life of Salvador Dali* (New York: Dial Press, 1961), as does the brilliant and tormented British painter Francis Bacon. See David Sylvester, *Interviews With Francis Bacon* (London: Thames and Hudson, 1975).

by-product of his genius?). Confirmations of the neuroses of creative people abound: from Berkeley's concern with the bowels to Einstein's eccentricities of dress and manner, from Bobby Fischer's tantrums to the unbelievable squalor of Francis Bacon's studio. But what of counter-examples? What of Mozart, Rembrandt, Hume? What of the argument that even if all creators have neuroses, not all neurotics are creative, and hence the creative value of what someone does cannot be fully understood in terms of their psychology? What makes the difference between Einstein's psychopathology and that of the schizophrenic who believes he is a piece of soap? The answer has to focus on the content of their ideas, and thus has to have reference to something like the objective existence of intellectual problems and traditions, and the further fact that Einstein's psychopathology resulted in his contributing to those rather than to the private world of insane fantasy. We cannot, as it were, direct neuroses into science and art rather than intellectual rubbish. This argument goes to undermine the idea that an explanation of creativity, even if found, will lead to practical knowledge of how to foster creativity. We might get further with folk tales and rules of thumb.

So much then for doubts about the utility of solving the basic problem of inexplicable uniqueness. Let me now argue that no such explanations of creativity are there to be found. The case I choose is the movies; not just because they are a specialty of mine, but also because their creative processes are less privatized than those of the traditional arts and sciences (I suppose it is a bit analogous to studying research teams rather than individual scientists). Producers of movies, obviously, have sought for many years to understand what makes a movie a success. Success is an aspect of creativity that cannot be gainsaid simply because popularity is one of its desiderata. In the classical arts, the crucial desideratum of success (so seldom mentioned) was to please the patron, the dedicatee, or God, as well as the artist himself.[6] One might

---

[6] When I was first introduced to Rembrandt's painting known as *The Night Watch*, it was remarked that its bold, active, almost chiaroscuro style had shocked those who commissioned it, and Rembrandt's intransigent artistic temperament on this point contributed to his financial downfall. The idea was that crass patrons always failed to understand geniuses, who had to be tough to maintain their integrity. Later, I noticed this story was declared a legend by contemporary historians, who claim that the picture was always hung, that Rembrandt's commissions did not dry up, and who attribute his downfall to expensive living (especially the house). The theory that all creative artists are misunderstood by hoi polloi is a widespread and pernicious one, since it can be used to rebut all criticism, and even self-criticism and doubt.

say that in movies, to be a creative success is to make something both interesting *and* popular. By this standard, the most creative periods in Hollywood were between 1914 and 1926, and, again, from the mid-thirties to the mid-forties. The first period marks the maturity and development of the silent movie, the second, maturity and development in the sound movie. What can explain such periods of creative success? Certainly no psychological theory of creativity will do, for this would be to reduce a creative era or a creative place to a fortuitous concatenation of individuals. To give so much to fortune seems excessive.

Two factors are widely bruited:[7] experiment and encouragement. While there may be exceptions, these factors do seem crucial, whether we think of Ingmar Bergman, the French New Wave, or the vintage periods of Hollywood. Freedom to (and security despite) experiment and continuing encouragement are entirely characteristic of Hollywood in the two periods mentioned, less as a policy than as an unintended consequence of institutional arrangements. By 1914, silent movies were twenty years old, technically accomplished, highly successful with the public, and hence not trammeled with rules, regulations, and restrictions. No one really knew for sure and in advance what would click at the box office and be something to be proud of as well. Hence many filmmakers were given their heads as soon as they had a success. This was institutional rather than attitudinal. Doubtless many movie moguls were crass and vulgar and concerned solely with catering to public taste. But they had to work through and with men who had a professional and creative pride; who were not and would not think of themselves as hacks. In some cases their self-estimation may have been excessive, but that is not important. What matters is that men of the caliber of D. W. Griffith, Eric von Stroheim, C. B. DeMille, King Vidor, John Ford, Buster Keaton, and other slapstick comedians were challenged and stimulated by a new medium to an unprecedented degree. At first, they simply enjoyed themselves immensely. Early Hollywood seems to have been a place where any crazy idea could get a hearing, and creators worked at a frantic pace.[8] What sorted out the sheep from

---

[7] See J. Agassi, "The Function of Intellectual Rubbish," *Research in the Sociology of Knowledge, Science, and Art* 2 (1979): 209–227.

[8] Charles Chaplin, *My Autobiography* (London: The Bodley Head, 1964; Penguin ed., 1966), 154. Chaplin was amazed when Mack Sennett said to him, "We have no scenario. We get an idea, then follow the natural sequence of events." So different from what he describes as the "rigid, non-deviating routine" of the theatre.

the goats was the popular touch, whether in a player or a director. Unawareness may have been something of a blessing, for with public acclaim came self-consciousness and, ultimately, pretension. Griffith and Stroheim are examples, as is Orson Welles in the forties. The most spectacular case, however, is Charlie Chaplin. This London street urchin, who became a brilliant vaudeville comedian of the English music hall, went to Los Angeles to try himself in films in 1913. He worked steadily and quickly until 1916. In that year he was negotiating a new contract with a different company, and this necessitated a trip to New York. He cabled his brother which train he was on, and settled down for the five-day journey. Remarking that in those days he was unrecognized when out of make-up and costume, he recalls being in the middle of shaving when the train was swamped with people in Amarillo, Texas. They were looking for him! Telegraph operators had spread the word that he was coming, and cities laid on formal welcoming ceremonies.[9] Chaplin himself does not say this, but I detect the beginnings of self-consciousness and decline in his movies from that experience, although there are occasional reversions to form. By 1918, Chaplin persuaded D. W. Griffith, Mary Pickford and Douglas Fairbanks to join him in creating their own film company under the title United Artists. Grandeur indeed.

After the introduction of sound, movies were in effect a new medium. Technical teething troubles over, they conquered the depression business slump and entered another golden age artistically and economically. It sounds incredible, but Los Angeles in the thirties seems to have been a cultural El Dorado. Gathered there were Hugh Walpole, Aldous Huxley, Christopher Isherwood, Thomas Mann, Bertolt Brecht, Thornton Wilder, F. Scott Fitzgerald, William Faulkner, Raymond Chandler, Nathanael West, Ben Hecht, Igor Stravinsky, Sir C. Aubrey Smith, Sir Cedric Hardwicke, Leslie Howard, Laurence Olivier, Orson Welles, John Houseman, and Vivien Leigh—to name only a few whose fame owed nothing to the movies. The combination of the attractions of California living with the intense creativity and excitement of Hollywood almost produced a cultural center to rival New York. In this atmosphere the individuals sometimes flourished and sometimes suffered, but the movies only flourished.[10]

---

[9] Ibid., 175–179.
[10] The most evocative account of Hollywood in the thirties and forties is by Charles Higham and Joel Greenberg, *Hollywood in the Forties* (London: A. Zwemmer, 1968). The

We can see then that there is some pattern to periods of great creativity. We cannot reproduce them at will. The fundamental strength of public demand for movies cannot be recovered, especially since the arrival of television. Hence, there have been long periods in which filmmakers have been offered anything but encouragement and certainly nothing like freedom. Recently a new phenomenon has appeared: desperate experimentation in the face of bankruptcy. Several of the major American movie companies have gone from success to collapse in the last six or seven years. For a time, there were unrivalled opportunities for innovation and experiment. But that has passed, and a pervading sense of insecurity co-exists with the most profitable year since 1946.[11]

In this section, I have argued that the first weakness in studies of creativity is poorly articulated aims. When the aims are articulated it seldom looks as though any of them could sustain the kinds of explorations of creativity that have been undertaken—practical or theoretical.

III   A Logical or a Psychological Issue?

Philosophers commonly distinguish between what they call the logic and the psychology of knowledge; between, that is, the rational reconstruction of the propositions and inferences which constitute knowledge, and the subjective mental processes that go on in those producing it. The aim of making the distinction is to free epistemology from psychology, to deny that knowledge has anything to do with belief. In a similar manner, I should like to distinguish between creativity as an objective matter, a property, so to speak, of created works; and creativity as a property of persons or their minds. Much of the research into creativity is in the latter category and, though I am skeptical of it for reasons already and yet to be stated, I do not want to discuss it directly. What I want to stress is the distinction and the consequences of its neglect. Unless there is an objective logic of creativity, a psychology of

---

only book I know which attempts seriously to discuss the creative process in movies without reference to individual genius, but rather to collective endeavor, is Lawrence Alloway, *Violent America: The Movies 1946–1964* (New York: Museum of Modern Art, distributed by the New York Graphic Society, Greenwich, Conn., 1971).

[11] See Pauline Kael, "On the Future of the Movies," *New Yorker* (5 August 1974): 43–59.

creativity can be of no interest. The psychology of scientists is interesting mainly because they are doing science, and science means something like exploring the way the world is. Presumably, creativity is interesting because there is something going on in creative people that results in objective results: creations. What are the objective achievements? Here the whole subject seems to become anecdotal: sayings and stories about the great geniuses are trundled out. Two things strike one: first, the *virtus dormativa* effect; second, that the achievements called creative can be characterized without the concept of creativity and without remainder. Originality, novelty, synthesis, insight, and so on suffice. The status of creativity as a property in its own right is highly questionable.

This is the main reason I have postponed saying anything direct about creativity until the end. So far, we have asked the simple question, what are the aims of studying creativity? This was an obvious question with which to begin a discussion of rationality and creativity, since a rational action is necessarily (though not sufficiently) a goal-directed action. But this question is also a second-order question: it is about the study of creativity, not about creativity. Here we begin to capture in a preliminary way some elements of what this paper is advocating. I believe that the rationality of creativity has to do not so much with the (psychological) creative process, as with the rationality of the creator towards his own creative process. In other words, rationality is to be located in the actions the creator takes, before, and especially after, any 'act of creation' occurs.

For various obvious reasons which I do not here want to go into,[12] Popperians often say that rational belief is only a special case of rational action; they subordinate or even absorb the act of belief or creation into action. Hence those who look on creativity psychologically, as bisociation, or psychoneurosis, and so on, as though there was a ghost in the machine, a Magic Moment when the Muse Speaks, a flash of blinding light, an urge to cry Eureka, are bypassed. Action before and action after eventually squeeze out what is in between.

Rational action is goal-directed action, where the tools are critically held theories. Rational thought is action directed to the goal of solving intellectual or artistic problems. The rationality of rational action shows itself in critical open-mindedness, trial and error. The rationality of

---

[12] See J. Agassi, "The Role of Corroboration in Popper's Methodology," *Australasian Journal of Philosophy* 39 (1961): 82–91; J. Agassi and I. C. Jarvie, "The Problem of the Rationality of Magic," *British Journal of Sociology* 18 (1967): 55–74.

rational thought consists of trial and error, which is a form of action. It is not the problem being tackled that is rational; no more is it the solution being offered that is rational; but the method of trying out the thought, inspiration, idea, against the problem, against other solutions and, in some interesting cases, against the facts, that is rational. This is the case whether the problem be called cognitive or artistic.[13]

One hears the response that this is all very well, but that the theory of creativity comes to explain the new thought, the very thing that is put on trial. This presupposes the mind, soul, ghost in the machine, that receives or creates the new thought, the inspiration, does the bisociation, or whatnot. My counter-suggestion would be that my account allows us to dispense with the mind reified in this sense, and hence creativity hypostatized in this sense, for the mind becomes the product rather than the producer of rational organization, of goal-directed, trial-and-error action. Einstein said: "my pencil is more intelligent than I."[14]

This view also proposes a rather different approach to the practical questions of increasing output, solving particular urgent problems. It suggests no recipe, but general social conditions of encouragement and freedom. Bisociation and the like are mental acts which—whether or not they lie at the root of creativity—is somehow irrelevant since there is no way to foster or induce them. Whereas an institutional setup that fosters freedom and encouragement—while not easy to construct—has been constructed from time to time, sometimes inadvertently. The other consequence of my view is that fostering creativity may turn out to be a less attractive prospect than it sounds. What I have in mind is this. Neither a favorable social setup nor an array of rules of thumb, are a recipe for creative achievement. So much expenditure may be undertaken without promise or even hope of results. Indeed, even if success is achieved, they predict that its cost will be a huge amount of what will later be designated waste: that is to say, we know beforehand that much of our expenditure will be afterwards declared waste, yet we cannot specify in advance what will be waste, and hence we cannot eliminate it. Thus we are denied the comfort of even thinking we can eliminate waste. (Although in my view we can dispense with the moral overtones on waste by declaring waste part of the costs of production.)

---

[13] What I have in mind is Gombrich's notion of art as "making and matching." See E. H. Gombrich, *Art and Illusion* (London: Phaidon Press, 1960).
[14] Einstein is quoted to this effect in K. R. Popper, *Objective Knowledge* (Oxford: The Clarendon Press, 1972), 225n.

If we divert the entire budget of the U.S. Pentagon into research into the causes of cancer, say, we can no more guarantee success (however that is defined) than we can assure the gambler that his number will come up (it will, but he could be dead before it does). No doubt, in time, scientific research on this scale would yield the bureaucracy, jobs, and contracting industry that the military budget does: and there are unattractive as well as attractive aspects to there being so many men and women in white coats. It is unlikely such expenditure and such waste would ever be agreed to because, while the military has a task at which it is very rarely tested, cancer research is tested every time a patient dies.

So much, then, for the question of what problems are being tackled in the literature on creativity. Not only are these problems not often formulated, formulating them inclines one to the conclusion that they cannot be solved: not simply because they are difficult or intractable but, much more seriously, because they reveal muddles that may vitiate the enterprise. Creativity may not give rise to clear problems because on no known theory is it presupposed as a definite property of the physical world or the world of mind. To avoid concluding it is chimerical we shall have to seek it elsewhere.

IV   *Creativity a World 3 Event*

The groundwork for the second main argument, about to be developed, has been extensively laid down in the discussion so far. Creativity, like knowledge or discovery, can be seen to have a logical as well as a psychological aspect. A solution to a problem can be judged creative; so can the mind which produced that solution. However, a solution that was in fact creative can fail to be recognized as such at the time, and its creator can similarly be thought not creative. The problems we are talking about can be cognitive or artistic. J. S. Bach is my favorite example: a composer virtually dismissed in his own time as a competent but rather pedestrian fellow, far outshone by his brilliant sons C. P. E. and J. C.[15] While those sons are by no means forgotten, they can hardly now be mentioned in the same breath as their father, who has serious claim to being one of the (if not the) greatest composers who ever lived.

---

[15] I. C. Jarvie, "The Objectivity of Criticism of the Arts," *Ratio* 9 (1967): 67–83. Tovey comments that Bach's art was neglected "as old-fashioned and crabbed" by his younger contemporaries. We owe his rediscovery to Mendelssohn and Schumann. (See "Bach, J. S." in *Encyclopedia Britannica*, 11th ed.).

With cognition, the question becomes more involved. For one thing, there is a popular prejudice in favor of positive science being called creative at the expense of negative science. Positive and negative are connected with the simpleminded distinction between, say, a theory (positive) and its criticism (negative). Sometimes, lord help us, a distinction is made between negative and constructive criticism. Hence, Copernicus is creative for inventing heliocentrism, but the many critics of Ptolemy are not even well-known. Along these lines one might as well say Plato was creative and Aristotle was not: but this shows up the absurdity. Aristotle created beautiful arguments against Plato which were enormous creative achievements in themselves. Isaac Newton was a creative genius, but so too was Berkeley, who picked holes in Newton's mathematics and metaphysics.

All this discussion is in the logical realm. Solving a problem is creative; devising a criticism of a theory is creative. Creativeness cannot be unpacked in any precise way, and indeed I have hinted earlier that it may be a dispensable term. What I want to emphasize here is the different point that whether or not an idea or a criticism is a creative one has nothing to do with psychology, with whether an act of creation, inspiration, or bisociation has occurred. Indeed, the extensive discussion of humor by both Koestler and Freud demonstrates this. So far as this paper is concerned, there is nothing creative about jokes. I find the expressions, 'what a creative joke,' or, 'he's a really creative comedian,' very odd. Odder, is the attention given to humor by those interested in creativity.

If there is rationality in creativity it is of course going to be located in the public, objective, logical realm, and not in the psychological one. Hence the importance of this distinction and the fact that it plays haywire with the literature on creativity. On this view, creativity is a cognate of 'simple,' 'powerful,' 'unifying,' 'exciting,' 'trail-blazing,' and other sorts of adjectives that might be attached to new theories, new criticisms, or new works of art. The rationality of creativity then consists of it being successful action directed at solving an artistic or cognitive problem. Calling something a 'creative failure,' might simply indicate ingenuity. Degrees of creativity are also sometimes alluded to, but I see no way of explicating these in any discussible manner.

Perhaps the notion of creativity, then, is that of a socially defined event in the world of ideas or art, what Popper has called the world of objective mind, or mind objectified, the third world or World 3.[16]

---

[16] K. R. Popper, *Objective Knowledge*, chap. 3, 4.

This rather than a 'property of the mind.' A new theory or work of art undoubtedly has its physical or World 1 aspects—marks on paper or daubs on canvas. It also undoubtedly in some sense had its origins in certain mental acts of its creator, in World 2. But neither of these is of much importance or interest. What makes a theory a new theory, a work of art an original work of art, is the objective relationship it bears as a World 3 object to other World 3 objects, other theories and works of art.[17] These in turn have gained their significance because of the bearing they have on those especially important World 3 entities known as problems, that is to say, former theories, or means of portraying the world in art that have now become inconsistent or otherwise unsatisfactory. The standards of what is new or what is a creative addition to art are similarly a judgment within World 3, constantly subject to World 3 debate. Art and cognition are the mind striving to achieve objective existence in the external World 3, transcending space and time, and they achieve that when something is created (a theory, a solution, a new problem, a new argument, a 'match,' a 'discovery,' etc.). Put it like this: to seek in the physical world a recipe for, or an explanation of, what physical conditions bring about Einstein's pencil marks is no more absurd than asking us what kinds of mind or mental process brings about Einstein's great thoughts. Just as Einstein's pencil marks have no meaning unless their significance in the third world is understood, so his thoughts have no interest unless there is a third world significance. This is precisely my objection to Storr's view of Einstein as a psychopath. What possible explanatory value does this hold? What counts is not psychopathy, but the world of objective ideas. This is the logical aspect of creation and cognition; creativity in a certain sense only exists as a vector in World 3.

V   *To Explain Away*

The third decisive argument undermining the entire enterprise of studying creativity in the manner it is currently studied has been most eloquently expressed by Einstein in his beautiful essay on Newton.

---

[17] This may explain my total opposition (not to modern art but) to modernism in art, the philosophy that traditions must be broken with. How someone trained as, or pretending to be, an artist can even think of this is something of a mystery; it is a bit like an English speaker deciding to utter only gibberish.

Conceding that reason is weak when measured against its never-ending task, Einstein hails Newton as the first to succeed in explaining a wide range of phenomena mathematically, logically, quantitatively, and in harmony with experience. How, he asks, 'did this miracle come to birth in his brain?' Then he apologizes for the 'illogical' question, "for if by reason we could deal with the problem of 'how,' then there would be no question of a miracle in the proper sense of the word."[18]

In other words, what Einstein is saying is that creativity is interesting precisely because and to the extent that it is uniquely mysterious. Were it not such, it would not be creativity. We can show this by imagining what the reaction would be were we to pinpoint the creative element in many cases of creation. I contend that what would happen then is that we would set out to isolate other, alternative special features of creativity as 'the miracle.'

The problem here is that this argument shows that creativity is such that were it to be explained it would be explained away. Usually an explanation of something does not explain it away. When it does, something is wrong.

VI   *Self-Reference*

The fourth decisive argument is this. Suppose we had an explanation of creativity. *A fortiori*, that would be an explanation of new explanations. *A fortiori*, it would be an explanation of that new explanation itself that we have just devised (namely of creativity).

Were we to say, (*T*) 'All creation is a product of neurosis,' we should also have to say that (*T*) itself, being a creation, was a product of neurosis—regardless of who first uttered it. But how are we to know that this neurotic manifestation is to be taken seriously, whereas the belief that someone is a piece of soap is not?

VII   *Trial and Error*

Having, then, looked at four arguments, which seem to me not only not met but quite impossible to meet, the grounds for my skepticism

---

[18] Albert Einstein, "Isaac Newton," in his *Out of My Later Years* (New York: Philosophical Library, 1950), 219–223, quote from 220.

towards the literature on creativity have been exposed. Toward the beginning of the paper, I said that what could be said about creativity was rather trite and rather scanty. At the risk of now being both trite and scanty, I present a few remarks on the matter additional to what has emerged in the foregoing discussion. Bertrand Russell, Mozart, and moviemaking are my examples of creativity; Russell in the cognitive area, Mozart in the area of individual artistic creation, movies in the area of collective artistic creation; Russell and Mozart fluent and individual geniuses, movies made by committees.[19]

In his essay, 'How I Write,'[20] Russell reports that, when bothered by a problem, he tried the method of writing and rewriting, but he invariably found the first version to be the best. This was a discovery about himself (his mind, but, more importantly, its World 3 achievements). Eventually, he adopted the following method. After concentrating reflection on the problem at hand, possibly writing nothing, he had planted it in his subconsciousness and would turn to other things. At some point the solution would re-emerge into his consciousness, and it only remained for him to write it out. This is a very striking passage in Russell. It gives concrete and helpful hints ("Turn to other things for a while"). It explains the sense of inspiration or revelation (as the rush created by the surfacing of subconscious mental work). It is also followed by a careful disclaimer. Russell points out that not everything he produced in this manner was creative or valuable or true. He says merely that this was his conscious method of working, which he had discovered by trial and error. After the fact, he decided whether what he had written was publishable. Even after he had published he might later decide that some of the things he had said were false. He emphasized, however, that his aim was simply to try to do the best he could at the time. The Russell Archives at McMaster University are filled with early drafts of books and articles that never saw the light of day. Hence, we see at work in Russell a conscious process of trial and error, a totally rational approach to creativity as ultimately a World 3 matter.[21]

---

[19] See I. C. Jarvie, *Towards a Sociology of the Cinema* (London: Routledge and Kegan Paul, 1970), chap. 1–3.

[20] In Bertrand Russell, *Portraits from Memory* (London: George Allen and Unwin, 1956), 194–197. Storr, *The Dynamics of Creation*, 42–43 attributes a similar idea to Graham Wallas.

[21] To show that Russell's cool detachment has nothing to do with his endeavors being logical and cognitive, one could cite the superb American painter Edward Hooper,

Similar in some ways is the fluency reported of Mozart, whose sub-conscious seems to have been working on music the whole time. Hence, he could compose in his head, play from memory, and write down the piece later; compose while playing billiards; even compose a prelude while copying down the already thought-out fugue.[22] He left very few notebooks or sketches, and yet is known to have corrected and improved works a great deal, often turning aside to easier, lighter commissions while struggling hard with problems in more intense works.

I have picked on examples like Russell and Mozart because on the surface they look so fluent and 'inspired,' the opposite of the hesitant, diffident, groping, trial-and-error creator I have in mind. In close-up, however, this impression disappears. Russell and Mozart have to be rational about their own creativity too. Russell reports a harrowing exception to his own method of work when he was writing *Principia Mathematica*. He tried consciously to work hard and creatively. The strain of working on the abstract and difficult problems of that book from 1902–1910 was so severe that "my intellect never quite recovered.... I have been ever since definitely less capable of dealing with difficult abstractions than I was before."[23]

Artists and intellectuals work as they can, as they find they have been most successful (in the World 3, not public opinion, sense) and exercise much of their critical faculties on the question of what is good enough to release. Painters throw away canvases, or store them away incomplete, perhaps to be finished one day, perhaps not; writers submit themselves to editors (who may be themselves, their wives, as well as others), the most startling case of which came to light recently with the publication of Ezra Pound's editing of T. S. Eliot's poem, *The Waste Land*. Some people went so far as to wonder whether publication

---

who not only creates by "painting, scraping off, and repainting," but also is dominated by the objective logic of creation: "I find, in working, always the distracting intrusion of elements not part of my most interested vision, and the inevitable obliteration and replacement of this vision by the work itself as it proceeds. The struggle to prevent this decay is, I think, the common lot of all painters to whom the invention of arbitrary forms has lesser interest. I believe that the great painters, with their intellect as master have attempted to force this unwitting medium of paint and canvas into a record of their emotions. I find any disgression from this large aim leads me to boredom." (Quoted in Lloyd Goodrich, *Edward Hoppper* [New York: H. N. Abrams, 1971], 161.).

[22] See the account in Erich Hertzmann, "Mozart's Creative Process," in *The Creative World of Mozart*, ed. Paul Henry Lang (New York: W. W. Norton, 1963), 17–30.

[23] Bertrand Russell, *The Autobiography of Bertrand Russell, 1872–1914* (London: George Allen and Unwin, 1967), 152–153.

did not detract from Eliot's stature as a creative innovator.[24] The short answer to that, I suppose, is that Eliot could have restored any cuts Pound made had it been his judgment that they did not serve to solve the poetic problem with which he was grappling. Furthermore, many artists and intellectuals show their work to friends, wives, children, professional peers, editors, publishers and the like long before it sees the light of day. Academe has a tradition of acknowledging such help. Because that tradition is not general does not at all imply the practice is not.

It is not hard, then, to see the process of trial and error not only at work, but consciously employed, in cognition and the individual arts. A *fortiori* it is not going to be difficult to detect it in collective arts, whether architecture or the cinema. Filmmaking not only employs trial and error, but, to the extent possible, institutionalizes—even bureaucratizes—it. This is not necessarily all to the good, as, obviously, excessive trial is a form of caution. Once Russell knew that earlier works he had written contained mistakes, or did not sell, he might have been justified in publishing nothing. Capable of error and yet wanting to avoid it, the cautious policy is to do nothing.[25] Capable of failure, yet desperately trying to avoid it, cautious movie producers compromise— that is to say, they interpret trial results too soon and too harshly. This permeates the creative process in movies, which is an institutionalized clash between art and commerce, each side with its own problems, its own integrity, its own series of trials and errors to be avoided. Money being the necessary, but by no means sufficient, condition of there ever being any films made at all, commerce holds a powerful position. The subtlety is not that the bureaucratic organization is split between commercial people and creative people, but that commerce and creation coexist in most film people. Hence, a script may be written and rewritten until it has shape and coherence; it then may be rewritten some more to improve its commercial possibilities. The same will apply to casting, to decisions on sets, costumes and locations, to editing the picture, to the manner in which it is publicized. The writer, the direc-

---

[24] T. S. Eliot, *The Waste Land*, a facsimile and transcript of the original drafts including the annotations of Ezra Pound, ed. Valerie Eliot (New York: Harcourt, Brace, Jovanovich, 1971).

[25] In the movies, this becomes interesting in the political dimension. From time to time Russia and China made it so difficult to avoid ideological error (because of unpredictable shifts in the party line) that filmmaking shrank almost to zero.

tor, the actor, the cameraman, the set designer, and the editor are all simultaneously in search of a solution to their creative problems which is also commercially viable. Some trials are creative (does that scene cut well?), some commercial (does the preview audience like it?), many are a mixture of both. For sure, the box office is neither physical nor psychological; I suggest that the creative side similarly is a sort of objective matter.

In film, as in the other arts, but less so in philosophy and still less so in science, there is a tedious avant-garde with a romantic view of creativity as mainly consisting in not interrupting while the Muse speaks through the favored individual. Life is easier that way. Being rational and self-critical is very hard and sometimes impossible. It is nevertheless the key to anything deserving the label creativity.

CHAPTER FOUR

CREATIVITY AS A DARWINIAN PHENOMENON:
THE BLIND-VARIATION AND
SELECTIVE-RETENTION MODEL

Dean Keith Simonton

I *Introduction*

In 1859, Charles Darwin advanced a theory that provided a scientific explanation for the evolution of life—the *Origin of Species* as the book's title has it.[1] Because Darwin argued that species evolved into new species through the process of natural selection, his explanation is often called 'selection theory.' However, selection does not constitute the sole process in Darwin's theory. On the contrary, selection depends on variation. Darwin assumed that organisms varied on numerous inheritable traits and that these traits conferred differential levels of adaptation. Those organisms that display superior fitness to the environment are more likely to survive the 'struggle for existence' and thereby pass their adaptive traits to the next generation. As should be apparent, without variation there can be no selection.

Even more to the point, the variation side of Darwin's theory is in many respects more provocative than the selection side. It may seem obvious, even tautological, to argue that those trait variants that bestow more fitness are most likely to survive in the gene pool. Yet Darwin's claims about the variations were more controversial in his own time, and continue to be so today: The variations displayed little volition nor intelligence. The variations are generated without any foresight into which variants were most likely to survive and reproduce. The variations are not pre-adapted, and many will be outright maladaptive. Although the species population as a whole might move toward enhanced environmental fitness, that movement could only be accomplished by producing many variants that will fail to outlast the

---

[1] Charles Darwin, *On the Origin of the Species by Means of Natural Selection: Or, The Preservation of Favoured Races in the Struggle for Life* (London: J. Murray, 1859).

selection process. Darwin's theory views variation as ignorant of future outcomes, and therefore inherently wasteful. Only a small proportion of all competing variants will prevail.

In a sense, Darwin's theory can be considered an implicit theory of creativity—albeit the creativity associated with life. It is a theory of how new forms emerge from the old. Indeed, the theory even features a direct relation with the definition of creativity favored by most researchers.[2] Specifically, creativity is defined as an idea that fulfills two independent requirements. First, a creative idea must be original, novel, or surprising. Repeating what has been done before does not count as creative. Second, a creative idea must work; that is, it must be adaptive or functional as judged by some criterion or set of criteria. Otherwise, it would be impossible to distinguish the creative from the crazy. Of course, both requirements are riddled with all sorts of niceties. Is originality, novelty, or surprise gauged with respect to the individual or society? Must an idea be adaptive for just the person or must it also work for other persons? Because satisfactory answers to these questions would demand another chapter, I will say no more here. The point I want to make is that the origin of species also arises from adaptive originality—the new variants that exhibit greater fitness.

Given this analytical connection, it may not be surprising that Darwin's theory soon influenced ideas about human creativity. The creative process in *Homo sapiens* could be perceived as functioning according to processes that were analogous to those responsible for the evolution of that species from common ancestors among the anthropoid apes. The first major thinker to make this connection was William James, the functionalist psychologist and pragmatist philosopher. Just a bit more than two decades after the first edition of *Origin*, James published, "Great Men, Great Thoughts, and the Environment" in which he sketched a Darwinian theory of creativity. James said:

> social evolution is a resultant of the interaction of two wholly distinct factors: the individual, deriving his peculiar gifts from the play of psychological and infra-social forces, but bearing all the power of initiative and origination in his hands; and, second, the social environment, with its power of adopting or rejecting both him and his gifts.[3]

---

[2] Dean Keith Simonton, "Creativity: Cognitive, Developmental, Personal, and Social Aspects," *American Psychologist* 55 (2000): 151–158.
[3] William James, "Great Men, Great Thoughts, and the Environment," *Atlantic Monthly* 46 (1880): 441–459; quote from 448.

He also described the cognitive processes by which the individual generates originality:

> Instead of thoughts of concrete things patiently following one another in a beaten track of habitual suggestion, we have the most abrupt cross-cuts and transitions from one idea to another, the most rarefied abstractions and discriminations, the most unheard of combination of elements, the subtlest associations of analogy; in a word, we seem suddenly introduced into a seething cauldron of ideas, where everything is fizzling and bobbling about in a state of bewildering activity, where partnerships can be joined or loosened in an instant, treadmill routine is unknown, and the unexpected seems only law.[4]

The process is chaotic rather than ordered, haphazard rather than deliberate, combinatorial rather than logical.

Unfortunately, James followed Darwin too closely insofar as he tended to view the individual creator as the unit of selection. Each creative individual was accepted or rejected according to that person's total ideational fitness. Although there can be no doubt that selection can occasionally take place at this level, it is often more useful to conceive selection as taking place within rather than across individuals.[5] In particular, individual creators themselves generate ideational variants that undergo selection by the individual. It is that conception of the creative process that I wish to make the focus of this chapter.

I begin by providing a summary of Donald Campbell's theory[6] and then offer an overview of empirical research findings that lend support to its basic tenants. I conclude by offering a broader discussion of the theory's advantages and disadvantages.

II   *The BVSR Model*

Campbell proposed that creativity occurred via the process of *blind variation and selective retention*, or what has been called a BVSR process.[7] The selective retention portion is governed by a set of criteria that

[4] Ibid., 456.
[5] Dean Keith Simonton, *Origins of Genius: Darwinian Perspectives on Creativity* (New York: Oxford University Press, 1999).
[6] Donal T. Campbell, "Blind Variation and Selective Retention in Creative Thought as in other Knowledge Processes," *Psychological Review* 67 (1960): 380–400.
[7] Gary A. Cziko, "From Blind to Creative: In Defense of Donald Campbell's *Selectionist Theory of Human Creativity.*" *Journal of Creative Behavior* 32 (1998): 192–208.

must be satisfied for an ideational variation to be retained for further use. For instance, of all potential solutions to a given problem, that one that meets the specified conditions will be preserved. Like in the case of Darwin's original theory, this is the least interesting and least controversial feature of the BVSR model. More provocative and contentious is the first step of the process—that which generates blind variations. Campbell maintained that true creativity required a certain amount of groping in the dark. The creator had to engage in some process in which the outcome of any given trial was uncertain. Any given ideational variant may or may not fulfill the twofold requirement of originality and adaptiveness, which is the hallmark of creativity.

It is critical to recognize that by *blind*, Campbell did not mean *random*. Although all random variations are blind, not all blind variations are random. He gave a specific example of 'systematic sweep scanning' to illustrate a mechanism that is blind but not random. Thus, when radar scans the horizon for aircraft at a fixed rate of motion and angle of search, each scan remains blind in the sense that the apparatus is not exploiting any *a priori* knowledge about the precise location of any approaching aircraft. This illustration also shows that the blindness is a quantitative rather than qualitative feature of the process. Obviously a radar installation will usually take advantage of some information about how to restrict the search. For example, radars at airports do not search for planes coming from straight overhead. Radars installed for defense purposes may limit the search to the direction from which an air assault must necessarily arrive. The scanning of defense radars is thus less blind than that of airport radars. But both are, to some degree, blind.

Because Campbell was a psychologist, he offered some suggestions about what kinds of mental processes would generate the blind variations behind creative thought. These suggestions built upon the previous speculations of such thinkers as Alexander Bain, Paul Souriau, Ernst Mach, and, especially, Henri Poincaré.[8] In essence, the variations emerge through some variety of combinatorial process, a process that involves some degree of chance or unpredictability.[9] In fact, the pro-

---

[8] Alexander Bain, *The Senses and the Intellect*, 3rd ed. (New York: Appleton, 1874); Paul Souriau, *Theorie de l'invention* (Paris: Hachette, 1881); Ernst Mach, "On the Part Played by Accident in Invention and Discovery," *Monist* 6 (1896): 161–175; Henri Poincaré, *The Foundations of Science: Science and Hypothesis, the Value of Science, Science and Method*, trans. George B. Halstead (New York: Science Press, 1921).

[9] Jacques Hadamard, *The Psychology of Invention in the Mathematical Field* (Princeton, N.J.: Princeton University Press, 1945).

posed mechanisms are roughly analogous to the genetic recombinations that provide the bulk of the variants for natural and sexual selection in biological evolution.

Regrettably, Campbell did not develop the BVSR model beyond the initial suggestions in his 1960 paper. Instead of elaborating the model into a complete theory of creativity, he chose to apply the same general framework to sociocultural evolution and evolutionary epistemology.[10] As a consequence, interest in the BVSR as a general model of creativity waned; but it would show up from time to time in theories of aesthetic evolution, economic innovation, and scientific discovery.[11] My initial involvement concerned the latter application,[12] but I eventually realized that the model could be enlarged into a truly comprehensive theory of creativity in the arts as well as the sciences.[13] The theory is comprehensive in that it supplies a coherent explanation for many diverse empirical findings that otherwise would appear unrelated to each other.

III   *Empirical Research*

The Darwinian theory of creativity accounts for key features of three core aspects of the phenomenon: the creative process, the creative personality, and creative development.

---

[10] Donald T. Campbell, "Variation and Selective Retention in Socio-Cultural Evolution," in *Social Change in Developing Areas*, eds. Herbert R. Barringer, George I. Blanksten, and Raymond W. Mack (Cambridge, Mass.: Schenkman, 1965), 19–49; "Evolutionary Epistemology," in *The Philosophy of Karl Popper*, ed. Paul A. Schlipp (La Salle, Ill.: Open Court, 1974), 413–463.

[11] Colin Martindale, *The Clockwork Muse: The Predictability of Artistic Styles* (New York: Basic Books, 1990); Barry M. Staw, "An Evolutionary Approach to Creativity and Innovations," in *Innovation and Creativity at Work: Psychological and Organizational Strategies*, eds. Michael A. West and James L. Farr (New York: Wiley, 1990), 287–308; Aharon Kantorovich, *Scientific Discovery: Logic and Tinkering* (Albany: State University of New York Press, 1993); Aharon Kantorovich and Yuval Ne'eman, "Serendipity as a Source of Evolutionary Progress in Science," *Studies in History and Philosophy of Science* 20 (1989): 505–529.

[12] Dean Keith Simonton, *Scientific Genius: A Psychology of Science* (Cambridge: Cambridge University Press. 1988); "The Chance-Configuration Theory of Scientific Creativity," in *The Psychology of Science: Contributions to Metascience*, eds. Barry Gholson, William R. Shadish, Jr., Robert A. Neimeyer, and Arthur C. Houts (Cambridge: Cambridge University Press, 1989), 170–213.

[13] Dean Keith Simonton, "Donald Campbell's Model of the Creative Process: Creativity as Blind Variation and Selective Retention," *Journal of Creative Behavior* 32 (1998): 153–158; "Creativity as Blind Variation and Selective Retention: Is the Creative Process Darwinian?" *Psychological Inquiry* 10 (1999): 309–328; *Origins of Genius*.

A. *Creative Process*

Cognitive psychologists tend to view creativity as a special form of problem solving.[14] Although not all problems require creativity, acts of creativity usually entail the solution of some given problem. Problem-solving behavior can be ordered along a continuous dimension that represents the amount of genuine creativity involved. At one extreme are problems that require no creativity at all. Such problems can be solved using well-defined 'strong methods,' such as algorithms.[15] Arithmetic and algebra problems are generally of this nature. With very minor exceptions (for example, the introduction of trial values), these problems cannot be said to require any form of BVSR process.

However, as problems become more novel and complex, with ill-defined goals and indefinite means to attain those goals, some kind of BVSR procedure becomes increasingly necessary. Domain-specific strong methods must be replaced with more general 'weak methods,' such has problem-solving heuristics that cannot guarantee a solution.[16] Besides some amount of blindness being involved in the application of these heuristics—because we cannot always know in advance which heuristic is optimal—one of the most commonplace heuristics is explicitly BVSR in operation, namely trial and error. In short, to the extent that the problem requires a high degree of creativity, the more the process must become Darwinian.[17]

Evidence for this conclusion comes from four sources: laboratory experiments, computer simulations, introspective reports, and archival data.

Laboratory Experiments. Most empirical research on creative problem solving uses laboratory experiments. This literature has amply documented the various processes that can contribute to the generation of ideational variations that are to some degree blind.[18] For instance, experiments have indicated how the incubation period preceding a

---

[14] Allan Newell and Herbert A. Simon, *Human Problem Solving* (Englewood Cliffs, N.J.: Prentice-Hall, 1972).

[15] David Klahr, *Exploring Science: The Cognition and Development of Discovery Processes* (Cambridge, Mass.: MIT Press, 2000).

[16] Klahr, *Exploring Science*.

[17] Simonton, *Origins of Genius*.

[18] Dean Keith Simonton, "Scientific Creativity as Constrained Stochastic Behavior: The Integration of Product, Process, and Person Perspectives," *Psychological Bulletin* 129 (2003): 475–494; *Creativity in Science: Chance, Logic, Genius,* and *Zeitgeist* (Cambridge, UK: Cambridge University Press, 2004).

creative insight may rely on the 'opportunistic assimilation' of haphazard environment stimulation that serendipitously primes the particular associative pathway that leads to a solution.[19] Experimental studies have shown how creativity can be enhanced by exposing the problem solver to random, incongruous, or ambiguous stimuli.[20] By broadening the scope of activated associative pathways, the probability is increased that one of those paths will suggest a creative solution. Needless to say, the broader the range of activation, the more blind will be the associative search.

Computer simulations. Computer programs that most successfully demonstrate creative problem solving tend to introduce at some level a blind-variation procedure, most often by means of some random combinatorial process.[21] The best examples are those programs that operate by strict Darwinian principles, namely, genetic algorithms and genetic programming.[22] In effect, these programs generate ideational variations using the software analog of the genetic recombination and mutation that drives biological evolution.[23]

Introspective reports. Several eminent creators have left autobiographical records of the mental processes by which they arrived at their major breakthroughs. Although quite varied, these most often support the

---

[19] Colleen M. Seifert, David E. Meyer, Natalie Davidson, Andrea L. Patalano, and Ilan Yaniv, "Demystification of Cognitive Insight: Opportunistic Assimilation and the Prepared-Mind Perspective," in *The Nature of Insight*, eds. Robert J. Sternberg and Janet E. Davidson (Cambridge, Mass.: MIT Press, 1995), 65–124.

[20] Ron A. Finke, Thomas B. Ward, and Steve M. Smith, *Creative Cognition: Theory, Research, Applications* (Cambridge, Mass.: MIT Press, 1992); R. A. Proctor, "Computer Stimulated Associations," *Creativity Research Journal* 6 (1993): 391–400; Albert Rothenberg, Artistic Creation as Stimulated by Superimposed Versus Combined-Composite Visual Images," *Journal of Personality and Social Psychology* 50 (1986): 370–381; Robert S. Sobel and Rothenberg, "Artistic Creation as Stimulated by Superimposed Versus Separated Visual Images," *Journal of Personality and Social Psychology* 39 (1980): 953–961; Wendy W. N. Wan and Chi-Yue Chiu, "Effects of Novel Conceptual Combination on Creativity," *Journal of Creative Behavior* 36 (2000): 227–240.

[21] Margaret A. Boden, *The Creative Mind: Myths & Mechanisms* (New York: Basic Books, 1991).

[22] John R. Koza, *Genetic Programming: On the Programming of Computers by Means of Natural Selection* (Cambridge, Mass.: MIT Press, 1992); *Genetic Programming II: Automatic Discovery of Reusable Programs* (Cambridge, Mass.: MIT Press, 1994); Koza, Forrest H. Bennett III, David Andre, and Martin A. Keane, *Genetic Programming III: Darwinian Invention and Problem Solving* (San Francisco, Calif.: Morgan Kaufmann, 1999).

[23] Colin Martindale, "Creativity and Connectionism," in *The Creative Cognition Approach*, eds. Steve M. Smith, Thomas B. Ward, and Ron A. Finke (Cambridge Mass.: MIT Press, 1995), 249–268.

involvement of some BVSR process.[24] To provide just one example, Hermann von Helmholtz admitted:

> I only succeeded in solving such problems after many devious ways, by the gradually increasing generalisation of favourable examples, and by a series of fortunate guesses. I had to compare myself with an Alpine climber, who, not knowing the way, ascends slowly and with toil, and is often compelled to retrace his steps because his progress is stopped; sometimes by reasoning, and sometimes by accident, he hits upon traces of a fresh path, which again leads him a little further; and finally, when he has reached the goal, he finds to his annoyance a royal road on which he might have ridden up if he had been clever enough to find the right starting-point at the outset. In my memoirs I have, of course, not given the reader an account of my wanderings, but I have described the beaten path on which he can now reach the summit without trouble.[25]

Interestingly, one heuristic in the inventory of problem-solving techniques is known as 'hill climbing.'[26] If you are trying to reach a peak, always go up. As Helmholtz demonstrates, this heuristic is frequently BVSR in operation. Because one cannot anticipate what obstacles may stand in the path or determine in advance whether one is heading toward a local rather than global maximum, the process must have an element of uncertainty or blindness. Every time the problem solver has to 'retrace steps' or 'start from scratch' it is an implicit admission that blindness had intruded into the process.

Archival data. Because introspective reports are inherently unreliable sources of data, it is fortunate that creators will sometimes leave behind more objective indicators of their creative process. These include notebooks, sketchbooks, diaries, and the like. Such records also point to the place that BVSR processes have in creative thought.[27] For instance, Picasso saved the sketches that he made in the process of creating *Guernica*, one of the most famous paintings in the history of modern art. Despite Picasso's exceptional artistic expertise, he did not begin with an initial compositional sketch and then fill in the details until he reached the final version. Instead of a simple honing process, the art-

[24] Simonton, *Origins of Genius*.

[25] Hermann von Helmholtz, "An Autobiographical Sketch," in *Popular Lectures on Scientific Subjects, Second Series*, trans. Edmund Atkinson (New York: Longmans, Green, 1898, orig. 1891), 266–291, quote from 282.

[26] David N. Perkins, *The Mind's Best Work* (Cambridge, Mass.: Harvard University Press, 1981).

[27] Simonton, *Origins of Genius*.

ist generated an extraordinary variety of sketches that explored various possible figures and their configurations.[28] Moreover, a detailed empirical analysis of these sketches demonstrated that they did not progress inevitably toward the final form.[29] Most often, the final version of a given figure would be closer to an earlier sketch than to a later one, showing that Picasso would often advance up a blind alley. He was patently engaged in the accumulation of diverse ideational variants from which he would select that subset that would contribute to the completed composition. In brief, *Guernica* was the clear upshot of a BVSR procedure.

Darwin's surviving scientific notebooks illustrate another critical feature of the creative career:[30] Rather than work on one project at a time, highly creative individuals tend to work on many projects simultaneously, jumping back and forth as obstacles are encountered or potential insights emerge.[31] This parallel processing of multiple problems has been styled a 'network of enterprises.'[32] An important repercussion of this modus operandi is that it permits considerable crosstalk across diverse and apparently unrelated topics.[33] This crosstalk functions, in effect, as a blind-variation process. This consequence is demonstrated in the following introspective report of Poincaré's:

> I turned my attention to the study of some arithmetical questions apparently without much success and without a suspicion of any connection with my preceding researches. Disgusted with my failure, I went to spend a few days at the seaside, and thought of something else. One morning, walking on the bluff, the idea came to me...that the arithmetic transformations of indeterminate ternary quadratic forms were identical with those of non-Euclidean geometry.[34]

---

[28] Rudolf Arnheim, *Picasso's Guernica: The Genesis of a Painting* (Berkeley: University of California Press, 1962).

[29] Dean Keith Simonton, "The Creative Process in Picasso's *Guernica*: Monotonic Improvements or Nonmonotonic Variants?" *Creativity Research Journal* (forthcoming).

[30] Howard E. Gruber, *Darwin on Man: A Psychological Study of Scientific Creativity* (New York: Dutton, 1974).

[31] Simonton, *Creativity in Science*.

[32] Howard E. Gruber, "Networks of Enterprise in Creative Scientific Work," in *The Psychology of Science: Contributions to Metascience*, eds. Barry Gholson, William R. Shadish, Jr., Robert A. Neimeyer, and Arthur C. Houts (Cambridge, Mass.: Cambridge University Press, 1989), 246–265.

[33] Dean Keith Simonton, *Creativity in Science*.

[34] Poincaré, *The Foundations of Science*, 388.

Poincaré could not solve one problem without first solving another problem that was seemingly unrelated to the earlier one.

B. *Creative Personality*

Researchers have made major headway in identifying the intellectual and personality traits that correlate with individual differences in creativity.[35] From our perspective, the most significant finding is that many of these correlates involve traits that should facilitate engagement in the hypothesized BVSR process.[36] For instance, creativity is positively correlated with the capacity to generate remote or unusual associations and to generate a diversity of responses to a given stimulus.[37] This capacity would clearly augment the span of activation produced by any set of stimuli.[38] Creativity is also correlated with openness to experience, including wide interests and a sensitivity to new ideas.[39] Consequently, highly creative individuals are open systems subjected to a variety of stimuli, thereby increasing the range of primed associations, some of which lead to serendipitous connections between hitherto unrelated ideas.

But perhaps the most telling correlate has to do with a person's ability to filter out extraneous information. This ability is negatively associated with both openness[40] and creativity.[41] Creative individuals are

---

[35] Gregory J. Feist, "A Meta-Analysis of Personality in Scientific and Artistic Creativity," *Personality and Social Psychology Review* 2 (1998): 290–309.

[36] Simonton, *Origins of Genius*.

[37] Harrison G. Gough, "Studying Creativity by Means of Word Association Tests," *Journal of Applied Psychology* 61 (1976): 348–353; J. P. Guilford, *The Nature of Intelligence* (New York: McGraw-Hill); Sarnoff A. Mednick, "The Associative Basis of the Creative Process," *Psychological Review* 69 (1962): 220–232.

[38] Martindale, "Creativity and Connectionism."

[39] Julie A. Harris, "Measured Intelligence, Achievement, Openness to Experience, and Creativity," *Personality and Individual Differences* 36 (2004): 913–929; Robert R. McCrae, "Creativity, Divergent Thinking, and Openness to Experience," *Journal of Personality and Social Psychology* 52 (1987): 1258–1265.

[40] Jordan B. Peterson and Shelley H. Carson, "Latent Inhibition and Openness to Experience in a High-Achieving Student Population," *Personality and Individual Differences* 28 (2000): 323–332; Peterson, Kathleen W. Smith, and Carson, "Openness and Extraversion Are Associated with Reduced Latent Inhibition: Replication and Commentary," *Personality and Individual Differences* 33 (2002): 1137–1147.

[41] Shelley H. Carson, Jordan B. Peterson, and Daniel M. Higgins, "Decreased Latent Inhibition Is Associated with Increased Creative Achievement in High-Functioning Individuals," *Journal of Personality and Social Psychology* 85 (2003): 499–506; Hans J. Eysenck, *Genius: The Natural History of Creativity* (Cambridge, England: Cambridge University Press, 1995).

less able to ignore supposedly irrelevant stimuli, paying attention to distractions rather than ignoring them. Although this inability is most likely a handicap in everyday life, it can prove an asset in creativity. As Mach pointed out long ago, noticing what others fail to notice provides the primary basis for serendipitous discoveries, and even in the absence of such a direct consequence such sensory input can again stimulate associations that might not otherwise emerge, associations that then end in a creative synthesis.[42]

Curiously, the inability to filter out extraneous stimuli is also positively correlated with psychopathology.[43] Indeed, this incapacity is associated with elevated scores on psychoticism, a measure of a person's leanings toward psychosis.[44] This linkage shows that there is some foundation for the notion of the 'mad genius.' Highly creative individuals do share an important cognitive disability with the mentally ill. At the same time, creators possess compensatory characteristics—such as high intelligence and ego-strength—that convert what otherwise would be a deficit into an asset.[45]

Nevertheless, to provide a dispositional profile of the creative person that does not take into consideration the domain of creative activity is impossible. This necessity ensues because domains vary according to their degree of dependence on some BVSR process.[46] This variation is portrayed schematically in the upper portion of Figure 1.

Scientific creativity, on the average, relies less on BVSR than does artistic creativity. The lesser reliance depends on the fact that a scientist's creativity tends to be more constrained by logic and mathematics and by accumulated empirical data, whereas the artist's creativity is only loosely restricted by a given aesthetic style. However, neither scientific nor artistic creativity are homogeneous domains with respect to the magnitude of BVSR. Within the arts, for instance, it is possible to distinguish between highly formal or classical forms, on the one hand,

---

[42] Ernst Mach, "On the Part Played by Accident in Invention and Discovery," *Monist* 6 (1896): 161–175.

[43] Hans J. Eysenck, "Creativity and Personality: Suggestions for a Theory," *Psychological Inquiry* 4 (1993): 147–178; *Genius*.

[44] Hans J. Eysenck, "Creativity and Personality: Word Association, Origence, and Psychoticism," *Creativity Research Journal* 7 (1994): 209–216.

[45] Frank X. Barron, *Creativity and Psychological Health: Origins of Personal Vitality and Creative Freedom* (Princeton, N.J.: Van Nostrand, 1963); Carson, Peterson, and Higgins, "Decreased Latent Inhibition Is Associated with Increased Creative Achievement in High-Functioning Individuals"; Eysenck, *Genius*.

[46] Simonton, *Origins of Genius; Creativity in Science*.

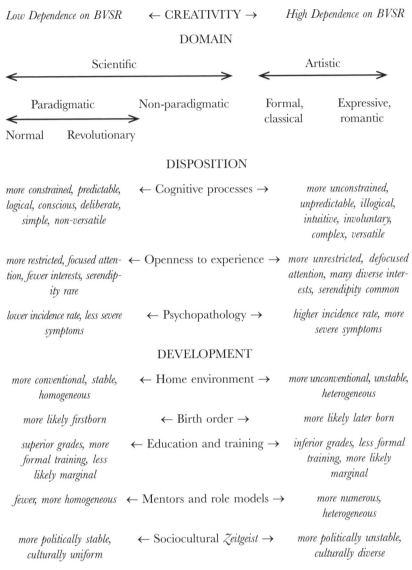

Figure 1. Domains of creativity are distinguished according to the extent to which they involve the participation of blind-variation and selective-retention processes. Placement along this dimension then determines the expected dispositional traits and developmental experiences for creators active within a given domain. Adapted from Dean Keith Simonton, *Creativity in Science: Chance, Logic, Genius, and* Zeitgeist (Cambridge, England: Cambridge University Press, 2004).

and highly expressive or romantic forms, on the other.[47] On the average, the former will be less Darwinian than the latter.

In the case of scientific creativity, it is first necessary to distinguish highly paradigmatic disciplines like the natural sciences from non-paradigmatic disciplines like the social sciences.[48] Because creativity in the former is far more constrained by theory, method, and data than is creativity in the latter,[49] the BVSR process should show a par-allel pattern. However, within the paradigmatic sciences it is necessary to distinguish normal 'everyday' creativity that operates within a given paradigm from revolutionary creativity in which a scientist offers a new paradigm to displaced one that has been discredited by accumulated anomalies.[50]

The cognitive processes, personality traits, and psychopathological tendencies are aligned along this same dimension (see Figure 1, middle section).[51] Thus, a physicist conducting normal science would have the attributes falling on the left side of the figure whereas a highly expressive romantic poet would have attributes falling on the right side of the figure. A large amount of research supports this alignment of individual differences.[52] For instance, artists have much higher rates of mental illness than do scientists, and among the latter social scientists have higher rates than do natural scientists.[53]

C. *Creative Development*

Research on this topic concentrates on two distinct phases of the life span. In the first phase, the individual acquires the internal capacity for creativity, whereas in the second the individual actualizes this capacity into external products.

---

[47] Arnold M. Ludwig, "Method and Madness in the Arts and Sciences," *Creativity Research Journal* 11 (1998): 93–101; Friedrich Nietzsche, *The Birth of Tragedy*, trans. Francis Golffing (Garden City, N.Y.: Doubleday, 1956; orig. 1872).

[48] Thomas S. Kuhn, *The Structure of Scientific Revolutions*, 2nd ed. (Chicago: University of Chicago Press, 1970).

[49] Dean Keith Simonton, "Psychology's Status as a Scientific Discipline: Its Empirical Placement within an Implicit Hierarchy of the Sciences," *Review of General Psychology* 8 (2004): 59–67.

[50] Kuhn, *The Structure of Scientific Revolutions*.

[51] Simonton, *Creativity in Science*.

[52] Ibid.

[53] Arnold M. Ludwig, *The Price of Greatness: Resolving the Creativity and Madness Controversy* (New York: Guilford Press, 1995).

Acquisition. A large amount of research has accumulated regarding the early childhood and adolescent experiences that enhance or impair the acquisition of creative potential.[54] These antecedents involved nature and nurture—that is, both natural endowment and environmental influences. In the former category is the genetic basis for the earlier observation that a connection exists between creativity and psychopathology. Outstanding creators are more likely to emerge in family lineages that feature higher-than-average rates of mental illness.[55] The more creative members of a pedigree are probably those who inherit the optimal intensity of symptoms, including the reduced cognitive filtering mentioned earlier. In line with what I said earlier, this familial linkage may be more noticeable among artists than scientists.

The category of environmental factors is much larger and probably more influential than the genetic category. Most of these factors operate to increase the person's intellectual openness and to reduce conformity to traditional ways of viewing the world.[56] For instance, creative development is enhanced when an individual is exposed to diverse cultures, languages, and ideas, when the person experiences unusual, even traumatic events in childhood and adolescence, and when the individual's educational experiences are less conventional. Even so, as was the case for dispositional traits, these antecedents vary according to the particular domain of creative achievement (See Figure 1, lower portion).[57] Of special interest is the impact of birth order, role models and mentors, and the sociocultural milieu. Disciplines that require a higher engagement of BVSR processes are more likely to feature later born children who studied or studied under numerous and diverse predecessors, and who grew up under more unstable political systems and more diverse cultural milieus. I hasten to point out that these associations, as usual in the social sciences, are statistical rather than deterministic. In the case for birth order, for instance, a specific set of circumstances can undermine and even reverse the effects.[58]

---

[54] Simonton, *Origins of Genius.*

[55] E.g., Kay R. Jamison, *Touched with Fire: Manic-Depressive Illness and the Artistic Temperament* (New York: Free Press, 1993); J. I. Karlson, "Genetic Association of Giftedness and Creativity with Schizophrenia," *Hereditas* 66 (1970): 177–182.

[56] Simonton, *Origins of Genius; Creativity in Science.*

[57] Simonton, *Creativity in Science.*

[58] Frank J. Sulloway, *Born to Rebel: Birth Order, Family Dynamics, and Creative Lives* (New York: Pantheon, 1996).

Actualization. Once development is complete, the person's creative potential must be actualized as creative products during the course of the career. This productive output also has features that are in accord with the conception of creativity as a Darwinian process.[59] A case in point is the relation between quantity and quality of output. The number of major works is positively correlated with the number of minor works, an association that holds both across and within careers. Those creators who produce the most high-impact publications also tend to produce the most low-impact publications; within the career of a single creator, the best work tends to appear during those periods in which the creator produces the most work regardless of quality. In short, the more variations a creator generates, the higher the odds that one will prove to have superior adaptive success. In addition, the hit rate, or the ratio of hits to total attempts tends to fluctuate randomly across and within careers.[60] Thus, with respect to across-career variation, those creators who produce the most hits also produce the most misses.

This statement should not be taken as saying that some creators cannot improve the odds of success with increased experience. On the contrary, such improvement is especially likely during the early phases of the career when the creator is still engaged in mastering the requisites for domain-specific achievement. But even after that mastery is attained, subsequent output will remain a hit or miss affair. A successful work will as likely be followed by an unsuccessful work as by another successful work. This unevenness in outcome shows that a residual amount of blindness remains in the creative process. Even a highly accomplished creator must still face moments of groping in the dark for something that is both original and functional.

IV *Discussion*

Given that Darwin's original theory of evolution provoked considerable controversy, it should not be surprising that the Darwinian theory of creativity has attracted extensive criticism as well.[61] Unfortunately, much

---

[59] Simonton, *Origins of Genius.*

[60] Simonton, *Creativity in Science.*

[61] Subrata Dasgupta, "Is Creativity a Darwinian Process?" *Creativity Research Journal* 16 (2004): 403–413; Liane Gabora, "Creative Thought as a Non-Darwinian Evolutionary Process," *Journal of Creative Behavior* 39 (2005): 262–283; David N. Perkins, "Creativity:

of the debate stems from fundamental misconceptions of what a BVSR process actually entails.[62] For example, some critics argue that the theory is exclusively predicated on unusual or exceptional cognitive processes, such as free or remote association.[63] Yet this argument is invalid.[64] Aside from the fact that the hypothesized associative processes are by no means strange or rare, a large number of non-associative processes can also give rise to blind variations. A systematic search through a set of permutations is a prime example. A person can solve an anagram problem using a step-by-step generate-and-test procedure, but that procedure will still incorporate blindness.

Permutation searches also illustrate another aspect of BVSR that is often misunderstood, namely that blindness is a continuous rather than discrete property.[65] The solution of crossword puzzles involves a search through permutations of letters of the alphabet. Yet seldom is the search totally blind. Most often, it will operate under a series of constraints, such as 'a five-letter word' that signifies 'a shelter for concealing hunters, especially duck hunters,' perhaps a little later additional hints emerging from the configuration of neighboring words, such as the fact that the second letter is an *l*. In some cases, the search will not be blind at all, either because the constraints are absolute (for example, 'three-letter definite article beginning with *t*') or because the puzzle-solver's expertise is so great (for example, the daily crossword puzzle enthusiast). In any case, creativity is not either blind or not blind, but varies in the degree of blindness involved in solving a given problem. In the main, as problems increase in novelty, ambiguity, or complexity, the amount of blindness required to attain a solution increases as well.

Beyond the Darwinian Paradigm," in *Dimensions of Creativity*, ed. Margaret A. Boden (Cambridge, Mass.: MIT Press, 1994), 119–142; Robert J. Sternberg, "Cognitive Mechanisms in Human Creativity: Is Variation Blind or Sighted?" *Journal of Creative Behavior* 32 (1998): 159–176.

[62] Cziko, "From Blind to Creative"; Dean Keith Simonton, "Darwin as Straw Man: Dasgupta's (2004) Evaluation of Creativity as a Darwinian Process," *Creativity Research Journal* 17 (2005): 299–208; "Picasso's *Guernica* Creativity as a Darwinian Process: Definitions, Clarifications, Misconceptions, and Applications," *Creativity Research Journal* (forthcoming).

[63] Michael D. Mumford and Alison L. Antes, "Debates about the 'General' Picture: Cognition and Creative Achievement," *Creativity Research Journal* (forthcoming); Robert W. Weisberg and Richard Hass, "We Are All Partly Right: Comment on Simonton," *Creativity Research Journal* 19:4 (2007) 345–360.

[64] Simonton, "Darwin as Straw Man."

[65] Simonton, "Picasso's *Guernica* Creativity as a Darwinian Process."

Other criticisms arise from the use of the adjective *Darwinian* to describe the process.[66] There are many ways that the origin of creative ideas does not operate like the origin of new species. For example, in the former case, the variants tend to be produced sequentially within a human brain whereas in the latter case they tend to emerge simultaneously within a population during a given reproductive cycle. Moreover, unlike what normally holds for biological evolution, human creativity can freely borrow ideas from distinct lineages. A horse cannot incorporate genes from a fly, but Picasso could easily assimilate graphic forms from African art. These and other differences cannot be denied. But the question reduces to what should be considered the essential features of a Darwinian process. For Campbell[67] and others like me, the essence is captured by the BVSR process. This process is then applied to a host of phenomena beyond biological evolution, such as neurological development and antibody formation.[68]

In conceiving such applications, it becomes useful to distinguish between two kinds of Darwinism: primary and secondary.[69] On the one hand, primary Darwinism is restricted to a single phenomenon—the evolution of life forms. This application now encompasses the wealth of concepts and processes subsumed under what is variously termed the modern evolutionary synthesis, the evolutionary synthesis, the modern synthesis, the new synthesis, the neo-Darwinian synthesis, or simply neo-Darwinism. In any event, primary Darwinism is only relevant to our understanding of creativity when it is used to account for the selection pressures that might have favored the emergence of a human brain capable of exhibiting creative behavior.[70]

On the other hand, secondary Darwinism applies a core aspect of Darwin's original formulation to some phenomenon besides biological evolution. Most often, the central feature chosen is the BVSR process,

---

[66] Liane Gabora, "Creative Thought as a Non-Darwinian Evolutionary Process"; "Why the Creative Process is Not Darwinian," *Creativity Research Journal* (forthcoming).

[67] Campbell "Blind Variation and Selective Retention in Creative Thought as in Other Knowledge Processes."

[68] E.g., Gerald M. Edelman, *Neural Darwinism: The Theory of Neuronal Group Selection* (New York: Basic Books, 1987); Thomas Söderqvist, "Darwinian Overtones: Niels K. Jerne and the Origin of the Selection Theory of Antibody Formation," *Journal of the History of Biology* 27 (1994): 481–529.

[69] Simonton, *Origins of Genius*.

[70] Dean Keith Simonton, "Human Creativity: Two Darwinian Analyses," in *Animal Innovation*, eds. Simon M. Reader and Kevin N. Laland (New York: Oxford University Press, 2003), 309–325.

but this need not be the only one. A classic example is Social Darwinism, a theory predicated on Darwin's concept of the struggle for existence—the title of *Origin*'s Chapter 3—and its involvement in weeding
out 'inferior' social groups. Briefly put, to say that something is Darwinian means merely to claim that it has some characteristics analogous
to those witnessed in Darwin's theory. To claim an analogy is not tan-
tamount to asserting an identity. It is perhaps for this reason that
scholars with established Darwinian credentials have not objected to
the application of this term to the phenomenon of human creativity.[71]

The analogical nature of the term is an asset insofar as it provides
a useful guide to theoretical and empirical research. On that score, I
maintain that a Darwinian theory of creativity has performed quite
well. Besides offering an integrative framework for coordinating all of
the diverse findings regarding the creative process, the creative personality, and creative development, it has led to specific theoretical models
and empirical inquiries that otherwise would not have been pursued.[72]
For instance, the BVSR process provided the foundation for a combinatorial model that yields precise predictions regarding individual differences and longitudinal changes in creative output.[73] That model has
also led to quantitative predictions regarding certain primary attributes
of the multiples phenomenon, that is, the occasion when a given discovery or invention is made by independent scientists.[74] Furthermore,
the testing of Darwinian-inspired models has produced new and important empirical results that would not have appeared otherwise. An
instance is the study of Picasso's *Guernica* sketches mentioned earlier in
this chapter.[75]

Even so, it must be acknowledged that the term Darwinian can be
a liability as well as an asset. For some critics, it is an emotionally-
charged word associated with sociobiology and evolutionary psychology,
two intellectual movements that are sometimes seen as more political
and even religious rather than strictly scientific.[76] One could, therefore,
argue that it might be better to find a more neutral word to designate

---

[71] Michael Ruse, "Review of *Origins of Genius: Darwinian Perspectives on Creativity* by
Dean Keith Simonton," *Isis* 92 (2001): 587–589.
[72] Simonton, *Origins of Genius*.
[73] Dean Keith Simonton, "Creative Productivity: A Predictive and Explanatory Model
of Career Trajectories and Landmarks," *Psychological Review* 104 (1997): 66–89.
[74] Simonton, "Psychology's Status as a Scientific Discipline."
[75] Simonton, "The Creative Process in Picasso's *Guernica*."
[76] Sternberg, "Cognitive Mechanisms in Human Creativity."

the set of ideas constituting the theory. For instance, rather than call the creative process Darwinian or even BVSR, we might better refer to it as a *combinatorial* or *constrained stochastic* process.[77] After all, would it be less valid if called by some other name?

My belief is that the benefits outweigh the costs. The study of creativity must be brought into the scientific mainstream. Rather than representing some mysterious process, creativity should be examined from a naturalistic perspective that links it with other phenomena of the same kind. Of all natural phenomena, the evolution of life comes closest to the creation of ideas. Notwithstanding the conspicuous differences between the two processes, they both can be subsumed under a generic BVSR mechanism. To the extent that Darwin can be credited with introducing that particular mechanism into organic evolution, so can he provide the eponym for the process underlying human creativity. That is just an act of giving credit where credit is due.

---

[77] Simonton, "Scientific Creativity as Constrained Stochastic Behavior"; "Darwin as a Straw Man."

CHAPTER FIVE

CREATIVITY AND SKILL

Berys Gaut

I *Introduction*

There is a long philosophical tradition, stretching from Plato to recent times, which denies that the core capacity involved in creativity is a matter of skill. Plato writes in the *Phaedrus*:

> if any man come to the gates of poetry without the madness of the Muses, persuaded that skill alone will make him a good poet, then shall he and his works of sanity with him be brought to nought by the poetry of madness, and behold, their place is nowhere to be found.[1]

This view of creativity was seconded by many of the Romantic poets, and has echoed throughout popular culture. The view of creativity as not being or involving a skill lies behind the thought that creativity is a natural (or supernatural) ability, not susceptible to the learning and teaching process, perhaps being completely inexplicable. I am going to argue that this view is mistaken, since it incorrectly adopts an anti-teleological view of the creative process and conflates what I shall call routinized with non-routinized skills. I will also show that the creative ability satisfies some plausible criteria for involving a skill. It will also emerge from the view defended here that the value of creativity is partly to be explained by the value of a kind of human freedom and the value of courage.

II *What Is Creativity?*

We need first to get clear about what creativity is. The traditional definition is two-part. The first part holds that a creative act or product

---

[1] Plato, *Phaedrus*, 245a, in *The Collected Dialogues*, eds. Edith Hamilton and Huntington Cairns (Princeton: Princeton University Press, 1961).

must be original.[2] Originality we can understand in terms of what is saliently new. The process of producing something saliently new I will refer to as 'innovation.'

What is saliently new is a matter of degree, and the standards applied have varied widely. John Dewey, in his educational and political writings, thinks of creativity as something to which all children have natural access. On the other hand, Immanuel Kant has a dauntingly high and restrictive standard. During the eighteenth century, the discussion of creativity was conducted largely in terms of the notion of genius; Kant recognizes genius as having a place only in the fine arts, and even there only at a very high standard of achievement.[3] So according to Kant, Kant was not a genius.

What is the correct standard for salient newness? Part of the answer is that, strictly speaking, creativity is a matter of degree, since things can be new to greater or lesser degrees, so as we become more demanding in what counts as saliently new, we should say that the activity is more creative. Another aspect of the answer is to recognize that standards of salience in what counts as new may legitimately vary, depending on the context, and that this is relevant to whether we judge whether something is creative *simpliciter*. We may judge some of children's activities as creative, even though those same activities done by adults would often not be, because we are (justifiably) less demanding in what counts as salient newness, given children's lesser skills and experience of the world. A further distinction in respect of newness that may be relevant in such cases is whether the idea is new to the person who comes up with it, as opposed to whether it is the first time that the idea appears in human history. This is Margaret Boden's distinction between psychological and historical creativity (P-creativity and H-creativity).[4]

The second part of the traditional definition holds that for an act to be creative, its product must be valuable because, it is held, originality alone does not suffice for creativity. For instance, Kant notes that there can be original nonsense, and had he been alive today he would at this point probably have added something rude about the Turner Prize. He

---

[2] The notion of a product should be understood broadly throughout this discussion: besides physical things, ideas, procedures, techniques, and so on, count as products.

[3] Immanuel Kant, *Critique of Judgment*, trans. Werner S. Pluhar (Indianapolis, Ind.: Hackett, 1987), sec. 46, Ak. 307–308.

[4] See Margaret Boden, *The Creative Mind: Myths and Mechanisms*, 2nd ed. (London: Routledge, 2004), 2.

requires that the products of genius (creativity) be 'exemplary,' that they serve as a standard or rule by which to judge other works. Therefore, transposing the view from genius to creativity, creativity is a matter of exemplary originality: an act is creative just in case it produces something innovative (saliently new) and valuable. Again, we should recognize that the value of things is a matter of degree (and therefore so is creativity), and that standards of how valuable something must be to count as creative *simpliciter* may vary, depending on the context.

The traditional definition is product-oriented: it places no constraints on the process that results in the creative output. As such, it is compatible with any story about that process, including Plato's story of supernatural intervention and human madness. But the definition is false, since the two conditions are insufficient for an act to be creative. Consider the inventor Charles Goodyear, who, in 1839, invented the vulcanization of rubber while he was in debtors' prison. Goodyear proceeded by systematically dropping into a liquid rubber solution all the substances on which he could lay his hands—including cream cheese (this did not work)—until he eventually came across sulfur, which did the job. Was Goodyear creative in what he did? He certainly produced something that was original and valuable, but his was not a terribly creative act, if it was creative at all. The reason lies in *how* he reached his discovery: by a brute, mechanical search process. Such a process did not require skill, insight, imaginative leaps, or anything other than sheer persistence—in short, it lacked flair. One could, indeed, mechanize this procedure, programming it into a computer, in the same way that drug companies mechanize the generation of innumerable chemical compounds to see which ones are effective in fighting diseases.

Consider another example: suppose that you kidnap me, strip me naked, cover me with paint, and lock me in a pitch-dark room for several hours. I thrash around, trying to escape. When eventually released, I discover that there was in the room a canvas, and in flailing around, I have produced a painted surface that is stunningly beautiful and completely unlike any other abstract painting yet seen. I have made something original and quite valuable. But I have not been creative, since my painting was completely accidental, produced independently of my knowledge, let alone any skills that I have.

The Goodyear and the painting examples show that the traditional definition of creativity is incorrect; for both of these activities satisfy it, in producing things which are original and valuable—vulcanization and the painting—but neither activity is creative. What more is required?

It is that the process of a thing's making involves, as I will say, *flair*. This should be understood to at least rule out the cases where I produce something by a mechanical search procedure, or in which I produce something purely by accident. Note that I say *purely* by accident, because one should allow a role for serendipity in creation: but that is the skillful exploitation of chance, rather than chance alone producing something.[5]

III *The Anti-Teleological Model of Creativity*

My claim is that flair involves a kind of skill. Why might one deny this? Let us start with Plato: why is the difference between the creative person and the drone not a difference in the possession of a kind of skill? In the *Ion*, Plato has Socrates argue that Ion, a rhapsode (a kind of creative recitor of poetry), does not have his ability to speak well on Homer's poetry by skill. If he did, he could explain not only the particular excellences in Homer, but also the particular merits and failures of other poets, on whom he admits he can say nothing. Moreover, Ion can offer no account of how it is that he can speak so well on Homer. (Socrates also claims that the creative process in Ion is irrational. Socrates has more than one reason for this; but one of them seems to rest on the thought that skill is a matter of bringing about one's ends by deploying suitable means. If one thinks of a rational process of making something as the taking of means to bring about the existence of the object, then if there is no skill, there is no taking of means, so one is not engaged in a process of rational making.)

Plato's reasons for denying the role of skill in Ion's creative process are peculiarly unconvincing. For there are specialized skills, and we are familiar with an academic world in which one person can write well on one poet, and have very little to say about another. Moreover, Ion's inarticulacy about his ability is a familiar feature of many kinds of skill: one cannot explain how one rides a bicycle, but it is a genuine skill for all that.

---

[5] For a related defense of the three-part definition, see my "Creativity and Imagination," in *The Creation of Art: New Essays in Philosophical Aesthetics*, eds. Berys Gaut and Paisley Livingston (Cambridge: Cambridge University Press, 2003), 149–151. The Goodyear example is taken from David Novitz, "Creativity and Constraint," *Australasian Journal of Philosophy* 77 (1999): 67–82, at 75, though Novitz employs it for a different purpose.

However, there is a way to defend the idea that creativity does not involve a kind of skill that is in the spirit of Plato's project. According to several influential writers, the creative process is not goal-directed, that is, it is not teleological. In being creative, I do not adopt the means to some already pre-determined end. R. G. Collingwood argued along these lines, and so did Monroe Beardsley and Vincent Tomas.

One version of the kinds of considerations to which these writers appeal can be reconstructed as a five-step argument. First, if one is to take the means to an end, one has to know the end. For instance, if I want to make a table, I must know what the table is to be like if I am to set about making it. Second, if, however, the process of making something is creative, then one cannot know the end: for if one knows the end, one has *already created the object*. For instance, a poet creating a poem cannot already know what the poem is, for if he knows this, he has *already* created the poem. To have conceived of it is to have made it. Contrast this with making something uncreatively, such as a table, where one can know what the table is to be like, without having made it, since one must go on physically to make it (by skill) before it exists. Third, it follows from the first two steps that creative making cannot consist in the taking of means to ends—the creative process cannot be teleological. Creating the poem cannot be a matter of taking means to an end. (Taking the means here can only mean writing the poem down, having already thought of it: but merely writing it down is something subsequent to the creative process, not part of it.) Fourth, exercising a skill requires the taking of means to bring about one's ends. Fifth, it follows from the last two steps that creativity cannot involve a skill.[6]

However, as just stated, the argument is open to an objection at step two about the proposed ontology of the artwork. Perhaps some kinds of artworks are abstract universals or types, such as poems and musical works, and so they do exist merely when conceived. But other artworks, such as paintings and sculptures, essentially involve material components. So the claim that conceiving of the artwork is identical

---

[6] R. G. Collingwood, *The Principles of Art* (Oxford: Oxford University Press, 1938 [reissued 1958]). Collingwood holds that "To create something means to make it non-technically, but yet consciously and voluntarily" (128); technical making is craft making, which involves a means-end structure and skill (16–18). Collingwood also holds that works of art are always created in this sense, and that they are imaginary objects, distinct from their physical embodiments (chap. 7). Collingwood does not explicitly link creation to creativity, but this version of the argument captures the spirit of his position.

with its creation is false in such cases. Hence, the anti-teleological argument would at best apply only to some artworks (and more generally only to the creation of abstract universals or types).

However, we need not enter into the ontological debate about the nature of artworks here, since an alternative version of the argument does not rely on the claim that the *artwork* is created when its idea is created. Rather, it holds that *the creative act* is completed when the artist has the idea of the artwork. It is the thinking up of the artwork that is the creative act. Some kinds of artworks (perhaps) essentially involve material objects, but the creative aspect of their making is nevertheless exhausted by the artist's conceiving of them. Their physical realization, in contrast, is a matter of noncreative manual labor in the case of sculpture and painting, or noncreative writing down of words or notation in the case of literature and music. So at step two, this variation of the argument holds that if the process of making something is creative, then one cannot know the end: for if one knows the end, one has *already been creative*. The argument then proceeds smoothly without the debatable ontological claim.

Something like this variation of the argument is adopted by Vincent Tomas:

> To create is to originate. And it follows from this that prior to creation the creator does not foresee what will result from it...[Otherwise he] would have to have the idea of it in mind. But if he already had the idea in mind, all that would remain to be done is to objectify the idea in paint or in stone, and this would be a matter of skill, or work....By the time they [sculptors] have the idea, the creative act, which in this case is the production of the idea, is finished. But to produce that original idea, the sculptor does not first have to produce an idea of it.[7]

So, according to Tomas, creativity cannot consist in finding the means to realize a pre-determined goal, and therefore does not involve skill; rather, it consists in thinking up an original idea. Thinking up this idea does not consist in finding the means to yet another idea, or there would be an infinite regress of ideas. Note that Tomas applies this claim not only to arts, such as poetry and music, whose products are abstract universals, but also to material arts such as sculpture. The sculptor thinks up an idea and in so doing is creative, but he can leave it to hired stonecutters to execute his plan.

---

[7] Vincent Tomas, "Creativity in Art," *Philosophical Review* 67 (1958): 1–15, at 4.

Instead, Tomas thinks of creativity as a kind of causal process: following Plato, there is a moment of inspiration, and then the original kernel of the creative idea develops over time in a non-teleological fashion. In this process, Tomas holds that the artist must exercise critical control, but this is a matter of the original inspiration causally controlling the creative process. Tomas talks of the inspiration 'kicking' the artist when he proceeds in a way inconsistent with it.[8] (Monroe Beardsley, in defending and elaborating Tomas's account, has characterized it as a propulsive as opposed to a finalistic theory.)[9] So creativity is a matter not of goal-directed activity, but of a causal process started in an admittedly mysterious act of inspiration, which then causally controls the development process through the artist's critical judgment. On this view, then, what I am calling flair cannot be a matter of skill, since skill, goes the claim, is always a matter of taking means to a preconceived end. The table-maker knows what the table that he is going to make looks like; his skill consists in following the techniques required to produce it. In contrast, the artist's creativity consists in thinking up something new, and its physical making, involving skill, can in principle be left to someone else.

I argue that this account is mistaken and that the creative process can be goal-directed, that skill plays an important part in it and that in particular flair involves skill. Indeed, there is a glaring problem with Tomas's account, for it leaves it utterly mysterious how the artist knows that he is on the wrong track. For unless he has some conception of his goal in mind, how can he know that he is going astray? Talk of inspiration kicking him when he is going wrong is a misleading metaphor, since it suggests a causal mechanism where there must be a goal-directed activity. For one's inspiration must have sufficient content—it must lay out the goal in sufficient detail so that one knows when one is deviating from it. 'That's not what I had in mind!' cries the artist, as she rejects a draft; but then she must have had *something* in mind, and know in outline what it was, to react in this way.[10]

So what is involved in the creative process, and what role is flair playing in it? The best way to approach this is by considering what is

---

[8] Ibid., 13.

[9] Monroe Beardsley, "On the Creation of Art," *Journal of Aesthetics and Art Criticism* 23 (1965): 291–304.

[10] John Hospers ("Artistic Creativity," *Journal of Aesthetics and Art Criticism* 43 [1984–1985]: 243–255) also notes this point at 245. However, he uses it to argue that there is no real difference between the teleological and propulsive theories.

required to change an activity from a non-creative one to a creative one. Let us consider cookery.

Start with a basic piece of cookery. I want to bake a chocolate cake. Finding my trusty cookbook, I consult the appropriate recipe. Each step involved in making the cake is laid out carefully: how much flour, raising agent, etc., I have to add, how long I have to place the mix in the oven, at what temperature, the sort of chocolate to choose, and the temperature at which to melt it and to pour it on the top, how long to let it stand. If I am competent and conscientious, I will have produced a perfectly serviceable chocolate cake by following the recipe. I have undoubtedly made something worth making, and I demonstrated some useful skills, but so far, except in the loosest sense, I have not been creative in my cooking. Why is this? Well, clearly, part of the answer is that there is nothing original about my cake. Part of the answer too is that I have simply followed the recipe laid down in the book. Even if by some fluke, caused by mislabeled packaging, so that my ingredients were wrong, or the oven was malfunctioning, and my cake came out radically original, I would not count as creative. Simply following the recipe meant that I was not engaged in a creative activity.

A recipe consists of a set of instructions for taking some steps that, if followed correctly, produce a pre-determined outcome. We can generalize the notion of a recipe to that of a routine: a routine is a set of rules that, if followed competently, produce a pre-determined outcome. Following these rules may be difficult and require a lot of training and skill. But as long as one simply follows a routine, one is not being creative, even though one may need to be highly skilled to do so. Practical life is full of routines: car mechanics and plumbers are skilled followers of routines.

To return to cookery, how might one start to be creative? One might decide to try to bake a better chocolate cake, perhaps a creamier, richer concoction. The problem is that one no longer has a recipe, so one cannot rely on a routine. The problem is twofold: one does not know the exact means to take (what ingredients to use, for instance), and one does not know the exact taste one is after (one cannot exactly specify the end). So one must experiment.

However, this cannot be done (if one is to be creative or even just plain sensible), by the Charles Goodyear method of randomly throwing in items into the cake mix to see what will happen. Rather, one experiments within bounds, trying out various possibilities, drawing on knowledge of other recipes which might help (perhaps there was a chocolate mousse recipe, found tasty in the past), varying the ingredients in quantity and type, and so on. So one deploys one's cookery skills, but does not follow a routine; if one's quest is successful, one will have developed a new routine (a new recipe) for a better chocolate cake, but one's actions did not, and could not, if they were creative, consist in following a routine. Moreover, one's actions could not be random, since otherwise (as in the case of my traumatic encounter with the paint and the darkened room) they would not be creative either.

I have been creative (albeit not at a terribly exalted level), if I produce a tastier chocolate cake. Yet that process was goal-directed throughout, *contra* Tomas. It also involved skills, though not the following of routines. So creativity is compatible with goal-directedness, for two reasons. First, creativity can consist in a greater specification of one's goal. I wanted to bake a better chocolate cake; but I initially had no idea as to the precise features of this end: how, precisely was it to taste? As I experimented further, I managed to get clearer about the exact qualities of the final product. So one way in which one can be creative is by further refining one's goal. A painter, for instance, can be creative by virtue of starting out with a rough idea of the sort of painting he wishes to make, and then get his goal more precise as he tries out various options. So creativity can involve teleological reasoning because one aspect of this reasoning is a more detailed specification of one's goal (a process sometimes put in terms of finding the constitutive means, as opposed to causal means, to one's ends).

Second, an aspect of creativity lies in finding the *means* to accomplish one's end. It is possible to be creative in finding the means to one's goal, even if the goal is completely precise. One may, have decided on the exact taste that one wants for one's cake, but not know how to achieve it. A similar process of controlled, skillful trying out of various options may lead one to reach it. Alternatively, imagine aiming to bake a five-foot high cake. One may know exactly what one is trying to make, but have no idea about how to go about making it, and be creative in finding those means. So there is such a thing as creativity of means as well as creativity of ends. The same applies to the arts: an architect, for instance, may be creative in thinking up the design of a building, but his structural engineer may also be creative in finding a way physically to realize the architect's apparently impossible design. Consider the creativity required to be Frank Gehry's structural engineer.

Talk of teleology may seem to miss something essential to creativity. What of inspiration, the creative idea that comes from one-knows-not-where? It seems to be essential to the creative process, but not to fit the teleological account. If inspiration strikes an artist, then there is no place for the end-specification and means-choosing processes that I have outlined. For in being inspired, he is completely passive: inspiration consists of 'poppings' into the mind, as Peter Kivy puts it in deflationary style.[11]

Moreover, since the artist is at the moment of inspiration passive, neither is there any conceptual room for skill. Talk of skill qualifies doings: when we display skill, we display it in doing something. When we are merely passive, there is no possibility of skill being exercised. It makes no sense, for instance, to talk of a skillful pain; in contrast, one can say that someone handled their pain skillfully: but that is a matter of how they acted and responded in respect of the pain, not in how they had the pain. So, for an essential aspect of creativity, teleology and skill have no place.

Now, to clarify, I do not maintain that creativity is necessarily a goal-directed process. My point is that it can be teleological, and indeed, that is almost always how it is. In any case, the passive aspect to creativity poses no threat to the account proposed here. For, there must be *some* psychological process that produces the moment of inspiration, and since it is a process, it can be teleological. For example, a widely accepted account of creativity is due to Graham Wallas, who describes the creative process as involving a process of preparation, followed by a perhaps lengthy period of incubation, when nothing consciously occurs to the creative person, followed by a sudden moment of illumination or inspiration, and ending in a period of verification or clarification in which the creative idea is elaborated and tested.[12] So, according to Wallas, the sudden moment of inspiration is standardly preceded by a long unconscious process and standardly leads to a further process. In developing this description, he drew on the writings of Henri Poincaré, who referred to "this appearance of sudden illumination, a manifest sign of long, unconscious, prior work."[13] Now nothing forbids this process

---

[11] Peter Kivy, *The Fine Art of Repetition: Essays in the Philosophy of Music* (Cambridge: Cambridge University Press, 1993), 68.

[12] Graham Wallas, *The Art of Thought*, ed. Jonathan Cape (London: Jonathan Cape, 1926), 79–96; reprinted in *Creativity*, ed. P. E. Vernon (Harmondsworth: Penguin, 1970).

[13] Henri Poincaré, *The Foundations of Science*, trans. G. B. Halstead (Science Press, Marrickville NSW, 1924), 383–394; reprinted in Vernon, *Creativity*, quote from 83 in Vernon.

from being teleological, or from involving skills: many skills are unconscious: those involved in riding a bike standardly are, for example.

However, the precise nature of the process is properly a matter of psychological investigation. What we need here is the simple point that, unless we deny the possibility of psychological explanation, then there is *some* psychological process that terminates in the moment of inspiration; there is no reason to deny that this process as a whole can be teleological and involve skills. In the same way, looking for something is an active process; the success-condition, seeing the thing looked for, is a passive occurrence; but the process *as a whole* is teleological and may involve skills by virtue of the active process of looking.

There is a second reply to the inspiration objection. Whether an idea for a work counts as an inspiration will crucially depend both on a person's skills and on his interests. Douglas Dunn once remarked in a lecture that he had had the idea for a poem when, talking with a friend, they both discovered that in their youths they had opened Blue Note jazz records imported from America and inhaled the odor of them: "The smell of America!"[14] What made this an inspiration? Well, Dunn was struck by a thought which he believed that, given his skills, he could likely work up into a good poem and because Dunn aims to write poetry. A non-poet might have merely gone on to think 'What a stink!'

On the other hand, a philosopher, such as Kant, might be inspired to produce a great philosophical work by the thought that events are individuated by the causal relations in which they stand. Even Douglas Dunn might be hard put to make a poem out of *that*. So what ideas count as inspirations is relative to what a person thinks that he can go on to do with them, and that depends on his abilities and interests.

Since one's interests specify one's goals, the notion of inspiration is thus conceptually related to that of one's goals. Indeed, one can think of the creative person's activity as involving a kind of search for ideas, which might be the germ for works: the searching might be active, or merely consist in openness to useful ideas or experiences thrown up by the world or by a person's unconscious. The creative person is thus on the lookout for ideas and experiences that may form the germs for achievements in her field, be it poetry or philosophy.

---

[14] Douglas Dunn, "Creativity in Poetry," Royal Institute of Philosophy Lecture, Dundee, 14 November 2003.

So the idea that the creative process cannot be teleological is mistaken. Even the process of thinking up new ideas can be goal-directed, since one can start with a general goal (to invent a better mousetrap), and then be creative in more exactly specifying the details (of the mousetrap). We have seen that one can be creative also in finding means to one's goals. Since the creative process can be teleological, the central reason for thinking that creativity cannot be a matter of skill lapses. We have also seen that what one must not do is simply follow routines if one is to be creative. So, the flair that the creative person shows involves skills, but not the following of routines.

Now it may be objected that this is not possible, for skills and routines are one and the same. But that is false. A routine is a set of rules, which if followed competently, will produce some pre-determined result; a rule is an abstract propositional structure. A skill, in contrast, is a kind of capacity, an ability to do something. Routines and skills are different kinds of things. Moreover, not all skills are plausibly specifiable in terms of rules. For the *application* of rules can require skill in hard cases. One might think that this skill could itself be specified by a rule; but that is not so, since one can also imagine hard cases for rules for applying rules, the adjudication of which would require the use of skills, and so on *ad infinitum*. Skills are often required to follow routines (one must know how to mix cake ingredients, for instance); but one can demonstrate skills in ways other than by following routines, as in my activity of trying to bake a better cake, or in knowing how to apply rules.

IV   *Criteria for Skills*

I have considered two prominent reasons for believing that creativity cannot involve a skill: it is alleged that the creative process cannot be teleological and that all skills are routinized. I have argued that both of these claims are false. But showing that this is so does not entail that creativity involves a skill, it merely demonstrates that we have been given no good reasons for believing that it does not involve a skill. To show that it does involve a skill requires showing that it satisfies the conditions for an ability to be a skill. But we must avoid a too-easy claim. I remarked earlier that a skill is a kind of a capacity, an ability to do something. If that were all that could be said about the notion of a skill, triviality would threaten the account. For creativity involves a capacity to produce saliently new and valuable outcomes, so it must be a skill, if a skill is a capacity or ability. No one ought to deny that creativity is a productive capacity.

So what more is required for a productive capacity to be a skill? I doubt if the notion of a skill is sufficiently determinate to be captured in terms of individually necessary and jointly sufficient conditions. Nevertheless, some criteria can be given, and the satisfaction of all of these is sufficient for an ability to be a skill. Some of the marks of skill are as follows. First, the capacity in some domain is special (not universally shared): we tend to talk of people as skilled in some activity when they have an ability that is not possessed by everyone who engages in that activity. Second, we talk of skills as a kind of accomplishment (the words 'skilled' and 'accomplished' are near-synonyms). Third, it makes sense to talk about practicing one's skills: in practicing music making, I thereby practice my music-making skills. Finally, skills are something that one can learn, so we oppose skills to purely natural abilities. Breathing is not a skill, because it is not something one learns; but music making is a skill, since it is learned, and (arguably) walking is also a skill, since that is something that is learned too. Note that I am not claiming that these marks are individually necessary conditions for a productive capacity to constitute a skill, but they are, rather, criteria for something to be a skill.[15]

Is a creative ability a skill on this criterial account? Clearly, creative activity in some domain is special and is an accomplishment. But does it make sense to talk of practicing creativity? The explanation for the apparent oddity of talking this way is simple: when we say that someone is creative, we have to specify the domain or domains in which this so. Charles Darwin and Pablo Picasso were both highly creative, but in very different fields. One standardly practices creativity by practicing creative something or other—short story writing, poetry, painting, philosophy, and so on. When one practices an activity in which one is creative, one can thereby practice the skills of creativity. Likewise, when one practices piano playing, one thereby practices one's piano playing skills. But there is also a disanalogy here, which helps explain the apparent oddity of talk of practicing creativity. Practice is most effective when one is following a routine, since there is a rule one can repeatedly follow, and so on which to strengthen one's grip. Because the skill involved in creativity is non-routinized, practice here runs the

---

[15] For more on the notion of a criterion, see my "'Art' as a Cluster Concept" in *Theories of Art Today*, ed. Noël Carroll (Madison: University of Wisconsin Press, 2000).

danger of merely hardening the grip of a routine on a person, rather than producing a genuinely creative outcome.

Can one learn to be creative, however? One might object that one cannot teach someone to be creative, so one cannot learn to be creative, and hence creativity cannot involve a skill. In reply, even if one denied that creativity can be taught, the claim that one can learn to be creative could still stand, for the fact that one can learn a skill does not require that one be taught it. Everyone from infants to research scientists can learn many things without being taught them, since they can learn them from experience, from trying something out. Further, it does not follow from the fact that something can be learned that everyone can learn it, still less that everyone can become equally accomplished in it. The ability to play a piano is a skill that can be learned, but it is not open to everyone (the tone-deaf and those who lack basic dexterity have a serious disadvantage), nor can everyone reach the same level of skill. As the music example also illustrates, skills rest on natural abilities, so saying that a skill can be learned is not to deny that it may also involve natural abilities.

Moreover, there are good reasons to think that creativity can be taught as well as learned. Edward de Bono and Tony Buzan have made highly successful careers out of teaching people to be more creative, and there is a plethora of books by educationalists dedicated to teaching creativity, by techniques ranging from imaginative play to fostering a supportive environment.[16] There are, in fact, many techniques for teaching creativity. One of the more august is Leonardo da Vinci's advice to the aspiring painter to look at a stained wall and see images in it. Philosophers have generally discussed this in the context of pictorial representation, to illustrate the phenomenon of 'seeing-in.'[17] But Da Vinci intended it as a piece of advice on how to foster the creativity of visual imagination: he described it as "of great utility in arousing the mind to various inventions."[18] By employing one's imagination and

---

[16] See for instance, Anna Craft, *Creativity across the Primary Curriculum: Framing and Developing Practice* (London: Routledge, 2000); Anna Craft, Bob Jeffrey and Mike Leibling, eds., *Creativity in Education* (London: Continuum, 2001); and Tina Bruce, *Cultivating Creativity in Babies, Toddlers and Young Children* (London: Hodder and Stoughton, 2004).

[17] E.g., Richard Wollheim, *Painting as an Art* (Princeton: Princeton University Press, 1987), 46.

[18] Martin Kemp, ed., *Leonardo on Painting*, trans. Martin Kemp and Margaret Walker (Yale University Press, 1989), 222.

exposing it to something outside one's control, one may find inspiration for new works.

Another technique for fostering creativity is to bind oneself in certain ways, so that one cannot do things in ways that one has customarily used. A good example is the Dogma 95 film movement, which abjured standard film techniques, such as recording final sound after shooting, allowing props to be brought in to locations and sets to be constructed, the use of optical work, filters, special lighting, and so on. The motivations of the movement for this were diverse, but it had the effect of enhancing creativity, by forcing filmmakers, such as Lars von Trier and Thomas Vinterberg, to find new ways of working that otherwise were susceptible to familiar solutions.[19]

The learning objection could still be pressed, however. Creativity is often associated with young children, yet young children may have little in the way of skills, so creativity cannot involve a skill. Moreover, education may function to make children less creative, undermining their spontaneous creativity.

These objections are not successful. Children will have learned a lot by the time they become creative in some activity such as drawing or painting, not least because they must have mastered many skills to be engaged in these activities, and some of these skills may be the skills involved in being creative. True, they will not have learned as much as a professional artist. But recall our earlier discussion about standards of creativity: creativity is a matter of degree, and what counts as creative *simpliciter* depends on how demanding we are about what counts as saliently new and about the degree of value that a product should exhibit. When we talk of children as being creative, we generally apply less demanding standards of salient newness and value than we would in assessing professional artists. A child's drawings are unlikely to show the degree of originality that we demand of professional artists, though they are perhaps charming and of considerable value to doting parents. While children have learned less than a professional artist, we also apply a less demanding standard of creativity to their works.

So learning skills and creativity are not in a disproportion here that would threaten the claim that creativity is learnable. Recall too the distinction between P- and H-creativity. That children's creativity

---

[19] For a general discussion of how constraints may promote creativity, see Jon Elster, *Ulysses Unbound: Studies in Rationality, Pre-Commitment and Constraint* (Cambridge: Cambridge University Press, 2000).

may be low on the H-creativity scale is not to deny that their ideas are highly saliently new to them: that they are often very P-creative. In addition, while it is true that education can sometimes undermine children's creativity, it does not follow that creativity cannot be taught: it only follows that some kinds of teaching can undermine rather than foster it.

So far, we have clarified the notion of a skill and discussed whether creativity involves a skill. But the question also arises of whether creativity is to be *identified* with a kind of skill, or whether it merely *involves* a skill, and something in addition is required. Consider mountain climbing. This involves many skills, but more is required to be a good mountain-climber than possessing these skills: one has to have the right attitudes and values as well. Someone scared of heights may possess the relevant skills, but be a very poor climber or no climber at all. The ability to climb mountains thus involves skills and the possession of certain attitudes and values. Creativity, I suggest, is like that. In parallel fashion, someone may have creative ability, but be poor at exercising the skill, because he or she is too timid to take the risks involved in being creative. As we will see shortly, there is an internal connection between being creative and possessing a kind of courage.

V   *Some Alternatives Considered*

It can seem hard to swallow the idea that creativity is an ability involving a skill, since so much of traditional discourse, both popular and philosophical, opposes creativity to skill. A brief survey of the alternatives may aid digestion.

The oldest alternative is the supernatural theory: Plato held in the *Ion*, as we saw, that the gods or muses speak through the poet: creativity is a supernatural force. That will be rejected by any even minimally naturalist psychology; and more importantly, it simply begs the question: for how do we explain the gods' creativity? Plato to support his case cites Tynnichus, the original one-hit wonder, who produced a famous praise-song, but nothing else of note, as an example of how the gods can pick on a person to demonstrate their creativity, but never again favor him.[20] However, it is striking that creative people tend to produce several creative things, not just one.

---

[20] Plato, *Ion*, 534d–e.

A second alternative is to hold that the creative process is completely inexplicable. Kant held this view: "*Genius* is the innate mental predisposition (*ingenium*) *through which* nature gives the rule to art"; and by 'nature,' he means "the supersensible substrate (unattainable by any concept of the understanding) of all his [man's] powers," the noumenal realm, which lies beyond the possibility of scientific explanation.[21] Yet complete inexplicability is incompatible with even the limited understanding that psychology has given us of creativity, and with the ability to enhance creative powers through teaching. Nor is there is any good argument for it. Some have thought that creativity is inexplicable because if something is explicable, it is predictable, and one cannot predict the creative outcome: for if one could do so, it would not be genuinely new, but could already be thought. Yet that argument has several problems, not least of which is that not all explanations have predictive power: historical explanations standardly cannot predict anything, but merely make sense of what happened.

A more modest alternative is that creativity is a purely innate, natural capacity; as such, it does not involve the learnable features of a skill; and not everyone has this capacity. Innate capacities are either bodily or mental. The capacity to become pregnant is innate, and it is no news to hear that not everyone has it. Is creativity like that, an ability to be impregnated with original ideas? Not so: creativity can be enhanced, as we have noted, through learning, but the ability to become pregnant is enhanced, if enhanced at all, by biological intervention. So is the innate capacity a mental one? It is surprisingly hard to find mental capacities that are purely innate. Perhaps the capacity to discriminate absolute musical pitch is an example of one (though even that is disputed). But, as we have already seen, an innate capacity can be a precondition for the possession of skills that are not universally possessed, such as musical ones; and a mark of a skill is improvement through learning. So the fact that we can improve creative abilities is incompatible with the pure innateness hypothesis, but is consistent with holding that, though creative ability requires some innate mental abilities, it also involves skills.

A final alternative is that the explanation for the difference between the competent artist and the creative one is not a difference in creative skills, but is entirely a reflection of their different personalities. There is a large and surprisingly robust psychological literature on the creative

---

[21] Immanuel Kant, *Critique of Judgment*, sec. 46, Ak. 307; sec. 57, Ak. 344.

personality. Creative scientists, compared to less creative ones, turn out to be open to experience, flexible in thought, have drive and ambition, are dominant, arrogant, hostile, introverted and independent. Artistic creative types tend to be open to experience, fantasy-oriented, impulsive, suffer from anxiety and affective illness, have drive and ambition, are nonconforming, independent, hostile, unfriendly and lack warmth.[22] However, this rather alarming empirical catalogue of personality traits does not show that personality traits alone suffice to make the difference between a competent and a creative artist or scientist. It is certainly possible to have these traits, be knowledgeable and competent in one's domain, and still not be creative. I suspect that many of us will be acquainted with real people just like that. Moreover, it is no part of my claim that personality plays no role in creativity: on the contrary, I have held that attitudes play a role; it is simply that skills do too.

So a brief survey of some of the alternatives to the skill view does not throw up any attractive alternatives, and this should help defuse some of the anxiety surrounding the claim.

VI   *The Value of Creativity*

Besides attacking the anti-teleological model, I have argued that the kind of skills involved in creativity are non-routinized. The latter thought has two interesting implications for the question of the value of creativity, one to do with freedom, the other with courage.

Why should we value the skills involved in creativity particularly highly? Part of the answer is that we value them on instrumental grounds, since their exercise can produce valuable things. But we also value creativity non-instrumentally, for its own sake. In general, we value skills for their own sake; but why do we particularly value creative skills? An explanation is available on the account defended here: creative persons exhibit a kind of freedom, they are not bound by routines, but they can stand back from them, consider whether they are for the good, and act in a way that is goal-directed but not routinized. Creative persons, then, are free in the sense that they are not bound by the established practice of routines. Creativity manifests a certain

---

[22] See Gregory J. Feist, "The Influence of Personality on Artistic and Scientific Creativity," who presents a comprehensive survey of the relevant literature, in *Handbook of Creativity*, ed. Robert J. Sternberg (Cambridge: Cambridge University Press, 1999).

kind of freedom in the domain of skills; and freedom is something we value for its own sake.

This claim must be understood carefully. I do not mean that creativity demonstrates freedom of the will in a sense that would show the hard determinist that he is mistaken. The freedom involved is less metaphysically weighty than that. It is the ability to stand back from one's course of action and consider whether one ought to continue to pursue it. This is a capacity that Christine Korsgaard has identified in another context as reflective freedom: when assailed by a desire, we may wonder whether we ought to adopt that desire, whether we should make it our own.[23] This is compatible with a deterministic account of the capacity, but it is nevertheless a recognizable sense of liberty in action. In parallel fashion, the creative person can step back from a pre-existing routine, and wonder whether she ought to adopt it, or find some other way in which to accomplish her task.

The connection of creativity to freedom emerges in another way. Creativity and play are often associated. For instance, in reflecting on his own creative process Albert Einstein wrote, "combinatory play seems to be the essential feature in productive thought."[24] Now people may play in two ways. Formalized games, such as football and rugby, have rules that must be obeyed to count as playing the game. These games are partly constituted by routines. In the second kind of game, not specified by rules, one can simply kick a ball around, for instance, without obeying any formal rules. So one's play-activity need not be governed by routines. This is clearly the kind of play that Einstein had in mind when he spoke of 'combinatory play': one plays freely with ideas to try out various combinations, to see what fruitful may come of them. This is not a blind, accidental process; it can involve considerable skills. Neither is it a matter of routines. Some play is free play. Free play can involve the transformation of one kind of procedure governed by routines into another, and so be the exercise of creativity. According to a (possibly apocryphal) story, rugby was invented by a pupil at Rugby school, who picked up a football and ran with it, thus violating the constitutive rules of one game and inventing another.

---

[23] See Christine Korsgaard, *The Sources of Normativity* (Cambridge: Cambridge University Press, 1996), 92–94.

[24] Albert Einstein, "Letter to Jacques Hadamard," in *The Creative Process*, ed. Brewster Ghiselin, (New York: Mentor, 1952), 43.

There is a related way in which the connection of the value of creativity to that of freedom emerges. Creativity is often associated with imagination: indeed, in some uses, 'imaginative' and 'creative' are synonyms. Imagination, unlike belief, is free of constitutive commitments to truth: a belief is what it is in part because it aims at the truth, so that the fact that a belief is not true is always a relevant criticism of it. Imagination, in contrast, is free of this constitutive commitment to truth: an act of imagining is not flawed merely by virtue of being about something that is not true. This lack of a constitutive commitment to truth means that imagination can be rationally employed to play with various hypotheses, to try them out, even though it might not be rational (yet) to believe them. So the kind of active creativity involved in trying out various ideas has imagination as its characteristic vehicle; and the vital property of imagination for this purpose is that it exhibits a kind of freedom: an ability rationally to stand back from what we believe, and consider the world in a different way.[25]

We value creativity for its own sake, then, in part because it expresses a certain kind of freedom. In being creative, we show ourselves to be capable of rising above the routines that govern so many of our activities, can rationally reflect on them, and can substitute for them a mode of activity that produces valuable results, and these results are not, insofar as they are original, achievable by previous routines. We see exhibited in this way a kind of practical freedom, an ability to stand back from the routines that govern our ordinary lives and reflect on whether there is another, better way to proceed.

Creativity is essentially connected to a second value. If creative activity is a kind of non-routinized activity, then it must by definition exhibit a kind of risk. A routine reliably produces a pre-determined outcome, if one conscientiously follows it. A creative act, not being governed by a routine, lacks this kind of reliability, so it is in that way, inherently risky. That is why an essential virtue of the creative person is courage exhibited in the realm of his creative activity. The creative person must have a high tolerance for risks. But since he is aiming at something valuable, his risk-taking is not mere foolhardiness, like someone who has jaywalking as a hobby. In aiming at the valuable, but knowingly being prepared to take risks to achieve it, the creative person fulfils the definitional conditions of courage. Picasso, looking

---

[25] For a defense of these claims and their greater elaboration, see my "Creativity and Imagination."

back on his co-invention of Cubism with Georges Braque, compared himself and Braque to two mountaineers roped together climbing a mountain: if one fell, the other would tumble after him. The metaphor not only strikingly captures the nature of their collaboration, but also well illustrates the courage that is required for the risk-taking, creative artist. The non-routinized skills involved in creativity thus exhibit not just the value of freedom, but also of courage.[26]

---

[26] Versions of this paper were read at Dundee University, Leeds University, Stirling University, the Institute of Education at London University, and the British Society of Aesthetics annual conference in 2005. I would like to thank the audiences at these occasions for their many helpful comments.

CHAPTER SIX

ON BRINGING A WORK INTO EXISTENCE

Peter Lamarque

I

The phrase 'completed work' has a pleasing ambiguity between process and product. When an artist's work is completed a completed work, so it seems, comes into existence. Completion of one kind signals completion of the other. When the (artist's) work stops the work (of art) starts. Indeed it seems a necessary condition for a work to come into existence that the work on it has been completed. The question is: what exactly occurs when a work comes into existence? If that question seems tendentious—as it will to some—then an alternative is this: what kind of change is wrought upon the world when the artist's work is completed?

It is far from clear what kind of thing a completed work is. Indeed given the diversity of the kinds of works at issue—paintings, prints, symphonies, songs, poems, novels, dramas, films, architectural works, sculptures, dance—it might seem unreasonable to expect any single or informative answer across the board. The intuitive differences between, say, sculptures and symphonies, the former apparently physical objects, the latter apparently abstract structures, immediately suggest there is no one 'kind of thing' that a work is, thus that it is pointless proceeding. But the focus for the discussion seeks to accommodate the obvious diversity of works and, as far as possible, stay neutral on pressing issues in work ontology.

The latter might not be realistic in all cases. For example, if you hold that musical works are eternal sound-structure-types then you will not be impressed by the phrase 'bringing a work into existence' for you hold that the work has always been in existence. However, you would be hard-pressed to deny that the 'composer' of the work actually worked at the composition (even if this work was a process of 'discovery') and completed it at some point. Then the question returns: what has changed in the world when the artist's work is completed? To suppose that the world was no different, in musical and artistic terms, after 1808, when Beethoven completed his *Fifth Symphony*—especially on the grounds that the *Fifth Symphony* has always existed as a sound-structure-type—is hyperbolic. The differences before and after this event are manifest and far-reaching. Perhaps, though, it might be argued, it is not the work itself that had this influence but the *discovery* of the work or the spreading *awareness* of the work. In any case, that a change was wrought upon the world when the compositional work was completed seems undeniable. So let us focus on that change.

The enquiry needs to be pinned down a bit more. For one thing, it does not need to be distracted with attempts to define art. Some of the works on the list will be works of art in an honorific sense, but many would not merit that title. There are paintings and poems and songs that are not normally considered *art* but are nonetheless completed works and need to be included. Questions of value, however, are inescapable in the enquiry. Michel Foucault, writing about linguistic works, nicely brings out the practical as well as theoretical problems in delimiting works, and the peculiar role of judgments of value:

> What is a work? What is this curious unity which we designate as a work?...If an individual were not an author, could we say that what he wrote, said, left behind in his papers, or what has been collected of his remarks, could be called a 'work'?...Even when an individual has been accepted as an author, we must still ask whether everything that he wrote, said, or left behind is part of his work. The problem is both theoretical and technical. When undertaking the publication of Nietzsche's works, for example, where should one stop? Surely everything should be published, but what is 'everything'? Everything that Nietzsche himself published certainly. And what about the rough drafts of his works? Obviously. The plans for his aphorisms? Yes. The deleted passages and the notes at the bottom of the page? Yes. What if, within the notebook filled with aphorisms, one finds a reference, the notation of a meeting or of an address, or a laundry list: Is it a work or not? Why not? And so on, ad infinitum. How can one define a work amid the millions of traces left by someone after his death? A theory of the work does not exist...[1]

Foucault despairs of finding a determinate answer to the practical questions he raises for the scholarly editor. Surely he is right that there is not always a clear line round what should count as an author's 'work' worthy of preservation. He is also right that value judgments relating to

---

[1] Michel Foucault, "What is an Author?" in *The Death and Resurrection of the Author*, ed. William Irwin (Westport, Conn.: Greenwood Press, 2002), 11.

an author's status can affect whether a product of a certain kind counts as a work; Friedrich Nietzsche's letters are works while the letters of an unknown bank clerk might not be. But we need stricter conditions on what counts as a work than the constraints imposed on a conscientious editor. That brings us back to 'completion' for the fragments and jottings that catch the eye of the editor are not completed works in the sense sought.

Of course, the idea of completion is not itself value-free. There is an aesthetic as well as a genetic conception of completion in the context of works.[2] A work-in-progress might seem aesthetically complete—well-structured, unified, pleasing—even though for its creator it is unfinished or has even been abandoned, just as a work completed by an artist, to that artist's satisfaction, might appear aesthetically incomplete. To deem a work aesthetically incomplete is to make an aesthetic judgment about it, to say that in certain respects it fails, it lacks unity, coherence, or appropriate closure. Genetic completion also involves a value judgment, this time by the artist. This is a judgment that now is the time to stop, that the work is complete. This is a decision that an artist must make. But aesthetic completeness, as we have seen, is neither necessary nor sufficient for this decision, for genetic completeness. An artist might stop working, believing the work to be aesthetically complete, in cases where the artist's objective critical opinion judges it aesthetically incomplete. Alternatively, the artist might stop working and be indifferent to aesthetic completeness. Of course there are many reasons why an artist might decide to stop work, not all of them resting on the belief that the work is complete. Some artists simply abandon their work. However, it would be wrong to endorse Paul Valéry's often quoted saying that "A poem is never finished, only abandoned" for the standard case remains that in which the artist decides the work is complete and therefore stops. In what follows, a completed work will be one that satisfies genetic completeness, in this sense, meaning: the work is completed as a result of a decision by its creator that the work is complete.

We need to be a bit wary also of conflating 'creation' and bringing into existence. Harry Deutsch has given reasons for keeping these distinct.[3] He cites the case of painting by numbers. Those who apply

---

[2] I borrow the terms from Paisley Livingston, whose discussion in "Counting Fragments, and Frenhofer's Paradox," (*British Journal of Aesthetics* 39 [1999]: 14–23), I have found very useful.

[3] Harry Deutsch, "The Creation Problem," *Topoi* 10 (1991): 209–225.

the paint have brought the painting into existence but all the creative work has been done for them. In general:

> (t)he creative part of creating a painting may in fact consist of doing less than bringing the painting into existence. It may consist in devising a scheme for where on the canvas the paint should go; or it might consist merely in creatively envisaging in some detail what the painting will be like.[4]

The problem is not peculiar to painting by numbers. Arguably an analogous situation arose in Renaissance studios where a Master painter would give instructions to teams of workers on what should be painted where. Creativity is credited to the Master although the underlings bring the painting into existence. It is not only creativity that is at issue in such cases. There are also issues of work identity. When avant-garde artists do something apparently similar, the question arises of what kind of works they are creating. Thus the conceptual artist Sol LeWitt laid down specifications for certain of his works without putting them into effect himself. One such, *Wall Drawing No. 623 Double asymmetrical pyramids with colour ink washes superimposed*, which has been realized (if that is the word) in a mural in the National Gallery of Canada, consists of instructions as follows: "colour ink wash: the background is grey, blue, grey, blue; left pyramid: the apex is left—four sides: 1—red, blue, blue, red, blue; 2—yellow, blue, grey, blue" and so on. But what is the work? Given that there can be different ways of realizing the work and given that LeWitt is a conceptual artist, it could be argued that the work is the *idea* rather than the painted mural itself.[5] (Even if this is right in this particular case, it should not be taken as a general endorsement of idealist theories of the work, such as R. G. Collingwood's, which identify the work in every case with something mental.) Clearly to know if and when a work has come into existence we need to know what kind of work it is. But it is worth distinguishing a value-free conception of creation where it literally means bringing into the world something that did not exist before, in contrast to an honorific sense implying originality or 'creativity.'

---

[4] Deutsch, "The Creation Problem," 211.

[5] The case is discussed by David Davies in *Art as Performance* (Oxford: Blackwell, 2004), who argues for the centrality of the idea in the work's identity: "The fact that there are actual enactments of LeWitt's constraints...bears upon the appreciation of the work only by, as we might put it, 'enlivening' the idea, supplementing the intensionality of the vehicle as verbally specified," 232.

II

An initial, if no doubt over-simple, description of what artists do in bringing a work into existence is that they are 'making something out of something.' In every case there seem to be 'materials' worked on, even if the materials take very different forms in different cases. A simple paradigm is that of the sculptor carving a sculpture out of stone or wood. The material is the physical material used (stone, wood) and a completed work appears after a process of carving and shaping and polishing. The sculpture is made out of the physical material. So much is obvious. Much less obvious is the relation that the work (the sculpture) has to the material out of which it is made. Indeed this becomes the pivotal issue in our enquiry. Is the sculpture identical with the shaped material out of which it was made or is the sculpture a distinct object, an object of a distinct kind, constituted by, but not identical with, this physical material? For those works with a similar physical base—painting, buildings, prints, even films—similar questions arise. It is common to call the materials out of which these works are made their 'medium'; in these cases the medium is physical, including a range of familiar kinds from canvas, paper, paint, charcoal, or bronze, to more exotic substances. But the idea of a medium in relation to works needs more refinement. For one thing, the medium is not always physical and there can be 'multi-media' works. To include musical and literary works we need a broader conception of materials to include abstract entities such as sound-types, word-types, and structure-types. But if such entities are admitted, then the parallels with physical material return. For it still looks as if the *work* of the artist can be described as a kind of patterning, shaping, configuring, in general manipulating, of a medium running up to the production of a completed work. The musical composer tries out sequences, patterns, and juxtapositions of sound-types, along with rhythms, pitches, tones, and harmonies, until the right final structure is in place and compositional work stops. This too is a kind of manipulation of a medium, not totally dissimilar to the work of a painter or sculptor—likewise for the author writing a sonnet or novel. The medium here is language, but a process of structuring and manipulating takes place; the materials are the words, meanings, and sentence structures afforded by the language and in a more literary context, the ideas, themes, genres, styles, character-types, and plot-types on which the author is drawing. The question that we asked of the physical works is directly applicable to works of these other kinds: what is the relation between the medium manipulated into a structure and the work itself? Is the musical work identical to the sound-structure-types of which it is constituted or is it something distinct? Is the literary work identical to its constitutive word-sequence-types (its *text*) or is it distinct?

Before addressing these questions directly, more needs to be said about the crucial idea of a medium. So far a medium has been identified with the materials, broadly conceived, of which works are constituted. These materials are not necessarily physical—they can take the form of abstract entities—but in each case it is not implausible to describe artists (or makers of works generally) as *manipulating* a medium as an essential part of the process of making a work. Works are made out of the materials of a medium. However, within aesthetics it is now common to distinguish a medium of this kind—the kind that David Davies calls a 'vehicular medium'[6]—with another kind, sometimes called an 'artistic' medium.[7] There is no settled view as to exactly how the latter should be defined. For Jerrold Levinson " 'Medium' in this sense is closer to 'art form' than to 'kind of stuff,' "[8] while for David Davies, "attention to the artistic medium of a work necessarily refers us to the intentionality of a maker who acts in light of these supposed understandings in manipulating a vehicular medium."[9]

Drawing on both these approaches, we might say that an artistic medium involves *the conception of a work by its maker as being a work of a certain kind*. The important point is the intentionality. A work's artistic medium is not determined (exclusively) by art, historical, or third person classification but by the way in which the work is conceived by the person making it. There might be cases where the artistic medium is unknown to art history (perhaps this is true of the prehistoric cave paintings), making the work virtually impossible to understand or appreciate.

The combination of vehicular and artistic medium allows for a richer understanding of what it is to make a work. For an artist is not just manipulating materials but is doing so under some conception of what kind of work is aimed for. Of course, it would be wrong to suppose this conception is always precise or unchanging. Artists might set out with only the vaguest conception of what they are doing and might

---

[6] Davies, *Art as Performance*, 56ff.
[7] The term comes from ibid.
[8] Jerrold Levinson, *Music, Art, and Metaphysics: Essays in Philosophical Aesthetics* (Ithaca, N.Y.: Cornell University Press, 1990), 29.
[9] Davies, *Art as Performance*, 60.

change their minds midway. But artists rarely work randomly—Jackson Pollock's 'action paintings,' for example, were far from random and issued from quite determinate conceptions of an artistic process—and, when they do, this itself helps determine the kind of work they produce. Furthermore, the way an artist conceives his work and the kind of work he conceives it to be do not arise in a cultural vacuum, but against a complex cultural background of practices, conventions, established modes (accepted or reacted against), prevailing ideas, political and social currents, as well as available materials, technology, and economic circumstances. Clearly, then, completing a work is not just deciding to stop—to stop manipulating the materials—but involves making that decision in the light of a conception of what has been achieved, against a background of cultural practices.

Now we can return to our questions about the relation between the materials out of which a work is made and the work itself. This closely ties in with the earlier question of what change has been wrought on the world by bringing a work into existence. Let us return again to the simplest case, that of the carved sculpture. Physical changes are wrought upon a physical medium. Is not the work, then, none other than the piece of stone as it appears at a certain point in time, viz. when the sculptor stops work on it? On this view, the only relevant change in the world when a work comes into existence is that something (the artist's activity) has stopped. The piece of stone in itself continues to exist but it is no longer being chiseled and worked. It is the same piece of stone that it was before the work stopped but now it has acquired a property it did not have before, namely, *being a sculpture*. The property of being a sculpture, on this account, is not different in kind from other properties possessed by the stone: *being white, being smooth-textured, being shaped like a person, being seven feet high*. Something that previously wasn't a sculpture is now a sculpture, just as something that previously was not smooth is now smooth. A work comes into existence when predicates like 'is a sculpture,' 'is a painting,' 'is a musical work' become truly applicable to some material such as a physical object or abstract entity.

This account has the appeal of simplicity but only I suggest because it combines truism with false analogies. It is a truism that when a work comes into existence, the predicate 'is a work' is truly applicable where it was not before. A true proposition can now be formulated about something in the world that would not have been true prior to the work's coming into existence. When Michelangelo finished the *Pietà*, it became true that the *Pietà* exists, something that was not true

while he was still working. But that says no more than that the work
was finished when the work was finished. We still do not know what
difference it made to the world that 'is the *Pietà*' became true of a piece
of marble, nor how that should be construed. The proposed account
is misleading in its comparison between the predicates 'is a sculpture'
and 'is smooth-textured' or 'is white.' Although it might be true that the
predicates are all applicable to one and the same object, the piece of
marble, only the latter two predicates identify intrinsic qualities of that
object. However the qualities came to be possessed by the marble, for
example, through polishing and cleaning, they remain physical qualities
of the object. Exactly those same qualities could have been possessed
by the object without any human intervention. Such, though, is not
the case with the property *being a sculpture*. That property is essentially
connected to human agency. Nothing is a sculpture—indeed nothing
is a work of any kind in the sense intended—except as a product of
human agency. But even more than that, if we apply our earlier finding,
there must be intentionality deep in the very concept of a work. A work
is the product of an agent's manipulation of a medium and becomes
a work, and the work that it is, only under a conception supplied by
the agent. A necessary condition for a piece of marble becoming a
sculpture is that it be conceived as a sculpture by its maker.[10] Without
that it remains just a piece of marble.

Behind the view discussed lies an analogy which, although initially
plausible, is flawed. It is an analogy with an activity like cooking. A
cook will 'manipulate' the ingredients until a dish is complete. When the
cooking is done new predicates are applicable to the finished product:
being a fried egg, being a sponge cake. It is tempting to see *being a sculpture*
as analogous, as the same kind of predicate. In both cases, there is a
process completed and the coming into existence of something that
was not there before. But disanalogies have already been identified.
Being a fried egg (like *being smooth-textured*) is a physical property, or
strictly *being fried* is a physical property of an egg. It is defined as such
independently of human intention. Most eggs are fried deliberately for
human ends but that might not always be the case. There could be

---

[10] There might be ancient or primitive works the creators of which did not possess
the concept of sculpture. We should be wary, though, of how to treat these. It might
be that they have been appropriated into the sculptural tradition by those who found
them. Arguably, those who found the works, not those who created them, *made* them
as sculptures.

fried eggs—even, however improbably, sponge cakes—without human agency. More importantly, a fried egg could come into existence without being conceived as such either by its maker or by others. That is not the case with works. Paintings, sculptures and symphonies do not happen by accident. The cooking paradigm can be put schematically. Cooking a φ with a set ψ of ingredients is such that when ψ has reached a certain physical state s then (by skill or good luck) ψ becomes a φ just in virtue of its attaining s. When the egg undergoes a certain physical change it becomes a fried egg. But in the case of works there is no physical state (or state of an abstract entity) the possession of which is sufficient for a work to come into existence. We cannot say that when the marble looks a certain way (for example, resembles so-and-so, has a smooth texture) then a sculpture exists, nor can we say in the musical case that when a certain combination of notes or a certain structure has been assembled then a musical work exists. A completed work, we have seen, depends not on the state of the materials used but on a decision by the maker, and its being the work it is depends on how it is conceived by its maker.

These seemingly innocuous observations already have far-reaching consequences for what can count as a work. If there can be no works without human agency and intentions and no works that are not conceived as such by those that fashion them then there can be no 'found' works, nor any eternally existing works. Beethoven's *Fifth Symphony* cannot exist eternally as an abstract sound-structure-type. That is not to say that there is not an abstract sound-structure-type associated with the work but void of any agency or any conception of the work that sound-structure-type per se could not *be* the work. Those who do wish to identify a musical work with an eternal sound-structure-type might respond by locating the required human agency in the *discovery* of the structure and the required intentionality in its becoming an object of *appreciation*. It is only when the sound-structure-type enters human consciousness, they might argue, that it becomes a *work* in the broader sense of the term but it always existed as a work in a generic sense. This, however, is already a retreat from the stronger conception of *work* mooted earlier.

Out of this response, we can develop another more refined version of the view that *being a painting, being a sculpture,* and *being a musical work* are properties that a vehicular medium—a physical object, an abstract type—acquires as a result of the work of an artist in manipulating that medium. This version has more to commend it, although ultimately it too must be rejected. A work is still essentially identified with the 'stuff' of which it is constituted but the change wrought in the world when the work comes into existence is that the constituting material acquires intentional and relational properties that previously it did not possess. To be a sculpture is to be a piece of marble (wood, for example) shaped and configured by human agency and which has come to possess intentional properties such as *being conceived as a sculpture, being an object of appreciation, being a representation of David, being in the classical style*. The parallel now is not between *being a sculpture* and *being smooth-textured* or even *being a fried egg* but between, say, *being a sculpture* and *being elected Mayor*. When Jones is elected Mayor something of a different order happens to him than when he puts on weight or loses his hair. The latter are physical changes, the former changes in status. Jones's election as Mayor brings with it a range of institutional powers and responsibilities. Acting as Mayor, Jones can formulate and implement policies on local matters, can represent the city on official occasions, can make appointments and award prizes; in addition, people will expect certain attitudes of him as Mayor, a degree of respect or deference, demanding of him an obligation to act with dignity and decorum, 'upholding the office.' Analogously, when a work comes into existence, it too acquires a status conventionally defined. Certain expectations arise for works, however humble. They are open to special kinds of appraisal, they are located in traditions and styles, they invite appreciation as works of a particular kind, and they can be attributed meaning or symbolism.

The idea that works, on becoming works, acquire a distinctive status and a distinctive range of intentional properties is correct and important.[11] The analogy with an institutional role like becoming a Mayor is illuminating. But how far can the analogy be pressed? Later we shall find reasons for caution. Is *being a work* a property that something can have at some times but not at others? Nelson Goodman, who invites us to ask not 'What is art?' but 'When is art?' answers in the affirmative:

> an object may be a work of art at some times and not at others. Indeed, just by virtue of functioning as a symbol in a certain way does an object become, while so functioning, a work of art. The stone is normally no work of art while in the driveway but may be so when on display in an art museum. In the driveway, it usually performs no symbolic function;

---

[11] See Peter Lamarque, "Work and Object," *Proceedings of the Aristotelian Society* 52, no. 2 (2002): 141–162.

in the art museum it exemplifies certain of its properties—e.g. shape, color, texture.... On the other hand, a Rembrandt painting may cease to function as a work of art when used to replace a broken window or as a blanket.[12]

As long as an object possesses the functions of a work of art, then it is art. But just as Jones may retire from the office of Mayor and lose his mayoral status so an object can cease to be art when it loses its relevant functions. According to Goodman, "That an object functions as art at a given time, that it has the status of art at that time, and that it is art at that time may all be taken as saying the same thing—so long as we take none of these as ascribing to the object any stable status."[13] Goodman retreats from the strong position apparently defended, "Perhaps to say that an object is art when and only when it so functions is to overstate the case or to speak elliptically. The Rembrandt painting remains a work of art, as it remains a painting, while functioning only as a blanket."[14] The point is that it does not so easily lose its function as a painting, just as a chair that is never sat on is still a chair.

The crucial part of the Mayor analogy is this: becoming Mayor is a status that some pre-existing object (Jones) acquires at a particular time. It is a status that could be given up. The change wrought on the world is a change of status not the introduction of anything new into the world. Jones-as-Mayor is identical to Jones; there is just one object here and Jones himself, *as a man*, stays the same before, during and after his elevation. It would be absurd to suggest that when Jones becomes Mayor a new object has appeared in the world. Is this true of works? Is it the case that to bring a work into existence is merely to change the status of something that already exists? Is a work identical to its constituting material? The view I will defend is that this is not a good analogy and that to bring a work into existence is indeed to bring something new into the world.

---

[12] Nelson Goodman, "When Is Art?" in *The Arts and Cognition*, eds. David Perkins & Barbara Leondat (Baltimore, Md.: The Johns Hopkins University Press, 1977), 17.
[13] Goodman, "When Is Art?" 10n, 19.
[14] Goodman, "When Is Art?," 18.

III

There has been considerable debate about constitution and identity, whether, in the familiar example, the statue is identical to the lump of clay that constitutes it.[15] The focus here is slightly different in asking what happens when a work comes into existence, but it draws on many of the same issues. The focus is evident in a question Roman Ingarden raises:

> whether a work of art is a physical object having a specific form or whether it is rather something that is constructed on the basis of a physical object as an entirely new creation brought into being by the creative activity of the artist.[16]

Eddy M. Zemach identifies the same issue but suggests its resolution lies more in a choice of conceptual systems than in further investigation of the objects themselves:

> The distinction between (1) a change *in* the object and (2) the object's going out of existence and replacement by another is relative to our concepts: it depends on a *choice* of a system of substance concepts. We cannot distinguish case 1 from case 2 by observing the object: what makes them different is not anything that a perceptive observer who is unaware of our system of substance concepts can discover. Yet the distinction between change and annihilation is very important to us; all things we identify and talk about have identity conditions; that is, we endow some of their properties with a privileged status.[17]

The core of the argument that a work (for example, a sculpture) is not identical to its constituting material (for example, clay, marble, or bronze) appeals to applications of Leibniz's Law or the Indiscernibility of Identicals. This law states that if an entity *a* is identical with entity *b* then, for any property, if *a* has that property then *b* has that property

---

[15] See, for example, Mark Johnston, "Constitution is Not Identity," *Mind* 101 (1992); Michael B. Burke, "Copper Statues and Pieces of Copper: A Challenge to the Standard Account," *Analysis* 52 (1992): 12–17; D. Zimmerman, "Theories of Masses and Problems of Constitution," *Philosophical Review* 104 (1995) 53–110; Lynne Rudder Baker, "Why Constitution is Not Identity," *Journal of Philosophy* 44 (1997): 599–621; Judith Jarvis Thompson, "The Statue and the Clay," *Nous* 32 (1998); Eric T Olson, "Material Coincidence and the Indiscernibility Problem," *Philosophical Quarterly* 51 (2001); Kit Fine, "The Non-Identity of a Material Thing and Its Matter," *Mind* (2003).

[16] Roman Ingarden, "Artistic and Aesthetic Values," *British Journal of Aesthetics* 4, no. 3 (1964): 198.

[17] Eddy M. Zemach, *Real Beauty* (University Park: The Pennsylvania State University Press, 1997), 147.

or, put another way, there can be no property possessed by *a* that is not also possessed by *b*. Should there be such a property then *a* cannot be identical with *b*. Philosophers have found the principle readily applicable to works of art. Thus, Joseph Margolis says:

> artworks possess, where 'mere real things' do not, Intentional properties: all representational, semiotic, symbolic, expressive, stylistic, historical, significative properties. If that is granted, then of course artworks cannot be numerically identical with 'mere real things.'[18]

A similar conclusion, drawn at a linguistic rather than metaphysical level, is reached by Kit Fine who observes that a range of descriptive predicates—for example, *defective, substandard, well* or *badly made, valuable, ugly, Romanesque, exchanged, insured*, or *admired*—might be truly applied to the statue but not to the piece of bronze.[19] The argument is not restricted to physical objects. Jerrold Levinson, who defends the thesis, "musical works must be such that they do *not* exist prior to the composer's compositional activity, but are *brought into* existence *by* that activity" (italics in original),[20] argues, by appeal to Leibniz's Law, that two musical works constituted by the same sound-structure-type would nevertheless not be identical because, being 'indicated' in different contexts, they would have different aesthetic and artistic properties.[21]

But the argument about different properties possessed by a work and by its constituting material needs to be handled with care. After all, might not Margolis's argument find an analogy with the Jones-as-Mayor case? If, as Margolis argues, artworks possess Intentional properties, but 'mere real things' do not, then can we not say that Jones-as-Mayor possesses Intentional properties, such as constitutional powers and obligations, that the man himself does not possess? Jones-the-man does not possess the power to legislate; that is only a power he acquires during his term of office and when acting in that role. Yet, as we have seen, it would be odd to conclude that Jones-the-Mayor is not identical with Jones. If that is correct, then perhaps we should hesitate to conclude, with Margolis, that artworks are not numerically identical with mere real things.

---

[18] Joseph Margolis, *What, After All, Is a Work of Art?* (University Park: The Pennsylvania State University Press, 1997), 34–35.

[19] Fine, "The Non-Identity of a Material Thing and Its Matter," 206.

[20] Levinson, *Music, Art & Metaphysics*, 68.

[21] Ibid., 69.

In this context, it is tempting for the identity theorist to deploy the idiom of qua objects, in spite of the controversial nature of that notion.[22] When we reflect on Jones qua Mayor we confine our reflections to certain aspects of his actions and interests. We might be ignorant of his other characteristics. Similarly it could be argued that it is only qua statue that the piece of bronze possesses, say, aesthetic properties; qua piece-of-bronze it does not possess such properties. After melting down, the bronze survives qua piece-of-bronze, but not qua statue. Being a work or being a painting or, more specifically, being a painting of Diana and Actaeon might, returning to our earlier hypothesis, be an aspect that a physical canvas possesses at some but not necessarily all times of its existence. Perceiving or thinking about the canvas qua work or the canvas qua representation-of-Diana-and-Actaeon might bring into salience a range of art-related properties, including aesthetic properties. On this account it is simply question-begging to say that objects, unlike works, cannot have such properties.

But the appeal to Leibniz's Law and differences in properties has not been defeated. The idea that something can have properties qua this but not qua that is fairly obscure. However, it becomes worse than obscure, incoherent, when *essential* properties are at issue. If we think of essential properties as *de re* necessities which hold of objects *under any description*, then there could be no essential properties of object O qua φ but not of O qua ψ. Yet in the art case, there do seem to be properties essential to works but not essential to the material that constitutes the works. Eddy Zemach gives an example:

> *Fountain* and the urinal are distinct things, since they have different essences. Being a part of a certain artworld is essential to *Fountain*; out of that context *Fountain* cannot exist, for it would lack its essential aesthetic property, its contrast to traditional artworks, which makes it the artwork it is. Its significance is due to its appearance as an artwork at a specific historical and art-historical period. For the urinal, on the other hand, its relation to that artworld is inessential; it can survive without it.[23]

---

[22] Criticisms of *qua*-objects appear in, for example, Harry Deutsch, "The Creation Problem," *Topoi* 10 (1991): 212–213; Mark Johnston, "Constitution is Not Identity," *Mind* 101 (1992): 91; Stefano Predelli, "Musical Ontology and the Argument from Creation," *British Journal of Aesthetics* 41 (2001): 288–289. For a more positive account, see Kit Fine, "The Problem of Non-Existents I. Internalism," *Topoi* 1 (1982): 97–140.

[23] Zemach, *Real Beauty*, 160.

An even simpler case might be this. Arguably, *being a sculpture* is an essential property of Michelangelo's *Pietà* such that the *Pietà* would cease to exist if it ceased to be a sculpture. But *being a sculpture* is not essential to the piece of marble, even in that configuration, because the marble might have issued from the wrong kinds of origins (for example, it might not have been the product of human agency or intention).

We need to distinguish a negative from a positive thesis. The negative thesis, which is widely held, is that a work is not identical to its constituting material. The positive thesis concerns what kind of entity a work is. Agreement on the negative thesis does not ensure agreement on the positive. However, the negative thesis does involve a commitment to there being a new kind of entity brought into existence with a work. This commitment comes out clearly in an example from Lynne Rudder Baker:

> When a large stone is placed in certain circumstances, it acquires new properties, and a new thing—a monument to those who died in battle—comes into being. And the constituted thing (the stone monument) has effects in virtue of having properties that the constituting thing (the stone) would not have had if it had not constituted a monument. The monument attracts speakers and small crowds on patriotic holidays; it brings tears to people's eyes; it arouses protests. Had it not constituted a monument, the large stone would have had none of these effects. When stones first came to constitute monuments, a new kind of thing with new properties—properties that are causally efficacious—came into being.[24]

Baker has developed the theory primarily in relation to persons[25] but sees it as applying also to "the relation that obtains between an octagonal piece of metal and a Stop sign, between strands of DNA molecules and genes, between pieces of paper and dollar bills, between stones and monument; between lumps of clay and statues—the list is endless."[26] Significantly, the example refers to causal properties. This suggests another weakness in the postulation of qua objects. How could O qua φ have causal properties not possessed by O qua ψ? But if Baker is right,

---

[24] Lynne Rudder Baker, *Persons and Bodies: a Constitution View* (Cambridge: Cambridge University Press, 2000), 32–33.
[25] For discussion, notably on the constitution issue, see D. Pereboom, "On Baker's *Persons and Bodies*," *Philosophy and Phenomenological Research* 64, no. 3 (2002): 615–622; M. Rea, "Lynne Baker on Material Constitution," *Philosophy and Phenomenological Research* 64, no. 2 (2002): 607–614; G. Wedeking, "Critical Notice: Lynne Rudder Baker, *Persons and Bodies*," *Canadian Journal of Philosophy* 32, no. 2 (2002): 267–290.
[26] Lynne Rudder Baker, *Persons and Bodies*, 27.

this can happen with the monument and the stone. The explanation is that the monument is 'a new kind of thing with new properties.'

Kit Fine also defends the negative thesis; he gives prime attention to the statue and the alloy from which it is made but views that example as paradigmatic of a wider relation between a material thing and its matter.[27] What is important for our purposes are not the detailed arguments for and against constitutionalism[28] but the metaphysical conclusion—intuitively disturbing—that two different material things might occupy the same space at the same time. A statue can be a material entity but is not *the very same* material entity as the piece of marble that constitutes it. One reason why this result is not repugnant to common-sense lies in a crucial feature, namely that the coincident objects are not of the *same kind*. The metaphysical principle that commonsense, if not logic itself, should preserve is that *no two objects of the same kind can occupy the same space at the same time.*[29] But acceptable versions of the positive thesis maintain that works and 'mere' physical things are *not* of the same kind, even in the cases where the works are physical things.[30]

Many aestheticians have advanced the negative thesis but it is striking how diverse are the views that emerge from a rejection of identity. Roman Ingarden, for example, insists:

> in its structure and properties a work of art always extends beyond its material substrate, the real 'thing' which ontologically supports it, although the properties of the substrate are not irrelevant to the properties of the work of art which depends upon it.[31]

From this starting point, he develops a view of the work as a collaborative effort between artist and observer centered on the notion of 'concretion':

---

[27] Kit Fine, "The Non-Identity of a Material Thing and Its Matter," *Mind* 112 (2003): 195–234.

[28] Kit Fine's argument in "The Non-Identity of a Material Thing and Its Matter" is primarily linguistic, showing that those defenders of the identity thesis who marshal arguments from "opacity" to combat putative exceptions to Leibniz's Law are themselves led to "intolerable consequences." Baker's argument, in contrast, is not primarily linguistic but metaphysical in showing that properties like *being a statue* are not only relational properties but are also essential in some cases.

[29] See David Wiggins, *Sameness and Substance* (Cambridge, Mass.: Harvard University Press, 1980).

[30] The point is also emphasised by Robert Stecker in *Interpretation and Construction: Art, Speech, and the Law* (Oxford: Blackwell, 2003), 91–92.

[31] Ingarden, "Artistic and Aesthetic Values," 198.

The *concretion* of the work is not only the reconstruction thanks to the activity of an observer of what was effectively present in the work, but also a completion of the work and the actualization of its moments of potentiality. It is thus in a way the common product of artist and observer.[32]

As the 'material substrate' is clearly not the common product of artist and observer the negative thesis is again reinforced although the latter on its own does not entail the positive thesis on offer. There is a role for observers (or interpreters) in the identity conditions of works but a somewhat different idiom, as we shall see, captures this better than Ingarden's.

A more radical version of the negative thesis distances works altogether from their physical substrates. On the idealist theory the work—even of ostensibly a physical kind—does not occupy space at all. Here is Collingwood:

A work of art in the proper sense of that phrase is not an artifact, not a bodily or perceptible thing fabricated by the artist, but something solely in the artist's head, a creature of his imagination; and not only a visual or auditory imagination, but a total imaginative experience. It follows that the painted picture is not the work of art in the proper sense of that phrase.[33]

However, Collingwood does not suppose that the act of putting paint on canvas is entirely fortuitous to the work itself for the act of painting is incorporated into the very experience that the painter expresses:

There is no question of 'externalizing' an inward experience that is complete in itself and by itself. There are two experiences, an inward and imaginative one called seeing and an outward or bodily one called painting, which in the painter's life are inseparable, and form one single indivisible experience, an experience, which may be described as painting imaginatively.[34]

Later he writes that "the painter 'records' in his picture the experience which he had in painting it" and:

the picture ... produces in [the audience] sensuous-emotional or psychical experiences which, when raised from impressions to ideas by the activity

---

[32] Ibid., 199.
[33] R. G. Collingwood, *The Principles of Art* (Oxford: Clarendon Press, 1938), 305.
[34] Ibid., 304–305.

of the spectator's consciousness, are transmuted into a total imaginative experience identical with that of the painter.[35]

So the material object, the painted picture, is both part of the artist's act of expression and causally connected to an audience's appreciative response but is nevertheless not identical with the work itself, which exists entirely in the mental realm.

Another, extreme, defense of the negative thesis seems to hold that works (of art) per se do not even exist, strictly speaking, but are projections of the imagination. They are not objects of perception but objects of the imagination and only objects of perception are *real*. Such is Jean-Paul Sartre's view. "The *Seventh Symphony*," he writes, "is in no way *in time*. It is therefore in no way real. It occurs *by itself*, but as absent, as being out of reach.... It is not only outside of time and space—as are essences, for instance—it is outside of the real, outside of existence."[36]

Something similar is true of pictures. Sartre thinks that paintings—that is, representational paintings—act much like images; to reveal their content, and thus their identity as pictures, requires an act of imaginative consciousness, a 'radical change' and 'negation' that shifts consciousness from perception to imagination. All that we can *perceive* is the paint and canvas; only when we attain an imaginative consciousness can we bring to mind what he calls the 'ethetic object,' in effect, the work itself.

Here then are three distinct views of the work consequent on accepting the negative thesis: that the work is a product of artist/audience collaboration, that it exists entirely in the mind of the artist, that it is a projection of the audience's imagination onto a material analogue. These views and others like them emerge under pressure of an assumption that a work is a different kind of entity from the materials underlying it. Works are not simply changes in pre-existing objects or rearranged items in the world. That at least is a view to be endorsed. Nor are these the only candidates for a theory of the work. Works have been characterized as action-types, performance-tokens, indicated structures, and culturally emergent entities.[37]

---

[35] Ibid., 308.
[36] Jean-Paul Sartre, *The Psychology of Imagination* (New York: Carol Publishing Group, 1991), 280.
[37] By, respectively, Gregory Currie, *An Ontology of Art* (Basingstoke: Macmillan, 1989); Davies, *Art as Performance*; Jerrold Levinson, "What a Musical Work Is," in *Music, Art,*

It is not necessary in this context to engage with all these theories. We already have the ingredients at hand to offer an answer of a *general* kind to our enquiry, about how the world changes when a work comes into existence. The important considerations are these: works are the product of human agency and intention; they emerge when work on them has been completed; work is completed, as opposed to abandoned, under a conception of the finished product; the work a maker undertakes in producing a completed work involves the manipulation of a vehicular medium constrained by an artistic medium; completed works possess intentional properties of an aesthetic, artistic or representational kind; the possession of those properties is made possible only in the appropriate cultural context.

Once we have embraced the negative thesis that a work is not simply a change of state in existing materials and once we have acknowledged the cultural embeddedness of works, there are few options in seeking a general characterization of the kind of entity that comes into existence when a work is completed. In short, a work must broadly be a 'cultural entity' of some sort. Herein lies what truth there is in institutional accounts of art. There have to be established 'practices'—perhaps something like an 'artworld,' though that idea is notoriously problematic—to make possible the existence of works (paintings, sculptures, symphonies). This is where the analogy with becoming a Mayor is at its most plausible. Mayors only exist where the appropriate constitutional and legal systems are in place. But, as we saw, being elected Mayor gives Jones a new status but does not introduce a new object. Becoming a work, in contrast, does introduce a new—'institutional'—object. Works are like schools, churches and laws. A new school is a genuinely new (institutional) object in a community not identical with the buildings that comprise it. The buildings might or might not be new themselves. A church ceases to be a church when it is sold, deconsecrated and turned into a coffee house. Something is lost, but not the building. To use a final hoary analogy, if I am missing a chess piece I might mould a bit of plasticine into a convincing shape and thereby *make* a rook. A new chess piece has come into the world but not a new bit of plasticine.

and Metaphysics: Essays in Philosophical Aesthetics (Ithaca, N.Y.: Cornell University Press, 1990); Joseph Margolis, "Works of Art as Physically Embodied and Culturally Emergent Entities," *British Journal of Aesthetics* 14 (1974).

The example calls to mind the perennial problem of 'readymades' in a theory of works. When Marcel Duchamp exhibited a bottle rack and called it *Bottlerack*, did a new object (a work) come into existence? To some this seems counterintuitive. But Margolis confidently uses the example to support the negative thesis, "Duchamp made something when he created *Bottlerack* but he did not make a bottle rack.... If the bottle rack were said to be identical with Duchamp's *Bottlerack*..., we should be contradicting ourselves."[38] This view can only be right if the example can satisfy our other conditions for workhood. Something analogous to manipulating a medium, forming a conception, and completing a work occurs in the readymade cases, as noted by George Dickie, in talking about the piece of driftwood that becomes a work, "Such a piece of driftwood would be being used as an artistic medium and thereby would become part of the more complex object—the-driftwood-used-as-an-artistic-medium. This complex object would be an artefact of an artworld system."[39] As such the artefact would acquire aesthetic and artistic properties and attain an identity in the artworld. There are parallels between Dickie's 'used-as-an-artistic-medium' and Levinson's indication; for Levinson by indicating a sound-structure-type a composer brings into existence a new kind of entity a 'structure-as-indicated-by-X-at-t.' Crucially, though, no such indication could be sufficient to make a new entity without there being an 'institutional' context—practices, conventions, accompanying expectations—where this is made possible.

The institutional requirement for work-existence casts doubt on the strongly mentalistic accounts offered by Collingwood and Sartre. Works cannot exist just in the mind or in the imagination. They need the cultural setting as outlined. But mentalistic elements are present. There have to be appropriate beliefs, attitudes, modes of appreciation, and expectations for works to come into, and be sustained in, existence; these are constrained by the conventions of established practices in the arts. Works cannot survive as works if these practices are lost. If no one remains in a position to judge that something is a work of a particular

---

[38] Joseph Margolis, *Art and Philosophy: Conceptual Issues in Aesthetics* (Atlantic Highlands, N.J.: Humanities Press, 1980), 20–21.
[39] George Dickie, "The New Institutional Theory of Art," in *Aesthetics and Art Criticism: The Analytic Tradition, An Anthology*, eds. Peter Lamarque and Stein Haugom Olsen (Oxford: Blackwell, 2003), 49.

kind then works of that kind no longer exist.[40] This is partly the truth behind Ingarden's observation that works are the 'common product of artist and observer.' It is only through a kind of social compact between people with like-minded interests that the recognition of a work as a work is possible.

We should conclude, then, that to bring a work into existence is indeed to bring a new entity into the world, not just to reorder what is there already. The conclusion is important, if hard won, because it means that whenever a work is completed there has been genuine creation even if in some cases we have to withhold the plaudits accompanying the more evaluative sense of artistic creativity.

---

[40] See Lamarque, "Work and Object," 155–156.

PART TWO

CREATIVITY, IMAGINATION, AND SELF

CHAPTER SEVEN

POINCARÉ'S 'DELICATE SIEVE': ON CREATIVITY AND CONSTRAINTS IN THE ARTS

Paisley Livingston

I *Introduction*

Testimony about episodes of artistic creativity often describes a puzzling combination of deliberate and involuntary elements. For example, Vincent Van Gogh wrote that it was possible for him to make an especially expressive picture, or as he put it, something with 'feeling' in it, because the picture had already spontaneously taken form in his mind before he started drawing. He added, however, that if there was something worthwhile in the picture, this was "not by accident but because of real intention and purpose."[1] Reflection on such testimony and on his own experience as a poet led Paul Valéry to conclude that artistic creation *always* involves a combination of 'conscious acts' and 'spontaneous formation'; only their relative proportion varies.[2] If this point is granted, the outstanding and notoriously difficult problem is to understand how such different elements combine in the creative process. In other words, how is inspiration, or the work of the muse, related to the artist's deliberations, plans, rational choices, and intentional actions? In what follows I shall develop a conjecture that falls within the conceptual space defined by two extreme theses—the popular, inspirationist idea that artistic creativity is a sudden, involuntary, and ultimately inexplicable event, and the dubious, rationalistic counter thesis, which characterizes artistic creation as a principled, deliberate selection from amongst an array of previously known options, each of which is associated with an expected quantity of artistic value. In Section II, I discuss Henri Poincaré's reflections on creativity in his 1908

---

[1] Vincent van Gogh, "Letter to Anton Ridder Van Rappard," in *The Creative Process*, ed. Brewster Ghiselin (New York: Mentor, 1952), 55.
[2] Paul Valéry, "*L'invention esthétique*," in *Oeuvres*, vol. 1, ed. Jean Hytier (Paris: Gallimard, 1957), 412–415.

essay, "*L'Invention mathématique.*"[3] Although some of Poincaré's ideas have been restated and elaborated upon in the literature on creativity, I contend that his most important claims still merit a closer look. Taking Poincairé's general model as my point of departure, I sketch a new conjecture about artistic creativity in Section III; I also discuss a kindred proposal by Jon Elster. In Section IV, I further illustrate and explain this conjecture with reference to Virginia Woolf's artistic breakthrough in the writing of *Jacob's Room.*[4] In my final section, I take up and respond to objections that may be raised against these claims about artistic creativity.

II   *Poincaré on Creativity*

Poincaré famously reported that some of his best mathematical ideas simply popped into his head while he was on holiday and not consciously doing mathematics:

> I then began to study arithmetical questions, apparently without any great result, and without suspecting that they could have the least connection with my previous investigations. Disgusted by my lack of success, I went away to spend a few days at the seaside, and thought about entirely different things. One day, as I was walking along the edge of the cliff, the idea came to me, again with the same characteristics of brevity, suddenness, and immediate certainty, that arithmetical transformations of indefinite ternary quadratic forms are identical with those of non-Euclidian geometry.[5]

Poincaré says that after a stint of hard work on these functions, he encountered new obstacles. His narrative continues:

> Thereupon I left for Mont-Valérien, where I had to serve my time in the army, and so my mind was preoccupied with very different matters. One day, as I was crossing the street, the solution of the difficulty which had brought me to a standstill came to me all at once. I did not try to fathom it immediately, and it was only after my service was finished that I

---

[3] Henri Poincaré, "*L'invention mathématique,*" *Bulletin de l'Institut Général Psychologique* 8 (1908): 175–187; reprinted in *Science et méthode* (Paris: Flammarion, 1908), 43–63; reprinted in *L'Invention mathématique* (Paris: Jacques Gabay, 1993), 35–51; trans. by George Bruce Halstead as "Mathematical Creation," in *The Foundations of Science* (London: Science Press, 1924), 383–394; all translations in this chapter are Paisley Livingston's.

[4] Virginia Woolf, *Jacob's Room* (Orlando, Fla: Harcourt, 1922).

[5] Poincaré, "*L'invention mathématique,*" 52.

returned to the question. I had all the elements, and had only to assemble and arrange them. Accordingly I composed my definitive treatise at a sitting and without any difficulty.[6]

At first glance, Poincaré may seem to be espousing an inspirationist conception of creativity—the idea that genuine creativity is largely if not entirely a matter of sudden, involuntary illumination or insight. A closer look at Poincaré's narrative reveals, however, that he is no straightforward exponent of a simple inspirationist thesis. Instead, Poincaré deserves to be acknowledged as an early exponent of the view that creative achievements are often the product of different sorts of interacting psychological processes, including the stages of preparation, incubation, insight, and revision that have become a commonplace in the literature on creativity.[7]

According to Poincaré, a necessary condition of what he calls "appearances of sudden illumination" is that they are "first preceded and then followed by a period of conscious work."[8] Prior, conscious work is necessary to inspiration because it sets in motion what Poincaré called *la machine inconsciente* (the unconscious machine).[9] The basic idea here is uncontroversial: someone who is truly idle, in the sense of not being at any time engaging in any relevant projects, will not be likely to experience the sort of episodes of inspiration that Poincaré and many other creative persons have described. Yet Poincaré gives other reasons why inspiration must be accompanied by conscious effort: unless the researcher or artist makes a prior selection of the elements upon which the mind is to operate, the search will be too open-ended and will most likely be fruitless as a result. Conscious, voluntary work *posterior* to moments of inspiration is necessary because the ideas that

---

[6] Ibid., 53.

[7] See, for example, Graham Wallas's influential pamphlet, *The Art of Thought* (London: Jonathan Cape, 1926). More recently, Poincaré's views have been taken up by Howard E. Gruber, "Insight and Affect in the History of Science," in *The Nature of Insight*, eds. Robert J. Sternberg and Janet E. Davidson (Cambridge: MIT Press, 1995), 397–432. One of the few authors who emphasizes Poincaré's historical importance on this topic is Robert W. Weisberg, *Creativity: Understanding Innovation in Problem Solving, Science, Invention, and the Arts* (Hoboken, N.J.: John Wiley & Sons, 2006), chap. 8; I first saw Weisberg's book while revising the notes to this essay. For additional philosophical background on artistic creativity, see "Introduction: The Creation of Art: Issues and Perspectives," in *The Creation of Art: New Essays in Philosophical Aesthetics*, eds. Berys Gaut and Paisley Livingston (New York and Cambridge: Cambridge University Press, 2003), 1–32.

[8] Poincaré, "*L'invention mathématique*," 53.

[9] Ibid., 54.

pop into one's mind usually require some development and polishing. Also, it is necessary to verify them: although inspiration tends to be accompanied by a second-order attitude, a belief or feeling, to the effect that the inspired thoughts are correct, worthwhile, or otherwise appropriate, sometimes this feeling of 'absolute certainty' is belied by subsequent examination or critical reflection.

To sum up, the moments of idleness or 'incubation,' when the artistic or scientist has set aside his or her work and takes up some unrelated pastime, can be crucial to the creative process. Yet if thinkers are, at such times, 'idle' in the sense of not being consciously occupied by work, in fact, their minds are not at all idle in the sense of being useless, empty, or unoccupied, for in an 'unconscious machine' has been set in motion and is hard at work. Or to shift to another image employed by Poincaré, one wheel on the pulley is idle so that the other wheels can work all the more efficiently.

One of the most original and fascinating aspects of Poincaré's discussion of creativity is his attempt to say something about how the process of incubation works, and more specifically, about how this process is functionally related to the efforts of the conscious ego or self. Poincaré repeatedly insists that the key to mathematical innovation, be it conscious or unconscious, cannot simply be the application of 'a tremendous power of attention' or of a heightened capacity of calculation. The symbolic combinations to be searched through are simply too numerous for this to be the key to discovery. The possible permutations are in principle infinite, and even if the unconscious mind has generative capacities that far exceed those of conscious attention or reasoning, its superior success cannot be explained in these terms: "Invention consists precisely in not constructing useless combinations, but in constructing those that are useful, which are a tiny minority. To invent is to discern, to choose."[10]

Should this point be granted, and if it is further allowed that some unconscious mental process is at times highly successful at realizing the relevant sort of discernment, it would seem to follow that the unconscious ego must employ tact and discernment so as to achieve a kind of selection or 'divination' of a (or even *the*) useful combination. Yet Poincaré rejects this conclusion. It is not a solution of the problem simply to assume that the unconscious mental processes can reliably identify a new, useful combination or idea without working through any of the

---

[10] Ibid., 48.

numerous possibilities. Talk of unconscious divination would merely relocate the mystery, since it is no good postulating the existence of an unconscious genius at work inside the mind of the genius. It can be added that the attribution of a capacity of discernment or divination to an unconscious homunculus does not square with Poincaré's observation that not all products of inspiration in fact prove to be good ideas.

With these problems in mind, Poincaré pursues the thought that the unconscious mental processes must in fact 'blindly' and rather rapidly generate a large number of combinations, most of which are of no interest or utility, but a few of which are truly genial. He suggests in passing that the unconscious machine can in a brief amount of time form more combinations than could be comprised in the whole life of a conscious being. He further observes that in the subliminal ego's symbolic operations or 'couplings,' there is a high degree of disorder or chance amounting to a kind of 'freedom.'[11] So a key ingredient to creative inspiration is a chaotic, rapid, unconscious recombination of ideas. This conjecture remains central to some (but not all) psychological theorizing and modeling in this domain, especially amongst connectionists and those who think of creativity as a kind of evolutionary process involving blind variation followed by the operation of a selective mechanism.[12]

Poincaré's conjecture about the extraordinary generative capacities of the unconscious mental machine raises a key question. How is it that in the oft-recounted experience of inspiration or 'insight,' a few of the results of the chaotic process of generation pop into mind and become candidates for verification and refinement? And how can we explain the fact that most of the unconsciously generated ideas go unnoticed, while most, *but not all*, of those that do pop into awareness are genuinely creative, in the sense of being innovative and valuable in the relevant context?[13]

---

[11] Ibid., 62.

[12] Colin Martindale, "Creativity and Connectionism," in *The Creative Cognition Approach*, eds. Steven M. Smith, Thomas B. Ward, and Ronald Finke (Cambridge, Mass.: MIT, 1995), 249–268; D. T. Campbell, "Blind Variation and Selective Retention in Creative Thought and Other Knowledge Processes," *Psychological Review* 67 (1960): 380–400; Dean K. Simonton, "Foresight in Insight? A Darwininan Answer," in *The Nature of Insight*, eds. Robert J. Sternberg and Janet E. Davidson (Cambridge, Mass.: MIT Press, 1995), 465–494.

[13] On the semantics of creativity and divergent conceptions of creation, see Gaut and Livingston, "Introduction," *The Creation of Art*; Margaret A. Boden, *The Creative Mind: Myths and Mechanisms* (London: Weidenfeld and Nicholson; 1990); 2nd ed. rev. (London: Routledge, 2004); Monroe C. Beardsley, "On the Creation of Art," *Journal*

In an effort to respond to this question, Poincaré hypothesizes that the good and useful mathematical ideas are harmonious and beautiful, and therefore are capable of affecting the mathematician's aesthetic sensibility, which somehow remains attuned to the outputs of unconscious cognitive processes. The arousal of this aesthetic sensibility is what directs conscious attention to these harmonious findings, in the form of the recognition of their apparent fittingness or correctness. In this context Poincaré makes a few relevant remarks about his notion of a specifically mathematical elegance or beauty. He contends that it is not 'the beauty of qualities and appearances' that strikes the senses. Instead, the talented mathematician has a sensibility attuned to the 'more intimate' beauty, which arises from the harmonious order of the parts of some whole, and which pure intelligence can grasp independently of sensorial perception. Elegance, he tells us, is a matter of the harmony between the parts; it is symmetry, a 'happy adjustment,' order, unity. With this in mind, Poincaré explicitly rules out the "garish colours and the blatant noise of the drum," which he castigated as the preferred objects of the 'barbarian' sensibility.[14]

Poincaré surmises that while one unconscious mental process blindly generates combinations, the aesthetic sensibility scans the results, singling out those that are especially pleasing, elegant, harmonious, or well-proportioned. In other words, when he was strolling idly along the cliff, Poincaré was not aware of the unconscious search going on in his unconscious mind, yet part of his mind—the mathematician's aesthetic sensibility—continued to monitor the ongoing calculations, and recognizing an especially harmonious or beautiful result, signaled this to the conscious ego, which thereby enjoyed the experience of inspiration. With these assumptions in place, Poincaré seeks to explain the advent of the occasional false inspiration. What he wants to say in this regard is that while all good mathematical ideas are beautiful, most, but not all beautiful ones are good. That some of the 'poppings' do not turn out to be true or useful meshes with the thought that false ideas can have features, such as elegance, that please the aesthetic

---

of Aesthetics and Art Criticism 23 (1965): 291–304; David Ecker, "The Artistic Process as Qualitative Problem Solving," *Journal of Aesthetics and Art Criticism* 21(1963): 283–90; Vincent Tomas, "Creativity in Art," *The Philosophical Review* 67 (1958): 1–15; R. Keith Sawyer, *Explaining Creativity: The Science of Human Innovation* (Oxford: Oxford University Press, 2006).
[14] Poincaré, "*L'invention mathématique*," in *Science et méthode*, 17.

sensibility sufficiently to call attention to themselves. Usually, however, unconsciously generated combinations that have the requisite aesthetic virtue to win recognition and pop into awareness turn out to have whatever other epistemic merits qualify them as genuine discoveries. Poincaré concludes, then, that the talented mathematician's special aesthetic sensibility "plays the part of a delicate sieve,"[15] singling out the elegant new combinations. Conscious deliberation must then take up the problem of deciding which products of the inspiration can be worked up into genuine discoveries and which cannot.

The adequacy of Poincaré's scheme to mathematical discovery is not my topic here. I shall instead focus in the next section on ways in which his basic conjecture might be adapted to account for some paradigmatic instances of artistic creativity.

III   *Artistic Creation and Aesthetic Commitments*

We have ample evidence supporting the idea that artistic creativity often arises from a multi-faceted process involving hard, deliberate work, periods of idleness, unconscious cognitive activity, and episodes of inspiration, appreciation, and revision. What is lacking is a better understanding of the relations between moments of inspiration and the artist's plans and choices; this is where Poincaré's evocation of the role of aesthetic intuition and sensibility may, if sufficiently reworked, lead to a new conjecture about artistic creativity and the relations between inspiration and constraints.

It was hardly an innovation on Poincaré's part to postulate a psychological faculty called the 'aesthetic sensibility.' It may seem easy to identify paradigmatic instances of its operation, such as 'our' instant recognition that a picture by Vincent Van Gogh is vibrant, well balanced, and so on. Yet it is anything but uncontroversial to postulate the existence of a compartmentalized or strongly modular faculty of a *formal and universal* aesthetic response capable of fulfilling the specific function Poincaré assigns to it. His assumptions about the intuition of mathematical truths cannot be carried over—without modification—to the question of the role of aesthetic sensibility in the process of artistic creation. One obvious reason for this is that we cannot accept the

---

[15] Ibid., 59.

assumption that the sole source of artistic value is a work of art's manifestation of a purely formal beauty. In modern and contemporary art, intentionally constituted ugliness and related aesthetic features often contribute to artistic value, as works by Otto Dix, George Grosz, Michael Kvium, and many other artists show. Even if we set such cases aside, the account of our responses to aesthetic beauty requires revision.

It is a truism to observe that the appreciation of some object's *aesthetic* qualities typically (if not always) depends on attunement to its perceptible features.[16] Yet such perceptual scrutiny is not a sufficient condition of the appreciation of aesthetic qualities, as such qualities depend as well on relations between perceptible features and a range of other factors, such as features of the artistic medium, the relevant art-historical context and genre, and the specific nature of the artist's project.[17] Features that clearly appear derivative, clumsy, and inelegant given one framework assumption about the artist and context can reveal rather different aesthetic valences when a better understanding of the context is gained.

To mention a few examples, the seemingly awkward compositional qualities and apparently clumsy narrative devices of some fifteenth-century Sienese pictures are better perceived as the skilful marks of a willfully anachronistic affirmation of a style associated with a proud, local authority and the favored, Sienese precedent of Duccio di Buon-insegna.[18] Again, the deliberately crafted and chosen cracks and asymmetries of a *wabi* tea bowl are incorrectly judged if we categorize them as mistakes or failures to achieve proper form. It is the advocates of a rival aesthetic who apply such negative labels.[19] Another example is Henri Matisse's exploration of unusual color combinations in *Woman with*

---

[16] Paisley Livingston, "On an Apparent Truism in Aesthetics," *British Journal of Aesthetics* 43 (2003): 260–278.

[17] Kendall L. Walton, "Categories of Art," *Philosophical Review* 79 (1970): 334–367; Richard Wollheim, "Criticism as Retrieval," in *Art and its Objects*, 2nd ed. (Cambridge: Cambridge University Press, 1980), 185–204. One way to couch the key idea here is to say that the "supervenience base" of aesthetic qualities is far broader than the perceptible features of some artistic structure or object on display.

[18] An example is a Sienese picture attributed variously to Sassetta, Sano di Pietro, and the Master of the Osservanza, *The Meeting of St Anthony and St Paul*, ca. 1430–1435 (47 × 33.6 cm), The National Gallery, Washington D.C.

[19] For example, the Seto stoneware teabowl named *Asaina* (Momyama period, 1568–1615). The neo-Confucian scholar Dazai Shundai, for example, called such items "filthy and damaged old bowls"; cited in Paul H. Varley, "Chanoyu: From the Genroku Epoch to Modern Times," in *Tea in Japan: Essays on the History of Chanoyu*, eds. Paul H. Varley and Kumakura Isao (Honolulu: University of Hawaii Press, 1989), 175.

a Hat (1905), which were pleasing to a sensibility attuned to such bold experimentation, but shocking to the many observers whose responses were informed by different conventions and expectations. What began as a negative label applied in outrage (*quels fauves!* [what wild animals!]) was to become a name for a successful new aesthetic.

More generally, we can say, along with Kendall Walton, Richard Wollheim, and others, that the apt appreciation of a work of art's valenced, aesthetic qualities requires scrutiny of the work against a background constituted by art forms, conventions, a level and history of achievement, recognition of the aims and standards to which the artist is committed, and a sensibility appropriately attuned to the latter. These are, I believe, relatively uncontroversial points about the determination and recognition of aesthetic and artistic qualities. The conclusion that has not been drawn in the literature is that these contextualist assumptions about the appreciation of aesthetic qualities have important implications for our understanding of artistic creation—a thought that follows from the observation that *one* of the artist's crucial tasks is the appreciation of his or her own emerging results.

As Poincaré conjectures, inspiration is not only the result of a generative or combinatorial device, but also requires a selective—an appreciative or evaluative, component. Poincaré also remarked that conscious work on a specific project is necessary to set the unconscious machine in motion, initiating its process of rapidly combining motifs or ideas. Yet it may also be conjectured that the function of prior, deliberate planning and work is not limited to the mere release or discharge of some generalized, unfocused unconscious activity, which would then be followed by the selective process guided by a universal, formal, aesthetic intuition. Instead, an artist's deliberations and intentional efforts help to establish a scheme that provides crucial guidance to subsequent activities that include deliberate experimentation with an artistic medium as well as unconscious or spontaneous explorations and responses that may extend through periods of apparent idleness or incubation.

What I have in mind in speaking of the artist's prior commitment to a scheme is the at least provisional choice of, and engagement with a given medium, art form, genre, and some more particular project. Some such constraints are inherent in a specific technology or craft; others may be proposed or imposed by a patron or producer, while others are more independently arrived at by the individual artist, or group of collaborating artists. Artistic movements and manifestos often reflect and influence this kind of commitment, as do projects whereby an artist undertakes to produce a series of interrelated works meant to fit together in valued ways. Another salient type of scheme to which an artist or group of artists may become committed is an 'aesthetic,' where an aesthetic is not a doctrine or theory, but a cluster of norms, expectations, and discriminations pertaining to artistic projects.

In the idiom of theories of rational choice and satisficing, we might say that what the artist's initial, more or less deliberate selection of a project and correlative aesthetic helps to establish are the parameters and threshold for an effective 'stopping rule' that can inform the spontaneous or deliberate termination of the process of combinatorial experimentation.[20] Yet this is not the insight we are after, as this idiom may suggest that the aesthetic valence of the options to be searched through exists entirely independently of the search and parameters in question, which in artistic contexts is misleading. What will count as a remarkable discovery worthy of a eureka-like response varies in function of the set of values and expectations established by the provisional scheme and project, and more generally by the artist's operative aesthetic.

The artist's commitment to or engagement with a scheme helps to establish and activate some valenced expectations that are the product of a more specific and context-sensitive counterpart to what Poincaré referred to as the aesthetic sensibility. Commitment to artistic constraints crucially orients the creative process by establishing formal as well as substantive, or content-related parameters, and corresponding normative expectations and dispositions. This is the case in part because the artist's response to options that emerge through hard work and inspiration involves the application not only of conscious criteria or principles, but also of a sensibility attuned to the orientations and purposes of a given project.

The importance of this function of prior constraints can be highlighted by reference to empirical investigations indicating that prompt and frequent self-evaluation is strongly correlated with artistic expertise.[21] A good artist, it would seem, is not only someone who has the gift of unconsciously generating new combinations and skillfully manipulating some medium, but someone who has the propensity to react sensitively

---

[20] David Schmidtz, "Satisficing as a Humanly Rational Strategy," in *Satisficing and Maximizing: Moral Theorists on Practical Reason*, ed. Michael Byron (Cambridge: Cambridge University Press, 2004), 30–58.
[21] Todd I. Lubart, "Models of the Creative Process: Past, Present, and Future," *Creativity Research Journal* 13 (2000–2001): 295–308.

to his or her own results, selecting those that correspond to a scheme of artistic value. Here is another point on which Poincaré's conjecture should be acknowledged as the source for contemporary observations about creativity; for example, a key refrain in criticism of algorithmic modeling of creative practices is that such models cannot perform the evaluative function that is essential to genuine creativity.[22]

Poincaré reasoned that a period of incubation or idleness can contribute to creativity because it involves a kind of chaotic, unconscious cognitive search. Although there is broad agreement that incubation is often helpful, the reason remains controversial amongst contemporary psychologists, and some even doubt that a chaotic unconscious search is part of the story.[23] It is hard to see, however, how a complicated new idea can pop into mind in the absence of any search or mental process whatsoever, and by definition a period of incubation involves no relevant, conscious effort or deliberate activity. In any case, another hypothesized function of incubation is that of deactivating fruitless assumptions about how a problem can be solved: a period of inactivity makes a fresh look possible, or as the French saying goes, *la nuit porte conseil*. There is an artistic analogue, at least in cases where the artist deems that his or her results have become too stale and predictable. The choice of new initial constraints, and the corresponding initiation of a period of related, unconscious cognitive activity, can serve to forestall or inhibit reliance upon overworked strategies, of which a tiresome personal mannerism or sterile and repetitive stylistic habit is the most evident symptom. So whatever else it may achieve, settling on a new scheme may help the artist resist a habitual way of working. This is, for example, one of the main motivations of the constraints adopted by members of the influential Dogma 95 movement.[24]

My conjecture can be further clarified with reference to a kindred proposal made by Elster, who explores the idea that strategies of rational pre-commitment or resolute choice are crucial to genuine artistic creativity. He defines 'inspiration' as the rate at which ideas move from the unconscious into the conscious mind, and conjectures that inspiration,

---

[22] This critique is stated, for example, in R. Keith Sawyer, *Explaining Creativity: The Science of Human Innovation* (Oxford: Oxford University Press, 2006), chap. 6.

[23] Eliaz Segal, "Incubation in Problem Solving," *Creativity Research Journal* 16 (2004): 141–148.

[24] Mette Hjort and Scott MacKenzie, eds. *Purity and Provocation: Dogma 95* (London: British Film Institute Press, 2003).

thus defined, "is an inversely U-shaped function of the tightness of the constraints."[25] Given this assumption, it makes sense that in a situation where the agent faces too many options, the self-imposition of constraints could be an effective way of enhancing inspiration.

Elster does not advocate any particular explanation as to why 'sufficiently' tight constraints contribute to inspiration. One of the themes of his ongoing research on human rationality and irrationality is the idea that pre-commitments and resolute choices have the characteristic function of allowing agents to overcome anticipated hyperbolic discounting, preference changes, strategic time inconsistency, and surges of passion. Thanks to Circe's helpful advice, Ulysses anticipates that hearing the song of the sirens will cause him to steer his ship to its destruction; so to enjoy their lovely song while resisting its fatal call, the hero has himself bound to the mast. More prosaically, someone struggling with an addiction, weakness of the will, or bad habits can plan ahead and employ various indirect strategies to preclude giving in when the time of temptation arrives. Yet it is not obvious that the same factors explain the importance of constraints in an artistic context. The artist, it might seem, is quite unlike Ulysses because in paradigmatic cases of artistic creation, there is no Circean advice, and no risk of any drastic preference shifts. How, then, are pre-commitments and inspiration related to each other in artistic cases? And why do constraints contribute to inspiration at all, other than for the trivial reason that one cannot do everything all at once? Even if we agree with Elster's notion that pre-commitments and resolute choices are important or even crucial to artistic creativity, it is dubious that their primary or characteristic function is that of overcoming anticipated inconsistencies across time. My Poincaré-inspired conjecture is that prior commitment in the case of artistic creativity involves the selection and activation of a system of artistic and aesthetic parameters crucial to the very occurrence of a determinate, valenced response to future output or performance. Pre-commitment, in the sense of a deliberate choice, or a more or less spontaneous engagement with a artistic scheme, project, or aesthetic, forestalls aesthetic indifference, directionless scrutiny, and the inability to experience a spontaneous judgment of the results of artistic experimentation. What artistic pre-commitments achieve, then, is not

---

[25] Jon Elster, *Ulysses Unbound: Studies in Rationality, Precommitment, and Constraints* (Cambridge: Cambridge University Press, 2000), 212.

the prevention of an unwanted shift of preference, but the attunement and enhanced activation of a capacity for response not directly under the artist's conscious control. To rephrase the point in terms of Elster's allegory, Ulysses prudently anticipates that hearing the lovely siren song will produce a disastrous change of preferences if he does not somehow pre-commit. What the artist risks in the absence of pre-commitment is the failure to hear any song at all, or better, any new song having what can be recognized as a determinate artistic value.

IV   *Virginia Woolf's Novelistic Breakthrough*

To flesh out my schematic indications with regard to the emergence and function of artists' commitments to artistic schemes, in this section, I shall briefly discuss a few relevant aspects of a particular episode of successful artistic creativity, namely, Virginia Woolf's composition of her first genuinely modernist novel, *Jacob's Room*.

    After Woolf had published her second novel, *Night and Day*,[26] in 1919, she was 'irritated' (as she put it) by criticisms raised in print by her friend and rival, Katherine Mansfield, who suggested that Woolf's long novel was far too traditional.[27] One reason why Woolf was genuinely bothered by this criticism was that she was basically in agreement with Mansfield and others about the tenets and values associated with modernism in the arts, and had come to understand her greatest ambition as that of contributing something important to the modernist revolution in literature.[28] Entries in her diaries express worries that such figures as James Joyce and T. S. Eliot might surpass her in this regard, and that Marcel Proust had already done so. In the period following the completion of *Night and Day*, Woolf was thinking and writing at a very general level about the very idea of modernist art. Her appreciation of her sister's paintings, and her engagement with the artistic interests and activities of such figures as Roger Fry, was part of an ongoing process through which she immersed herself in a modernist aesthetic. She began to

---

[26] Virginia Woolf, *Night and Day* (London: Flamingo, 1919).
[27] For Mansfield's criticisms, see Clare Hanson, ed., *The Critical Writings of Katherine Mansfield* (London: Macmillan, 1987), 56–63; for plausible comments on Woolf's reaction and more general relation to Mansfield, see Angela Smith, *Katherine Mansfield and Virginia Woolf: A Public of Two* (Oxford: Clarendon, 1999).
[28] For background on Woolf and artistic modernism, see Hermione Lee, *The Novels of Virginia Woolf* (London: Methuen, 1977), 11–24.

write a number of episodic and impressionistic short stories (including a short fiction entitled "An Unwritten Novel")[29] that eschewed the sorts of characterizations and descriptions that Woolf had come to associate with Victorian fiction. Her deliberations and writings, guided by the very general scheme of achieving a truly modern form of literature, led to the emergence of a new, more specific leading idea, namely, a scheme for the creation of a modernist, experimental novel. Having come up with exciting new thoughts in this vein, Woolf wrote with enthusiasm in her diary:

> The day after my birthday; in fact I'm 38. Well, no doubt I'm a great deal happier than I was at 28; & happier today than I was yesterday having this afternoon arrived at some idea of a new form for a new novel. Suppose one thing should open out of another—as in "An Unwritten Novel"—only not for 10 pages but for 200 or so—Doesn't that give the looseness and lightness I want: doesnt [sic] that get closer & yet keep form & speed, & enclose everything? My doubt is how far it will enclose the human heart—Am I sufficiently mistress of my dialogue to net it there? For I figure that the approach will be entirely different this time: no scaffolding; scarcely a brick to be seen; all crepuscular, but the heart, the passion, the humour, everything as bright as fire in the mist. Then I'll find room for so much—a gaiety—an inconsequence—a light spirited stepping at my sweet will. Whether I'm sufficiently mistress of things—thats [sic] the doubt; but conceive mark on the wall, K. G. [Kew Gardens] & unwritten novel taking hands & dancing in unity. What the unity shall be I have yet to discover: the theme is a blank to me; but I see immense possibilities in the form I hit upon more or less by chance 2 weeks ago. I suppose the danger is the damned egotistical self; which ruins Joyce & Richardson to my mind…I must grope and experiment but this afternoon I had a gleam of light. Indeed, I think from the ease which I'm developing the unwritten novel there must be a path for me there.[30]

Woolf explicitly records here her decision to pursue a scheme for the writing of her next novel, a scheme labeled, 'a new form for a new novel.' This scheme receives various other, metaphorical characterizations in the diary entry, including an architectural image. She clearly has in mind a style or narrative 'voice' that has emerged here and there in some of her most recent writings. The more proximate 'breakthrough' idea, which seems to have crystallized some two weeks after

---

[29] Virginia Woolf, "An Unwritten Novel," in *Monday or Tuesday* (New York: Harcourt, Brace, 1921).

[30] Entry of Monday 26 January 1920, *The Diary of Virginia Woolf*, vol. 2, ed. Anne Olivier Bell (Harmondsworth: Penguin, 1981), 13–14.

these stylistic experiments, is that of making this sort of 'free' narrative form the organizational principle for an entire novel. Thus the artist is simultaneously engaged in a retrospective appreciation of her own earlier efforts, in which she culls what she now perceives as promising moments, and an anticipatory plan for combining those elements so as to generate a result of even greater value in this same vein. In her anticipation of future efforts to apply this scheme, Woolf expresses worries about possible shortcomings of the 'path' or approach she has in mind. She knows she will need to find a theme for her new novel, and she worries whether this new form she has in view will truly serve as a vehicle for psychological insights. Woolf's discovery of a general scheme or formal strategy was accompanied by a high level of excitement, and was followed by a burst of deliberate, conscious work and spontaneous, unconscious mental activities. (In Poincaré's terms, the 'unconscious machine' had been set in motion.) Woolf's own manner of talking about this aspect of the writerly process reads as follows:

> After a hard day's work, trudging round, seeing all he can, feeling all he can, taking in the book of his mind innumerable notes, the writer becomes—if he can—unconscious. In fact, his under mind works at top speed while his upper mind drowses. Then, after a pause the veil lifts; and there is the thing—the thing he wants to write about—simplified, composed.[31]

In the months that followed her experience of the 'gleam of light' about a new form for a new novel, Woolf made swift progress on *Jacob's Room*, continuing to monitor her results in terms of the initial scheme and ambition. She recorded in her diary how, when things were going well, she got ideas for her narrator's flights of fancy while she was out on her daily walk. When her first draft was completed, she edited and rewrote some of her pages in function of her initial scheme, deleting, for example, passages which were taken as having recourse to more traditional plot development and explanatory and descriptive devices.[32] Although not everyone agrees about the merits of her results, it is fairly uncontroversial to recognize *Jacob's Room* as an important modernist work, and it is clear that it was a major breakthrough for Woolf in

---

[31] Virgina Woolf, "The Leaning Tower," in *A Woman's Essays: Selected Essays*, ed. Rachel Bowlby (London: Penquin, 1992), 163.

[32] For this general claim about Woolf's revisions and an example, see James King, *Virginia Woolf* (London: Hamish Hamilton, 1994), 315.

that it pointed the way towards such masterpieces as *Orlando, To the Lighthouse,* and *The Waves.*[33]

To sum up, I have not suggested that episodes of creative artistry are reducible to, or can be fully reconstructed as, sequences of rational choice, if by rational choice is meant the deliberate singling out of an option expected to maximize some function. In the case of Virginia Woolf, the scheme she settles on before she begins writing *Jacob's Room* is indeed a highly schematic notion about a kind of work that she wants to create, a path and not a definite result or destination. This scheme is, however, sufficiently particularized in her mind to have a generative and evaluative function: Woolf is in a position to assess her own results, and subsequent readers can follow her at least part of the way in this regard. It would appear, then, that strategies of rational problem-solving, including planning and pre-commitments, are an important part of the story of artistic creation and reception. These strategies are functionally related even to those aspects of creativity that seem most suited to an a-rationalist, inspirationist account, namely, the 'top speed' work of an 'under mind' that is not under the agent's direct control, as well as those moments when valuable new ideas suddenly pop into awareness following a period of incubation. Yet the operation of a universal, formal sensibility does not make such spontaneous, selective responses possible. Instead, it is an operative aesthetic, partly shaped and generated through an artist's context-bound selection of, and engagement with, a prior scheme or project, which in happy cases, is at least partly a product of a moderately rational choice made from a range of worthwhile artistic goals.

V   *Objections and Replies*

I turn now to a series of objections to these conjectures about creativity and commitment to constraints. In his probing comments on Elster's proposal, Jerrold Levinson claims that artists are typically free to change their minds and abandon or revise whatever prior commitments they may engage in, in which case there may be no correla-

---

[33] Virginia Woolf, *Orlando: A Biography* (New York: Harcourt, Brace, 1928); *To the Lighthouse* (New York: Harcourt, Brace, 1927); *Jacob's Room & The Waves* (New York: Harcourt, Brace, 1923 © 1931).

tive to Ulysses' strategy of self-binding or resolute choice.[34] After all, someone who starts out trying to draft a serious philosophical novel could, if things went wrong, bail out and reclassify the results as an ironic fragment. To this one may respond that although such cases no doubt obtain, in many others the commitment is much more binding, if only because of the degree to which the artist's attitudes effectively become entrenched, psychologically as well as legally and economically. Artists often refrain from an opportunistic abandonment of prior engagements, in part because the artist's own critical judgment remains informed by a given project and by related norms determining what can and cannot be experienced as an artistically successful result. The relevant device or method of pre-commitment, then, is the creation of a disposition to respond. What at one point appears as one distant and schematic option amongst others finally becomes the object of an irresistible desire and 'self-evident' judgment. In some cases, the means of artistic pre-commitment is a public proclamation of intent (as in the programmatic statements of a manifesto), the unexplained repudiation or abandonment of which would have serious repercussions for the artist's self-understanding and status.

Levinson levels another objection against what he characterizes as the overly 'inflexible' model proposed by Elster, namely, that Ulysses' enters into self-binding explicitly and deliberately, whereas this is not the case with artists. I think the correct response here is to split the difference. In other words, we should acknowledge that some artists do deliberately and explicitly settle on, and commit to a scheme, whereas in other cases the operative scheme or aesthetic spontaneously emerges against a background of factors that are not entirely or even predominantly a matter of the artist's doings. Mixed or hybrid cases are no doubt common. Pre-commitment is often, but not always, then, the product of the artist's deliberation and choice. A similar point can be made about Elster's postulation of the existence of a definite, overall objective in the artist's mind, namely, the maximization of artistic value: at least some of the schemes that motivate and guide subsequent activities are indeed oriented towards the creation of artistically valuable works, given a suitably broad and plausible conception of this kind of value. This moderate thesis is not contradicted by the existence of cases where an artist deliberately makes an artistically less valuable work

---

[34] Jerrold Levinson, "Elster on Artistic Creativity," in *The Creation of Art*, 235–256.

to achieve some other goal, such as the maximization of an expected economic payoff.

Another objection that may come to mind here is that it is viciously circular to propose that creativity is explicable in terms of a prior, *creative*, and rational selection of the constraints corresponding to an aesthetic or to some general artistic project. Indeed, it would be hopeless to propose that to be creative at making a particular work, the artist must first be creative in selecting an entire aesthetic, where the latter feat remains a perfect mystery. However, my proposal is not that all prior constraints and schemes are the products of great creativity. The mistaken thesis would be what R. G. Collingwood called 'aesthetic individualism,' the idea that the artist is a perfectly self-sufficient individual who creatively generates everything—including the medium, art form, themes, techniques, and genres.[35] Sometimes new artistic constraints are devised, but then the artist relies on a background of traditional artistic conventions and methods, as well as received orientations and norms.[36] Yet deliberate experimentation with seemingly arbitrary constraints is sometimes an important part of the story, and can indeed establish a scheme within which unanticipated yet viable aesthetic discernments become possible. In other cases, the attunement of the requisite sensibility and capacities of discernment is a product of training and experience that are only partly the object of the artist's deliberate selection.[37]

---

[35] R. G. Collingwood, *The Principles of Art* (Oxford: Oxford University Press, 1938), 316.

[36] This point is underscored and developed by Stein Haugom Olsen in "Culture, Convention, and Creativity," and by Noël Carroll in "Art, Creativity, and Tradition," in *The Creation of Art*, eds. Gaut and Livingston, 192–207, 208–234 respectively.

[37] A first version of this paper was initially presented at Stanford University at a conference on rational choice and the humanities organized by David Palumbo-Liu. I think David for his helpful editorial advice. Another version was presented in Providence, Rhode Island at the annual meeting of the American Society for Aesthetics. I thank my respondent on that occasion, Gary Fuller, for his comments and encouragement. David Davies and other members of the audience raised some helpful questions. The work described in this paper was partially supported by a grant from the Research Grants Council of the Hong Kong Special Administrative Region, China (Project No. LU3401/06H). I am very grateful for this support.

CHAPTER EIGHT

THE CREATIVE IMAGINATION[1]

Michael Polanyi

The enterprise that I am undertaking here has been severely discouraged by contemporary philosophers. They do not deny that the imagination can produce new ideas which help the pursuit of science or that our personal hunches and intuitions are often to the point. But since our imagination can roam unhindered by argument and our intuitions cannot be accounted for, neither imagination nor intuition are deemed rational ways of making discoveries. They are excluded from the logic of scientific discovery, which can deal then only with the verification or refutation of ideas after they have turned up as possible contributions to science.

However, the distinction between the production and testing of scientific ideas is not really so sharp. No scientific discovery can be strictly verified, or even proved to be probable, yet we bet our lives every day on the correctness of scientific generalizations, for example, those underlying medicine and technology. Admittedly, Sir Karl Popper has pointed out that, though not strictly verifiable, scientific generalizations can be strictly refuted. But the application of this principle cannot be strictly prescribed. It is true that a single piece of contradictory evidence refutes a generalization, but experience can present us only with *apparent contradictions*, and there is no strict rule by which to tell whether any apparent contradiction is an *actual contradiction*. The falsification of a scientific statement can therefore no more be strictly established than can its verification. Verification and falsification are *both formally indeterminate* procedures.

There is in fact no sharp division between science in the making and science in the textbook. The vision which guided the scientist to

[1] Reprinted from *Chemical and Engineering News* 44 (1966): 85–93. © 1966 American Chemical Society, and *The Concept of Creativity in Science and Art*, eds. Denis Dutton and Michael Krausz (The Hague/Boston/London: Martinus Nijhoff Publishers, 1981), 91–108, *all rights reserved*.

success lives on in his discovery and is shared by those who recognize it. It is reflected in the confidence they place in the reality of that which has been discovered and in the way in which they sense the depth and fruitfulness of a discovery.

Any student of science will understand—must understand—what I mean by these words. But their teachers in philosophy are likely to raise their eyebrows at such a vague emotional description of scientific discovery. Yet the great controversy over the Copernican system, which first established modern science, turned on just such vague emotional qualities attributed to the system by Nicolaus Copernicus and his followers, which proved in their view that the system was real.

Moreover, after Isaac Newton's confirmation of the Copernican system, Copernicus and his followers—Kepler and Galileo—were universally recognized to have been right. For two centuries their steadfastness in defending science against its adversaries was unquestioningly honored. I myself was still brought up on these sentiments. But at that time some eminent writers were already throwing cold water on them. Henri Poincaré wrote that Galileo's insistence that the earth was really circling round the sun was pointless, since all he could legitimately claim was that this view was more convenient. The distinguished physicist, historian, and philosopher, Pierre Duhem, went further and concluded that it was the adversaries of Copernicus and his followers who had recognized the true meaning of science, which the Copernicans had misunderstood. While this extreme form of modern positivism is no longer widely held today, I see no essential alternative to it emerging so far.

Let us look then once more at the facts. Copernicus discovered the solar system by signs which convinced him. But these signs convinced few others. For the Copernican system was far more complicated than that of Ptolemy: it was a veritable jungle of *ad hoc* assumptions. Moreover, the attribution of physical reality to the system met with serious mechanical objections and also involved staggering assumptions about the distance of the fixed stars. Yet Copernicus claimed that his system had unique harmonies which proved it to be real even though he could describe these harmonies only in a few vague emotional passages.[2] He did not stop to consider how many assumptions he had to make in formulating his system, nor how many difficulties he ignored in doing

---

[2] *De Revolutionibus* [*On the Revolutions of the Heavenly Spheres*] (Nuremberg, 1543), Preface and bk. 1, chap. 10.

so. Since his vision showed him an outline of reality, he ignored all its complications and unanswered questions.

Nor did Copernicus remain without followers in his own century. In spite of its vagueness and its extravagances, his vision was shared by great scientists like Kepler and Galileo. Admittedly, their discoveries bore out the reality of the Copernican system, but they could make these discoveries only because they already believed in the reality of that system.

We can see here what is meant by attributing reality to a scientific discovery. It is to believe that it refers to no chance configuration of things, but to a persistent connection of certain features, a connection which, being real, will yet manifest itself in numberless ways, inexhaustibly. It is to believe that it is there, existing independently of us, and that for that reason its consequences can never be fully predicted.

Our knowledge of reality has, then, an essentially indeterminate content: it deserves to be called a *vision*. The vast indeterminacy of the Copernican vision showed itself in the fact that discoveries made later, in the light of this vision, would have horrified its author. Copernicus would have rejected the elliptic planetary paths of Kepler and, likewise, the extension of terrestrial mechanics to the planets by Galileo and Newton.[3] Kepler noted this by saying that Copernicus had never realized the riches which his theory contained.[4]

This vision, the vision of a hidden reality, which guides a scientist in his quest, is a dynamic force. At the end of the quest the vision is becalmed in the contemplation of the reality revealed by a discovery; but the vision is renewed and becomes dynamic again in other scientists and guides them to new discoveries. I shall now try to show how both the dynamic and the static phases of a scientific vision are due to the strength of the imagination guided by intuition. We shall understand then both the grounds on which established scientific knowledge rests and the powers by which scientific discovery is achieved.

I have pursued this problem for many years by considering science as an extension of ordinary perception. When I look at my hand and move it about, it would keep changing its shape, its size, and its color but for my power of seeing the joint meaning of a host of rapidly changing clues, and seeing that this joint meaning remains unchanged.

---

[3] Ibid., bk. 1, chap. 4.
[4] See H. Dingle, *The Scientific Adventure* (London: Pitman, 1952), 46.

I recognize a real object before me from my joint awareness of the clues which bear upon it.

Many of these clues cannot be sensed in themselves at all. The contraction of my eye muscles, for example, I cannot experience in itself. Yet I am very much aware of the working of these muscles indirectly, in the way they make me see the object at the right distance and as having the right size. Some clues to this we see from the corner of our eyes. An object looks very different when we see it through a blackened tube, which cuts out these marginal clues.

We can recognize here *two kinds of awareness*. We are obviously aware of the object we are looking at, but are aware also—in a much less positive way—of a hundred different clues which we integrate to the sight of the object. When integrating these clues, we are attending fully to the object while we are aware of the clues themselves without attending to them. We are aware of these clues only as *pointing to the object we are looking at*. I shall say that we have a *subsidiary awareness* of the clues in their bearing on the object to which we are *focally attending*.

While an object on which we are focusing our attention is always identifiable, the clues through which we are attending to the object may often be unspecifiable. We may well be uncertain of clues seen from the corner of our eyes, and we cannot experience in themselves at all such subliminal clues, as for example the effort of contracting our eye muscles.

But it is a mistake to identify subsidiary awareness with unconscious or preconscious awareness, or with the Jamesian fringe of awareness. What makes an awareness subsidiary is *the function it fulfills*; it can have any degree of consciousness so long as it functions as a clue to the object of our focal attention. To perceive something as a clue is sufficient by itself, therefore, to make its identification uncertain.

Let me return now to science. If science is a manner of perceiving things in nature, we might find the prototype of scientific discovery in the way we solve a difficult perceptual problem. Take for example the way we learn to find our way about while wearing inverting spectacles. When you put on spectacles that show things upside down, you feel completely lost and remain helpless for days on end. But if you persist in groping around for a week or more, you find your way again and eventually can even drive a car or climb rocks with the spectacles on. This fact, well-known today, was in essence discovered by Stratton seventy years ago. It is usually said to show that after a time the visual image switches round to the way we normally see it. But some more recent observations have shown that this interpretation is false.

It happened, for example, that a person perfectly trained to get around with upside-down spectacles was shown a row of houses from a distance, and he was then asked whether he saw the houses right side up or upside down. The question puzzled the subject and he replied after a moment that he had not thought about the matter before, but that now that he was asked about it he found that he saw the houses upside down.[5]

Such a reply shows that the visual image of the houses has not turned back to normal; it has remained inverted, but the inverted image no longer means to the subject that the houses themselves are upside down. The inverted image has been reconnected to other sensory clues, to touch and sound and weight. These all hang together with the image once more, and hence, though the image remains inverted, the subject can again find his way by it safely. *A new way of seeing things rightly has been established.* And since the meaning of the upside-down image has changed, the term 'upside down' has lost its previous meaning, so that now it is confusing to inquire whether something is seen upside down or right side up. The new kind of right seeing can be talked about only in terms of a new vocabulary.

We see how the wearer of inverting spectacles reorganizes scrambled clues into a new coherence. He again sees *objects*, instead of meaningless impressions. He again sees *real things*, which he can pick up and handle, which have weights pulling in the right direction and make sounds that come from the place at which he sees them. He has made sense out of chaos.

In science, I find the closest parallel to this perceptual achievement in the discovery of relativity. Einstein has told the story of how from the age of sixteen, he was obsessed by the following kind of speculations.[6] Experiments with falling bodies were known to give the same results on board a ship in motion as on solid ground. But what would happen to the light which a lamp would emit on board a moving ship?

---

[5] See F. W. Snyder and N. H. Pronko, *Vision with Spatial Inversion* (Wichita, Kans.: University of Wichita Press, 1952). For fuller evidence and its interpretation in the sense given here, see H. Kottenhoff, "*Was ist richtiges Sehen mit Umkehrbrillen und in welchem Sinne stellt sich das Sehen um?*" *Psychologia Universalis* 5 (1961).

[6] See P. A. Schilpp, ed., *Albert Einstein, Philosopher-Scientist* (New York: Tudor, 1951), 53.

Supposing the ship moved fast enough, would it overtake the beams of its own light, as a bullet overtakes its own sound by crossing the sonic barrier? Einstein thought that this was inconceivable, and, persisting in this assumption, he eventually succeeded in renewing the conceptions of space and time in a way which would make it inconceivable for the ship to overtake, however slightly, its own light rays. After this, questions about a definite span of time or space became meaningless and confusing—exactly as questions of 'above' and 'below' became meaningless and confusing to a subject who had adapted his vision to inverting spectacles.

It is no accident that it is the most radical innovation in the history of science that appears most similar to the way we acquire the capacity for seeing inverted images rightly. For only a comprehensive problem like relativity can require that we organize such basic conceptions as we do in learning to see rightly through inverting spectacles. Relativity alone involves conceptual innovations as strange and paradoxical as those we make in righting an inverted vision.

The experimental verifications of relativity have shown that the coherence discerned by Einstein was real. One of these confirmations has a curious history. Einstein had assumed that a light source would never overtake a beam sent out by it, a fact that had already been established before by Michelson and Morley. In his autobiography, Einstein says that he made this assumption intuitively from the start. But this account failed to convince his contemporaries, for intuition was not regarded as legitimate ground for knowledge. Textbooks of physics therefore described Einstein's theory as his answer to the experiments of Michelson. When I tried to put the record right by accepting Einstein's claim that he had intuitively recognized the facts already demonstrated by Michelson, I was attacked and ridiculed by Professor Grünbaum who argued that Einstein must have known of Michelson's experiments, since he could not otherwise have based himself on the facts established by these experiments.[7]

However, if science is a generalized form of perception, Einstein's story of his intuition is clear enough. He had started from the principle that it is impossible to observe absolute motion in mechanics, and when he came across the question whether this principle holds also when light is emitted, he felt that it must still hold, but he could not quite

---

[7] See A. Grünbaum, *Philosophical Problems of Space and Time* (New York: Knopf, 1963), 378–385.

tell why he assumed this. However, such unaccountable assumptions are common in the way we perceive things, and this can also affect the way scientists see them. Newton's assumption of absolute rest itself, which Einstein was to refute, owed its convincing power to the way we commonly see things. We see a car traveling along a road and never the road sliding away under the car. We see the road at absolute rest. We generally see things as we do, because this establishes coherence within the context of our experience. So when Einstein extended his vision to the universe and included the case of a light source emitting a beam, he could make sense of what he then faced only by seeing it in such a way that the beam was never overtaken, however slightly, by its source. This is what he meant by saying that he knew intuitively that this was in fact the case.

We understand now also why the grounds on which Copernicus claimed that his system was real could be convincing to him, though not convincing to others. We have seen that the intuitive powers that are at work in perception integrate clues which, being subsidiarily known, are largely unspecifiable; we have seen further that the intuition by which Einstein shaped his novel conceptions of time and space was also based on clues which were largely unspecifiable; we may assume then that this was also true for Copernicus in shaping his vision of reality.

And we may say this generally. Science is based on clues that have a bearing on reality. These clues are not fully specifiable; nor is the process of integration which connects them fully definable; and the future manifestations of the reality indicated by this coherence are inexhaustible. These three indeterminacies defeat any attempt at a strict theory of scientific validity and offer space for the powers of the imagination and intuition.

This gives us a general idea of the way scientific knowledge is established at the end of an inquiry; it tells us how we judge that our result is coherent and real. But it does not show us where to start an inquiry, nor how we know, once we have started, which way to turn for a solution. At the beginning of a quest we can know only quite vaguely what we may hope to discover; we may ask, therefore, how we can ever start and go on with an inquiry without knowing what exactly we are looking for.

This question goes back to antiquity. Plato set it in the *Meno*. He said that if we know the solution of a problem, there is no problem—and if we don't know the solution, we do not know what we are looking for and cannot expect to find anything. He concluded that when we do solve problems, we do it by remembering past incarnations. This strange solution of the dilemma may have prevented it from being taken seriously. Yet the problem is ineluctable and can be answered only be recognizing a kind of intuition more dynamic than the one I have described so far.

I have spoken of our powers to perceive a coherence bearing on reality, with its yet hidden future manifestations. But there exists also a more intensely pointed knowledge of hidden coherence: the kind of foreknowledge we call a problem. And we know that the scientist produces problems, has hunches, and, elated by these anticipations, pursues the quest that should fulfill these anticipations. This quest is guided throughout by feelings of a deepening coherence and these feelings have a fair chance of proving right. We may recognize here the powers of a dynamic intuition.

The mechanism of this power can be illuminated by an analogy. Physics speaks of potential energy that is released when a weight slides down a slope. Our search for deeper coherence is likewise guided by a potentiality. We feel the slope toward deeper insight as we feel the direction in which a heavy weight is pulled along a steep incline. It is this dynamic intuition which guides the pursuit of discovery.

This is how I would resolve the paradox of the *Meno*: we can pursue scientific discovery without knowing what we are looking for, because the gradient of deepening coherence tells us where to start and which way to turn, and eventually brings us to the point where we may stop and claim a discovery.

But we must yet acknowledge further powers of intuition, without which inventors and scientists could neither rationally decide to choose a particular problem nor pursue any chosen problem successfully. Think of Stratton devising his clumsy inverting spectacles and then groping about guided by the inverted vision of a single, narrowly restricted eye for days on end. He must have been firmly convinced that he would learn to find his way about within a reasonable time, and also that the result would be worth all the trouble of his strange enterprise—and he proved right. Or think of Einstein, when as a boy he came across the speculative dilemma of a light source pursuing its own ray. He did not brush the matter aside as a mere oddity, as anybody else would have done. His intuition told him that there must exist a principle which would assure the impossibility of observing absolute motion in any circumstances. Through years of sometimes despairing inquiry, he kept up his conviction that the discovery he was seeking was within his ultimate reach and that it would prove worth the torment of its pursuit; and again, Einstein proved right. Kepler too might reasonably have concluded, after some five years of vain efforts, that he was wasting his time, but he persisted and proved right.

The power by which such long-range assessments are made may be called a *strategic intuition*. It is practiced every day on a high level of responsibility in industrial research laboratories. The director of such a laboratory does not usually make inventions, but is responsible for assessing the value of problems suggested to him, be it from out-side or from members of his laboratory. For each such problem the director must jointly estimate the chances of its successful pursuit, the value of its possible solution, and also the cost of achieving it. He must compare this combination with the joint assessment of the same characteristics for rival problems. On these grounds he has to decide whether the pursuit of a problem should be undertaken or not, and if undertaken, what grade of priority should be given to it in the use of available resources.

The scientist is faced with similar decisions. The kind of intuition which points out problems to him cannot tell him which problem to choose. He must be able to estimate the gap separating him from discov-ery, and he must also be able roughly to assess whether the importance of a possible discovery would warrant the investment of the powers and resources needed for its pursuit. Without this kind of strategic intuition, he would waste his opportunities on wild goose chases and soon be out of a job.

The kind of intuition I have recognized here is clearly quite different from the supreme immediate knowledge called intuition by Gottfried Leibniz or Benedict (Baruch) Spinoza or Edmund Husserl. It is a skill for guessing with a reasonable chance of guessing right, a skill guided by an innate sensibility to coherence, improved by schooling. The fact that this faculty often fails does not discredit it; a method for guessing 10 percent above average chance on roulette would be worth millions.

But to know what to look for does not lead us to the power to find it. That power lies in the imagination.

I call all thoughts of things that are not present, or not yet present—or perhaps never to be present—acts of the imagination. When I intend to lift my arm, this intention is an act of my imagination. In this case imagining is not visual but muscular. An athlete keyed up for a high jump is engaged in an intense act of muscular imagination. But even in the effortless lifting of an arm, we can recognize a conscious intention, an act of the imagination, distinct from its muscular execution. For we never decree this muscular performance in itself, since we have no direct control over it. This delicately coordinated feat of muscular contractions can be made to take place only spontaneously, as a sequel to our imaginative act.

This dual structure of deliberate movement was first described by William James seventy years ago. We see now that it corresponds to the two kinds of awareness that we have met in the act of perception. We may say that we *have a focal awareness of lifting our arm, and that this focal act is implemented by the integration of subsidiary muscular particulars.* We may put it exactly as in the case of perception, that we are focally aware of our intended performance and aware of its particulars only subsidiarily, by attending to the performance which they jointly constitute.

A new life, a new intensity, enters into this two-leveled structure the moment our resolve meets with difficulties. The two levels then fall apart, and the imagination sallies forward, seeking to close the gap between them. Take the example of learning to ride a bicycle. The imagination is fixed on this aim, but, our present capabilities being insufficient, its execution falls behind. By straining every nerve to close this gap, we gradually learn to keep our balance on a bicycle.

This effort results in an amazingly sophisticated policy of which we know nothing. Our muscles are set so as to counteract our accidental imbalance at every moment, by turning the bicycle into a curve with a radius proportional to the square of our velocity divided by the angle of our imbalance. Millions of people are cycling all over the world by skillfully applying this formula which they could not remotely understand if they were told about it. This puzzling fact is explained by the two-leveled structure of intentional action. The use of the formula is invented on the subsidiary level in response to the efforts to close the gap between intention and performance; and since the performance has been produced subsidiarily, it can remain focally unknown.

There are many experiments showing how an imaginative intention can evoke covertly, inside our body, the means of its implementation. Spontaneous muscular twitches, imperceptible to the subject, have been singled out by an experimenter and rewarded by a brief pause in an unpleasant noise; and as soon as this was done, the frequency of the twitches—of which the subject knew nothing—multiplied about threefold. Moreover, when the subject's imagination was stimulated by showing him the electrical effect of his twitches on a galvanometer, the frequency of the twitches shot up to about six times their normal rate.[8]

This is the mechanism to which I ascribe the evocation of helpful clues by the scientist's imagination in the pursuit of an inquiry. But we have to remember here that scientific problems are not definite tasks. The scientist knows his aim only in broad terms and must rely on his sense of deepening coherence to guide him to discovery. He must keep his imagination fixed on these growing points and force his way to what lies hidden beyond them. We must see how this is done.

Take once more the example of the way we discover how to see rightly through inverting spectacles. We cannot aim specifically at reconnecting sight, touch, and hearing. Any attempt to overcome spatial inversion by telling ourselves that what we see above is really below may actually hinder our progress, since the meaning of the words we would use is inappropriate. We must go on groping our way by sight and touch, and learn to get about in this way. Only by keeping our imagination fixed *on the global result* we are seeking can we induce the requisite sensory reintegration and the accompanying conceptual innovation.

No quest could have been more indeterminate in its aim than Einstein's inquiry, which led to the discovery of relativity. Yet he has told how during all the years of his inquiry, "there was a feeling of direction, of going straight towards something definite. Of course," he said, "it is very hard to express that feeling in words; but it was definitely so, and clearly to be distinguished from later thoughts about the rational form of the solution." We meet here the integration of still largely unspecifiable elements into a gradually narrowing context, the coherence of which has not yet become explicit.

The surmises made by Kepler during six years of toil before hitting on the elliptical path of Mars were often explicit. But Arthur Koestler has shown that Kepler's distinctive guiding idea, to which he owed his success, was the firm conviction that the path of the planet Mars was somehow determined by a kind of mechanical interaction with the

---

[8] See R. F. Hefferline, et al., "Escape and Avoidance Conditioning in Human Subjects without Their Observation of the Response," *Science* 130 (1959): 1338–1339; R. F. Hefferline, "Learning Theory in Clinical Psychology," in *Experimental Foundations of Clinical Psychology*, ed. A. J. Bachrach (New York: Basic Books, 1962).

sun.[9] This vague vision—foreshadowing Newton's theory—had enough truth in it to make him exclude all epicycles and send his imagination in search of a single formula, covering the whole planetary path both in its speed and in its shape. This is how Kepler hit upon his two laws of elliptical revolution.

We begin to see now how the scientist's vision is formed. The imagination sallies forward, and intuition integrates what the imagination has lit upon. But a fundamental complication comes into sight here. I have acknowledged that the final sanction of discovery lies in the sight of a coherence which our intuition detects and accepts as real; but history suggests that there are no universal standards for assessing such coherence.

Copernicus criticized the Ptolemaic system for its coherence in assuming other than steady circular planetary paths, and fought for the recognition of the heliocentric system as real because of its superior consistency. But his follower, Kepler, abandoned the postulate of circular paths, as causing meaningless complications in the Copernican system, and boasted that by doing so he had cleansed an Augean stable.[10] Kepler based his first two laws on his vision that geometrical coherence is the product of some mechanical interaction,[11] but this conception of reality underwent another radical transformation when Galileo, Descartes, and Newton found ultimate reality in the smallest particles of matter obeying the mathematical laws of mechanics.

I have described at some length elsewhere some of the irreconcilable scientific controversies which have risen when two sides base their arguments on different conceptions of reality. When this happens neither side can accept the evidence brought up by the other, and the schism leads to a violent mutual rejection of the opponent's whole position. The great controversies about hypnosis, about fermentation, about the bacterial origin of disease, and about spontaneous generation are cases in point.[12]

It becomes necessary to ask, therefore, by what standards we can change the very standards of coherence on which our convictions rest.

---

[9] See Arthur Koestler, *The Sleepwalkers* (London: Hutchinson, 1959).

[10] Ibid., 334.

[11] Ibid., 316.

[12] Michael Polanyi, *Personal Knowledge* (Chicago: University of Chicago Press, 1958), 150–160.

On what grounds can we change our grounds? We are faced with the existentialist dilemma: how values of our own choosing can have authority over us who decreed them.

We must look once more, then, at the mechanism by which imagination and intuition carry out their joint task. We lift our arm and find that our imagination has issued a command which has evoked its implementation. But the moment feasibility is obstructed, a gap opens up between our faculties and the end at which we are aiming, and our imagination fixes on this gap and evokes attempts to reduce it. Such a quest can go on for years; it will be persistent, deliberate, and transitive; yet its whole purpose is directed on ourselves; it attempts to make us produce ideas. We say then that we are *racking our brain* or *ransacking our brain*; that we are *cudgeling* or *cracking* it, or *beating our brain in trying to get it to work.*

And the action induced in us by this ransacking *is felt as something that is happening to us.* We say that we *tumble* to an idea; or that an idea *crosses* our mind; or that it *comes into* our head; or that it *strikes* us or *dawns* on us, or that it just *presents itself* to us. We are actually surprised and exclaim: Aha! when we suddenly do produce an idea. Ideas may indeed come to us unbidden, hours or even days after we have ceased to rack our brains.

Discovery is made therefore in two moves: one deliberate, the other spontaneous, the spontaneous move being evoked in ourselves by the action of our deliberate effort. The deliberate thrust is a focal act of the imagination, while the spontaneous response to it, which brings discovery, belongs to the same class as the spontaneous coordination of muscles responding to our intention to lift our arm, or the spontaneous coordination of visual clues in response to our looking at something. This spontaneous act of discovery deserves to be recognized as *creative intuition.*

But where does this leave the *creative imagination?* It is there; it is not displaced by intuition but imbued with it. When recognizing a problem and engaging in its pursuit, our imagination is guided both by our dynamic and by our strategic intuition; it ransacks our available faculties, guided by creative intuition. The imaginative effort can evoke its own implementation only because it follows intuitive intimations of its own feasibility. Remember, as an analogy, that a lost memory can be brought back only if we have clues to it; we cannot even start racking our brain for a memory that is wholly forgotten. The imagination must attach itself to clues of feasibility supplied to it by the very intuition that it is stimulating; sallies of the imagination that have no such guidance are idle fancies.

The honors of creativity are due then in one part to the imagination, which imposes on intuition a feasible task, and, in the other part, to intuition, which rises to this task and reveals the discovery that the quest was due to bring forth. *Intuition informs the imagination, which in its turn, releases the powers of intuition.*

But where, then, does the responsibility for changing our criteria of reality rest? To find that place we must probe still deeper. When the quest has ended, imagination and intuition do not vanish from the scene. Our intuition recognizes our final result to be valid, and our imagination points to the inexhaustible future manifestations of it. We return to the quiescent state of mind from which the inquiry started, but return to it with a new vision of coherence and reality. Herein lies the final acceptance of this vision; any new standards of coherence implied in it have become our own standards; we are committed to them.

But can this be true? In his treatise on *The Concept of Law*, Professor H. L. A. Hart rightly observes that, while it can be reasonable to decide that something will be illegal from tomorrow morning, it is nonsense to decide that something that is immoral today will be morally right from tomorrow. Morality, Hart says, is "immune against deliberate change"[13] and the same clearly holds also for beauty and truth. Our allegiance to such standards implies that they are not of our making. This existentialist dilemma still faces us unresolved.

But I shall deal with it now. The first step is to remember that scientific discoveries are made in search of reality—of a reality that is there, whether we know it or not. The search is of our own making, but reality is not. We send out our imagination deliberately to ransack promising avenues, but the promise of these paths is already there to guide us; we sense it by our spontaneous intuitive powers. We induce the work of intuition but do not control its operations.

And since our intuition works on a subsidiary level, neither the clues which it uses nor the principles by which it integrates them are fully known. It is difficult to tell what were the clues, which convinced Copernicus that his system was real. We have seen that his vision was fraught with implications so far beyond his own ken that, had they

---

[13] H. L. A. Hart, *The Concept of Law* (Oxford: The Clarendon Press, 1961).

been shown to him, he would have rejected them. The discovery of relativity is just as full of unreconciled thoughts. Einstein tells in his autobiography that it was the example of the two great fundamental impossibilities underlying thermodynamics that suggested to him the absolute impossibility of observing absolute motion. But today we can see no connection at all between thermodynamics and relativity. Einstein acknowledged his debt to Mach, and it is generally thought, therefore, that he confirmed Mach's thesis that the Newtonian doctrine of absolute rest is meaningless; but what Einstein actually proved was, on the contrary, that Newton's doctrine, far from being meaningless, was false. Again, Einstein's redefinition of simultaneity originated modern operationalism, but he himself sharply opposed the way Mach would replace the conception of atoms by their directly observable manifestations.[14]

The solution of our problem is approaching here. For the latency of the principles entailed in a discovery indicates how we can change our standards and still uphold their authority over us. It suggests that while we cannot decree our standards *explicitly*, in the abstract, we may change them *covertly* in practice. The deliberate aim of scientific inquiry is to solve a problem, but our intuition may respond to our efforts with a solution entailing new standards of coherence, new values. In affirming the solution we tacitly obey these new values and thus recognize their authority over ourselves, over us who tacitly conceived them.

This is indeed how new values are introduced, whether in science, or in the arts, or in human relations. They enter subsidiarily, embodied in creative action. Only after this can they be spelled out and professed in abstract terms, and this makes them appear to have been deliberately chosen, which is absurd. The actual grounds of a value, and its very meaning, will ever lie hidden in the commitment, which originally bore witness to that value.

I must not speculate here about the kind of universe, which may justify our reliance on our truth-bearing intuitive powers. I shall speak only of their part in our endorsement of scientific truth. A scientist's originality lies in seeing a problem where others see none and finding a way to its pursuit where others lose their bearings. These acts of his mind are strictly personal, attributable to him and only to him. But they derive their power and receive their guidance from an aim that

---

[14] See Schilpp, *Albert Einstein, Philosopher-Scientist*, 49.

is impersonal. For the scientist's quest presupposes the existence of an external reality. Research is conducted on these terms from the start and goes on then groping for a hidden truth toward which our clues are pointing; and when discovery terminates the pursuit, its validity is sustained by a vision of reality pointing still further beyond it.

Having relied throughout his inquiry on the presence of something real hidden out there, the scientist will necessarily also rely on that external presence for claiming the validity of the result that satisfies his quest. And as he has accepted throughout the discipline which this external pole of his endeavor imposed upon him, he expects that others, similarly equipped, will likewise recognize the authority that guided him. On the grounds of the self-command, which bound him to the quest of reality, he must claim that his results are universally valid; such is the universal intent of a scientific discovery.

I speak not of universality, but of universal intent, for the scientist cannot know whether his claims will be accepted; they may be true and yet fail to carry conviction. He may have reason to expect that this is likely to happen. Nor can he regard a possible acceptance of his claims as a guarantee of their truth. To claim universal validity for a statement indicates merely that it *ought* to be accepted by all. The affirmation of scientific truth has an obligatory character, which it shares with other valuations, declared universal by our own respect for them.

Both the anticipation of discovery and discovery itself may be a delusion. But it is fertile to seek for explicit impersonal criteria of their validity. The content of any empirical statement is three times indeterminate. It relies on clues which are largely unspecifiable, integrates them by principles which are undefinable, and speaks of a reality which is inexhaustible. Attempts to eliminate these indeterminacies of science merely replace science by a meaningless fiction.

To accept science, in spite of its essential indeterminacies, is an act of our personal judgment. It is to share the kind of commitment on which scientists enter by undertaking an inquiry. You cannot formalize commitment, for you cannot express your commitment noncommittally; to attempt this is to perform the kind of analysis, which destroys its subject matter.

We should be glad to recognize that science has come into existence by mental endowments akin to those in which all hopes of excellence are rooted and that science rests ultimately on such intangible powers of our mind. This will help to restore legitimacy to our convictions, which the specious ideals of strict exactitude and detachment have discredited. These false ideals do no harm to physicists, who only pay lip service to them, but they play havoc with other parts of science and with our whole culture, which try to live by them. They will be well lost for truer ideals of science, which will allow us once more to place first things first: the living above the inanimate, man above the animal, and man's duties above man.

CHAPTER NINE

EVERY HORSE HAS A MOUTH: A PERSONAL POETICS[1]

F. E. Sparshott

I

This essay does not seek to anatomize the creative process, but looks at
the credentials of the very idea of such a process in the field of poetry.
It is in three parts, somewhat loosely interrelated. The first part inquires
into the legitimacy of inquiring into the 'creative process'; the second
describes some aspects of my own experience, to see whether anything
in the processes of my creating deserves to be called a creative process;
and the third asks why one should try to effect a union between such
disparate concepts as those of creation and process.

II

It may seem reasonable that someone who has both published extensively on aesthetic theory and made a public profession of poetry should
be asked to testify from personal experience on the creative process.
Yet a poet's first impulse when asked how he writes poems is usually to
resist the question. 'With pencil on paper,' he will say; or 'in English';
or 'with difficulty'; and so on. These may be truths, but the questioner
is likely to feel they are the wrong truths. Yet why should these not
be the only truths there are? Why should there be a further question?
Anything that ends in a poem must be a poetic process, and anything
that ends in an original poem must be a creative process. What more
could one say? A way of writing should have no interest for the public
independent of what is written and published, and when the worth of

---

[1] Reprinted from *Philosophy and Literature 1* (Dearborn: The University of Michigan
Press, 1977), reprinted in *The Concept of Creativity in Science and Art*, eds. D. Dutton and
M. Krausz (The Hague/Boston/London: Martinus Nijhoff Publishers, 1981), 47–73,
all rights reserved.

what is written is established, it can be of no consequence whether it was written in this way or that. It is notorious that when poets talk among themselves they find little to say about the processes and procedures whereby they write. These have nothing interesting in common, and confessional anecdotes soon grow tedious. The problems in which poets show an engrossing common interest are those of publicity and finance: how to get their work before a sufficient public at a rate that makes it not quite suicidal to devote some reasonable proportion of their lives to their exacting art. The process of writing enters into this concern only insofar as it is related to skill or luck in attracting commissions and similar opportunities. This has been said often; but, however often and emphatically it is said, it always needs to be said again.

Yet people persist in asking about the creative process as though that were something above and beyond writing poems or painting pictures. What makes them persist in the face of such discouragement? Perhaps there are two things that seem so puzzling that they feel they must return to their question. First, since poetry for most poets is not a living and never has been, and is less likely to bring fame than to incur rejections and contemptuous reviews, one wonders what drives anyone to choose it for a career. And second, since poems are seldom asked for and even less often fill any social or economic need, how does one decide on any particular occasion to write a poem, and how does one decide what poem one shall write?

Those do seem to be good questions. Yet to ask them presupposes one or both of two things, both strange or absurd. The first presupposition is that any activity that is not justified either by socio-economic yield or by an outcome successful in some other fashion is at best inexplicable and at worst suspect. But that is absurd, as Aristotle showed: some activities must be valued for themselves alone, or nothing can have value. The second supposition is that to write poetry is to do something odd or at least something requiring explanation: that poetry is somehow not normal. But that would be a strange thing to suppose. The occasional practice of poetry seems to be very widespread. A large proportion of our young people commit themselves to verse at least once in their lives, and regular poets are not especially rare; history fails to record any society in which poetry was not practiced, or in which the poet was not a recognized figure. Nor is it unusual, even in a society so dominated as ours is by its economic structure, for a person to devote time and energy to an uneconomic activity that interests him. So a poet asked about the poetic process may resent the question as expecting him to assume responsibility for an oddness and eccentricity that no tenable view of civilization would impute to him: the oddity, he may retort, is that civilization should have decayed to a point where a merely banausic viewpoint could claim such privilege.

The poet does not need to be so touchy. The presupposition might after all be not that the poet is a crank but that his role is of such singular importance that we are interested in how anyone comes to take it on and, having assumed it, fulfills its requirements. And there is after all a difficulty in principle in understanding how poets write poems. It is this difficulty that gives rise to the concept of a creative process and is reflected in the seemingly paradoxical nature of that concept. Poets and other artists engage in creative production on a regular basis. This regularity seems to show that there is a dependable or at least repeatable process or procedure they go through; otherwise, one could not say of a person that he was now a poet, but only that he had been one. To say that he is now a poet suggests that he will go on writing. Yet this seems something not even the poet could know, since our notion of a poem requires that it be original, hence unprecedented, hence unpredictable. Thus, to say that one is a poet is to predict the unpredictable.

Strictly, one does not know that one is still a poet, for every poet must one day write his last poem, and will not then know that it is his last poem he has written. But one may have good reason to believe that one is. And that good reason may not be that one has access to some creative process, or some Muse who will continue to call on one when she is called on. Any one who knows he is a poet also has some knowledge of what sort of poet he is. His poems, however original, will be his poems and will manifest to himself as well as to his readers something of his characteristic style. The poet knows he is a poet because he has a way of writing, which he knows. When he stops writing it will most likely be because he is no longer interested in writing that way. If there is such a thing as a creative process it may lie in this, that every poet develops his own way of finding themes and his own way of working them. The process is to find a theme and work it.

That might be another good place to stop. Psychoanalysts and historians might find something more to say in general terms about how themes are found and worked. But the philosopher cannot: he can only insist that a theme must be found, and worked too. And the poet can only tread his own regress: somewhere at the end of his technique and at the bottom of his bag of tricks there must be an absolute starting point. But so it is with all skills, even the most rudimentary. How do you raise your arm? Philosophers have liked to ask that question, and conclude that though the arm-raiser may invent or discover means, procedures, or re-descriptions, sooner or later he must come to something that he admits he just *does*. Otherwise he would never get his arm up. One might postulate an 'arm-raising process,' just as one speaks of a creative process, as a fancy way of saying that people just raise their arms, as poets just write poems, without being able to say altogether how. A poet is someone to whom writing a poem has become something as intimately familiar as raising his arm, the difference being that what he is intimately familiar with is the way of doing it that he has developed for himself.

In this more reasonable frame of mind, one can after all say something more general about the creative process. How does the poet think of something to write about? The answer must be: it just comes to him. And how does it come to him? Maybe somebody brings it. Bridegrooms evoke epithalamia as editors elicit articles. But if nobody brings anything, if there is no commission or request, how does it come to him? And now the inexperienced or very infrequent writer cannot say. It simply does. That is exactly what it is to be an inexperienced or infrequent writer, that there is no set condition on which he writes. But the experienced writer can say. He keeps on the watch for occasions, seeks them out. He scrutinizes his world for occasions of just such poems as he knows how to write. And how does he recognize such an occasion? Because he sees in it the possibility of just such development as lies within the scope of his practice. Again, that has to be exactly what it is to be an experienced writer. To have experience is nothing other than to be able to recognize and exploit occasions for skill. It might be thought that what this describes is the practice of the unoriginal and uncreative writer, but it is not so. Even the most astonishing innovator astonishes in the sum of his work, or the total development of his practice, or in one or two works that are new departures, and not in each work taken singly in relation to the others. On the other hand, the experience of the poet is not that of the farmer. The farmer must recognize the right day for grubbing the rutabagas, and it is the same day that another farmer would recognize, and would be an equally good day for anyone placed as he is placed to get them in. But what the poet has to recognize is the proper occasion for the exercise of his own style and no other, and it is rarely that even a sympathetic poet can suggest to another what such an occasion would be.

When the poet has thought of something to write about, how does he know what to write about it? The answer is almost as before: it comes to him. But not quite as before, because it must already have come to him. In recognizing an occasion or an opportunity, he must have recognized it as an occasion for doing this or that. But we may set that aside, for unless the completed work springs to his mind ready-made there is work yet to do. How does he know how to do this work? It comes to him. And how does it come? Again, it may be brought, or some of it may. It is possible that someone should tell him what meter to use, what rhymes, what analogies, and so on to any extent. His ignorance may be thus aided, his expertness thus tested. If I give a child a paint-by-numbers set I suggest at once that he shall paint, what he shall paint, and how he shall paint it; and a less explicit variant on this procedure might stimulate production without quite excluding creation. But, of course, any part played by such intrusion is outside our interest when it is specifically the creative process that engages our attention.

Given a *donnée*, then, how does the knowledge of how to develop it come to the poet? Once more, the poet who lacks experience cannot say. He can know how to follow a rule, but not how to depart from it, and if he departs he must do it in fear and trembling or in foolhardiness. With the experienced poet it must be otherwise. Strictly, he cannot *say* how it comes to him, for anything he could say would amount to a rule he could cite. But, though he cannot describe it fully, there is nothing he knows better than his own way of proceeding. That, and nothing else, is what his art is. He knows what to do next, and this is not what the rule of his art prescribes but what determines his style. And the truly original and creative artist is the one whose style determines a way of developing and changing his ways of proceeding themselves, who sees in the next occasion for his art not an opportunity to do what he knows how to do but an opportunity to do what he knows to be the next thing.

But how does the poet know it will continue to come to him? The artist's perpetual fear that the sources of his inspiration will suddenly dry up seems real and reasonable, but there is something factitious about it, as though a man were to fear he might forget how to speak his native tongue—or how to raise his arm. Such things do happen. But in the ordinary course of events, as Aristotle remarks in opposing the suggestion that a man might 'forget' his moral principles, one does not forget what one does all the time. I forget my French, which

I speak seldom, but not my English, which I speak every hour and in which I frame all my thoughts.

Here is the heart of the matter. The artist, the poet, is to be known by his sustained habit of attention. As he scrutinizes his world for themes, so he looks ceaselessly up and down for ways of proceeding. His style is a style of search, not a habit of acceptance. His mind is a restless scanner, an inward rat. The other day an inventor was interviewed on television and asked if he might not run out of ideas. He said he would not. "I think all the time. If you think for forty hours a week, you'll think of something." The layman who asks the writer how he gets his ideas seems to think that such ideas would be forcing themselves spontaneously on a mind as idle as his own. But nothing is more evident to the artist than that he is working at his art, and the layman is not. What poets have most evidently in common is not a mysterious contact with secret springs, and certainly not any shared mental process, but simply a steady application to the actual writing of poetry. Anybody can be a poet who really wants to be, though wanting will not make him a good one. What the layman does not do, and probably could not do, is bring himself to attend steadily, day after day and year after year, to the business of the art.

To ask a poet to describe the creative process is to ask him to formulate a rule, or something that will do in place of a rule, by following which any idle ninny could make a poem. But writing poems is something idle ninnies cannot expect to do without forfeiting their idleness and ninnyhood. A poet is not an idle ninny who just happens to own a sort of magical sausage-machine that he might lend (or of which he might deliver the patent) to his neighbor, like lending him a power-mower. If there is a creative process it cannot be a substitute for intelligent work. It must be a way such work is done.

III

Talk of the creative process, it seems, covers two questions the poet may be asked: how he came to bend his attention steadily in that unremunerative direction, and how he comes to write this or that poem. If I now answer these questions for my part, it is not because I wish to speak for 'the poet,' since each must answer for himself, but because what I think about these matters must reflect what has happened to me, and the way I interpret my experience must be colored by my theories.

My answers will be honest, within limits, but I cannot answer for their truth. The way I now recall my life may not be at all the way it was.

In my assumption of the vatic mantle—a suitably portentous phrase, stressing the self-image rather than the work to be done; and a mantle, unlike a *persona*, covers the contours but leaves the face exposed—I recognize five stages and look to a possible sixth.

The first stage was my realization that the poetry we were taught at school was something I understood better than my teachers—or rather, understood in a way they did not. I had a feel for what was going on, like someone watching players at a game he knows. That was when I was a child, eleven or twelve. The second stage came a year or two years later. It was the realization that I knew how poetry worked, what governed the choice to say this rather than that. The poems I was then writing were not good ones, even by the standards appropriate to children's verse, but they were rooted in a confidence that I knew what I was doing—a confidence that I have never lost, and have never experienced in any other form of activity, even in those in which my practice seems objectively to have been more successful.

I have sharp and vivid recollections of the occasions on which the two realizations I have mentioned came to me—or rather, perhaps, of the moments that have come to stand for these discoveries. The difference between the two stages thus marked seems very real and evident to me, though I am less sure that I can put the sense of it into words: it is the difference between finding something congenial and finding it rational, between a feel for the whole and a grasp of its workings. But it may after all be that the real difference is between the two images I retain, and the two incidents they purport to stand for.

The third stage begins with the recognition, at fifteen or so, that poetry was what I came into the world to do: not something I *could* do, but something it was my business to do. R. G. Collingwood, in his *Autobiography*, tells how the conviction that philosophy was his business was precipitated in him at the age of eight, though he did not then know what the business was.[2] I recognize in his account something akin to my own experience, and suspect it may be a common one in the onset of prophetic vocations.

The fourth stage is not linked to any date or event. It was the realization, somewhere in my twenties, that it was not in me to be a first-rate

---

[2] R. G. Collingwood, *An Autobiography* (London/N. Y.: Oxford University Press, 1939).

poet; specifically, that my gift was not such that it would be rational to organize my life around it or sacrifice all other pursuits and interests to it. I have called this a realization; but it may rather have been a decision, or even the entry on a new style of self-dramatization. But a decision or self-assessment was in any case called for. It is part of our romantic orthodoxy that devotion to any art must conflict (or demands readiness to conflict) with moral and social obligations; and even without that orthodoxy everyone must confront the question of what weight each of his major concerns is to have in the economy of his life. So I decided to be a minor poet. Poetry would be something interstitial, something I did when not preoccupied. But this was a change of policy, not of attitude; poetry still was, and still is, the only thing I took completely seriously. But I encased my seriousness with irony and formed my life around the inwardly farcical but outwardly respectable career of the academic philosopher.

The fifth stage began in 1958, when at the prompting and with the help of a friend, I began to publish my work. From this point, poetry was no longer a private affair, a matter of my self-image, but part of my ordinary engagement in the world. Publication normalizes poetry.

A sixth stage would begin if I were to begin to write, or to believe myself to be able to write, extremely good poems. Poetry would then be something I would think it proper to give things up for. But this does not seem likely.

Such is my poetic process (wholesale). There seems to be a clear enough pattern to it: first seeing that a practice is congenial, then seeing it as a field for confident operation, then the sense that practice in this field is not merely possible but called for, and at the same time the recognition of the associated role and the decision to present oneself in one of its versions; and finally, in maturity, the recognition that the role is to be played in a certain fashion and under certain conditions suggested by an adult assessment of social reality and one's own place in it. But this clear pattern turns out not to be very interesting, because on inspection it proves to be one that everyone must follow who is to adopt a career on the basis of its attraction rather than because it is socially accessible. In fact, it seems likely that an analogous path must be traced even by those who merely drift along the line of least resistance into a hereditary niche. It too must seem at first merely congenial, because one has grown up with it; then feasible and intelligible; then, as one confronts adulthood, it must begin to figure as what one is going to do with one's life; then, as one matures in one's occupation, one comes to know one's place in it both as a set of skills and as a social position. And at last one simply occupies one's place, and no longer needs to think about that. So I could have spared my autobiography, had it not been that it was only by reflecting on it that I have come to recognize this form of development that the very nature of the case seems almost to demand.

But how about the poetic process (retail)? How do my poems get started? For anyone who makes a profession of poetry, there can be only one answer to this: in every way possible. In the practice of my profession I direct my attention upon all my surroundings in a hunt for occasions of writing. It must therefore be the case, and it is, that everything that could serve as such an occasion will actually serve as one. If I knew of any other sorts of occasion than those I find, I would make use of them at once. A poem may start from the following. An incident. A recollected incident. An incident read about. A mood, or more likely something seen and experienced through the mood, for a mood in itself is nothing. A phrase that suggests a verbal structure. A word that sticks in the mind, or a line or a snatch of rhythm that comes from nowhere. Some words chosen at random by sticking a pin in a dictionary—rather tricky, that. An idea for a kind of poem, or a scheme to be filled in. In fact, anything that a poem could be about, or that could go into a poem, or any way of writing a poem. Whatever. All that is necessary is that one should be able to say 'I could use that'; one need not even know at once how one could use it.

Sometimes an idea for a poem, or a part for a poem, may occur to one when one is not on the watch and not in the mood for poetry. It may then stay around for years until eventually it germinates or is abandoned as after all boring or irrelevant. Sometimes a line, or a phrase or a rhythm, comes together with the adumbration of its own completion, a shadowy notion of a larger structure in which the fragment should occupy a place already determined. But in my case the adumbrated structures are usually large and complex, and I recall no case in which such a structure came to fruition: the pattern completed has always been a smaller one. No doubt that is part of what it is to be a minor poet: that the settled tendency of one's work is towards a diminution of scale.

One possible source of ideas I have seldom used: dreams often yield poetic fragments, but these seldom lead beyond themselves or sustain their promise of interest. And I have chosen not to resort to drugs for the release of inhibition or the derangement of the senses.

Of a very few poems I cannot say how they originated because they appeared spontaneously completed, requiring only to be written down and slightly revised. These poems do not seem on the whole to be better or worse than those in whose genesis deliberation played a greater part, and differ from them in only two ways: that they contain rather more banal Freudian imagery (of pegs and holes, birds and oceans), and that they tend to contain weak elements that for a long time escape notice or resist revision. These spontaneous poems seem neither more nor less characteristic of me than the others. And indeed one does not see why any great gulf should be fixed between the willed and the unwilled. Someone who habitually writes verse might be expected to develop such a facility that he could and sometimes would do so without thinking about it, much as an experienced driver can direct his car through heavy traffic without giving any thought to where he is going.

It is often thought that the operations of the unconscious mind in composition (to which the 'instantaneous' or 'spontaneous' poetizing I have referred to might be thought to attest) are accompanied by agonies of 'incubation' and other psychological disturbances, and that these are an integral part of the creative process. My own experience has been that such pains, irritabilities, abstractions, fatigues, and other signs of unconscious effort are not particularly associated with poetry or creative writing. They occur at a certain phase in the composition of philosophical writings, or the solution of personal or administrative problems, or any complex matter. As many have reported, the phase is that at which a problem is mooted but the terms in which it is formulated are too nebulous, or too complex, to repay systematic problem-solving, any attempt at systematic or step-by-step procedures being at once frustrated by the conviction that the terms of the problem are unclear or just wrong. It is then that one waits and agonizes, contracts a migraine, quarrels with one's family, goes for long walks, dreams, or tosses in insomnia. These distressing episodes seem in my own experience to be related to the phase in the problem to be solved, and to have no connection with antecedent or current events in my personal life. The popular image of 'the oyster and the pearl,' according to which such distresses bear witness to the nacreous covering of an intrusive irritant in one's psyche, seems based on an interpretation of only one class of cases—and, I suspect, a conjectural interpretation at that. The painful incubation marks rather the phase in problem solving that calls for intensive work of a kind one cannot consciously do.

My reference to unconscious labors is open to the objection that, even if the very notion of an unconscious mental activity does not embody a contradiction, unconscious activities are *ex hypothesi* unobservable and hence merely hypothetical constructs: all that is observably happening is that one is interrupting one's work with a bad conscience. The objection is easy and has point, but it is misleading to speak thus of 'all that is observably happening,' for that is not sufficiently described unless one says that everything goes on as if an internal energy-consumer and attention-distracter were scanning one's problem for a system of ordering that would allow the work of conscious problem-solving and monitoring to go forward fruitfully in a systematic or serial fashion. Unconscious mental activity is a dispensable or an empty hypothesis only in the sense that the physical world is so.

In addition to the occasions for verse mentioned, there are commissions—requests for a piece of writing of a certain sort, for a certain occasion, of a certain dimension, on a given topic—any or all of these. In this regard a poem is no different from a philosophical paper or lecture. I can accept such a commission in full confidence that I will come up with something on schedule that will fulfill the requirements, although of course I cannot answer for the quality beyond a certain minimal competence. Why should I not be confident? It is my business to do so.[3] Between the acceptance of the commission and the fulfillment I shall expect the pains of incubation to intervene, but sometimes they do not; sometimes I am visited by what seems to me an 'inspiration' in the form of a genuinely novel and exciting idea and sometimes I am not; and the occurrence of episodes of either kind bears no observable relation to the degree or kind of satisfaction the relevant public takes in the outcome.

In outlining my career as a poet and cataloguing the occasions of my poems, I have answered both the questions that inquiry into the creative process seemed to comprise. But I have left out what is superficially the most striking aspect of my experience, which in this respect parallels that of another academic part-time poet, Alfred Edward Housman. Aside from my adolescence, when one writes verse as a baby dribbles, there

---

[3] It is my good fortune that my productive processes are properly synchronized with anticipated deadlines. Many unfortunate artists and writers are so constituted that the passing of a deadline is needed to initiate the process, just as some people are unable to set out for the opera before curtain-time.

have been four periods in my life when I wrote verse regularly, a poem or a large part of one more or less everyday. In Housman's case, these periods were by his own account times of excitement, answering no doubt to gusts of inspirational afflatus or surges of hormonal flow. In my case, no such disturbance is easy to discern, though of course there is no knowing what an analyst or a lie detector might dredge up.

The first of these periods of regular production, from January 1 to the middle of March, 1944, was undertaken as a matter of policy in the context of adoption of the role of verse-writer, the date fixed in advance—one begins diaries with the new year. So any relation to personal disturbance must at least have been mediated.

The second period, in January 1966, had a double occasion that again called for no troubling of the waters by angels. In the first place, a hiatus between teaching engagements had left my mind free from preoccupations for the first time in years; in the second place, recent publication of a volume had depleted my stock of unpublished poems. Again, the decision to go into regular production on a certain date and for a certain time was taken beforehand. On this occasion I confirmed that I could, given a clear mind, sit down with a sheet of paper and be sure that in no more than an hour I would certainly have come up with a poem or a substantial part of one; though that does not mean that I did not, or need not, keep on the watch for the rest of the day.

The third period of regular composition, from late August to October, 1969, was different. A reading of Matsuo Bassho's *Journey to the Deep North* reactivated an old interest in Japanese verse and occasioned the project of writing a series of occasional poems in Japanese forms, at least one every day. These, being very short, could be composed in short times of peace, without needing protracted freedom from preoccupations. Not surprisingly in view of the nature of the initial stimulus, the series of poems that resulted tended to be on the theme of travel, but in fact it turned out to be more cohesive than that and ended in a sequence that took on the evident though unheralded character of an end. One might therefore postulate some internal unconscious dynamic governing the form of the whole that some form of structural or psychological analysis might lay bare. However, the poems did not, as a sequence or individually, come from any felt disturbance or other specific experience other than that of reading a book that suggested a model.

The fourth period, from June to October 1970, presents a more complex case. Superficially, the situation was as in 1966. The recent publication of a book had depleted my unpublished store, and the start of a sabbatical year provided the necessary freedom from constraining preoccupations. But although I might, conformably with past practice, have provided for a period of regular poetizing, I made no such plans. Rather, the book was occasioned by a curious incident. I had a dream in which I arrived at a meeting where I was to read from my poems, and found I had brought none with me. I hurried home and searched in vain for my manuscripts, but at last found in a drawer a book I had forgotten. This proved to be full of poems I did not recall writing but knew I had written; they were full of a strange power. On waking, I wrote down what I had dreamed—something I do not usually do. Some time later, I found in my office a mimeographed document that I recognized at once as the book of my dream, and which I knew at once that it was laid upon me to fill with poems. So I did so, one or more on every day when I was not sick or traveling. This time, though, there was no conclusion. It simply happened that by late September there were fewer and fewer days when I could summon the composure to wait in stillness. The initial sense of something akin to obligation had given way to a mere habit of continuing, and after a while, there seemed no reason to push it further; besides, I was becoming more engrossed in a complex piece of philosophizing. So the series dwindled away, its last members perfunctory and fragmentary, and the book remains unfilled. The poems, of course, do not have the special power of the poems I dreamed, and differ from other things I have written only in the absence of any large and complex structures. The reason I call this incident curious is that next winter I found the account of the dream I had written, and found that the book I had dreamed was not really the book I 'recognized'—it was in fact a book I knew well, the account book I keep for the income-tax people. It is as if the dream and the false recognition were part of some unconscious dynamic in me, though the outcome fitted well into what would have been a normal and sensible strategy for me to pursue deliberately. And I note in myself an unreasoned urge to tell the story, in one form or another—in fact, it is only to provide a setting for it that I accepted an editor's suggestion that I might exploit my own experience for this article.

So much for anecdote. I infer from my experience that there may well be an unconscious dynamic of composition, but that it is useless to look to it for any characteristic significance, idle to expect that it will correlate with any character discernible in the outcome, and rash to suppose that it always works in a way that is independent of the conscious strategies of its host.

A caution is needed. Obviously I recall much in my life that I have left out, although it could affect the interpretation of what I have written. For instance, the occurrence of sustained but widely separated bursts of poetic activity might seem odder than it is, because my narrative did not mention that my writing of philosophical prose has accustomed me to regular writing for protracted periods on set themes. But so it is with all those anecdotes of sudden inspirations and dream-compositions and emotional disturbances that figure so often in writings on the creative process. Such accounts necessarily come to us as parts of stories that are the products of selection and editing; and it often happens that the selecting and editing are carried out in order to present a certain image of creative procedure, and may therefore omit material that could have been used to tell a very different story—one, perhaps, in which the striking incidents would not figure at all, or would not appear striking.

IV

The phrase the creative process is used in two different ways. Sometimes it is used generically to refer to all processes, whatever they may be, whose outcome meets some appropriate criteria for originality. At other times it is used to refer to some specific process whose characteristic outcome is supposed to be original work. It is not always clear in which sense the phrase is being used, and the distinction is not always recognized. Yet the distinction must be made, for if original work is ever produced it must be produced somehow or other and the phrase cannot lack application in the former sense; but it does not follow that the phrase has any application in its latter sense.

Three different accounts of the creative process have achieved some currency. One, associated with Paul Valéry,[4] and ultimately inspired by Edgar Allan Poe,[5] is exemplified in Part II of this paper: it reduces to saying that some possible component or aspect of a poem serves as a starting point and is then elaborated, partly heuristically and partly systematically. Since all this says is that one must start and then continue, this is clearly taking creative process in the former of the senses distin-

---

[4] For example, Paul Valéry, *Aesthetics* (New York: Pantheon, 1964), 130ff.
[5] E. A. Poe, "The Philosophy of Composition," *Collected Works* (New York: Crowell, 1902), vol. 14.

guished above. It tells nothing about how poems are made, except that they are poems and they are made. A second account of the creative process is associated with Robert Graves,[6] T. S. Eliot,[7] and a host of romantic writers.[8] A schematized version of it might go as follows. First comes the original formulation of a problem or conceiving of a theme (preceded possibly by the poet finding himself in an excited, troubled, or sensitized condition). Second comes a period of random search not directed by the will, unconscious incubation, and so on. Third comes a flash of insight, a relief from suspenseful tension, a sense of how things will go together. Fourth comes the deliberate elaboration of this insight; and fifth is the criticism and refinement of the elaborated solution. This five-stage model will be referred to from now on as 'the standard version,' and seems to take creative process in its second sense, for it appears to describe a psychological process whose correlation with creative solutions to problems or original achievements would need to be established empirically.[9] The third account of the creative process to achieve currency is that elaborated by Arthur Koestler from a hint of Sigmund Freud's.[10] Here, creativity is attributed to the unforeseen interaction of two or more thought-patterns previously elaborated independently. But does this take creative process in the former or the latter of the senses we distinguished? It might be either. Although it seems merely to say how originality actually comes about in typical cases, it might be construed to mean that in every truly original work one must be able to find a complexity of the kind indicated, so that we are merely performing a logical analysis that must in some form or

---

[6] Robert Graves, *The Crowning Privilege* (Harmondsworth: Penguin Books, 1959), 214.

[7] T. S. Eliot, "Tradition and the Individual Talent," in *The Sacred Wood* (London: Methuen, 1920).

[8] Cf. F. E. Sparshott, "Xanthippe," in *Looking for Philosophy* (Montreal: McGill-Queen's University Press, 1972).

[9] At a recent general meeting of the League of Canadian Poets at Fredericton, N.B., the three contributors to a panel on the writing of a poem gave accounts all of which conformed to the following pattern. The poet is attracted by a large public or personal theme, which seems to call for a poem, but sees no way of setting about it. Then, an incident in the poet's life reminds of him of an incident connected with the troublesome theme, and in a state of excitement, he writes a shortish poem or fragment interpreting one in terms of the other. On the basis of this he is then able to work systematically at the large theme. The pattern itself seems as interesting as the coincidence: this might be a typical way of finding an authentic mode of entry into a major theme.

[10] See Arthur Koestler, *The Act of Creation* (New York: Macmillan, 1964), and the article by Koestler contained in this volume. ["This volume" refers to the original publication in which this chapter appeared.—Eds.]

other be presumed to have its counterpart in the process of production. The reason it is hard to tell which is meant is that many authors who write in this field think in terms of a natural necessity: the mind is a logical engine, so that in describing what takes place we are at the same time performing a logical analysis, and vice versa. I return to this question later.

In whichever sense the phrase the creative process is taken, and whichever of the three models we adopt, we may be met by the objection that the very phrase embodies a *contradictio in adjecto*. The idea of creation is that of production from nothing, production of absolute novelty, and the absoluteness of the novelty requires that there be no rule, no method, no series of stages, and accordingly no process whereby it came. The model of creation is the unqualified fiat of God, applied to names whose sense is eternally or instantly complete and only awaits its reference. But the model of a process is something like digestion, in which one can identify initial and terminal stages and enumerate and explain the steps whereby beginning is transformed into end.

To see that the concept of a creative process is not so paradoxical after all, one might compare Aristotle's seemingly innocuous account of the requirements of a whole.[11] It must, he says, have a beginning, a middle, and an end: the beginning is what has no necessary antecedent but has a necessary or normal consequent, the end is what comes naturally—necessarily or normally—from an antecedent but has no consequent, and the middle of course has both antecedent and consequent. So we have a process divisible into linked stages; but the accounts of beginning and end are not symmetrical. The end is not said to necessitate its antecedents: it is not a ground of explanation, but something explained. The beginning, by contrast, is a ground of explanation but is unexplained. The concept of a beginning thus defined is that of a novelty that is absolute but fertile.[12] But if the beginning is an unexampled beginning, the necessary steps by which the inevitable end is reached cannot be known in advance. It must be a necessity retrospectively revealed. And if we recall the way Aristotle usually speaks of natural necessities we may suggest that what is retrospectively revealed is how the intermediate steps were needed to bring about the inevitability of the result. So

---

[11] Aristotle, *Poetics* vii, 1450b26–31.

[12] The notion of an absolute end brings an analogous inexplicability. How can anything have no consequences? Only in the hererocosms, the separate universes, of art, can an end be a completion that is not also the beginning of something.

we may say that a creative process differs from a non-creative process in that the causal connections are not known in advance, as they are in processes where the initial stage is itself explicable as how what regularly happens normally begins. One might still complain that the notion of a process is misapplied, as though anatomizing a whole were tracing the steps of its genesis; but the charge of paradox will not stand. In fact, recent philosophical discussions of creativity take two forms. One inquires into how something akin to rules and methods, right and wrong ways of proceeding, can enter into the processes of producing unprecedented objects. The other inquiries into the nature and locus of the novelty in the created work, without supposing anything about the way it came into being. The former is no more open to the charge of paradox than the latter.

Let us consider further our Aristotelian model of a creative process as one with an absolute beginning and a series of subsequent stages whose necessity is therefore only retrospectively revealed. A poem or other work of art obviously functions as some sort of communication among people, and one might therefore expect to reduce it to terms of the simplest model of communication theory. This model assumes that one starts with something determinate to be communicated. This is encoded, the encoded message is transmitted, then at the other end it is decoded and the original message recovered. The model calls for no absolute beginning: the original message is a structured datum that enters into the communicative process for reasons congruent with the formulation of the message and the devising of the process itself. Let us contrast with this R. G. Collingwood's account of artistic expression, which we may construe as a standard philosophical account of the creative process.[13] Here there is no determinate first stage, no known and structured message to be encoded. There is only an encoding that is at the same time a deciphering. The creative process is a passage from unclarity to clarity, the imparting of structure to inchoate feeling. But this is seen not as a passage from beginning to end, as though the clarification were brought about by the successive application of ever finer filters, but as the arrival at an absolute beginning. So there is and there is not a process: there is, because the artist has progressed from unclarity to clarity, and what he has clarified is in an unexplained

---

[13] See R. G. Collingwood, *The Principles of Art* (Oxford: Clarendon Press, 1938).

sense the 'same feeling' that he began with;[14] but there is not, because
the end has the status of an absolute beginning in the light of which
earlier phases are of no account, sublated, *aufgehoben*, or something.
And what is transmitted from artist to public is supposed not to be in
a code or to admit of decoding, because the artist's encoding was also
a deciphering and all paths of transmission are magically bypassed.
This is strange stuff indeed, but the strangeness may be demanded by
the nature of the case. Attempts to apply information theory to art
seems to fail just because they see no need for such oddness.[15] They
simply take it for granted that a work of art is the encoded version
of a pre-existing message that the artist wishes to transmit. It is only
on this supposition that the concept of redundancy can be pressed
into service to give precision to the notion of style. But if in fact there
was no original message—for otherwise the process would have been
reproductive rather than creative—there is no way it is transmitted,
no code, no bits of information, no redundancy. The model cannot
be applied at all.

Where there is no initial message to be encoded and transmitted, we
cannot tell message from noise. The creative process is thus necessarily
indeterminate. Yet it must be strongly ordered, since the end is ordered.
Vincent Tomas has spelled out how this is possible, in an account that
we could crudely adapt to the terms of Part I of this paper as follows.[16]
The work must start from a *donnée* that has to be regarded as gratuitous,
an absolute starting point. But the artist perceives it as structured in
a way that permits and calls for a line of further development. It is
fidelity to this line of development that serves to regulate his continuing
creation. Normally, it is the author's style, which includes his style of
changing his style that serves as a matrix both for the structures originally discerned and for the continuations suggested, though of course
it may happen that the development envisaged is in some ways, even
in many ways, unprecedented. In any case what serves as controlling
factor is the present condition of the uncompleted work in the light of
the possibilities originally contemplated. But we have to add that every
recognizable intermediate stage in the work's progress serves as a new

---

[14] See, however, Collingwood's *Essays on Philosophical Method* (Oxford: Clarendon,
Press, 1933) for an explication of the patterns of thought involved.
[15] Cf. A. A. Moles, *Information Theory and Esthetic Perception* (Urbana: University of
Illinois Press, 1966).
[16] Vincent Thomas, "Creativity in Art," *Philosophical Review* 67 (1958): 1–15.

donnée suggesting a partially new set of possibilities for development. The work is presumed complete when a stage is reached that calls for no development.

This modest account of something that is both truly creative and truly a process, controlled in a way that can be rationally accounted for and retrospectively described but is at the same time unprecedented and free from rules and routines, is meant to exclude an account in Collingwood's manner that supposes the end of a work to be somehow implicit in its beginning. To see a way of proceeding is not to sense the way to a goal. True, but one feels that the sense of an end must be operative in some way or other. The artist's activity is inexplicable unless he has a hunch that a completed work might result from his working; and his sense of work to be done and progress to be made is unintelligible without some adumbration of a sort of completion. Accounts of the sort I have outlined should be taken not as denying that such a sense of an end is necessary but as denying that it can be understood as determining the course a work takes. The envisaged end is likely to change as the work already done reveals an unsuspected character and suggests unforeseen possibilities.[17]

It seems that one can produce at least one account of what a creative process would be that is coherent and free of paradox. But we have not described a definite process. All we have done is show that the notion of creation does not exclude everything that might be termed a process, and suggest how such a process might be articulated. This is not to say that the notion of creativity includes or implies any sort of process. To speak of creation or creativity is not to say that a sort of procedure has been followed, but only that certain sorts of procedures, namely routines, have not been followed. What, for instance, do we mean when we call a person 'creative'? Sometimes we mean that his solutions to problems are unexpected and fruitful—unexpected, or they would be routine; fruitful, or nothing would have been brought into being. Sometimes we are merely classifying his job as one that involves neither routine production nor dealing with the public: he works in the creative department, no matter what the merits of his work. Sometimes I think we call a person creative if his rate of production in the fine

---

[17] Conformably with this recognition, Mikel Dufrenne, who speaks of the artist as responding to the call of the as yet uncreated work, describes it as an "indeterminate" call. See Mikel Dufrenne, *Phenomenology of Aesthetic Experience* (Evanston: Northwestern University Press, 1973), 35.

arts or some other creative activity is unusually high: if he is fertile in fruitful solutions, or if he is full of ideas. In general, a person is called creative because of a tendency to produce things of a novel sort, or things of a sort in which novelty is important, in a variety of contexts. In no case do we suggest anything about his procedures of production. One might go further and insist that it is absurd to suppose that a single process would characterize such a tendency in all fields alike. Creative activity is not a special sort of activity, but any sort of activity that issues in new being. The idea of a creative process is not paradoxical, but gratuitous.

Those who think of the creative process as a characteristic sort of sequence of psychological events are exposed by the foregoing considerations to a familiar philosophical attack that seems crushing.[18] The occurrence of any such process, it is said, is logically incapable of being either a necessary or sufficient condition of creativity in the sense sketched above. Novelty and fruitfulness in solutions can be identified without knowing their psychological antecedents, and a hackneyed or eccentric solution is not redeemed by any anecdote about its origins. But this argument, though valid and important, does not suffice to show that the occurrence of a certain sort of process in a context where the novelty of the outcome is an important issue has merely anecdotal significance. It shows only that the process cannot serve as hallmark for the product, as some writers have seemed to think it could. But that is not the only significance it could have.

Suppose someone were to put forward our five-stage standard version as a characteristic way of producing novel solutions, in the arts or elsewhere. This might indeed be put forward merely as a generalization about how originators in fact originate. Even that would not be merely nugatory: if we are interested in a result, it is natural that we should be interested in how it came about, and the way things tend to happen in the human world is a proper matter for concern. Alternatively, one might propose it, not as necessary or sufficient condition of creativity already recognized, but as actually defining a sense of 'originality'—that sense, in fact, which is relevant to art. In some cultures, a pot is not deemed properly made unless its design was revealed in a dream.[19] To do this is of course to propose a radical revision of our ideas. Art is

---

[18] For example, see John Hospers, "The Concept of Artistic Expression," *Proceedings of the Aristotelian Society* (1954): 55.

[19] Ruth L. Bunzel, *The Pueblo Potter* (New York: Columbia University Press, 1929).

transformed into something of which a psychological process could be the necessary and sufficient condition—that is, a psychological episode. The work of art is reduced to the status of evidence that 'art has taken place.'[20] All criticism is reduced to foolishness because the evident object is replaced by an unverifiable claim. And, because the alleged dynamic is common to creative work in any field and not in the arts alone, it replaces the role of 'artist' in our hagiography by that of the creative person conceived as a psychological type, a sort of holy fool. Such a revision seems to me preposterous, but a few years ago there were many to propose it.

These extreme interpretations of our standard version, as anecdotal and as definitive, are not the only ones possible. One could for instance argue that the occurrence of the process, because its very description seems to testify both to a serious churning and to some sort of resolution in the outcome, constitutes a claim that the outcome merits attention. This might not be a claim of actual worth, for one might well concede that puddings are proved in eatings, but a claim that what has emerged merits scrutiny for possible worth. This point may be obscured by an inevitable but misleading tendency in collections of reports on the creative process. Only successful artists are asked to provide anecdotes of how they create, so that what they say may appear to be a recipe for success even though a thousand bunglers might have told precisely similar stories if anyone had thought to ask them. Similarly, the handful of exemplary anecdotes that are endlessly repeated from the annals of scientific discovery report only those dreams and inspirations whose outcome was a successful discovery or invention. We are not told of the inspiration that proved abortive, the dream that dissolved on waking, the unconscious incubation and flash of insight whose elaboration disclosed an egregious blunder, the 'got it' phenomenon whose sequel was a 'lost it' experience. So, if we attach any weight to the occurrence of any psychological process, it would be wiser to do so on the basis of our general expectations about human affairs than on the basis of analogies from success stories.

There is a better reason for invoking the creative process as a clue to seriousness in the arts than in the sciences. Notoriously, the work of a

---

[20] Here is an example plucked from the remainder table: "It could be argued... that the painting was a kind of relic, a kind of certificate or guarantee that certain activities had taken place previously which you were not there to witness." Donald Carroll and Edward Lucie-Smith, *Movements in Modern Art* (New York: Horizon, 1973), 132.

truly original artist may be misprized until familiarity has revealed the right way to look at his work, the perspective from which his patterns are visible. We are therefore tempted to look to something other than what we find in the work for testimony to its seriousness or even to its worth. This extraneous aid could be the testimony of an informed critic, or the artist's proved reputation won by work in a more familiar mode. But it could also be something extraneous in the production of his work, such as his labor and eventual satisfaction; or, perhaps rather less extraneous, the occurrence of a process that we deem likely on the face of it to issue in serious work. We may think of the creative process as guaranteeing at least some sort of novelty, and, if the novelty for which it is a recipe is by no means the originality of the highest form of art, our description of it may serve as a guarantee that in a serious and experienced worker the outcome can be neither hackwork nor a mere flash in the brain pan. Even so qualified an assurance may be of comfort to the humble camp-follower of the arts in these difficult days.

If occurrence of the sort of process sketched in our standard version can be taken as presumptive evidence of seriousness, part of the reason may be that what the version describes is what we think ought to take place when something truly original is done. It may be that the standard version and its variants are popular, not because there is any reason to think that anything of the sort often or ever takes place, but because it seems fitting: a work of art is as if it were the outcome of such a process. As human beings, we feel able to pronounce on the fittingness and congruence of human affairs and attitudes. We do not feel the need to have recourse to the behavioral sciences to assure us that our sense of how life goes has empirical backing. On the contrary, we feel free to deride these sciences if they either otiosely confirm or absurdly conflict with our lifelong experience of being human.

It seems then that our standard version may function less as an inductive generalization than as an expression of our untutored and uncriticized sense of what ought to be the case, our way of imagining what it must be to create. It is but one step more to claim for it the status of a myth. Plato in his *Symposium* metaphorically describes artistic and intellectual creation as 'giving birth in beauty.'[21] Our standard account may be construed as an explanation of this metaphor. The triggering experience answers to insemination, the initial formulation

---

[21] Plato, *Symposium* 206b–212a.

of the problem corresponds to conception. Unconscious incubation is transparently an image of gestation, and the moment of intuition is the moment of birth. Then nature yields to nurture: the phases of elaboration and criticism answer respectively to the phases of development in which the infant masters first bodily movement and speech, and then social skills. Our reasons for adopting this natal metaphor are doubtless as much religious as evidential. It testifies to our sense of the dignity of art, to the importance we assign to the birth of new being, to the status of the work of art or the scientific discovery as a new and almost living force come into the world. It is a late survival of the eighteenth-century notion of the 'genius' as someone who is less a fabricator than the place where an autonomous and natural evolution occurs.[22]

Our reasons for accepting this or that description of a creative process as what inevitably, or usually, or typically, or properly, or occasionally but interestingly takes place, may be of many kinds. But, as the examples of Tomas and Koestler may suggest, we might arrive at the notion of such a process simply by considering the conditions without which the emergence of something that was both unexampled and significant would not be possible. As a loaf must be baked, a poem must be created, and it is not clear why there can be no necessary conditions for either process. But at this point we would do well to abandon psychology for phenomenology or conceptual analysis. The alleged 'process' becomes an elucidation of origination as such. If there is to be origination there must be a starting point of some kind; if the originated whole is to be original the principles of its organization must themselves be unprecedented, and must therefore represent a second origin; if there is organization, there must be elaboration; and if there is to be a public outcome it must have been promulgated and must therefore have passed the critical scrutiny of the creator or his custodian. Our standard version does little more than spell out these requirements in psychological terms, assigning each phase a place in a temporal sequence. The one item in the standard version quite unaccounted for is the 'unconscious incubation,' which from the present point of view is either a gratuitous piece of psychologizing (or theologizing)[23] embroidery, or else a dramatization of our recognition that

---

[22] See M. H. Abrams, *The Mirror and the Lamp* (New York: Oxford University Press, 1953), chap. 8.

[23] The phrase unconscious incubation seems to have had its original home in William James's *The Varieties of Religious Experience* (London: Longman's, Green and Co., 1902), with the phenomena of religious conversion.

the two starting points are in principle separate and that each is a true beginning. The transposition of the creative process from psychological and genetical to analytical terms is exemplified in a vigorous argument by Monroe C. Beardsley, who urges that what we call creativity and originality is properly to be located within the work of art itself, and is the emergence of complex resultant qualities that could not have been inferred from an enumeration of the constituents and their relations: this non-inferrability is popularly construed as unpredictability, put into a temporal frame of reference, and projected back onto the artist—as though works of art were produced by human beings instead of appearing, as we all know, ready made on the walls of galleries.[24]

Although proponents of the old 'new' criticism may be contented with an account of creativity and originality in analytical or phenomenological terms, there are reasons why artists and cultural critics cannot be. There is an important difference between human and divine creation: the Creator's claim to originality is (in orthodox theology) unimpeachable, but human beings must establish their bona fides. Creation, properly, is the production of new being, of something that did not before exist but now has a being of its own and in its own right. The concept of creation is then basically less that of process and outcome than that of an achievement. What matters is that there should now be something that owes its being to another, God or man, but in itself is perfectly real. In the paradigm case of the divine creation, this suffices: before, there was no world, but now there is a world, and God will answer for it. But when we speak of human achievements an ambiguity creeps in. With half our minds we think that achievement, creation and originality are relative to their point of origin. We do not deny originality or creativity to either Charles Darwin or Alfred Russel Wallace on the other's account, and there is a sense in which Darwin's achievement would have been no less if Wallace had reached his conclusions a decade before but left them unpublished. So it is that to sustain a plagiarism suit the plaintiff must show not only that the form produced by the alleged plagiarist coincides with the preexisting form, but that he had access to it. It may be in part because memory is delusive, the external history of creation often unknown and unverifiable, and the channels whereby ideas are transmitted manifold and hard to trace, that we like to invoke a creative process, an agonizing labor that at least shows that

---

[24] Monroe C. Beardsley, "On the Creation of Art," *Journal of Aesthetics and Art Criticism* 23 (1965): 291–305.

the alleged creator did not know he was doing anything so undemanding as plagiarizing. Just so, councilors were at one time summoned to attend the birth of a prince, lest some low-born brat be smuggled in a warming-pan; but, if decorum precludes observation of the royal childbed, some reassurance may be had from the observation that the Queen was previously pregnant and is pregnant no more, and that the putative birth was heralded by appropriate groans.

It may be that the status of our standard version is more that of a parable than of a myth. The hard-headed will say that when the Pueblo potter says she dreamed her design the real purport of her claim is that she did not copy it. So it may be that to claim to have undergone the creative process is but a dramatic way of claiming true authorship. And why claim true authorship? Copyrights may be involved, and the artist must live. But that is not all. The value of originality has become deeply embedded in our whole way of thinking about art and even about science.[25] We think of art in terms of its history. The truest work of art, perhaps the only true work of art, we think, is one fit to figure in the history of art: the only true point is a turning point.

---

[25] For an early manifestation cf. Edward Young, *Conjectures on Original Composition in a Letter to the Author of Sir Charles Grandison* (London: Printed for A. Millar and R. and J. Dodsley, 1759).

CHAPTER TEN

CREATIVITY AND SELF-TRANSFORMATION

Michael Krausz

I

I work with special handmade brushes. They are made of the hairs of deer, elk, and fox. They have their own life. After dipped in a solution—like India ink or dried pigment mixed in water—with a slight pressure on museum board, they make very fine, thin lines. With greater pressure a brush's bulbous base releases a swath of pigment on to the surface.

I usually have a general idea of what the painting will look like. But the materials take on a life of their own. They suggest their own possibilities. The unintended spontaneous movements of my fingers and arms allow brush and pigment to respond as they may. Sometimes the unintended emergent results are welcome, sometimes not. Sometimes brush and pigment respond with extreme delicacy, variety, and wit. Other times they respond with ponderous contortions. Sometimes the result is a scene that I could not have imagined. Sometimes the scene provides a space that invites my entry.

As I work on a particular piece, I do so with the foreknowledge of its place in a series of works. Just as a single work may give rise to emergent features, so too may a series of related works give rise to emergent features. These features may become apparent when the series is viewed as a whole, as in a solo exhibition. Creating a given artwork provides an occasion to discover and explore its emerging scapes.

My art-making has a history closely related to my self-transformation. In 1971, I had a nondualistic experience in the studio of a friend. When being surrounded by her large abstract shaped canvases, I suddenly experienced myself *in* the space of the work instead of looking *at* it. More than that: I experienced an 'interpenetration' of my self and the space of the painting.[1]

---

[1] I borrow this apt term from John Dewey, who describes such experiences as: "complete interpenetration of self and the world of objects and events," in *Art as Experience* (New York: Capricorn Books, 1934), 19.

In that space, I suddenly became much more highly visually sensitive—to spatial relations, to coloration and more. As a consequence of that nondualistic experience I *needed* to paint. As a matter of 'inner necessity,' I *had* to paint.[2] After one year of intense work, I had my first one-person exhibition. Since then, I have had twenty.

As a consequence of my nondualistic experience (which I shall discuss later), I now experience more clearly, more expansively, more richly, more perspicuously.[3] Such changes in my *ways* of experiencing in turn affect what I produce. What I produce has affected my ways of experiencing. I think of my art-making as a process in which *who I am* is enriched and transformed. In short, my art-production fosters my self-transformation, and my self-transformation fosters my art-production.

Upon reflection, the reader may be tempted to distinguish several distinct transformations whereby one transformation took me into the space of the painting. Another would have involved the interpenetration of myself and the space of the painting. Yet another transformation would have involved my becoming visually sensitive, and a still further transformation would have involved my need to paint. Could I have had a transformation in *how* I experience as opposed to *what* I experience, and *not* associate it with anything particular to art? Could I have had the same experience but not be compelled to make art myself? Could I have had that experience but simply develop a need to experience more of my friend's work and that of others? Could I have had that experience and not have any related experiences when making my art? In my experience, these logically distinguishable possibilities are inextricably intertwined and symbiotic.

More fully, my painting is integrally related to my self-transformation, and my self-transformation is integrally related to my painting. I value both painting and self-transformation as ends in themselves. My artistic production motivates my self-transformation and my self-transformation motivates my artistic production. Such is my *personal program*.

---

[2] Wassily Kandinsky elaborates the idea of inner necessity in his book, *Concerning the Spiritual in Art, and Painting in Particular* (New York: Wittenborn, Schultz, 1963). See also my *Interpretation and Transformation: Explorations in Art and the Self* (Amsterdam: Rodopi, 2006), chap. 9, 10.

[3] See J. N. Findlay, "The Perspicuous and the Poignant," in *Aesthetics*, ed. Harold Osborn, ed. (London: Oxford University Press, 1972).

II

I periodically invoke my personal program as part of my understanding of who I am. I bring it to mind as need arises, as I confront vocational challenges or life decisions. It plays a significant role as I periodically assess what I am making of my life. I revise my personal program as my aims and interests change and develop.

I do not propound this personal program for others. Others might not connect artistic production with self-transformation, or, self-transformation with artistic production, in these ways, or not at all. Quite possibly, for others, no meaningful relationship exists between artistic production and self-transformation. Or, possibly artistic production ought to take *precedence* over self-transformation; perhaps self-transformation should be the overriding aim, with artistic production contributing to that aim. Maybe the aim of self-transformation and the aim of artistic production should be co-equal; or the aims of self-transformation and artistic production may be symbiotic. In the course of life, one may take precedence over the other in different ways at different times. There is no single right personal program.

My personal program values process over product, seeks to foster self-transformation, and accommodates nondualistic experiences. It recognizes nondualistic experiences as benchmarks of my creative life's journey. It does so chiefly, but not exclusively, through art-making. It could do so as well (and sometimes does) through making music, writing, or other such activities.

Yet one could embrace a personal program that excludes any or all of these ingredients. An individual could, for example, embrace a personal program that values product over process; or that excludes or is indifferent to self-transformation; or excludes or is indifferent to nondualistic experiences. A personal program might exclude or be indifferent to art-making, music making or any other such activities. It could value process to the exclusion of products entirely; or, as in the case to the ascetic, disvalue or exclude process and product.

More generally, personal programs indicate our present place in relation to our projected future, informed by our emerging interests and purposes. They help to identify *who we are* to ourselves as our lives unfold. Personal programs situate what David Novitz calls a narrative identity. He says, "The construction of narrative identities, like that of works of art, is often highly inventive. Both are usually constructed with immaculate care, often with insight and sensitivity, and in a way, moreover, which must alter and contribute to the sorts of people we are."[4] He continues, "Our narrative identities are neither God-given nor innate, but are painstakingly acquired as we grow, develop, and interact with the people around us." [5]

In this way, *who* we are—our self—transforms. Sometimes our self may exhibit opposing or incongruent characteristics. The need and extent of their 'resolution'—whether a single self should answer to a single set of fully congruent characteristics or numerous incongruent ones—also depends upon the requirements of our personal program. Novitz says, "Most of us have, at best, a fragmented and changing view of self. We see ourselves successively in different, sometimes incompat- ible, ways, and we do so, on my view, because we are inclined to tell more than one story about ourselves."[6]

Nondualistic experiences might be variously described as nirvanic, epiphanic, numinous, religious, flow, ecstatic, or oceanic—depending upon one's preferred philosophical or soteriological tradition. Charac- terizations of nondualistic experiences might deploy such metaphors as 'interpenetration' of subject and object, or 'fusion' of artist and work, or 'overcoming,' or 'dissolving,' or 'transcending' such binary oppositions as subjective and objective reality. All these idioms suggest that, under particular circumstances, sharp distinctions between such binary terms as self and other, or subject and object, are undone.[7]

Arthur Danto describes such nondualistic experiences as:

> high moments of artistic work, those moments of pure creativity, when artist and work are not separated by a gap of any sort, but fuse in such a way that the work seems to bring itself into existence. At such points—and any creative person lives for these—there is none of the struggle and externality that marks those phases of artistic labor in which inspiration fails and the work itself refuses to cooperate... [Materials] are...agents of selflessness, which is the state at which...so much of Oriental philosophy...aims.[8]

---

[4] David Novitz, "Art, Narrative and Human Nature," *Philosophy and Literature* 13, no. 1 (April 1989): 72.

[5] Ibid. 65.

[6] Ibid. 62.

[7] For his discussion of "peak experiences," see A. H. Maslow, *Religions, Values, and Peak Experiences* (New York: Viking Press, 1963). Also, for his discussion of "flow," see Mihaly Csikszentmihalyi, *Creativity: Flow and the Psychology of Discovery and Invention* (New York: Harper Collins Publisher, 1996).

[8] Arthur Danto, *Mysticism and Morality* (New York: Basic Books, 1972), 110–111 (my emphasis).

Noted British composer Alexander Goehr comments that at special moments:

> [T]he music writes itself.... There is no longer a composer who pushes the material about, but only its servant, carrying out what the notes themselves imply. This is the exact experience I seek and which justifies all else. For me such experience exceeds all other satisfactions that I know or can imagine... for, at this moment, I find myself overcome by an *oceanic sensation of oneness* with all around me.[9]

Chang Chung-yuan speaks of states of nonduality or 'Oneness' when he asks, "What is Tao-painting?" He answers:

> Tao is the ontological experience by which subjective and objective reality are fused into one.... This interfusion initiates the process of creativity, which in turn establishes unity in multiplicity, the changeless in the ever-changing. [The work of] the artist who has reached this state of oneness will be far beyond what his egoform self could accomplish. [Chang continues:] Robert Henri (1865–1929), speaking of modern art, expresses somewhat the same idea: The object, which is back of every true work of art, is the attainment of a state of being, a state of high functioning, a more than ordinary moment of existence. In such moments activity is inevitable, and whether this activity is with brush, pen, chisel, or tongue, its result is but a by-product of this state, a trace, the footprint of the state. The work of art is, indeed, the by-product of a state of high functioning. This state of spiritual exaltation is fundamental to creative activity, while skills and measurements are secondary. It is the manifestation of an ontological experience.[10]

In addition, according to the Advaita Vedantic Hindu tradition for example, the state of realization of Brahman is also a state of 'nonduality,' where all consciousness of diversity and multiplicity is negated.[11]

So understood, nondualistic experiences differ from the more common experience of 'losing oneself' in one's work, understood simply as concentrating on one's work. In the latter case, a sharp distinction remains between the self and work.

---

[9] Alexander Goehr, *Independent* (1 June 1991), quoted in Anthony Storr, *Music and the Mind* (New York: Ballantine books, 1992), 97 (my emphasis).

[10] Chang Chung-yuan, *Creativity and Taoism: A Study of Chinese Philosophy, Art and Poetry* (New York: Harper Colophon Books, 1970), 203–204 (my emphasis).

[11] See Vibha Chaturvedi, "Reflections on the Interpretation of Religious Texts," in *Interpretation and its Objects: Studies in the Philosophy of Michael Krausz*, ed. Andreea Deciu Ritivoi (Amsterdam: Rodopi Publishers, 2003), 308.

Larry Briskman assigns logical priority to the production of creative products.[12] He agrees that there can be a connection between creative activity and self-transformation. But he sees self-transformation as an unintended consequence or by-product of creative production. Ironically, Briskman argues that, if we give priority to artistic production we will be in a better position to benefit from the potential self-development or self-transformation that can follow in its wake. Indeed, Briskman holds that self-development or self-transformation should not be pursued as an aim as such. He argues that losing oneself in one's work—whether of the more common variety or of the nonduality variety—depends upon focusing upon making the work and not upon the self.

Yet an individual might have an aim without making it a perpetual focus of attention. Such an aim may be invoked periodically to make sense of the process as a whole. For example, I may aim to have a meaningful relationship or a rewarding career without continually focusing upon those aims at every waking moment. Still, I may periodically call upon an aim and choose among various personal or vocational possibilities in light of it. Having an aim does not require that it be the object of my continual focus. In this manner, we can keep self-transformation as an aim, even if it is best only occasionally to call it to mind.

Indeed, for their duration, nondualistic experiences do inhibit creative activity. For the ability of emergent properties of a work to affect their creator depends upon a duality between creator and work (or, more generally, the Other.) Such duality is necessary for the creator to be 'carried by' or 'influenced by' the creator's work in progress. As well, nonduality inhibits criticism and critical interaction between creator and work.

Yet, nondualistic experiences characteristically arise only periodically. Only during nondualistic periods would creative activity be interrupted. Such activity can be resumed with the reinstallation of duality, later to be informed by the 'afterglow' of nondualistic experience. Put otherwise, since creative activity demands the duality between self and work, the pursuit of creative activity will be inhibited in moments of nondual-

---

[12] See Larry Briskman "Creativity and Self-Development: Comments on Michael Krausz's 'Creating and Becoming'" unpublished. An abridged version of this paper was presented at a symposium on "Creating and Becoming," at the annual meeting of the Society for Philosophy of Creativity, Eastern Division Meeting of the American Philosophical Association, Washington, D.C. (28 December, 1978). A version of the APA presentation was published as Larry Briskman, "Creating and Self-Development: A Reply to Michael Krausz," *Leonardo* 13, no. 4 (Autumn 1980): 323–325.

ity. Yet from such moments of nonduality we can draw inspiration for subsequent creative activity.

To consider a work's strengths and weaknesses, criticism and commentary demand looking at works apart from oneself. They must occur in a dualistic mode. But nondualistic experiences are not outside the range of creativity. While nonduality can inhibit productivity, we should not dismiss nonduality as irrelevant to creative processes. It can be an ingredient of a creative life journey, a part of a larger project of self-transformation.

III

Consider Briskman's tri-partite distinction among creative persons, creative processes, and creative products. To draw out the consequences of his view I will adopt a less personalistic voice than that of Part I.

In contrast to my concerns about personal programs that accommodate nondualistic experiences, Briskman's treatment concerns the logical priority of creative products. He draws sharp distinctions among creative persons, creative processes, and creative products. *He takes these terms to be fundamentally independent.* His central concern addresses the question how we are to identify a creative product, creative person, and creative product. He holds that creative products are logically prior to creative persons and to creative processes. Creative persons and creative processes can be identified only after creative products have been identified as such. Briskman says:

> Creative people and creative processes can only be identified *via* our prior identification of their...products as themselves creative. That is, the person is a creative one and the process was a creative process only in the light of our prior evaluation of the product itself as a creative product. If this is correct, then it follows that a[n] artistic product is not creative because it was produced by a creative person or a creative process, but rather that both the psychological process involved, and the person involved, are deemed to be creative because they succeed in producing a product deemed to be creative. It is the creativity of the product which has, so to speak, logical priority.[13]

---

[13] Larry Briskman, "Creative Product and Creative Process in Science and Art," *The Concept of Creativity in Science and Art*, eds. Denis Dutton and Michael Krausz (The Hague: Martinus Nijhoff Publishers, 1981), 135. Reprinted in this volume, chap. 2.

Briskman summarizes his view:

> A creative…artistic, product has, I suggest, the following characteristics.
> First, relative to the background of prior products, it is a *novel* product.
> Second, it puts this novelty to a desirable purpose by *solving a problem*, such
> problems being themselves relative to this background and emerging from
> it. Third, it does so in such a way as to actually *conflict* with parts of this
> background, to necessitate its partial modification, and to supplant and
> improve upon parts of it. Finally, this novel, conflicting problem-solution
> must be favorably evaluated; it must meet certain exacting standards which
> are themselves part of the background it partially supplants.[14]

I agree that "creative people and creative processes can only be identified
via our prior identification of their…artistic products as themselves
creative." Yet, as my earlier discussion suggests, I qualify my agreement. Sometimes, the very distinctions among persons, processes and
products cannot be sharply sustained.

For the moment, let us pursue Briskman's tripartite distinction and
see where it leads us. Briskman's three terms—person, process, and
product—generate eight formal possibilities: (1) creative person, creative process, and creative product; (2) uncreative person, uncreative
process, uncreative product; (3) uncreative person, creative process,
creative product; (4) creative person, uncreative process, and creative
product; (5) creative person, uncreative process, uncreative product;
(6) creative person, creative process, uncreative product; (7) uncreative person, creative process, uncreative product; and (8) uncreative
person, uncreative process, creative product. These permutations are
formal possibilities.

(1) It is natural to assume that a creative product is an outcome
of a creative person and a creative process. And (2) it is natural to
assume that an uncreative person and uncreative process will lead to
an uncreative product. But (3) a creative product might arise from a
creative process, while its originating person is uncreative. This would
be so if the product exhibited emergent properties that the originating
person never intended or imagined.

Whatever might be said about the originating person, some creative
process is required for a creative product to arise. So, a product may be
creative and its process may be creative, while its originating person—
with respect to the product first identified—is uncreative. Accordingly,
from the logical priority of a creative product, it does not follow that

---

[14] Ibid., 144.

the originating person was creative. If we disallow miraculous creation from nothing, given a creative product, the antecedent processes must be creative. In turn, according to possibility (4), a product is creative and its originating person is creative, but its antecedent process is uncreative. This formal possibility is implausible because, again, without some creative process, a creative product would be miraculous. A creative product minimally requires a creative process. It may but need not involve a creative person. In turn, possibility (5) allows for an uncreative product, an uncreative process, and a creative person. How could a person be creative if the product and the process are uncreative? Now a creative person might be creative in relation to some product *other than that which was first identified*. That allows the possibility that a creative person might (and usually does) produce some failures.

Consider possibility (6) in which a person and a process is creative but the product is not. Suppose that we ask whether a particular composer is creative by considering his or her very latest work. Suppose further that that latest work is unimaginative, derivative, pretentious, boring, and breaks no existing compositional tradition. We judge it to be uncreative. But it does not follow that the composer is altogether uncreative if we take into consideration the creativity of other products besides this latest work. We could deem the composer to be a creative person by virtue of the creativity of the other products. So the question whether a person is altogether creative could be considered in relation to a body of work other than a particular one initially identified for consideration. Possibility (7) suggests a product and its originating person is uncreative, while the process is creative. Without the product being creative, it is implausible to infer that its process was creative. Yet, a process may be creative but in relation to a creative product other than the one first identified. Finally, possibility (8) suggests that a product is creative and its originating person and its process are uncreative. This possibility is implausible, since the creativity of the product would be miraculous. Again, the creative product would have been a miraculous creation from nothing. In sum, unless qualified, (1), (2), and (3) are the most plausible of the eight formal possibilities. In turn, (5), (6) and (7) appear to be implausible. But they become plausible when we do not follow Briskman in identifying the creativity of a person or a process only in relation to a given product that is first identified. He assumes that we should judge the creativity of persons and processes by isolating a given product from the family of products with which it resides.

In private correspondence (2 July 2007), Karen Bardsley raises an interesting puzzle concerning the uniqueness of a creative product. It concerns two individuals, who generate a product, say, a solution to a problem, almost but not quite in tandem. Suppose both pursued a common process to address the same problem. Unbeknownst to the second person, the first person hits upon the solution a month before the second person does. When the second person puts it forward, the community of pertinent practitioners rejects it as uncreative because they already accepted the solution as offered by the first person. Briskman's account suggests that the uniqueness of a creative product—and thus the creativity of its person and process—is inextricably connected with historical circumstance. The breaking of a tradition is, among its problem-solving virtues, a matter of historical achievement. When only one of the two individuals actually succeeds in uniquely breaking a tradition—where his or her solution actually has an impact on pertinent practitioners—it follows from Briskman's suggestion that the solution of only one of the individuals could be creative. According to the tradition-breaking criterion, the second person who produced the same solution was not creative, nor was the process that gave rise to it. But the two solutions are identical. This is a puzzling result. Why not regard both instances of the same product as creative? Why not regard both persons and their respective processes as creative? The answer depends upon whether we regard tradition-breaking in historical terms. If so, then only one individual could be creative. If not, more than one individual could be creative.

Still assuming Briskman's fundamentally independent tripartite distinctions among persons, processes, and products, let us collect our findings. For a product to be creative a pertinent creative process is necessary. No creative product can be produced without its creative process. These findings are compatible with Briskman's overall (though roughly put) claim that creative products are logically prior to creative persons and processes in the sense that we can identify creative persons and creative processes as such only via our prior identification of creative products.

But even within the terms that Briskman embraces, the situation is more complicated. First, creators need not be individuals; they may be groups of individuals. They may even be holistic collectives like institutions. Creators need not be persons. They may be other sorts of beings, either non-mechanical (like elephants and dogs) or mechanical (like computers). Products may be multiple rather than singular, as in a series of works—some but not all of which, taken separately, might be deemed creative. Finally, more than one converging process may precede a creative product. This possibility raises issues about how we should count or individuate such processes. These considerations—only mentioned here—complicate the logical possibilities that arise from Briskman's relatively simple tripartite distinction.

IV

The issues surrounding self-transformation further complicate Briskman's taxonomy. For we may regard self-transformation per se (still in Briskman's idiom) as a creative product, thus undermining a general and sharp distinction between creative process and creative product, or, in terms of Briskman's mentor, Karl Popper, between World 2 and World 3 entities. (Popper argues that inhabitants of World 3 are 'objective contents of thought,' inhabitants of World 2 are subjective mental states, and inhabitants of World 1 are physical states.) Briskman relegates self-transformation to the subjective World 2 realm. On his account self-transformation could not be regarded as a creative product. In accord with Popper's ontology, Briskman identifies both creative products and non-creative products as World 3 entities. As he puts it:

> If creativity were to be located as an event in World 3—if creativity was held to be, in a logical sense, *fundamentally independent* of events in World 2—then it would follow that living per se, and self-development per se [or self-transformation per se], could not be considered creative.[15]

According to Briskman, to say that self-transformation can be creative we must make self-transformation an objective World 3 product. So he generates a dilemma: either we must abandon his Popperian objectivist World 3 requirement for creativity. Or we must somehow 'objectify' the subjective self-transformation. Actually, we must do both. We must reject Briskman's construal of subjective and objective states as 'fundamentally independent,' and we must allow that self-transformation may be taken up as a possibly creative activity. Put otherwise, we may take up our self-transformation as our *work*. To speak this way requires an adjustment to Briskman's idea of a product.

---

[15] Briskman "Creativity and Self-Development," 4 (my emphasis).

Indeed, my underlying misgivings about Briskman's tripartite distinctions are captured by the thought that the idea of a product carries with it the suggestion that a product is an objectified *entity*, with the valence of 'thingliness.' The idea of a product is too restrictive. In contrast, we should substitute the idea of a *work* that is not restricted to thingliness. It allows for both a process and a product. It allows for bracketing a project such as self-transformation as one's work. It allows for a vocation as one's work; it allows for a personal relationship as one's work; it allows for one's life as one's work. No doubt, thingly products partly constitute one's life; they punctuate it; they serve as its signposts. But we need the more ample idea of a work or a 'life-work' to provide the normative context in virtue of which thingly products may have meaning and significance. It is in that larger notion of work that my personal program finds its place.

We can easily identify the thingliness of a work in such plastic arts as painting or sculpture. Their products are physically embodied in palpable ways. The thingliness in other artistic endeavors such as music, dance, or conceptual art is not so easily identified. In these domains, the distinction between process and product is not easily drawn. Where is the distinction between process and product when in 1917, by exhibiting his *Fountain*, Marcel Duchamp debunks the tradition of precious objects in the artworld? Where is the distinction between process and product in Leonard Bernstein's performance of Beethoven's *Ninth Symphony* to celebrate the fall of the Berlin Wall in November 1989? Where is the distinction between process and product in Christo and Jeanne-Claude's wrapping and unwrapping of the Reichstag in June and July of 1995? Such examples suggest that we cannot draw a general and sharp distinction between process and product.

The idea of work incorporates processes and products. It is both a verb and a noun. It is both an act and a resultant product. A work is a doing as well as that which is done. Accordingly, we can take up the self and its life as a creative work. Indeed, such a notion of work is commonplace in psychotherapy and soteriology. This idea of work is encapsulated in John Dewey's idea when he says:

> We have an experience...when the material experienced runs its course to fulfillment. Then and only then is it integrated within and demarcated in the general stream of experience from other experiences. A piece of *work* is finished in a way that is satisfactory; a problem receives its solution; a game is played through; a situation, whether that of eating a meal, playing a game of chess, carrying on a conversation, writing a

book, or taking part in a political campaign, is so rounded out that its close is a consummation and not a cessation. Such an *experience* is a whole and carries with it its own individualizing quality and self-sufficiency. It is an experience.[16]

So understood, our work may include more than thingly products. It may include our self-transformation. And, in some personal programs, it may accommodate nondualistic experiences amongst its ingredients. Yet conceding this much requires a taxonomy somewhat different from one that takes creative persons, creative processes, and creative products as fundamentally independent.[17]

[16] John Dewey, *Art as Experience* (New York: Capricorn Books, 1934), 35 (my emphasis).

[17] This essay revisits and develops my, "Creating and Becoming" in *The Concept of Creativity in Science and Art*, eds. Dutton and Krausz, 187–200. For their helpful comments and suggestions, I thank Karen Bardsley, Elizabeth D. Boepple, Larry Briskman, Roy Fitzgerald, Mark Harris, Peter Lamarque, Thomas Leddy, Anne Sclufer, Jill Stauffer, Ulli Wiesner, and Mary Wiseman.

CHAPTER ELEVEN

ON THE DIALECTICAL PHENOMENOLOGY OF CREATIVITY[1]

Albert Hofstadter

I would like to present to you the idea of thinking about creativity in terms of the basic concepts of dialectical phenomenology. It is unnecessary to stop to examine the notion of dialectical phenomenology. Illustration of it is already before us in the shape of Hegel's *Phenomenology of Spirit* and his later writings about the philosophy of mind. We need not adopt Hegel's own monistic spiritualistic metaphysics in taking over the basic ideas of dialectical phenomenology, nor need we presuppose a logically necessary and single-track line of development, whether in individual life, social life, or world history. What I wish to suggest is only the dialectical structure and meaning of the creative process, with the thought that study of this process in terms of dialectical phenomenology could open it up to a genuine mode of comprehension.

It is generally agreed that creation is not a one-sided mechanical making according to a fixed formula or routine. So, for example, creative photography is not like the process by which the passport photographer takes your picture. He already knows what content and what form he wants the picture to have, and he needs only to fit you, as subject, into the frame to produce your picture. He has a content and form already decided beforehand, and has only to fit the new matter into it. He could take the same picture of anyone else; and the degree to which the process is routine is measured by the comic effect that would be produced if he substituted a horse or a camel for a human being. The creative photographer, on the other hand, finds that the very idea of a picture is already a challenge. He does not know beforehand what content it is to have, what its form is to be. His task, indeed, is precisely to find a content and a form and the unity of the two, to determine the being of a picture. 'Picture' first gets a meaning for him

---

[1] Reprinted from *The Concept of Creativity in Science and Art*, eds. D. Dutton and M. Krausz (The Hague/Boston/London: Martinus Nijhoff Publishers, The Hague/Boston/London, 1981), 201–208, *all rights reserved*.

in this process of finding/inventing the new unity of form, content, and subject. Instead of following a routine he has to develop the new totality itself: the new unity of form, content, and matter, which is to be the new picture.

What is it that differentiates the routine from the creative photographer? The routine photographer, like the passport photographer, already has his general form-content unity fixed, and he swings his lens around to the prefixed type of subject so as to produce the normally expected result—the expertly done photograph, the arty picture. The creative photographer, to the contrary, is first in a quandary. He does not have a prefixed form-content idea with its correlated subject matter class. He looks upon all that as not his dish of tea; he finds himself estranged from it, finds it alien to his spirit. He has to find in the whole situation a form-content unity and its correlative subject matter to which he can give himself and which will give itself to him. He is in search of a new totality, which will be own to him and to which he will give himself as its own. He is in search of a new reconciliation of the factors of opposition and difference—form, content, subject matter on the one hand, and his own living spirit on the other—which he can experience as real truth, as genuine actuality, a totality in which inner and outer factors have come together in a living, not a mechanical, unity.

I use the example of the photographer because it is so easy to see the difference almost immediately, since the routine mechanical photographer depends chiefly on mechanical means—predetermined content, form, subject, instrument, equipment—all of them so ready at hand that anyone can be such a photographer, whereas the creative photographer is in the same general fix as any creative being: everything around him has fallen into flux, he himself swims in the midst of the turbulent stream without any shores, and he has to find his way to safety by bringing the flux into the rhythm of a living form.

But the photographer is only the image of us all. Wherever we are, in private life or public, art or religion, action or thinking, the same general problem faces us. We can approach the context with our prefixed formula for the given sphere of life—prefixed meanings, forms of procedure, subjects to which they are applied, habits of feeling, willing, and thinking, capacities and skills—and try to put things together in the same way as before. And as long as this works, we can persist in it. When, however, life inside or out rebels against this mechanical way of constraining it, we are confronted with the problematics of creativity. We have to become creative, since we have to find and invent a new totality of form-content, matter, and spirit, which will enliven the life process.

This life-quandary is widespread today. The people who are most involved in it, that is, the younger people who are now confronted with the task of determining the form and content of their life, experience the rebellion of life within their own selves, and they find themselves in profound alienation from much of the traditional culture. So they are in the midst of the crisis that is characteristic of creativity generally: the crisis of estrangement, alienation, otherness, difference.

This language of alienation, estrangement, otherness, and difference brings us directly into touch with the context of dialectical phenomenology. If anything is characteristic of the dialectic, it is the appearance of the phenomenon of alienation or estrangement, or more generally of difference, opposition, and otherness. These are one half of the story of the dialectic; the other half is given in the correlative names for unity: reconciliation, appropriation, and ownness. Hegel says '*Versöhnung*,' Heidegger '*Ereignis*,' and both ultimately come to the same thing as 'appropriation' and 'ownness.' It is ultimately in the structures of ownness that human creativity shows itself and its products. The meaning of creativity lies in the attainment of genuine ownness.

In thinking about creativity we tend to think first of the artist as creator and his activity as creation. In earlier days one thought first, rather, of God and of His act of creation. Our present tendency is a reverberation of the romantic movement in life and art, which placed the artistic individual at the center, and which put special accent on his subjectivity as the source of truth rather than on submitting his subjectivity to a reality outside him as foundation of truth. But creativity belongs everywhere, and perhaps it would be better if we looked more frequently to spheres outside art for subjects of investigation. We shall recollect that Whitehead thought creativity to be so pervasive, present in every pulse of process that gave rise to a new actual entity, that he declared it to be the first and most universal of all the categories. Therefore, in what immediately follows, I would like to bring to your attention, as an instance of creativity a nonartistic matter, the apparently unlikely matter of the master-slave relationship. Since it is one of the most achieved parts of Hegel's phenomenology and has been much examined in recent years, and since it lies at the basis of the possibility of advanced socialized life, it is of particular interest as a means of directing our attention to creativity in life and experience apart from art.

The master-slave or lord-bondsman relationship arises out of the struggle for recognition. Two egos stand in confrontation. Each, as an ego, seeks recognition by the other as being 'I.' Each seeks to be the essence of their mutual relationship. Each needs an other to be its own: the one needs to appropriate the other, needs the other to be reconciled within a unity in which the ego is recognized as the essence. In an other alone can the ego find its own, so that it can truly be ego. Its basic drive as ego is to be with its other as its own. The problem is: how is this being-with to be achieved?

The two egos are not themselves self-conscious about this need they share. It is we, who look on from 'above the battle' (for we have already been through it and are now reflecting backwards), who can apprehend with conscious awareness what is going on there. The two involved egos are there in the throes of their own desires and passions, basically the passion to be free—that is, to find selfhood in and with what is not self, and in this case particularly to find self-recognition in the other. They do not yet know this passion to be theirs—they are, rather, inside it, moving in and moved by it; the knowledge of it will come, and can only come, as it gets realized, so that they can see in the realized form what it is they were struggling for. (As Croce maintained: the creative one does not know what he has been striving to create until he has created it.)

Before the master-slave relationship developed in human culture there was the immediate relationship of being-with, as in the hunting band, where no one is chief, ruler, lord, but everyone has his say and his part in determining what is to be done. The life of the Mbuti pygmies in the African Congo region (as described by Colin Turnbull in *Wayward Servants*)[2] gives a beautiful picture of what a life is like which dispenses with the master-slave foundation—although, perhaps, a closer look would indicate how powerfully the forest itself is given the role of master in relation to all members as its servants. There is here a necessary suppression of individuality so as to prevent any particular member from asserting himself—no matter how great his talent, skill, even genius—beyond the average level of sociality. This book is indeed a fascinating story of how a people can create, with genuine and continuing creativity, a form of social life that is essentially free, equal, and

---

[2] Colin Turnbull, *Wayward Servants* (Garden City, N.Y.: Natural History Press, 1965).

fraternal within itself, but also, within the confines of a very limited geography and socio-psychological topography. But all advanced culture depends on the prior establishment of political power and the relation of ruler to ruled. Much of human history has lain in the production and transformation of this relationship towards the point at which eventually its asymmetry can be entirely removed.

The theme I wish to stress, then, is that the master-slave relationship, as such, is something that is created in the struggle between the confronting egos as the mode of unity—the mutual appropriation, reconciliation, or ownness—which sublates (*aufhebt*—cancels, preserves, while transcending) the opposition of the two agents, raising them up into being the subjects of a new totality, with a new content and form, which gives (albeit only a passing one, nevertheless) a fulfillment to their mutual need for recognition.

The idea of master-slave, lord-bondsman, was an indispensable creation in the history of the development of human society, and it still remains as an indispensable creation in the history of human individuality. Much of childhood's suffering, as well as its fulfillment and security, lies in the recognition it is compelled, by its own weakness, to give to the adult-parent ego, finding its own selfhood in the maturity, strength, and above all credible authority of the parent. The suffering is greater when that authority later comes into question and when, therefore, a new creative art of social appropriation of self and other is needed—that is, the achievement of a new unified totality of content, form, and the subjectivity of its own selfhood. This is part of the search for one's identity as outcome of the identity crisis and is the clear counterpart, in the actual struggle for life, of the artist's search for artistic identity as he grows out of dependence on earlier forms, traditions, and masters and finds himself cast into the outsideness and indeterminateness of new existence.

Let us try to see how the master-slave relationship—despite the negative attitude we presently have towards the subjection of ruled to ruler, political subject to despotic king or dictator, serf to lord, slave to slave owner—was nevertheless an actual creation, a step forward into novelty and constructive order.

The egos, to begin with, are isolated within themselves; each, outside the other, is not the other, and the other is not it; they are really different. But difference among egos cannot remain as mere otherness: the different is the strange and alien, and what is strange and alien is, or rapidly becomes, hostile, an enemy. The further off people are from us, the easier it is for us to regard them, and for them to regard us, as actually or potentially hostile. We approach one another with caution, for, being distant, without nearness, we are not neighbors, and so it does not grieve one when the other is mishandled; on the contrary, even we, who have been educated and disciplined in the values of the high religions of the East and the West, find it easy enough to take the position of master to the other as slave, determiner to determined.

The two thus become enemies. It is tempting to think that they could have started at the very beginning as friends; but one does not know how to think 'friend' except through thinking 'enemy.' Friendship needs the long discipline of living together in the security of a social environment that cares for both. Enmity needs only the initial encounter of those who are other to one another.

The two become enemies, however, because they need one another. For outside the relationship of ego to ego, self to self, the ego cannot find the ownness it needs in order to be itself. Without the alter ego the ego is outside the *Ereignis*—outside the appropriation of being to being, outside the reconciliation, the *Versöhnung*, which it needs in order to come to its own. The step into enmity is already the first step on the road to the creation of a genuinely human life. Instead of passing one another by, the two are attracted to each other and in need of one another. Egos are beings who, being an I, can have a 'mine.' And this means that a further possibility—amazingly new, fecund, fraught with the deepest potentialities of existence and truth—begins to appear. For, if an ego can apprehend and appropriate something as mine, it is on the point of being able to turn around and *give* itself also as 'thine.' It needs only another ego, in whom it can recognize also the power of owning, to which it is able to yield.

Both the mine and the thine are necessary for the new unity that comes about between separate egos who have become enemies. In its primitiveness each can think first only of possessing the other as its own, as mine. To possess an other ego as mine means that the other ego must *give* itself to me, so that I am its thine. Neither has as yet learned how to give itself. They know only how to demand and try to take what is other as their own. Each wants the other to belong to it, but in the way in which an ego can belong to an ego—that is, by recognition, acknowledgment, giving of itself to the other (as gift) so that the other's self is its own self, its own essence—what is mine is thine, even to the point of my own self. This is what the one ego wants of the other; and the struggle to the death to achieve it is itself the creative process of realizing this new, profound, soul-shaking idea.

Both egos are engaged in this process. The creative agent is neither the one alone nor the other, but the two of them in a mutual structure of consciousness of other and of self. There is a We in process of self-formation, creating itself in and out of the I's, first by developing in and through their animosity as alien and estranged, and then by the struggle of this animosity to bring itself into being in the definite shape of the master-slave condition.

Underlying the process is the fundamental need and desire, the passion to be free, to find ownness and otherness, self-recognition in the other, or, as Heidegger's phrase goes, to be 'gathered in the appropriation.' This passion is the source of the dialectical structure of the creative process. Gathering in appropriation needs, first of all, the *Enteignung*, the de-appropriating, which is at the same time a readying of the appropriate to the appropriate, so that there can be a true appropriation, an *Ereignung*, in which the others find their own. From the mere sameness, the abstract difference, of the two egos, there had to develop first their real difference, their opposition and alienation, precisely in order that the struggle should begin in which they might find in each other their own.

I have not the space to specify in detail how not only the master finds his own in the slave, but also how the slave first begins to find what is truly *man's* own, and not merely this individual's own, in the discipline of rule, so that a creative process is started that looks towards reconciliation at a level of ultimacy.

The struggle of the artist with his medium, and also with his society and culture, his artistic competitors, his own past education, his habits and the pregiven cast of his mind, the temptations of popular success, and so many other factors of difference, is also a struggle to be with all these as own, to transform others and self into a new shape, gathering them all into a new appropriation in which they fit so as to be able to live in freedom.

The struggle of every creative person—and this means every person so long as he or she tries to continue to live in a meaningful way—is this same dialectic of plunging into the alienation in order to reach towards the appropriation, opening one's self and one's situation to the factors of difference, opposition, and estrangement so as to permit the possibility of a new living gathering.

As the bridge gathers the opposing shores of the river, the country and city, the fields and streets, the one life and the other, into a reciprocal totality of ever-moving life, so the creative person bridges otherness to gather what is alien into a new ownness.

The categories we must use to comprehend creativeness, wherever it is, are those of identity, differentiation, and recovery, of estrangement and reconciliation, the alien and the own, the gathering of differents and opposites into the appropriation of a reciprocal ownness.

These are the categories of dialectical phenomenology, which have yet to be tried for their power of enlightenment.

CHAPTER TWELVE

THE ARTISTIC RELEVANCE OF CREATIVITY

David Davies

I

Art historians tell us many fascinating things about the activities of artists. From Kenneth Clark, we learn that Turner's *Snowstorm* was painted after Turner had himself fastened to the mast of a small boat in a snowstorm, risking his life, and that in painting the picture, he used a new method for representing light that was developed through years of experimentation.[1] Philip Steadman and David Hockney have each argued, in different ways, that artists such as Jan van Eyck and JohannesVermeer used various kinds of optical devices, including the camera obscura, in generating their paintings.[2] We also learn, from scholars who have scrutinized canvasses with x-ray photography, that many paintings (for example, Vermeer's *Woman with a Wine Glass*) have *pentimenti* that have been hidden from view through overpainting, and that some paintings (for example, the *Disciples at Emmaus*, originally attributed to Vermeer) have a completely different history of making from the one previously assumed.

Turning to the other arts, Livingstone Lowes's *The Road to Xanadu* suggests that Samuel Taylor Coleridge wrote "Kubla Khan" after taking opium, the poem being the unfinished transcription of something that came to him in his reverie, and that the poem is unfinished due to the untimely arrival of the person from Porlock.[3] We learn that artists sometimes fail to realize their artistic intentions in their work, as, perhaps, in the case of Gerald Manley Hopkins whose poem "Henry Purcell" arguably contains a line that says something different from what

---

[1] Kenneth Clark, *Looking at Pictures* (London: John Murray, 1960).
[2] P. Steadman, *Vermeer's Camera* (New York: Oxford University Press, 2001); D. Hockney, *Secret Knowledge* (London: Thames and Hudson, 2001).
[3] J. Livingston Lowes, *The Road to Xanadu* (New York: Houghton Mifflin, 1927).

Hopkins intended it to say.[4] Film scholars reveal to us the sometimes
Byzantine processes whereby the films we see have been constructed
through the collaborative, or competitive, activities of directors, actors,
cinematographers, editors, and producers. They also inform us that
Thomas Vinterberg's *Festen* was made according to the strict requirements of the Dogme 95 'vow of chastity,' which prohibits inter alia
the use of artificial lighting, bringing standard props to the shoot, and
the use of fixed camera and non-diegetic music.

Such examples lead us to ask, what bearing our knowledge of the
history of making of an artwork—of 'provenential properties' of the
work, as we may call them—has upon our attempts to properly appreciate and evaluate the work as art. Under what conditions can such
knowledge be 'artistically relevant' in the sense of having such a bearing?
In the present context, our interest is more specialized. For to view at
least some artistic activities of the sort just canvassed as manifestations
of the *creative* powers of the artist is natural.

As writers on the nature of creativity have stressed, we view an action
or process occurring in a given practice as creative only if it manifests
novelty that we view as valuable in the context of that practice, and
does so in a way that is attributable to the intentional and imaginative
agency of the individual(s) concerned.[5] Some of the foregoing cases
are paradigm examples of artistic creativity so construed—for example,
Turner's experimentation with the pictorial representation of light in
the medium of oil paint whose conclusions are manifest in *Snowstorm*,[6]
and Vinterburg's re-explorations of the possibilities of the cinematic
medium using his restricted cinematic 'palette.'

Conversely, we might view with a more jaundiced eye the relevant
activities of Vermeer, Coleridge, and Hopkins on the basis of what we
learn, in that certain valued features of the artistic products will now
be seen as the result of mechanical, accidental, or externally driven

---

[4] For a discussion of this example, see G. Iseminger, "An Intentional Demonstration,"
in *Intention and Interpretation* (Philadelphia: Temple University Press, 1992), 76–96.

[5] See for example, C. R. Hausman, "Criteria of Creativity," in *The Concept of Creativity
in Science and Art*, eds. Dutton and Krausz (The Hague: Martinus Nijhoff, 1981), 75–90.;
B. Gaut, B. and P. Livingston, *The Creation of Art* (Cambridge: Cambridge University
Press, 2003), 8–11; Gaut, "Creativity and Imagination," in Gaut and Livingston, *The
Creation of Art*, 149–151.

[6] Consider also Monet's experimentation in capturing *l'effet du neige*, culminating
in pictures where this is captured with no use of white pigment at all, or Morris
Louis's exploitation of the possibilities of the newly developed acrylics in his staining
technique.

processes, rather than as manifestations of the artist's creativity. Do these judgments, which are perhaps most naturally seen as bearing upon our assessment of the activities of the artists themselves, also have some bearing on the appreciation and evaluation of their works? Is creativity, conceived as a characteristic of the process whereby an artist generates an artistic product, artistically relevant in the sense defined above?

How we answer this question seems to depend upon how we rule as to the artistic relevance of provenential properties in general, and this in turn, as we shall see below, will depend upon how we understand those activities in terms of which we have defined artistic relevance, namely, the proper appreciation and evaluation of artworks as art. Our pretheoretical intuitions as to the artistic relevance of provenential properties certainly vary. For, in spite of the interest accorded them by critics and curators, there is considerable disagreement and uncertainty within the philosophical community as to whether the sorts of provenential properties cited above *are* artistically relevant.[7] This suggests that we should begin by asking which, if any, provenential properties are artistically relevant, and, if this holds for some, but not all, such properties, what principle serves to effect such a distinction. Given an answer to these questions, we can turn to our more specific concern with the artistic relevance of creativity.

II

Before putting such a strategy into operation, however, three preliminary matters require attention. First, a little more needs to be said about the notion of artistic relevance, A property is artistically relevant for a given work *W*, we have said, if it bears upon the proper appreciation and evaluation of *W* as art. Some properties bear their artistic relevance on their sleeve, in that they are the very properties to which we attend in our appreciative engagement with an instance of the work and which thereby play a part in our assessment of its value—for example, the representational or expressive content of a painting. Such properties might be said to be *directly* artistically relevant for *W*. Other properties of *W*, however, while not directly artistically relevant, may be said to

---

[7] See for example, J. Crook and T. Learner *The Impact of Modern Paints* (London: Tate Gallery, 2000); D. Bomford, *Art in the Making: Degas* (London: National Gallery, 2004).

be *indirectly* artistically relevant if they play a role in determining those properties of the work that *are* directly artistically relevant. A natural assumption, which we will have cause to question, is that provenential properties will have at best indirect artistic relevance, through their bearing on those properties of a work that are the proper objects of artistic appreciation and evaluation.

Second, we must counter a possible objection arising from the broader philosophical literature on creativity. I assumed above that the issue concerning the artistic relevance of creativity pertains to aspects of a work's history of making. But some have argued that creativity is first and foremost a property of the artistic product, not of the process generative of that product. Larry Briskman, for example, claims:

> the scientific or artistic product is not creative *because* it was produced by a creative person or a creative process, but rather...both the psychological processes involved, and the person involved, are deemed to be creative *because* they succeeded in producing a product deemed to be creative. It is the creativity of the product which has, so to speak, logical priority.... The creativity of the product resides not in its psychological origins, but in its objective relations to other, previous, products.[8]

He offers two arguments for the priority of the product. First, he maintains that, while we can study certain personality traits and certain psychological processes as facts, "we cannot *identify* these traits or processes as *creative ones* independently of our standards and values."[9] This is because creativity is only rightly ascribed to that which we think should be highly valued. But, he argues, such ascriptions of value can be made only on the basis of a person's 'output,' the 'products' of their activity. Second, he argues that we cannot even describe the creative process without referring to the products that are its outcome, since 'intermediary' products are the focus of the artist's ongoing generative activity. The creativity of an artistic product, Briskman maintains, can only be assessed relative to the artistic background of a given artistic act, since only thus can we determine whether a product meets two preconditions for being creative: (1) being novel, and (2) being valuable as a solution to a problem which is not soluble by appeal to established methods and mechanisms. Noël Carroll, citing Briskman, has proposed a similar view, stressing that creativity is possible only given a tradition

---

[8] L. Briskman, "Creative Product and Creative Process in Science and Art," in *The Concept of Creativity in Science and Art*, eds. Dutton and Krausz, 135–136.
[9] Ibid., 137.

which underwrites the intelligibility of novelty. Carroll contrasts his view of artistic creativity:

> with the perhaps more common view that creative artworks are the ones that flow from genius. That conception of creativity correlates it with certain inner psychological processes—whatever happens when genius does its work. My conception of artistic creativity has more to do with the place of the artwork in outwardly observable social and historical processes—the evolution of the relevant artwork.[10]

But we can grant the 'priority of the product,' as argued for by Briskman and Carroll, without impugning the suggestion that, in asking about the artistic relevance of creativity, we should focus upon the generative activity of the artist. For both Briskman and Carroll are targeting the idea that creativity is a quality of psychological processes occurring in the artist. I, however, am concerned with creativity as a quality ascribable to a manifest process whereby an artist engages in an ongoing interaction with an artistic medium. The latter process evades Briskman's second 'priority' argument, since it involves an engagement with the very intermediary products in terms of which the creative process has to be described. The first priority argument is also evaded, in that we are ascribing creativity to the *performative* output of the artist. Furthermore, since our characterization of the artist's engagement with the artistic medium will locate that activity in an artistic context to which various artistic moves can be seen as responses, we can also agree with Briskman and Carroll that creativity itself, and ascriptions of creativity, make sense only against the background of a tradition.

Finally, to clarify our question about the artistic relevance of provenential properties in general and to facilitate the discussion in the remainder of the paper, it will be helpful to introduce some terminology.[11] I shall use the term 'focus of appreciation' to denote certain aspects of the product of the generative act through which an artwork comes into existence. The focus of appreciation is that which, as the *final outcome* or *product* of a generative act on the part of one or more individuals, is *relevant to the appreciation* of the artwork brought into existence through that act. We can think of the focus of appreciation in the following manner. Artworks, we may say, come into being

---

[10] N. Carroll, "Art, Creativity, and Tradition," in *The Creation of Art*, eds. Gaut and Livingston, 208–234.

[11] I develop this terminology at much greater length in chap. 3 of my *Art as Performance* (Oxford: Blackwell, 2004).

because something is done in a context where this doing counts as doing something else. For example, an individual applies oil paint to a canvas, and this counts as the production of a painting to which various representational, expressive, and formal properties can be ascribed by receivers. An artist, then, creates a work by generating something that receivers will interpret as having certain properties that bear on the work's appreciation. We can call the thing that the artist produces which is open to such interpretation the *artistic vehicle*—for example, the painted canvas by Turner titled *Snowstorm* which hangs on the wall of the Tate Gallery in London. We can then term the meaningful properties that viewers ascribe to that vehicle in their attempts to appreciate the work the *artistic content* they take to be articulated through that vehicle—for example, what they take the canvas to represent or express or what formal or material properties they take it to make manifest.

The provenential properties of a work, then, pertain to the artistic activity whereby a vehicular medium has been manipulated with the intention of articulating an artistic content. They will comprise both general relational features of that activity—when and where the activity took place, what other activities preceded or were contemporaneous with it, etc.—and specific, generally non-relational features of the activity—who performed it, what materials were employed, what specific actions made up the activity, the order in which they were performed, and the aims of the agent.

III

For philosophers who subscribe to what Gregory Currie has termed 'aesthetic empiricism' (AE), the answer to our question about the artistic relevance of provenential properties is simple: only those features of provenance that are directly perceptible in an otherwise unmediated experiential engagement with a genuine instance of the work are artistically relevant.[12] Works, it is assumed, are given for appreciation in an experiential encounter with a perceptible entity—a canvas on a gallery wall, for example, or the sequence of sounds produced by an

---

[12] G. Currie, *An Ontology of Art* (New York: St Martin's Press, 1989), chap. 2. For an AE response to our question about the artistic relevance of provenential properties, see M. C. Beardsley, "On the Creation of Art," *Journal of Aesthetics and Art Criticism* 23 (1965): 291–304.

orchestra—and only properties of W that are available to receivers in such an encounter are artistically relevant. A widely voiced criticism of AE, however, is that it greatly impoverishes our appreciation of artworks, because much of a work's specific artistic content depends not just upon the manifest properties of the artistic vehicle but also, in many subtle ways, upon the artistic context in which that vehicle was produced with the aim of articulating a specific artistic content.[13] Thus, it may be said, we can identify a work's focus of appreciation, and thereby appreciate the work, only if we locate the manifest product—the vehicle—in the context of its history of making. In arguing against AE, critics have offered hypothetical examples where what are arguably distinct works with distinct artistic contents would be indistinguishable on empiricist grounds. Whether we consider Arthur Danto's gallery of perceptually indistinguishable 'red rectangles,'[14] Levinson's 'musical doppelgangers,'[15] or philosophers' appeals to Borges's 'textually indistinguishable works,'[16] the intended lesson is the same. We cannot properly appreciate the artistic content articulated through a work's artistic vehicle and thus properly ascribe artistic value to the work without attending to the history of making of that vehicle—its place in the wider oeuvre of the artist, the artistic context in which the artist is working, and the broader tradition upon which the artist is drawing.[17]

IV

My concern in the present context, however, is not to rehearse well-worn objections to AE, but to look at the status of provenential properties if AE is rejected. If we agree that *some* features of the history of making of an artwork not given in an immediate experiential encounter with the work's artistic vehicle are, in this way, artistically relevant,

---

[13] See, for example, J. Levinson, "What a Musical Work Is," *Journal of Philosophy* 77 (1980): 5–28; Arthur Danto, *Transfiguration of the Commonplace* (Cambridge Mass.: Harvard University Press, 1981), chap. 1; Currie, *An Ontology of Art*, chap. 2; Davies, *Art as Performance*, chap. 2, 3.

[14] Danto, *Transfiguration of the Commonplace*, chap. 1.

[15] Levinson, "What a Musical Work Is."

[16] J. L. Borges, *Labyrinths* (Harmondsworth: Penguin, 1970), 62–71.

[17] For those allergic to such hypothetical examples, consider the 'white canvasses' of Kasimir Malevich, Robert Ryman, Yves Klein, and Hélio Oiticica, the artistic differences among which are in no way explicable in terms of perceptible differences among the canvasses.

what principle determines *which* such features are artistically relevant? The critique of AE suggests the following answer: those provenential properties that determine contentful aspects of the work-focus. We may describe such provenential properties as 'focus-determining,' If a work, with vehicle *V*, has artistic content *M* because *V*, with manifest properties *p*1, *p*2..., was generated in context *C*, or using material *X*, then these provenential properties are focus-determining.

The kinds of provenential properties cited at the beginning of this paper, however, do not in any obvious way play such a focus-determining role. Such properties will include overpainting, visible only through x-ray technology; the use of devices such as the camera obscura; early drafts or sketches of works whose design elements are superseded in the finished vehicle; failed or unrealized semantic intentions on the part of artists; experiments with the vehicular medium on which artists draw in their manipulations of that medium in a given work; and more broadly, biographical facts about how the artist acquired various skills, dispositions, or interests bearing upon those manipulations. To take one example, the artistic content articulated in Vermeer's paintings do not appear to depend upon whether he employed the camera obscura or whether he overpainted. However the artistic vehicle was produced, and whatever changes it underwent, it seems to bear on our grasp of the work's focus of appreciation simply as the resulting painted surface.

We might respond to this situation in two ways. First, we might insist that, if provenential properties are to be artistically relevant, they must enter in *some* way into our experiential engagement with the artistic vehicle. Suppose we say that a property *p* of an artwork *W* is *experientially relevant* to the appreciation of *W* just in case the belief that *W* has *p* makes a difference to those experiential engagements with an instance of *W* that bear upon its proper appreciation and evaluation. Then we might insist that provenential properties are artistically relevant only if they are experientially relevant. Term this an 'experiential criterion' of artistic relevance. Such a criterion entails that provenential properties, if artistically relevant, can only be *indirectly* so unless they are somehow directly accessible in the receiver's experiential engagement with an instance of the work.[18] The challenge, in this case, to one who wishes

---

[18] Patrick Maynard ("Drawing as Drawn: An Approach to Creation in an Art," in *The Creation of Art*, eds. Gaut and Livingston, 53–86) argues that how a drawing is made is indeed directly accessible in this way.

to artistically enfranchise provenential properties that are not in any obvious way focus-determining is to show how they can nonetheless be experientially relevant.

Second, we might claim that provenential properties can be artistically relevant independently of being experientially relevant, because the 'achievement' of the artist in generating a particular focus of appreciation is itself an appreciable feature of the work that bears upon both its proper appreciation and its artistic value. We might claim for example, that 'achievement properties' of the sort that might be ascribed to Turner, Vermeer, and Vinterberg bear directly upon the appreciation and evaluation of their works independently of how, if at all, our knowledge of such properties affects our experiential engagement with instances of the work. The claim here will be that some provenential properties can be directly artistically relevant in this way. We may term this the 'augmented criterion' of artistic relevance, since it allows for both experiential and non-experiential elements entering directly into the proper appreciation and evaluation of a work as art.

It is easy to see how one might argue for the artistic relevance of such properties as originality and creativity if one adopts some form of the augmented criterion. One writer who has argued in this way is Jerrold Levinson. He claims that not only is art-making an activity that can involve *achievement*, but also that the resulting work is the embodiment of this achievement. It follows, for Levinson, that the work is logically and appreciably inseparable from the activity that generates it. Since originality (and creativity) can be qualities of the artist's generative activity, they are aspects of the work, and, so Levinson further claims, aspects of the work that bear upon its proper appreciation and evaluation. Those who deny that originality (and presumably creativity) are artistically relevant are, he claims, guilty of equating artistic value with aesthetic value—value that pertains to "the experienced rewards that a work affords its audience."[19]

Levinson nicely brings out here the view of artistic value that underlies experiential criteria of artistic relevance, a view that I have elsewhere termed 'enlightened empiricism.' The enlightened empiricist, while acknowledging the failings of AE and taking appropriate account of the epistemological relevance of provenance, continues to uphold the basic principle of empiricist axiology: the artistic value of a work resides in

[19] J. Levinson, "Elster on Artistic Creativity," in *The Creation of Art*, eds. Gaut and Livingston, 235–256.

qualities of the experience it elicits in an appropriately primed receiver. I have argued elsewhere that we should reject enlightened empiricism,[20] and I concur with Levinson in thinking that, once we have done so, we can view without problem the originality and creativity manifest in the artist's generative activity as having direct artistic relevance. Where I disagree with Levinson is over the implications of proceeding in this way. Levinson (and Denis Dutton)[21] maintain that we can accommodate the direct artistic relevance of an artist's achievement (*qua* process) by taking the resulting product to somehow 'embody' that achievement. Differently, Gregory Currie and I have argued, in separate ways, that the rejection of enlightened empiricism and the espousal of an augmented criterion of artistic relevance require that we identify the artwork not with the product of the artist's activity so viewed, but with the action-type enacted, or the token 'doing' performed, by the artist.[22]

Rather than rehearse these matters here, however, I want to consider the options open for the enlightened empiricist who favors an experiential constraint on artistic relevance that might, but need not, enfranchise certain provenential properties that are not, at least on the surface, focus-determining. I shall briefly survey two possible constraints, before elaborating upon a third that I think is more promising. As we shall see, whether artistic originality and creativity can satisfy any of these constraints, save in a very limited class of cases, is questionable. Thus, if we wish to uphold the artistic relevance of creativity for works in general, we must pursue the second strategy. If creativity is artistically relevant, then, I shall suggest, it must be directly relevant in virtue of satisfying an augmented criterion of artistic relevance.

V

Consider, then, the claim that, to be artistically relevant, a provenential property must be experientially relevant—must make some difference to how we experience the art object in arriving at a proper appreciation and evaluation of the work. In the case of focus-determining properties,

---

[20] D. Davies, "Against 'Enlightened Empiricism,'" in *Contemporary Debates in Aesthetics and the Philosophy of Art*, ed. Matthew Kieran (Oxford: Blackwell, 2005), 22–34.

[21] D. Dutton, "Artistic Crimes: The Problem of Forgery in the Arts," *British Journal of Aesthetics* 19 no. 4 (1979): 304–314.

[22] See Currie, *An Ontology of Art*, chap. 3; Davies, *Art as Performance*, esp. chap. 8.

we already have an experientially relevant sufficient condition for artistic relevance which might be expressed as follows: a provenential property p of a work W is artistically relevant if knowledge of p is necessary for the receiver to grasp some feature f of W's artistic content, given W's artistic vehicle. For example, knowing that one of Danto's red squares is by a formalist painter and is intended to be non-representational and non-expressive is necessary if I am to grasp that the canvas exemplifies its redness and squareness, but lacks any expressive or representational content. Call this the focus-determining criterion of artistic relevance. It might be suggested, austerely, that a provenential property p that fails to satisfy this criterion can be experientially relevant only if there is some manifest feature of the artistic vehicle that provides defeasible evidence for p. Term this an 'evidential' criterion of the artistic relevance of provenential properties. A painter's use of a camera obscura might satisfy this criterion if there is some perspectival distortion in the picture of the kind produced by cameras in general: this would be defeasible evidence that a camera obscura was used. Then we might consider a disjunctive experiential criterion of artistic relevance for provenential properties of works, whose disjuncts are the evidential criterion and the focus-determining criterion.[23] Term this disjunctive criterion *C1*.

The evidential component in *C1* faces difficulties, however. First, its extension is unclear. Suppose, for example, that I know how difficult it is to represent a given object without using a certain kind of optical device. Then the excellence with which that object is depicted in a painting might seem to be defeasible evidence of the use of such a device. Indeed, this is precisely how David Hockney argues for the use of a camera obscura to represent the chandelier in van Eyck's *Arnolfini Wedding*.[24] Does this count as a legitimate application of the evidential criterion? Second, on its most obvious reading, the evidential criterion cannot admit the artistic relevance of provenential properties of which the artistic vehicle once provided, but no longer provides, perceptual evidence. For example, 'having originally been painted' as a property of Greek statues, 'having been completed in manner x,' as a property of damaged paintings or frescoes, and 'having originally been brightly colored,' as a property of Turner's watercolors, executed, by choice,

---

[23] I take it that this is what Kathleen Stock's proposal ("On Davies' Argument from Relational Properties," *Acta Analytica* 20 [2005]: 24–31) amounts to, given the non-empiricist gloss that she provides for talk of 'manifest' properties.

[24] Hockney, *Secret Knowledge*.

using 'fugitive' pigments. To accord with our reflective artistic practice in such cases, it seems that we must allow that a provenential property that fails to satisfy the focus-determining criterion may be artistically relevant *now* even when there is no present perceptual evidence. But this calls into question the rationale for having an evidential criterion of artistic relevance in the first place. If evidence need not be evidence for us, why is it crucial to artistic relevance?

Derek Matravers has proposed an experiential criterion of artistic relevance that eschews any kind of evidential criterion. He proposes, instead, what might be seen as a development of the focus-determining criterion in *C1*.[25] Generalizing from the example of a piece of music played with the left hand, Matravers suggests that provenential properties that are not obviously focus-determining can be artistically relevant in virtue of the fact that the work product WP can possess the following property:

It is appropriate that we have an experience-of-WP-as-being-produced-by-method-Q.

I assume that this is intended to yield something like the following criterion:

C2: A provenential property p is artistically relevant iff (or only if?) it is appropriate to experience the work-product as being produced by p.

This criterion, unlike the disjunctive *C1*, seems to apply to both focus-determining and some non-focus-determining provenential properties of works. Thus Vermeer's presumed use of a camera obscura in producing a painting is artistically relevant just in case it is appropriate, in appreciating the work, to experience the canvas as having been so produced. On the other hand, Coleridge's consumption of opium prior to writing "Kubla Khan" is *not* artistically relevant if it is not appropriate to experience the text as having been written by someone who had just consumed opium. As Matravers points out, if we accept *C2*, then which provenential properties enter into the proper appreciation of works will depend upon: (1) when it makes sense to claim that a fact about the generative process can enter into experience of the work-product in this way; and (2) when it makes sense to say that

---

[25] D. Matravers, "Two Comments and a Problem for Davies' Performance Theory," *Acta Analytica* 20 (2005): 32–40.

it is 'appropriate' to experience the work-product as having a given provenential property.

Given that we currently lack a well-founded and generally accepted account of what can enter into the content of experience, there will, as he notes, be a crucial indeterminacy in this answer to our original question about the bearing of provenance on appreciation. There is a further aspect of *C2* which requires clarification. According to *C2*, which provenential properties are artistically relevant depends not only upon how we view the possible contents of experience, but also upon what makes it *appropriate* to experience the work as having been produced in a given manner. In the 'played with the left hand' example, if we know the piece was composed for a pianist who only had a left hand, the warrant for hearing it as played with the left hand is similar to that for hearing a piece scored for a given instrument as played on that instrument rather than as played on a perfect timbral synthesiser. But what might make it appropriate to experience a Vermeer painting as generated with the help of a camera obscura?

VI

C2 is on the right track, however, if we are to formulate a principled and adequate experiential criterion of artistic relevance. Such a criterion must tie artistic relevance in some way—but not evidentially—to our experiential engagement with the product of artistic activity. Rather than appeal here to norms prescribing what a work product should be experienced as, we might tie artistic relevance to a determinate role played in our appreciative engagement with the work-product in something like the following manner:

> *C3*: provenential property *p* of a work *W* is artistically relevant iff *our taking W to have p* affects *the way in which we experientially attend to* the artistic vehicle of *W* in correctly determining *W*'s focus of appreciation, and in particular the artistic content articulated through that vehicle.

The restriction, in *C3*, to experiential attention that determines the focus of appreciation is required because all sorts of information about a work—intuitively quite irrelevant to its proper appreciation as art—may affect how we 'experientially attend to an artistic vehicle' if this notion is not so restricted. For example, I may look at a painting differently if I know it was purchased for an immense sum, or was once stolen from the gallery, or was painted in order to settle a gambling debt. But in none of these cases does such experiential attention to the picture seem to enter into determining the nature of the artistic vehicle or what the picture represents, or expresses, or manifests as a design.

To put some flesh on this proposal, we must clarify how knowledge of a vehicle's history of making *can* affect the experiential attention through which we determine the work-focus, and more particularly the artistic content articulated in a work. With focus-determining properties, this seems fairly clear. But our question is whether, and how, provenential properties that are not focus-determining can nonetheless be artistically relevant by *C3*. The following proposal merits consideration. What we take a work to represent, express, or exemplify depends not merely upon the undifferentiated manifold presented to us through the artistic vehicle, but, more crucially, on the kind of order we find in the elements making up that manifold, and the sense we find in that order. Faced with such an array of elements, we must always ask, 'why *those* elements in *that* order?' In our attempts to determine the order of elements in an artistic manifold and the sense to be given to that order, we posit an intentional process of ordering those elements to some purpose. Knowledge of provenential properties that are not focus-determining may then affect how we relate the elements in a manifold to such an intentional process.

For example, early drafts or sketches may reveal how the original conception of a work such as Picasso's *Les Demoiselles d'Avignon* differs from its final form and thus affect the order and sense we see in the latter, and evidence of *pentimenti* may clarify why the manifest aspects of the painting are as they are.[26] Many of the problematic provenential properties cited at the beginning of this paper can be seen to be artistically relevant through applying *C3* so construed. For example, where we take some element in a work to be unintended, or where we take a poem to be unfinished because its composition was interrupted, we operate with different standards of adequacy in assessing whether an interpretation of the work is sufficiently accountable to the elements that make up the artistic manifold. Where the use of a camera obscura or some other manipulative technique *does* manifest itself in some perceivable feature of the artistic vehicle, we do not look for some

---

[26] For a development of this idea in defense of a moderate intentionalist view of interpretation, see P. Livingston, "*Pentimento*," in *The Creation of Art*, eds. Gaut and Livingston.

deeper explanation of why the vehicle possesses that feature. This is why it can sometimes be relevant that there is an experienceable mark of provenance, although this cannot serve as a criterion of artistic relevance as wrongly assumed in *C1*. Similarly, knowing that *Festen* is a Dogme 95 film, we do not require a more substantive explanation of those features of the artistic vehicle that reflect adherence to the vow of chastity in the making of the film.

On the other hand, it might be said that neither Turner's maritime adventures nor Coleridge's consumption of opium satisfy *C3*'s constraints on artistic relevance. In neither case, it would seem, would knowledge of such facts affect the experiential attention through which we determine the artistic statement articulated through the artistic vehicle. Note, though, that both of these provenential properties *might* satisfy *C3* under certain circumstances—where, for example, there are certain distinctive features of verbal processing under the influence of opium that can be cited to explain otherwise puzzling aspects of the poem "Kubla Khan." But this may be a strength of *C3*, since it seems to be on a par with explaining puzzling features of a Renaissance painting ('What is that dog doing there?') in terms of what was specified by a patron.

VII

Something like *C3* is, I think, the most promising option if we seek an experiential criterion of artistic relevance that will both accommodate focus-determining properties of the sort advanced as objections to AE, and provide us with a principled way of allowing some, but not all, other provenential properties to have artistic relevance in appropriate circumstances. Expressed in terms of our earlier terminology, *C3* allows that provenential properties that are not focus-determining in any direct sense can play a crucial role in our appreciation of the contextualized product of the artist's activity, by *indirectly* contributing to the experiential attention through which we determine the focus of appreciation. But clearly *C3*, if understood in the manner elaborated, will deny artistic relevance to features of provenance that cannot be seen to bear either directly or in this indirect way on our grasp of the artistic content articulated in a work. This might apply to the extensive experimentation upon which Turner drew in rendering light through color in *Snowstorm*: while a knowledge of the conclusions which Turner drew from such experimentation may indeed help us to make sense of way in which pigment is distributed on canvas in the painting, it is unclear that knowledge of the process whereby Turner arrived at such conclusions can bear in this indirect way upon the experiential engagement with the canvas whereby we determine the work's focus of appreciation. If we share Kenneth Clark's judgment that the 'major feat of pictorial intelligence' involved in Turner's use of color to represent light in *Snowstorm* is crucial to appreciating *Snowstorm* as a painting,[27] then there may still be provenential properties for whose intuitive artistic relevance *C3* is unable to account. Similar reasoning might rule against ascribing artistic relevance to Monet's experimentation in using the medium of oil paint to capture '*l'effet de neige*,' or to Morris Louis's development of the 'staining' technique using acrylic paint that gives his paintings their translucent qualities.

But—and here we can finally bring our reflections thus far to bear on our central theme—while diverse activities entering into the history of making of an artistic vehicle may, through *C3*, be seen to have artistic relevance, it is difficult to see how this can be extended to the *creativity* manifested in those activities. For, as we saw earlier, talk of the creativity manifested in the activities generative of an artistic vehicle is talk of something *achieved* in the carrying out of those activities—something in the doing which is novel, and is viewed as making a valuable contribution to artistic practice and the achievement of its goals, whatever the latter be taken to be. *C3* poses a direct challenge to the artistic relevance of creativity so construed because it denies that features of provenance can be artistically relevant simply in virtue of their bearing on the *doing* generative of an artistic vehicle that articulates a particular artistic statement. *C3* entails that, unless they are somehow manifest in artistic product, achievement properties can be artistically relevant only *indirectly*, through their contribution to the experiential attention to the artistic vehicle through which we try to grasp what is thereby articulated. This appears to entail that it is only by virtue of contributing to *the achievement construed as product*, rather than of being a feature of *the achievement viewed as process*, that an artist's generative achievement can satisfy *C3*. But creativity as we are understanding it for the purposes of this paper is a characteristic of the *process*, not of the *product*, even

---

27 Clark, *Looking at Pictures*.

though it is only in virtue of certain merits of the product as embedded in its context of generation that the process is properly so viewed.

VIII

But can creativity or originality ever count as artistically relevant on an experiential criterion such as *C3*? It will be illuminating here to consider an argument offered against the artistic relevance of *originality* which might seem to extend very naturally to creativity. Originality, Bruce Vermazen has maintained, has no bearing on a work's 'artistic value,' its value *as* a work of art.[28] Originality can be thought to contribute to artistic value only if it is taken to involve not just newness, but newness in some respect that we take to be of independent value. He suggests the following analysis:

> A work is original if and only if it is new with respect to some property *p*, that is, it has property *p* and no work (or no work in that medium), so far as the maker knew, had p before that point, and property *p* is an aesthetically valuable property.[29] But then we may pose the following question: 'Where originality amounts to newness with respect to some-thing good.... what reason is there to count the originality as a merit of the work over and above the merit the thing or property has aside from its originality?'[30]

Vermazen offers two arguments in support of his contention that there is in fact no good reason to view originality as itself a merit. First, he argues that, if originality is to make a separate contribution to the good-ness of a work, we require a situation in which two works, $O1$ and $O2$, satisfy the following three conditions: (1) $O1$ and $O2$ are alike in all their aesthetically valuable properties; aside from originality; (2) $O1$ is new in some respect in which $O2$ is not; (3) we feel compelled to say that $O1$ is better. But, he argues, we have good reason to think there can be no such situations. For consider Franz Hals's portraits, which resemble one another in style and differ only in their subjects. Does the first of these portraits have a distinct artistic value in virtue of being the one in which Hals initiated the style of portraiture manifest in the rest of the

---

[28] B. Vermazen, "The Aesthetic Value of Originality," *Midwest Studies in Philosophy* 16 (1991): 266–279.
[29] Ibid., 271.
[30] Ibid., 270.

oeuvre? Vermazen maintains that any preference for the first portrait can pertain only to its historical value, not to its artistic value.

Vermazen's second argument focuses on a possible counter-example to his claim about the artistic relevance of originality. Russian formalists held that the proper goal of a literary work is to defamiliarize either the objects represented or the subject's act of receiving the text. On one version of this view, the poet's task is to 'deautonomize' its act of creation and the reader's act of reception by means of foregrounding, and successful foregrounding seems to require that the text of the poem depart from what has been done before in striking ways. Thus, it might be argued, striking originality in what the poet does is a necessary condition for achieving the proper goal of poetry, and thus of artistic value. Vermazen counters this line of argument by claiming that, if originality is tied to foregrounding, it is not an enduring property of the work even if it is an enduring property of the generative act of the poet. For how a stylistic property of the text affects the readers depends upon the background that they bring to their encounter with the text. While certain stylistic features may have deautonomized the reading experience for contemporaries of the poet, they will cease to have that effect as readers become familiar with the poem, or as the stylistic 'novelties' become an accepted part of the literary culture. Thus foregrounding is not an enduring feature of the work required for its proper appreciation, and originality, even if it is a precondition for foregrounding, is not thereby artistically relevant.

Given the nature of Vermazen's arguments, and given the conceptual links between originality and creativity as characteristics of an agent's generative activity, it seems that, if these arguments count against the relevance for artistic value of originality, they extend to the purported artistic relevance of creativity. Where an artist's creativity results in a valuable innovation in the use of an artistic medium, for example, it might be argued that appreciating and assessing the value of the work itself depends only on grasping the artistic qualities realized through the innovation and neither on the originality nor the creativity of the artistic activity that brought that innovation about.

I think we have good reason to question at least the second of Vermazen's arguments, which rests on the assumption that the artistic qualities rightly ascribed to a work in its proper appreciation depend upon how its strikes the receiver in whatever context the receiver finds itself. This assumption, or something like it, is necessary if, as Vermezen claims, we are to count the 'foregrounding' effect sought by the formalist poet as a property of the poet's action but not of the poem because only receivers contemporary with the poet will achieve this effect. But this assumption seems highly questionable if we look at the kinds of properties we want to ascribe to works. Marcel Duchamp's *Readymades*, for example, strike the artistically informed modern viewer as familiar, unthreatening, and almost endearing given the much more extreme offerings of late modern visual art. But to appreciate Duchamp's works, and to correctly assess their artistic value, we must characterize them as shocking, radical, provocative, and subversive. What matters in determining the experienced artistic qualities of a work that bear upon its appreciation and evaluation is how the work would affect an *appropriate* receiver. In the case of certain affective properties that depend upon the anticipated context of reception for the work, our own responses may not track those of an appropriate receiver, and our failure to experience a particular quality does not show that the work, qua object of artistic appreciation, lacks that property or has lost it. Rather, it only shows that certain appreciable properties of the work may not be directly available to us since we fail to share the anticipated context of reception for the work. We can recognize the shocking and radical nature of Duchamp's *Fountain* because we can gauge how the work struck members of the target audience, not because we ourselves find it shocking. So, returning to the case of the Russian formalist poems, that certain stylistic features are foregrounded is a feature of the poem and not just of the artist's activity, even though they are not foregrounded for us when we read the poem.

Suppose that we grant that originality is a *precondition* for foregrounding, and that foregrounding can be a property of the work. Vermazen's first argument can still hold that it does not follow that originality has some independent bearing on a work's artistic value. What contributes to the work's artistic value, he might claim, is the foregrounding itself, and the work acquires no additional value, qua work, from the originality that is a precondition for that foregrounding. But, even if we grant this claim about artistic value, it seems that originality, in the case in question, is artistically relevant in the sense of *C3*. Knowledge of originality bears crucially upon the work's proper appreciation, and thereby on its proper evaluation. For foregrounding to work for a particular receiver, the medium must be manipulated in a manner with which she is unfamiliar, and for foregrounding to be a property of the work itself this must be the case for all appropriately informed receivers. But a given receiver for whom a feature of the work is foregrounded can justifiably

impute foregrounding to the work only if she assumes that she is react-
ing in the way an appropriately informed receiver would react—in
other words, only if she recognizes that what is unfamiliar for her will
be unfamiliar for such a receiver—that is, that the relevant features of
the work are original for such a receiver. In other words, even if it is
foregrounding, and not originality, that contributes to a work's artistic
value, it is only in virtue of recognizing the work's originality that the
receiver can justifiably ascribe the property of foregrounding and the
consequent artistic value. So, in at least this special case, originality is
artistically relevant by *C3*.

Again, in this special case, the same considerations apply if we
consider those stylistic originalities that are rightly viewed as creative—
where the originality, given the context, is traceable to what the artist
intentionally did. For intending to do *X* is plausibly taken to be at least
a necessary condition for *X*'s being part of what one achieves, even if
some of the properties rightly attributed to a work are not intended by
the artist: for such unintended properties are not part of what the artist
achieved. But then, to the extent that we take what an artist achieves,
in the product sense, to bear on the appreciation of the artist's work,
foregrounding will be part of the its concrete achievement only if the
artist's manipulations of the medium are not only original for appropriate receivers but also intended to be original. The deliberate and
intentional generation of something novel that contributes to the value
of a work seems to be just what is involved in artistic creativity. So, in
the special case under consideration, the originality of a work and the
creativity of the artistic process seem to be artistically relevant in the
sense of *C3* in that knowledge of both of these dimensions of a work
is required for its proper appreciation, even if we agree with Vermazen
that the originality (and by extension the creativity) does not make an
independent contribution to the work's artistic value.

IX

Foregrounding, I have suggested, may represent an example of an appreciable property of a work whose recognition presupposes the receiver's
apprehension of both the originality of the work and the creativity of
the process generative of the artistic product. But this is a limited vic-
tory at best for the proponent of the artistic relevance of creativity. For
the argument offered above with respect to foregrounding seems to be

limited to the special case—it does not, for example, admit of any extension to the Franz Hals case cited by Vermazen. Furthermore, creativity is deemed to be artistically relevant only indirectly, through its bearing on the ascription of contentful features bearing on the work's artistic value. No artistic value has been shown to attach to creativity itself. As suggested earlier, our reflections strongly suggests that, if a case is to be made for the artistic relevance of creativity in any richer sense, that case must be made by taking aspects of the generative process to bear directly upon the artistic value of a work, rather than seeing any such bearing as necessarily mediated by what was achieved or produced by that activity. In other words, to defend the artistic relevance of creativity in anything other than the very limited sense for which I have just argued, we need to espouse an augmented, rather than an experiential, criterion of artistic relevance. But this, as I also suggested earlier, may have wider ramifications for our conception of artworks.

PART THREE

FORMS AND DOMAINS OF CREATIVITY

CHAPTER THIRTEEN

CREATIVITY: HOW DOES IT WORK?

Margaret Boden

I   *Introduction*

Creativity is the ability to come up with ideas that are new, surprising, and valuable.[1] I am using 'idea' as shorthand, catchall term here. It can be a concept, a poetic image, a scientific theory, or even a particular form of taxation, all of which are commonly called ideas. But it can also mean a style of painting or dancing, a way of building a bridge or skinning a cat, a millinery design, a cooking recipe, a recipe for home-made bombs—or even a plan for delivering them to maximum effect.

As that long list suggests, we find creativity in every area of life: not just art, science, or business. Moreover, it is an aspect of normal adult human intelligence. So every one of us has it, although some of us display it more often, and more convincingly, than others do. By 'more convincingly,' I mean that some people repeatedly produce ideas highly regarded as valuable—and which, so far as is known, no one else has ever had before. (They are 'historically' creative, or H-creative.) Most people, by contrast, produce only moderately interesting ideas, many of which are already known by other people, even if new for the individual concerned. (They are 'psychologically,' or 'personally,' creative: P-creative, for short.)

What different people regard as interesting varies, so new ideas can be valuable in many different ways. Encyclopedia writers, gallery curators, chemists, sculptors, property developers, entrepreneurs, and advertising executives focus on different sorts of creative idea, different sorts of value. But for all these groups, they are most interested in H-creativity. However, if an idea is H-creative it must necessarily be P-creative too.

---

[1] Margaret Boden, *The Creative Mind: Myths and Mechanisms* (London, Routledge, 2004).

So the first step to understanding H-creativity is to understand P-creativity. We need to ask how someone can come up with an idea that they have never had before. Some of those ideas will turn out to be H-creative also, but the core processes—though not the details—of idea generation are much the same in all cases.

Understanding how P-creativity works would be interesting in itself, as an exercise in psychology. But it would also be useful because if we want to encourage creativity, in our schoolchildren or in the workforce, we had better have some idea of just what sorts of mental process are involved. We will see, in Section IV below, that different types of creativity can be fostered in different ways. Although all of them can be—and, sadly, too often are—discouraged in much the same way.

Some people appear to be offended by questions about how creativity works, believing that it is not possible for us to understand this. If they merely mean that we cannot usually know, in every detail, how this or that novel idea (poetic image, symphony, mathematical proof) came about on a particular occasion, then they are right. Quite apart from anything else, we do not usually know enough about the contents of the individual creator's mind—even if that individual is oneself. But if they mean that we cannot understand the general principles by which creative ideas arise, then they are mistaken. Creativity does not work by magic or by divine inspiration. We cannot explain it in terms of intuition. It is true, to be sure, that creativity involves intuition, but to say that does not tell us much, since the word 'intuition' is just a placeholder for some unknown psychological process, invisible even to creative persons. If we want to understand how creativity is possible, how human minds can come up with ideas that are both new and valuable, we cannot rely on appeals to intuition. Something more constructive needs to be said. In other words, we need to understand how intuition works.

Creativity is not the only mental ability that depends on 'invisible' (non-introspectible) processes. For instance, we are unaware of the processes that enable us, most of the time, to speak in perfectly grammatical sentences. But creativity seems especially mysterious because its results, unlike grammatical sentences, are always surprising—and sometimes utterly amazing. If one compares the surprise we experience in various cases of creativity, one will find three different sorts of surprise.

We may be surprised because a new idea is statistically unusual, contrary to commonsense expectations—like an outsider winning the Kentucky Derby. We may be surprised because we had not realized that the new idea had been a possibility all along. For example, compare discovering a beautiful village tucked away in a hollow between two spurs of the Motorway. Its location had always been marked on the map, but we had not examined the whole map closely. Or, we may be surprised by something that we had previously thought impossible, and which we still see as utterly counterintuitive. For example, think of the very first exhibition of Impressionist paintings, or imagine the impact on non-physicists of the introduction of wireless, or television. In such cases, a particular creative idea appears as if it simply could not have arisen—yet it did. These three sorts of surprise correspond to three ways of coming up with new ideas, three different answers to our question, How does creativity work? In other words, they point to three types of creativity—discussed in Section II, below.

Another kind of surprise focuses not on the nature or likelihood of the idea itself but on its being offered to us as something valuable. As remarked above, values in many areas are disputable—and even highly changeable. Sometimes, they can change virtually overnight—due to commercial decisions in the fashion industry for instance (enticing the public to buy new clothes even though they are not strictly needed), or to what some widely admired 'celebrity' happened to wear to a high-profile party. At other times, the change may take years to happen. The first Impressionist paintings had to be shown in a special hall because the official exhibition would not accept them. After having been nearly universally rejected at first, they can now be seen every day on birthday cards and boxes of chocolates. This gradual change from disgusted rejection to clichéd acceptance is a special case of the value-change that typically accompanies the third type of creativity discussed below.

There may, of course, be some universal (or nearly universal) values, more resistant to cultural change. Two possible examples are the preference for symmetry and shininess. Quite apart from their cross-cultural popularity, there are good biological reasons why valuing these two characteristics has evolved.[2] In addition, psychologists have identified other naturally evolved tendencies to favor perceptible features, and behave towards them in a particular way; certain shapes or textures, for instance, suggest opportunities for locomotion, feeding, holding, stroking, or courting. These nearly-universal values are prominent in

---

[2] Margaret Boden, *Mind as Machine: Myths and Mechanisms*, two vol. (London: Routledge, 2006), vol. 1, 553–556.

craftworks, which is why the crafts are readily intelligible across cultures.[3] But even biologically based values can be deliberately transgressed and their opposites admired in their stead. Think of the highly asymmetrical architecture of Daniel Libeskind, for example.

In short, the surprise we feel on encountering a creative idea is sometimes due, in part, to the unfamiliar values that we are being invited to adopt. Mostly, however, it is due to the novelty of the idea in itself. We are surprised that it even happened, regardless whether it is obviously 'valuable.' Here, the three sorts of surprise listed above correspond to three different ways of coming up with new ideas, three different answers to the question, How does creativity work?

II   *Three Types of Creativity*

Three types of creativity are combinational, exploratory, and transformational.[4] These types are distinguished by the types of psychological process involved in generating the new idea. The exercise and appreciation of each of these forms of creativity depends upon specific cultural knowledge. Someone from a different culture may not even be able to recognize the novelty involved, and *a fortiori* may not be able to understand or value it. The 'someone from a different culture' need not be a foreigner: they may be your next-door neighbor, equipped with a range of knowledge and cultural interests different from yours. If so, they will have to undergo a learning process if they are ever to understand the novelty and to appreciate its value.

Combinational creativity involves the generation of unfamiliar (and interesting) combinations of familiar ideas. In general, it gives rise to the first type of surprise mentioned above. Just as one does not expect the outsider to win the Derby because that is, statistically unusual, so one does not expect ideas X and Y to be combined. On the contrary, they are normally regarded as being mutually irrelevant.

Everyday examples of combinational creativity include visual collage (in advertisements and MTV videos, for instance), much poetic imagery, all types of analogy (verbal, visual, or musical), and the unexpected juxtapositions of ideas found in political cartoons in newspapers. Each of

---

[3] Margaret Boden, "Crafts, Perception, and the Possibilities of the Body," *British Journal of Aesthetics* 40 (2000): 289–301.
[4] Boden, *The Creative Mind*, chap. 3–6.

these can sometimes be both startlingly novel and hugely appropriate—highly creative. Think of the most telling images in your favorite poetry, or of the last newspaper cartoon that made you laugh aloud on your train journey. In either case, the two (or more) conjoined ideas are not obviously relevant to each other—hence part of your surprise. Yet, on further consideration, you can see that they allow an interpretation wherein they are closely, perhaps very closely, linked—hence the other, and especially satisfying, part of your surprise.

Many attempts to define creativity, even within the specialist psychological literature, confine it to this first type alone. Thinking that forming unfamiliar combinations is the only creative game in town is a mistake, for exploratory and transformational creativity are different. They are both grounded in some previously existing, and culturally accepted, structured style of thinking—what one can call a 'conceptual space.' Of course, combinational creativity depends on a shared conceptual base—but this is, potentially, the entire range of concepts and world knowledge in someone's mind. A conceptual space is both more limited and more tightly structured. It may be a board game, for example, or a particular type of music or painting, or a way of visualizing the structure of molecules in chemistry.

In exploratory creativity, the existing stylistic rules or conventions are used to generate novel structures (ideas), whose possibility may or may not have been realized before the exploration took place. To continue the analogy mentioned in Section I, you may or may not have had some reasons to expect to find an unknown village nestling between the Motorways. The vast majority of creative work in the arts and sciences is of this kind (philosophers of science call exploratory creativity 'normal' science).[5]

Exploratory creativity is not to be sneezed at. There are three reasons for this. First, most artists and scientists spend their working time engaged in exploratory creativity. Only very few go beyond it, and they do so only occasionally. Second, exploratory creativity can produce highly valued (beautiful, useful, interesting) structures, or ideas. Even if you were already familiar with nineteenth-century Impressionism, upon entering a room full of previously-unseen Impressionist canvasses, only a mind-numbing glut of chocolate boxes would lead you to say "Oh no! Not more Monets!"

---

[5] Thomas S. Kuhn, *The Structure of Scientific Revolutions* (Chicago, Ill., University of Chicago Press, 1962).

Finally, exploratory creativity can often offer surprises deeper than merely seeing the previously unseen. For it need not be a matter of adopting the current style unthinkingly. It can also involve the deliberate search for, and testing of, the specific stylistic limits concerned. To do that is to discover just which types of structure can be generated within this space, and which cannot. If you have ever visited a retrospective exhibition of a painter's life-work, with canvasses arranged chronologically, you will have seen this process. (Had it not, there would be little interest in showing the years-long collection of work. Only a doting family member, with more money than sense, would have arranged such an exhibition.)

In testing the potential and limits of the adopted style, exploratory creativity sometimes involves varying it too. Some of the rules, conventions, or constraints that define the style can be slightly altered or 'tweaked' (again, this is readily visible in a retrospective exhibition). In that case, the new ideas that arise would not—could not—have arisen without the tweaking. Nevertheless, they will clearly be 'of a piece with' (in the same general style as) the earlier, more familiar, examples. As such, they will be readily intelligible, in terms of the methods of interpretation already in place to understand the style. They may cause an extra frisson of excitement, but no amazement—and certainly no bewildered incomprehension. Instead, amazement, bewilderment, and incomprehension are caused by transformational creativity. For it is this which leads to 'impossibilist' surprise because some deep dimension of the thinking style, or conceptual space, is altered—so that structures can now be generated which could not be generated before, and which are not all of a piece with the previous style.

Imagine altering the rule of chess that says pawns cannot jump over other pieces so they are now allowed to do this, as knights always were. The result would be that some games could now be played, which were literally impossible before. Similarly, to start painting abstract pictures, where previously the paintings had all been representational, is to invite incomprehension as well as to cause surprise. The greater the alteration, and the more fundamental the stylistic dimension concerned, the greater the shock of impossibilist surprise.

The distinction between tweaking and 'transforming,' and therefore between exploratory and transformational creativity, is a matter of degree. After all, I said above that the novel ideas occurring after the exploratory tweaking 'could not have arisen' before. However, in exploratory creativity, the variation in style is relatively minor and relatively superficial. That is why the result is readily intelligible, even though it is a novel variation as well as a novel structure. It is also why the result is immediately accepted as valuable, not rejected as disturbing—still less, as absurd.

Transformational creativity is different, because here the variation is greater and the stylistic dimension being varied is deeper. The resulting change is so marked that the new idea may be difficult to accept, or even to understand. Sometimes, many years will have to pass before it can be valued by anyone outside a small group of aficionados. Picasso's pioneering cubist canvas of *Les Demoiselles d'Avignon*, for instance, was initially spurned even by his close circle of fellow artists. He kept it hidden in his studio for several years before exhibiting it.

Even in transformational creativity, not every dimension of the style will have been changed. So there will be both structural continuities and structural discontinuties between the untransformed space and its seemingly impossible successor. The nature of these continuities and discontinuities will affect the valuation of the new idea. Consider our example of the transformed chess game, for instance. If some feature of the game, which you had enjoyed before the change, is retained, then you will find something to enjoy in the transformed version. You may, however, be so averse to jumping pawns—perhaps doing so makes you feel giddy—that you decide to revert to old-style chess. Transformationally creative thinkers may add new rules and drop or vary old ones. They may then engage on a lengthy process of exploring the new style more fully.

One illustrative example concerns the composer Arnold Schoenberg.[6] He transformed the space of Western tonal music by dropping the fundamental home key constraint: no longer did every composition have to favor one of a finite number of sets of seven notes (the major and minor scales). Atonality was born. But besides dropping this constraint, Schoenberg experimented by adding new ones. At one point, for instance, he said that each composition should contain every note of the chromatic scale. Musical exploration could then ensue on this basis. But the more radical transformation was the decision to drop the constraint of a home key. In general, transformational creativity is valued more highly than the other two types. (That is less true in literature than the other arts because language offers scope for especially

---

[6] Charles Rosen, *Arnold Schoenberg* (New York: Viking, 1975).

rich creative combinations the theme of human motivation offers huge exploratory potential.)

However, novel transformations are relatively rare. We usually remember artists and scientists whose names are recorded in history books above all for changing the accepted style. (Again, that is somewhat less true of writers.) The three types of creativity are analytically distinct, in that they involve different types of psychological process for generating P-novel ideas. But these processes sometimes occur together. For instance, an advertising graphic may both explore a recognizable visual style (specific to the brand concerned) and combine two or more images normally kept apart. That is partly why it is usually more sensible to ask whether this or that aspect of an artwork or scientific theory is creative, and in what way, rather than asking, Is this new idea creative: yes or no?

III   *Creativity in Computers?*

If we could say 'just which' psychological processes underlie creativity, we should be able to model them in computers. Indeed, over the last twenty years, an increasing amount of work has been done in this area.[7] I am not referring to computer art, which began during the late 1950s and has burgeoned since then. For computer art (with a few exceptions) is done only with the aim of producing something visually/musically interesting, not with the aim of understanding how human artists' minds work.

Modeling creative processes as such is a different enterprise. All three types of creativity have been modeled in this way. The most successful examples concern exploratory creativity. This requires, of course, that the programmer, or a close collaborator, knows enough about the domain concerned (math, chemistry, graphics, music) to be able to identify the constraints that define the style being investigated. For example, only someone very familiar with Bach fugues, and preferably with what musicologists have written about them, could write a plausible fugue-generating program. Many people believe that no program could possibly generate 'plausible' Bach fugues, or Chopin nocturnes. They are wrong. The composer, David Cope, wrote a program in the

---

[7] Boden, *The Creative Mind*, chap. 6–8, 12; Boden, *Mind as Machine*, vol. 2, 1059–1068.

1980s, which could produce very convincing pastiches of a wide range of famous composers. Indeed, it is not clear that 'pastiche' is always the right word. For when these pieces are played by human musicians in the concert hall, they often 'fool' even the best musical experts.[8]

Similarly, an architectural program based on Frank Lloyd Wright's Prairie House style has come up with every one of the 40-odd houses he designed, plus others—clearly within the same general style—which no one, Wright included, has ever seen before.[9] One can certainly say that these house designs and musical compositions are new. That is, they are newly discovered structures within the space of possibilities defined by the style concerned. Moreover, they are valuable: after all, exploratory creativity in general is grounded in some already accepted (valued) style.

But the style itself is not new. In other words, these programs model exploratory, not transformational, creativity. Whether a computer could ever come up with a new style is a hotly disputed question. It is not obvious that it could not, because some programs are able to alter their own rules in unpredictable ways, so that they can generate structures on Tuesday, which they could not have generated on Monday. These are the so-called evolutionary programs, which contain mechanisms—'genetic algorithms'—that can make random changes in the program's rules and select the most promising for further 'breeding.' Sometimes, the selection is done at each generation by a human being. But sometimes, the programmer chooses a list of criteria—the 'fitness function'—by means of which the program itself selects the winners automatically.

There are three problems with these self-transforming programs, however. First, if the 'mutations' allowed are so radical that a seemingly new type of structure does result then it may be so different from what went before that the human beings using the program see it as having little or no value. Second, radical transformations will not lead to a sustained new style (unless the transformed program is immediately 'frozen' by the programmer) because another, very different, radical change may happen within a few generations. Third, some people argue that genuine novelty is not available even from evolutionary programs, because every structure generated by the computer must lie within the

---

[8] David Cope, *Computer Models of Musical Creativity* (Cambridge, Mass.: MIT Press, 2006).

[9] Hank Koning and Julie Eisenberg, "The Language of the Prairie: Frank Lloyd Wright's Prairie Houses," *Environment and Planning* 8, no. 3 (1981): 295–323.

possibility-space defined by the program itself. (If the program is allowed
to interact with the physical world, however, a genuine novelty may arise:
for instance, a new—not merely an improved—type of sensor.)[10]

One might think that there would be no problem modeling combinational creativity on a computer. After all, a computer program could
come up with novel combinations of ideas until kingdom come. It could
even do this by using mechanisms broadly comparable to associative
memory in human beings.[11] Here, however, the problem—again—is
the assignment of value. Most of the associations produced by the
program will have little or no interest for human users. Conceivably,
someone looking for novel ideas for an advertising campaign might
find it worthwhile to sift through the novel associations generated by a
computer—but they would probably be far better off relying on their
own powers of association and world-knowledge. (Kim Binsted and
Graeme D. Ritchie discuss an example of computerized combinational
creativity used for generating simple jokes.)[12]

Computer models of creativity can help us to think clearly about how
creativity works. That is true even in the cases where their performance
is disappointing, for then we can ask just why they failed to come up with
the expected results. We have seen that they can sometimes give results
that match human creativity, especially of the exploratory type. Whether
even those examples are 'really' creative, however, is a quite different
question—philosophical, not scientific. Maybe only the programmers
are truly creative and we should attribute any apparent 'creativity' in
the computer to them. That very common opinion is often based one
or more of four highly controversial philosophical assumptions (about
consciousness, brain-stuff, and meaning, for example).[13] We cannot go
into them here, but notice that, being 'highly controversial,' we cannot take them for granted. There is a fifth reason for people denying
that computers can be creative, which is that they doubt whether even
human creativity can be scientifically understood. If the argument of
the previous sections is correct, however, they are mistaken.

---

[10] Jon Bird and Paul Layzell, "The Evolved Radio and its Implications for Modeling
the Evolution of Novel Sensors," in *Proceedings of Congress on Evolutionary Computation,
CEC '02* (Brighton, UK: Sussex University, 2002), 1836–1841.

[11] Boden, *The Creative Mind*, chap. 6.

[12] Kim Binsted and Graeme D. Ritchie, "Computational Rules for Punning Riddles'
Humor," *International Journal of Humor Research* 10 (1997): 25–76.

[13] Boden, *The Creative Mind*, 286–300.

IV *How Creativity Can Be Encouraged*

If we want to know how creativity can be discouraged, the answer is simple. Since all types of creativity involve novelty and surprise, any cultural attitudes that punish people for providing these will thereby hinder their creativity. Suppose that someone—schoolchild or adult—comes up with an unexpected (surprising) answer to a question. If their answer is immediately dismissed as a 'mistake,' or—still worse—if the individual is scorned as 'stupid,' they will be much less likely to offer new answers (or perhaps any answers) in the future.

Of course, people do sometimes make mistakes. But there are ways of conveying this without also implying that the person is stupid. Indeed, there are often ways of conveying it in a constructive fashion, so that the person can see how their (mistaken) idea could have been on the right lines if the question/problem had been slightly different. The more one hopes for truly surprising ideas, the more important it is not to undermine people's self-confidence. Evidence suggests that what makes for an especially H-creative person is not their having any special idea-generating mechanisms in their heads. Rather, it is their motivation, self-confidence, and single-minded commitment to the domain in question.[14]

Indeed, high-profile H-creators are often monsters of egotism and selfishness.[15] In the case of transformational creativity in particular, this makes sense. For transformational creativity (by definition) breaks the commonly accepted rules, and challenges other people to adopt new values in accepting the novel idea. It is therefore likely to meet with incomprehension, bewilderment, and even scorn.

The H-creator needs plenty of self-belief to weather such storms. Turning to the happier topic of how to encourage creativity, the answer is not quite so simple. For here, we must distinguish carefully among the three types. The sort of experience or training best suited to fostering one type will differ from that best suited to fostering another.

Combinational creativity, as we have seen, depends on two things: making unfamiliar combinations of familiar ideas, and doing so aptly, or appropriately. Several forms of encouragement are relevant here.

---

[14] David N. Perkins, *The Mind's Best Work* (Cambridge, Mass.: Harvard University Press, 1981); Boden, *The Creative Mind*, chap. 10.

[15] Howard Gardner, *Creating Minds: An Anatomy of Creativity Seen through the Lives of Freud, Einstein, Picasso, Stravinsky, Eliot, Graham, and Gandhi* (New York: Basic Books, 1993).

The first is to enlarge the variety of concepts in the person's mind. Someone who does not possess a host of concepts, drawn from a wide range of domains, will be very unlikely to come up with startling new combinations. So an essential part of helping someone to be creative in this particular way is to widen their general knowledge, encouraging them to engage in many different interests and activities, and perhaps also to draw on more than one culture. However, there is no guarantee that a well-stocked mind will generate large numbers of novel associations.

In addition, then, one should foster a habit of experimenting with unfamiliar conceptual 'mixtures.' For example, a child (or adult) could be given two or more ideas drawn—possibly at random—from different areas, and asked to make up a story, or compose a sentence, in which all those ideas feature. Or one could encourage the person to ask, What does that remind you of? in the expectation that at least a dozen things will come to mind. In this sort of way, the various exercises recommended in the many self-help books on creativity can induce people to think more adventurously than they normally do.[16]

Finally (the most difficult of all), one should help the person to learn how to judge the results, to pick out the more interesting combinations. This may involve making explicit comparisons and contrasts between the newly joined ideas, a process helped by giving the person the experience of existing examples of combinational creativity and asking them just what is 'interesting' about the different cases. Careful consideration of the imagery in poems, for instance, can awaken the reader to conceptual connections that they had not consciously realized before.

Self-help books on creativity usually provide helpful hints on how to assess novel mixes of ideas. As for exploratory creativity, mere general knowledge and richness of associations will not be enough. Persons will also need prolonged experience of, and perhaps special training in, the thinking style concerned. If that style is interestingly complex, or if it requires special skills (such as mixing oil paints, playing a keyboard, or synthesizing chemical molecules), it may take years to become competent in it, so that one can produce new structures satisfying the stylistic constraints in question. Learning how to test and tweak the style will take even longer. (Renowned composers, even including child prodigies

---

[16] Tony Buzan, *Mind Maps at Work: How to Be the Best at Work and Still Have Time to Play* (London: Thorsons, 2004); Edward De Bono, *De Bono's Thinking Course* (London: BBC, 1982); De Bono, *Six Thinking Hats* (London: Penguin, 2000).

such as Mozart, seem to need about twelve years of total immersion in music before they can write something 'creative' rather than merely competent. On the other hand, even 'ordinary' people, if given enough training, can reach unusual heights in musical creativity.)[17]

It follows that exploratory creativity is not primarily an exercise in 'free thinking.' Indeed, even combinational creativity is not wholly unconstrained, since the novel association (which may have been—though usually is not—produced by random processes) must be evaluated for aptness. In other words, the belief that one can best equip children (or adults) for creativity by encouraging them to ignore all conceptual constraints and think only 'for themselves,' is mistaken. As that term 'constraints' suggests, creativity involves personal discipline as well as freedom. Where exploratory creativity is in question, that discipline may require years of painstaking practice. Ultimately, to be sure, the style may become so familiar that the person can explore it effortlessly. But a great deal of effort will have been needed to learn it in the first place.

Transformational creativity, as we have seen, is built on the exploratory variety. For here, the style is not merely tested and tweaked, but to some extent transcended. That is done by altering, adding, or deleting dimensions of the original conceptual space, which implies that those dimensions must already have been learnt by the person concerned. Some forms of alteration will apply only to a specific dimension of a specific conceptual space. For instance, we saw in Section II that Schoenberg altered tonality partly by insisting on using every note of the chromatic scale.

Others are more general: these include the negation of an existing dimension, or its deletion, or its iteration. For instance, in discovering the structure of benzene, the chemist Friedrich von Kekule transformed his idea of a chemical molecule from an open string to its opposite, a closed string.[18] Schoenberg dropped the seven-note scales that defined tonal music.

One way of encouraging transformational creativity is to present the person with many such examples, asking them to consider just what dimension/s has/have been changed, and how. Once they understand the nature of transformational creativity they will be in a better

---

[17] Joseph H. Kunkel, "Vivaldi in Venice: An Historical Test of Psychological Propositions," *Psychological Record* 35 (1985): 445–457.

[18] Boden, *The Creative Mind*, 25–28, 62–71.

position to experiment with it. As always, however, they will also need to be able to evaluate their own novel ideas. Learners are especially likely to resist this form of creativity—perhaps rightly so: not all transformations are valuable. Whereas mere exploratory tweaking is unlikely to destroy the interest of the novel idea (although it may lessen it), a radical transformation can do so.

It would be helpful, too, if the 'transformational' creator could be encouraged to present ideas in ways that will help other people to understand and accept, them. Understanding requires a realization of the similarities between the new style and the previous one, and a sensitive explanation on the part of the originator should be able to provide this. Acceptance is even more elusive, and may require additional persuasion on the part of the creator, for which there can be no set formula.

Here we come full circle, for the self-confidence needed to persevere—and perhaps eventually to persuade—in transformational creativity is the greatest of all. Whichever form of originality we are trying to encourage, however, the person's motivation must be fostered in addition to their 'brain power.'

CHAPTER FOURTEEN

THE THREE DOMAINS OF CREATIVITY[1]

Arthur Koestler

I *Introduction*

This paper attempts to give a condensed outline of a theory I have
set out in detail in my book on creativity and to carry that theory to
the next step.[2] The proposition I shall submit is, in a nutshell, that the
conscious and unconscious processes which enter into all three forms of
creative activity have a basic pattern in common. When I speak of *three*
forms of creativity, I mean the domains of artistic originality, scientific
discovery, and comic inspiration. I believe that all creative activity falls
into one or another of these three categories or, more frequently, into
some combination of them. If you speak, for instance, of cooking as
'creative,' you automatically imply that cooking is either an art, or a
science, or both.

As a first step toward describing that pattern, let us try something
simple like this: The creative act consists in combining previously
unrelated structures in such a way that you get more out of the emergent whole than you have put in. This sounds like making a *perpetuum
mobile*, and in a sense it is, because mental evolution, like biological
evolution, seems to contradict the second law of thermodynamics,
which contends that the universe is running down as if afflicted by
mental fatigue. But we will not go into this; instead, let me illustrate by
a few schoolbook examples what I mean by combining two previously
unrelated structures.

---

[1] Originally appeared in *Challenges of Humanistic Psychology*, ed. James F. T. Bugental
(New York: McGraw-Hill, 1967), 30–40; reprinted in *The Concept of Creativity in Science
and Art*, eds. D. Dutton and M. Krausz, eds., (The Hague/Boston/London: Martinus
Nijhoff Publishers, 1981), 1–17, *all rights reserved*.
[2] Arthur Koestler, *The Act of Creation* (New York: Macmillan, 1964).

II   *Association and Bisociation*

The motions of the tides have been known to man since time immemorial. So have the motions of the moon. But the idea to relate the two, the idea that the tides were due to the attraction of the moon, occurred, as far as we know, for the first time to a German astronomer in the seventeenth century, and when Galileo read about it, he laughed it off as an occult fancy.[3] Moral: The more familiar each of the previously unrelated structures are, the more striking the new synthesis and the more obvious it seems in the driver's mirror of hindsight.

The history of science is a history of marriages between ideas, which were previously strangers to each other, and frequently considered incompatible. Lodestones—magnets—were known in antiquity as some curiosity of nature. During the Middle Ages, they were used for two purposes: as navigators' compasses and as a means to attract an estranged wife back to her husband. Equally well known were the curious properties of amber, which, when rubbed, acquires the virtue of attracting flimsy objects. The Greek word for amber is *elektron*, but the Greeks were not much interested in electricity, nor were the Middle Ages. For nearly two thousand years, electricity and magnetism were considered separate phenomena, in no way related to each other. In 1820, Hans Christian Oersted discovered that an electric current flowing through a wire deflected a compass needle, which happened to be lying on his table. At that moment the two contexts began to fuse into one—electromagnetism—creating a kind of chain reaction which is still continuing and gaining in momentum; forever amber.

From Pythagoras, who combined arithmetic and geometry, to Einstein, who unified energy and matter in a single sinister equation, the pattern is always the same. The Latin word *cogito* comes from *coagitare*, 'to shake together.' The creative act does not create something out of nothing, like the God of the Old Testament; it combines, reshuffles, and relates already existing but hitherto separate ideas, facts, frames of perception, associative contexts. This act of cross-fertilization—or self-fertilization within a single brain—seems to be the essence of creativity. I have proposed for it the term *bisociation*. It is not a pretty word, but it helps us to make a distinction between the sudden leap

---

[3] I owe the term "*Haha* reaction" to Dr. Brennig James's paper, "The Function of Jokes," (unpublished), which he kindly sent me.

of the creative act and the more normal, more pedestrian, associative routines of thinking.

The difference between the two could be described as follows: Orderly thinking (as distinct from daydreaming) is always controlled by certain rules of the game. In the psychological laboratory, the experimenter lays down the rule: 'name opposites.' Then he says 'dark,' and the subject promptly says, 'light.' But if the rule is 'synonyms,' then the subject will associate 'dark' with 'black' or 'night' or 'shadow.' To talk of stimuli in a vacuum is meaningless; what response a stimulus will evoke depends on the game we are playing at the time.

But we do not live in laboratories where the rules of the game are laid down by explicit orders; in normal life, the rules control our thinking unconsciously—and there's the rub. When talking, the laws of grammar and syntax function below the level of awareness, in the gaps between the words. So do certain simple rules of common or garden-variety logic and of courtesy and convention, and also the complex and specialized rules which we call 'frames of reference' or 'universes of discourse' or 'thinking in terms of' this or that—of physiological explanations or ethical value judgments. All thinking is playing a game according to fixed rules and more or less flexible strategies. The game of chess allows you a vast number of strategic choices among the moves permitted by the rules, but there is a limit to them. There are hopeless situations in chess when the most subtle strategies will not save you—short of offering your opponent a jumbo-sized martini. Now in fact there is no rule in chess preventing you from offering your opponent a martini. But making a person drunk while remaining sober oneself is a different sort of game with a different context. Combining the two games is a bisociation. In other words, associative routine means thinking according to a given set of rules, on a single plane, as it were. The bisociative act means combining two different sets of rules, to live on several planes at once.

III   *Three Kinds of Reactions*

I do not mean to belittle the value of law-abiding routines. They lend coherence and stability to behavior and structured order to thought. But they have their obvious limitations. For one thing, every game tends to become monotonous after awhile and fails to satisfy the artist's craving for self-expression and the scientist's search for explanations. In the second place, the world moves on, and new problems arise which cannot be solved within the conventional frames of reference by applying to them the accepted rules of the game. Then a crisis occurs: The position on the scientist's checkerboard is blocked; the artist's vision is blurred; the search is on, the fumbling and groping for that happy combination of ideas—of lodestone and amber—which will lead to the new synthesis.

The Aha Reaction. Gestalt psychologists have coined a word for that moment of truth, the flash of illumination, when bits of the puzzle suddenly click into place. They call it the *Aha* experience. One may regard it as a synonym for the 'Eureka!' cry. Imagine it written on a blackboard, thus:

    Aha

We shall see in a moment the reason for this display. There is an empty panel on each side—for the *Aha* response represents only *one* type of reaction after the bisociative click. There are others. Let me tell my favorite anecdote:

> A nobleman at the court of Louis XV had unexpectedly returned from a journey and, on entering his wife's boudoir, found her in the arms of a bishop. After a short hesitation, the nobleman walked calmly to the window and went through the motions of blessing the people in the street.
> "What are you doing?" cried the anguished wife.
> "Monseigneur is performing my functions," replied the nobleman, "so I am performing his."

Well, some readers will be kind enough to laugh; let us call this the *Haha* reaction:[4]

    Haha   Aha

The Haha Reaction. Now let us inquire into the difference between the *Haha* and the *Aha* reactions. Why do we laugh? Let me try to analyze first the intellectual and then the emotional aspect of this odd reaction. The nobleman's behavior is both unexpected and perfectly logical—but of a logic not usually applied to this type of situation. It is the logic of the division of labor, where the rule of the game is the *quid pro quo*, the give-and-take. But we expected, of course, that his reactions would

---

[4] I owe the term *Haha* reaction to Dr. Brennig James's paper, "The Function of Jokes."

be governed by a quite different logic or rule of the game. It is the interaction between these two mutually exclusive associative contexts, which produces the comic effect. It compels us to perceive the situation at the same time in two self-consistent but habitually incompatible frames of reference; it makes us function on two wavelengths simultaneously, as it were. While this unusual condition lasts, the event is not, as is normally the case, perceived in a single frame of reference but is bisociated with two.

But the unusual condition does not last for long. The act of discovery leads to a lasting synthesis, a *fusion* of the two previously unrelated frames of reference; in the comic bisociation, you have a *collision* between incompatible frames, which for a brief moment cross each other's path. But whether the frames are compatible or not, whether they will collide or merge, depends on subjective factors, on the attitudes of the audience—for, after all, the colliding or merging takes place in the audience's heads. The history of science abounds with examples of discoveries greeted with howls of laughter because they seemed to be a marriage of incompatibles—until the marriage bore fruit and the alleged incompatibility of the partners turned out to derive from prejudice. The humorist, on the other hand, deliberately chooses discordant codes of behavior or universes of discourse to expose their hidden incongruities in the resulting clash. Comic discovery is paradox stated—scientific discovery is paradox resolved.

Let me return for a moment to our poor nobleman blessing the crowd through the window. His gesture was a truly original inspiration. If he had followed the conventional rules of the game, he would have had to beat up or kill the bishop. But at the court of Louis XV, assassinating a Monseigneur would have been considered, if not exactly a crime, still in very bad taste. It simply could not be done; the chessboard was blocked. To solve the problem, that is, to save his face and at the same time to humiliate his opponent, the nobleman had to bring into the situation a second frame of reference, governed by different rules of the game, and combine it with the first. All original comic invention is a creative act, a malicious discovery.

The Emotional Dynamics of Laughter. The emphasis is on malicious, and this brings us from the *logic* of humor to the *emotional factor* in the *Haha* reaction. When the expert humorist tells an anecdote, he creates a certain tension, which mounts as the narrative progresses. But it never reaches its expected climax. The punch line acts like a guillotine, which cuts across the logical development of the situation; it debunks our dramatic expectations, and the tension becomes redundant and is exploded in laughter. To put it differently, laughter disposes of the overflow of emotion which has become pointless, is denied by reason, and has to be somehow worked off along physiological channels of least resistance.[5]

I shall not bore you with physiological explanations because if you look at the coarse and brutal merriment in a tavern scene by William Hogarth or Thomas Rowlandson, you realize at once that the revelers are working off their surplus of adrenalin by contractions of the face muscles, slapping of thighs, and explosive exhalations of breath from the half-closed glottis. The emotions worked off in laughter are aggression, sexual gloating, conscious or unconscious sadism—all operating through the sympathicoadrenal system. On the other hand, when you look at a clever *New Yorker* cartoon, Homeric laughter yields to an amused and rarefied smile; the ample flow of adrenalin has been distilled into a grain of Attic salt. Think, for instance, of that classic definition: What is a sadist? A person who is kind to a masochist.

The word "witticism" is derived from 'wit' in its original sense of 'ingenuity.' The clown is brother to the sage; their domains are continuous, without a sharp dividing line. As we move from the coarse toward the higher forms of humor, the joke shades into epigram and riddle, the comic simile into the discovery of hidden analogies; and the emotions involved show a similar transition. The emotive voltage discharged in coarse laughter is aggression robbed of its purpose; the tension discharged in the *Aha* reaction is derived from an intellectual challenge. It snaps at the moment when the penny drops—when we have solved the riddle hidden in the *New Yorker* cartoon, in a brainteaser, or in a scientific problem.

The Ah Reaction. Let me repeat, the two domains of humor and discovery form a continuum. As we travel across it, from left to center, so to speak, the emotional climate gradually changes from the malice of the jester to the detached objectivity of the sage. If we now continue the journey in the same direction, we find equally gradual transitions into a third domain, that of the artist. The artist hints rather than states, and he poses riddles. So we get a symmetrically reversed transition toward the other end of the spectrum, from highly intellectualized art

---

[5] For a review of the theories on laughter, see Arthur Koestler, *The Act of Creation* (New York: Macmillan, 1969), chap. 1–2; Koestler, *Insight and Outlook* (New York: Macmillan, 1949), pt. 1, Appendix 2.

forms toward the more sensual and emotive, ending in the thought-free beatitude of the oceanic feeling—the cloud of unknowing.

But how does one define the emotional climate of art? How does one classify the emotions which give rise to the experience of beauty? If you leaf through textbooks of experimental psychology, you will not find much mention of it. When behaviorists use the word 'emotion,' they nearly always refer to hunger, sex, rage, and fear and to the related effects of the release of adrenalin. They have no explanations to offer for the curious reaction one experiences when listening to Mozart of looking at the ocean or reading for the first time John Donne's *Holy Sonnets*. Nor will you find in the textbooks a description of the physiological processes accompanying the reaction: the moistening of the eyes, perhaps a quiet overflow of the lachrymal glands, the catching of one's breath, followed by a kind of rapt tranquility, the draining of all tensions. Let us call this the *Ah* reaction and thus complete our trinity.

> *Haha!   Aha   Ah….*

Laughter and weeping, the Greek masks of comedy and tragedy, mark the two extremes of a continuous spectrum; both are overflow reflexes, but they are in every respect physiological opposites. Laughter is mediated by the sympathicoadrenal branch of the autonomous nervous system, weeping by the parasympathetic branch. The first tends to galvanize the body into action; the second tends toward passivity and catharsis. Watch how you breathe when you laugh: long, deep intakes of air, followed by bursts of exhalatory puffs—'Ha, ha, ha.' In weeping, you do the opposite: short, gasping inspirations—sobs—are followed by long, sighing expirations—'a-a-h, aah.'[6]

IV   *Self-Assertion and Self-Transcendence*

In keeping with this, the emotions, which overflow in the *Ah* reaction, are the direct opposites of those exploded in laughter. The latter belong to the familiar adrenergic hunger-rage-fear category; let us call them the *aggressive-defensive* or self-assertive emotions. Their opposites we might call the *self-transcending* or participatory or integrative emotions. They are

---

[6] Cf. Koestler, *The Act of Creation*, 271, 284; and, for a bibliography on the psychology and physiology of weeping, 725–728.

epitomized in what Sigmund Freud called the 'oceanic feeling': When you listen to a Johann Sebastian Bach toccata thundering through the cathedral, you experience that expansion and depersonalization of awareness in which the self seems to dissolve like a grain of salt in a lot of water.

This class of emotions shows a wide range of variety. They may be joyous or sad, tragic or lyrical; but they have a common denominator: the feeling of participation in an experience which transcends the boundaries of the self. That higher entity, of which the self feels a part, to which it surrenders its identity, may be nature, God, the anima mundi, the magic of forms, or the ocean of sound.

The self-assertive emotions are expressed in bodily actions; the self-transcending emotions operate through the passive processes of empathy, rapport, projection, and identification. In laughter, tension is suddenly exploded, emotion debunked; in weeping, it is drained away in a gradual process, which does not break the continuity of mood. The self-transcending emotions do not tend toward action but toward quiescence and catharsis. Respiration and pulse rate are slowed down; 'entrancement' is a step toward the trancelike states induced by contemplative techniques or drugs. The self-transcending emotions cannot be consummated by any specific, voluntary action. You cannot take the mountain panorama home with you; you cannot merge with the infinite by any exertion of the body. To be 'overwhelmed' by awe and wonder, 'enraptured' by a smile, 'entranced' by beauty—each of these verbs expresses a passive surrender. The surplus of emotion cannot be worked off in action; it can be consummated only in internal, visceral, and glandular processes.[7]

The participatory or self-transcending tendencies, these stepchildren of psychology, are as powerful and deeply rooted in man's nature as his self-assertive drives. Freud and Piaget, among others, have emphasized the fact that the very young child does not differentiate between ego and environment. The nourishing breast appears to it as a more intimate possession than the toes of its own body. It is aware of events but not of itself as a separate entity. It lives in a state of mental symbiosis with the outer world, a continuation of the biological symbiosis in the womb. The universe is focused in the self, and the self *is* the universe—a condition which Jean Piaget called 'protoplasmic consciousness.' It may be

---

[7] Ibid., 285–300.

likened to a liquid, fluid universe, traversed by dynamic currents, the rise and fall of physiological needs causing minor storms which come and go without leaving solid traces. Gradually the floods recede, and the first islands of objective reality emerge; the contours grow firmer and sharper; the islands grow into continents, the dry territories of reality are mapped out; but side by side with it, the liquid world coexists, surrounding it, interpenetrating it by canals and inland lakes, the vestigial relics of the erstwhile symbiotic communion. Here, then, we have the origin of that oceanic feeling which the artist and the mystic strive to recapture on a higher level of development, at a higher turn of the spiral.

V   *Art and Self-Transcendence*

Children and primitives are apt to confuse dream and reality; they not only believe in miracles but also believe themselves capable of performing them. When the medicine man disguises himself as the rain god, he produces rain. Drawing a picture of a slain bison assures a successful hunt. This is the ancient unitary source out of which the ritual dance and song, the mystery plays of the Achaeans, and the calendars of the Babylonian priest-astronomers were derived. The shadows in Plato's cave are symbols of man's loneliness; the paintings in the Altamira Caves are symbols of his magic powers.

We have traveled a long way from Altamira and Lascaux, but the artist's inspirations and the scientist's intuitions are still fed by that same unitary source—though by now we should rather call it an underground river. Wishes do not displace mountains, but in our dreams, they still do. Symbiotic consciousness is never completely defeated but merely relegated underground to those unconscious levels in the mental hierarchy where the boundaries of the ego are still fluid and blurred—as blurred as the distinction between the actor and the hero whom he impersonates and with whom the spectator identifies. The actor on the stage is himself and somebody else at the same time—he is both the dancer and the rain god.

Dramatic illusion is the coexistence in the spectator's mind of two universes, which are logically incompatible; his awareness, suspended between the two planes, exemplifies the bisociative process in its most striking form. All the more striking because he produces physical symptoms—palpitations, sweating, or tears—in response to the perils of a Desdemona whom he *knows* to exist merely as a shadow on the television screen or as dry printer's ink in the pages of a book. Yet let Othello but get the hiccups, and instead of coexistence between the two planes juxtaposed in the spectator's mind, you get collision between them. Comic impersonation produces the *Haha* reaction because the parodist arouses aggression and malice; dramatic stagecraft achieves the suspension of disbelief, the coexistence of incompatible planes, because it induces the spectator to identify. It excites the self-transcending and inhibits or neutralizes the self-assertive emotions. Even when fear and anger are aroused in the spectator, these are vicarious emotions, derived from his identification with the hero, which in itself is a self-transcending act. Vicarious emotions aroused in this manner carry a dominant element of sympathy, which facilitates catharsis in conformity with the Aristotelian definition—'through incidents arousing horror and pity to accomplish the purgation of such emotions.' Art is a school of self-transcendence.

We thus arrive at a further generalization: *The* Haha *reaction signals the collision of bisociated contexts; the* Aha *reaction signals their fusion; and the* Ah *reaction signals their juxtaposition.*

This difference is reflected in the quasicumulative progression of science through a series of successive mergers, compared with the quasi-timeless character of art in its continuous restatement of basic patterns of experience in changing idioms. I said 'quasi' because it can be shown that this, too, is a matter of degrees, because the progress of science is not cumulative in the strict sense. It is moving in a dizzy, zigzag course rather than in a straight line.[8] On the other hand, the development of a given art form over a period of time often displays a cumulative progression.[9] I shall return to this in a moment, but first let me briefly mention a few more types of the combinatorial activities which enter into the fabric of art.

VI   *Bisociative Structures in Art*

When we listen to poetry, two frames of reference interact in our minds: one governed by meaning, the other by rhythmic patterns of sound.

---

[8] See T. S. Kuhn, *The Structure of Scientific Revolutions* (Chicago: University of Chicago Press, 1962); K. R. Popper, *The Logic of Scientific Discovery* (London: Hutchinson, 1959).
[9] See E. H. Gombrich, *Art and Illusion* (London: Phaidon Press, 1962).

Moreover, the two frames operate on two different levels of awareness: the first in broad daylight, the other much deeper down. The rhythmic beat of poetry is designed, in the words of Yeats, 'to lull the mind into a waking trance.' Rhythmic pulsation is a fundamental characteristic of life; our ready responses to it arise from the depths of the nervous system, from those archaic strata which reverberate to the shaman's drum and which make us particularly receptive to, and suggestible by, messages which arrive in a rhythmic pattern or are accompanied by such a pattern.

The rhyme has equally ancient roots. It repeats the last syllable of a line. Now the repetition of syllables is a conspicuous phenomenon at the very origins of language. The young child is addicted to babbling, 'obble-gobble,' 'humpty-dumpty,' and so on. In primitive languages, words like 'kala-kala' or 'moku-moku' abound. Closely related to it is association by pure sound. The rhyme is in fact nothing but a glorified pun—two strings of ideas tied together in a phonetic knot. Its ancient origins are revealed in the punning mania of children and in certain forms of mental disorder and in the frequent recurrence of puns in dreams. 'What could be moister than the tears of an oyster?' The statement that the oyster is a wet creature and that therefore its tears must be particularly wet would not make much of an impression, but when meaning is bisociated with sound, there is magic. This is what I meant when I said that routine thinking involves a single matrix, whereas creative thinking always involves more than one plane. Needless to say, it is difficult to identify with an oyster, so the reaction will be *Haha*, not *Ah*.

Thus rhythm and meter, rhyme and euphony, are not artificial ornaments of language but combinations of contemporary, sophisticated frames of reference with archaic and emotionally more powerful games of the mind. In other words, creative activity always implies a *temporary regression* to these archaic levels, while a simultaneous process goes on in parallel on the highest, most articulate and critical level: the poet is like a skin diver with a breathing tube.

The same applies, of course, to poetic imagery. Visual thinking is an earlier form of mental activity than thinking in verbal concepts; we dream mostly in pictures and visual symbols. It has been said that scientific discovery consists in seeing an analogy where nobody has seen one before. When in the *Song of Songs*, Solomon compared the Shulamite's neck to a tower of ivory, he saw an analogy which nobody had seen before; when Harvey compared the heart of a fish to a mechanical pump, he did the same; and when the caricaturist draws a nose like a cucumber, he again does just that. In fact, all combinatorial, bisociative patterns are trivalent—they can enter the service of humor, discovery, or art, as the case may be.

Let me give you another example of this trivalence. Man has always looked at nature by superimposing a second frame on the retinal image—mythological, anthropomorphic, scientific frames. The artist sees in terms of his medium—stone, clay, charcoal, pigment—and in terms of his preferential emphasis on contours or surfaces, stability or motion, curves or cubes. So, of course, does the caricaturist, only his motives are different. And so does the scientist. A geographical map has the same relation to a landscape that a character sketch has to a face. Every diagram or model, every schematic or symbolic representation of physical or mental processes is an unemotional caricature of reality—at least unemotional in the sense that the bias is not of an obvious kind, although some models of the human mind as a conditioned-reflex auto-mation seem to be crude caricatures inspired by unconscious bias.

In the language of behaviorist psychology, we would have to say that Cézanne, glancing at a landscape, receives a stimulus, to which he responds by putting a dab of paint on the canvas, and that is all there is to it. But in fact, the two activities take place on two different planes. The stimulus comes from one environment, the distant land-scape. The response acts on a different environment, a square surface of 10 by 15 inches. The two environments obey two different sets of laws. An isolated brushstroke does not represent an isolated detail in the landscape. There are no point-to-point correspondences between the two planes; each obeys a different rule of the game. The artist's vision is bifocal, just as the poet's voice is bivocal, as he bisociates sound and meaning.

VII *Extraconscious Factors in Discovery*

Let me return for a moment to science. I said at the beginning of this paper that the essence of discovery is the coagitation, the shaking together, of already existing frames of reference or areas of knowledge. Now we arrive at the crucial question: Just how does the creative mind hit upon that happy combination of ideas, which nobody had thought of combining before?

Artists are inclined to believe that scientists reason in strictly rational, precise verbal terms. They do, of course, nothing of the sort. In 1945, a famous inquiry was organized by Jacques Hadamard among eminent mathematicians in America to find out their working methods.[10] The results showed that all of them, with only two exceptions, thought neither in verbal terms nor in algebraic symbols but relied on visual imagery of a vague, hazy kind. Einstein was among those who answered the questionnaire; he wrote:

> The words of the language as they are written or spoken do not seem to play any role in my mechanism of thought, which relies on more or less clear images of a visual and some of a muscular type. It seems to be that what you call full consciousness is a limiting case which can never be fully accomplished because consciousness is a narrow thing.

Einstein's statement is typical. On the testimony of those original thinkers who have taken the trouble to record their methods of work, *not only verbal thinking but conscious thinking in general plays only a subordinate part in the brief, decisive phase of the creative act itself.* Their virtually unanimous emphasis on spontaneous intuitions and hunches of unconscious origin, which they are at a loss to explain, suggests that the role of strictly rational and verbal processes in scientific discovery has been vastly overestimated since the Age of Enlightenment. There are always large chunks of irrationality embedded in the creative process, not only in art (where we are ready to accept it) but in the exact sciences as well.

The scientist who, facing his blocked problem, regresses from precise verbal thinking to vague visual imagery seems to follow William Wordsworth's advice: "Often we have to get away from speech in order to think clearly." Words crystallize thoughts, but a crystal is no longer a liquid. Language can act as a screen between the thinker and reality. Creativity often starts where language ends, that is, by regressing to preverbal levels, to more fluid and uncommitted forms of mental activity.

Now I do not mean, of course, that there is a little Socratic demon housed in the scientist's or artist's skull who does his homework for him; nor should one confuse unconscious mentation with Freud's primary process. The primary process is defined by Freud as devoid of logic,

---

[10] J. Hadamard, *The Psychology of Invention in the Mathematical Field* (Princeton: Princeton University Press, 1949).

governed by the pleasure principle, apt to confuse perception and hallucination, and accompanied by massive discharges of affect. It seems that between this very primary process and the so-called secondary process governed by the reality principle, we must interpolate a whole hierarchy of cognitive structures, which are not simply mixtures of primary and secondary, but are autonomous systems in their own right, each governed by a distinct set of rules. The paranoid delusion, the dream, the daydream, free association, the mentalities of children of various ages, and of primatives at various stages, should not be lumped together, for each has its own logic or rules of the game. But while clearly different in many respects, all these forms of mentation have certain features in common, since they are ontogenetically, and perhaps phylogenetically, older than those of the civilized adult. They are less rigid, more tolerant, and more ready to combine seemingly incompatible ideas and to perceive hidden analogies between cabbages and kings. One might call them 'games of the underground,' because if not kept under restraint, they would play havoc with the routines of disciplined thinking. But under exceptional conditions, when disciplined thinking is at the end of its tether, a temporary indulgence in these underground games may suddenly produce a solution—some farfetched, reckless combination which would be beyond the reach of, or seem to be unacceptable to, the sober, rational mind. The place for the rendezvous of ideas is underground.

Illumination and Catharsis. What I have been trying to suggest is that the common pattern underlying scientific discovery and artistic inspiration is a temporary regression, culminating in the bisociative act, that is, the bringing together of previously separate frames of perception or universes of discourse. I suppose that is what Ernst Kris meant by his frequently quoted but somewhat cryptic remarks about regression in the service of the ego.[11] The boundaries between science and art, between the *Ah* reaction and the *Aha* reaction, are fluid, whether we consider architecture or cooking or psychiatry or the writing of history. There is nowhere a sharp break where witticism changes into wit or where science stops and art begins. Science, the hoary cliché goes, aims at truth, art at beauty. But the criteria of truth, such as verification by experiment, are not as hard and clean as we tend to believe, for the same experimental data can often be interpreted in more than one way.

---

[11] E. Kris, *Psychoanalytic Explorations in Art* (New York: International Universities Press, 1952).

That is why the history of science echoes with as many bitter and venomous controversies as the history of literary criticism. Moreover, the verification of a discovery comes after the act; the creative act itself is for the scientist, as it is for the artist, a leap into the dark, where both are equally dependent on their fallible intuitions. The greatest mathematicians and physicists have confessed that, at those decisive moments when taking the plunge, they were guided not by logic but by a sense of beauty, which they were unable to define. Vice versa, painters and sculptors, not to mention architects, have always been guided, and often obsessed, by scientific or pseudo-scientific theories and criteria of truth: the golden section, the laws of perspective, Dürer and Leonardo's laws of proportion representing the human body, Cézanne's doctrine that everything in nature is modeled on the cylinder and cone, Braque's alternative theory that cubes should be substituted for spheres, Le Corbusier's modulator theory, Buckminster Fuller's geodesic domes. The same goes, of course, for literature, from the formal laws imposed on Greek tragedy to the various recent and contemporary schools—romanticism, classicism, naturalism, symbolism, stream of consciousness, socialist realism, the *nouveau roman*, and so forth—not to mention the intricate rules of harmony and counterpoint in music. The English physicist Paul Dirac, a Nobel laureate, said recently, "It is more important to have beauty in one's equations than that they should fit experiment."[12] The counterpart to this is the statement by Georges-Pierre Seurat on his pointillist method, "They see poetry in what I have done. No, I apply my method, and that is all there is to it." In other words, the experience of truth, however subjective, must be present for the experience of beauty to arise, and vice versa: An elegant solution of a problem gives rise in the connoisseur to the experience of beauty. Intellectual illumination and emotional catharsis are complementary aspects of an indivisible process.

VIII   *Regression and Rebound*

I would like to conclude this discussion with a remark, which is no more than a hint, to place the phenomena of human creativity into a wider biological perspective. I have talked of temporary regression, followed

---

[12] P. A. M. Dirac, "Evolution of the Physicist's Picture of Nature," *Scientific American* 208 (1963): 45–53.

by a rebound, as a characteristic of the creative act. Now biologists are familiar with a similar phenomenon on lower levels of the evolutionary scale. I mean the phenomenon of regeneration.[13] It consists in the reshaping of bodily structures—or the reorganization of functions—in response to traumatic challenges from the environment. It involves the regression of bodily tissues to a quasi-embryonic state and the release of genetic growth potentials which are normally under restraint in the adult organism—just as in the moment of discovery the creative potentials of the earlier forms of intuitive thinking are released from the censorship of the conscious adult mind. Psychotherapy reflects the same process on a higher level. It aims at inducing a temporary regression in the emotionally traumatized patient in the hope that he will regenerate into a pattern, which eliminates the conflict. The creative act could be called a kind of do-it-yourself psychotherapy where the traumatic challenge is intellectual instead of emotional, for instance, new data which shake the foundation of a well-established theory, observations which contradict each other, problems which cause frustration and conflict—or the artist's perplexities in trying to communicate his experiences through the blocked matrices of conventional techniques.

And finally, we find the same pattern reflected in the death-and-resurrection motif in mythology, in Toynbee's *Withdrawal and Return*, in Jung's *Night Journey*. Joseph is thrown into a well, Mohammed goes out into the desert, Jesus is resurrected from the tomb, Jonah is reborn out of the belly of the whale. The mystic's dark night of the soul reflects the same archetype. It appears to be a principle of universal validity in the evolution of individuals and cultures.

---

[13] Koestler, *The Act of Creation*, 447–474.

CHAPTER FIFTEEN

CREATIVITY IN SCIENCE[1]

Rom Harré

I   *Novelty and Creativity*

To create is to produce or generate what did not exist before, and most importantly, it is to produce not only an individual that did not exist before but one of a new and hitherto unknown kind. In science the most obvious product of creativity is a sort of discourse, the flow of theory. But theory is itself a secondary product, a description of potent things and products which produce the phenomena we experience. And yet, at least initially, the potent things and processes described in theory are not part of that experience. It is in our conceiving of ideas about them, by imagining possible potent things in which and among which causal activity occurs, that creativity is exercised.

But if theory is to provide understanding, it must be intelligible, and that intelligibility must derive ultimately from the intelligibility of the novel entities and forms conceived in the creative scientific imagination. So novelty must be tempered by connection with the known, or at least with that amongst the known which we take to be intelligible. What it is for something to be intelligible will emerge in the course of the discussion. But the only possible connection that would allow both intelligibility and novelty is that of analogy. New things and processes must be like known things and processes in some ways, but must be unlike them in others. The forms of unlikeness may be very various. Unlikeness may derive from the absence of some common property, as photons have no rest mass, or it may derive from a combination of a set of properties never found together in ordinary experience, as the spatio-temporal continuum must be both continuous and infinitely divisible. Sometimes, as in the latter case, the resolution of the consequent

---

[1] Originally published in *The Concept of Creativity in Science and Art*, eds. D. Dutton and M. Krausz (The Hague/Boston/London: Martinus Nijhoff Publishers, 1981), 19–46, *all rights reserved*.

paradoxical intuitions is achieved only by proofs of consistency created
in the formal domain of mathematics.

In this chapter, I shall follow the creative scientific imagination in
some of its acts and examine some of the constraints and disciplines
which have developed to banish fantasy from the theorizing of scientists.
These, we shall see, derive from stricter and stricter ideas of what is
possible. And in doing this we shall be pursuing the philosophical issue
of realism, since we shall soon confront the problem that the realm of
the real seems to extend far beyond the realm of the experienceable.

II   *False Theories of Creativity*

The importance of creativity will vary with different views of science.
In a simple inductivist or positivist view of science, the passage from
fact to theory is achieved by a purely formal addition of generality to
observed fact, and logical axiomatization of the 'laws' so derived.
Scientific creativity is then, at bottom, no more than formal invention.
To someone taking science seriously as it appears to be, namely an
intellectual enterprise in which ever-new content is added to the rev-
elations of experience, the creativity involved in the invention of new
concepts can only be an illusion of the advancement of possible experience for an inductivist. On the positivist view, this burgeoning of new
concepts can have at best a literary purpose, providing a kind of attractive appearance to propositional structures and linking concepts that
have only logical importance as bridges from one observation statement
to another. Indeed, the creative act is strictly dispensable, since all that
is essential to science is contained in descriptive concepts and the
logical and grammatical particles that are the connectives of their
structure as a discourse, if we follow the inductivist-positivist view.

According to realist views of science, the concepts of theory do refer
to possible real processes in real structures of things, and thus the
introduction of a novel concept enlarges the possibility of experience
and adds something to our conception of the world. But realist philosophers of science differ fundamentally on the issue of whether the
appearance of a new theory or of its component concepts in the
scientific community, and presumably once in the mind of an individual scientist, is a process which is susceptible to rational analysis,
and then to reduction of the obedient following of certain canons.
Thus some realist philosophers hold a purely psychological (and thus

serendipitous) theory of scientific creation. According to Arthur Koestler in *The Sleepwalkers*,[2] scientific invention is some kind of accidental occurrence mediated by psychological processes, mysterious to the inventor himself, and amenable only to the kind of analysis he provides of Kepler's mind: part history, part biography, and part psychology. But his analysis of Kepler's intellectual life lays bare certain preparations, which anyone must undertake if he is to hope for a 'discovery,' in the sense of the invention of a new concept bringing order to the data. Kepler *already* had the ellipse, as a form, both geometrical and analytical, before he could creatively apply it to the problem of making sense of the orbit of Mars. There is then a two-stage process, the invention or acquisition of the required concept, and then the novel use of this concept bringing out something new in the data. In just this way in microsociology, once we have acquired Goffman's concept of the 'with,' the symbolically displayed pairing, etc., of people in public places, the world is suddenly full of withs.[3] And what is more, not only must the specific form of the image or concept be present to the mind of the creator, but it must inhabit a mind prepared for that kind of form, as Kepler's was prepared for *an* orbit of harmonious proportions, by his adherence to a general metaphysics, or supra-theory, according to which all the processes of nature were compounded of processes involving forms having harmonious proportions. As I shall argue in detail later, Kepler's situation corresponds precisely with the scheme for rational analysis of scientific invention which merges from the theory I shall propose. Kepler had already studied a highly specific analogue of the orbit of Mars, namely the geometrical ellipse, and was thoroughly acquainted with its properties, and with the various consequences which followed from such properties as the ratio of semi-diameters. And, from his earliest studies, he had been convinced of the verisimilitude of a world picture of the universe, in terms of which the attempt to find a regular geometrical form to correspond to and represent the orbit of Mars made perfect sense.

In the same vein, the fallibilist theory of Karl Popper rightly lays stress on the role of invention in science and the role of the imagination in that invention.[4] But the discipline under which that faculty works,

---

[2] Arthur Koestler, *The Sleepwalkers: A History of Man's Changing Vision of the Universe* (London: Hutchinson, 1959).

[3] E. Goffman, *Relations in Public* (New York: Harper and Row, 1972).

[4] K. R. Popper, *Conjectures and Refutations* (London: Routledge and Kegan Paul, 1963).

making it the imagination of a scientist, rather than the fantasy of a crank, is left unanalyzed by Popper, and assigned to the 'psychological.' This unfortunate move is clearly connected with Popper's very narrow vein of rationality, identified by him throughout his works with adherence to the canons of deductive formal logic. Of course the way invention occurs in science must be a topic for psychological study alone, and can conform to no schema, and have no canons of rationality, if rationality is confined to the principles of deductive logic. But one must take great care to distinguish the bogus claim to rationality of the inductivist, who purports to pass beyond experience in the dimension of generality, and the genuine claim of the realist, who sees the imagination of scientists generating conceptions of things, properties and processes that pass beyond any actual experience, not because they make some claim to universality, but rather provide an inkling of the way the world is here and now in those regions like the very small and the very distant, to which we have neither sensory nor instrumental access. The defender of the rationality of creativity seeks the canons of reasonableness in accordance with which such imaginative constructions of conceptions of the unknown can be rated proper or improper, plausible or implausible.

III   *Science as Icon of Natural Structures and Powers*

An adequate theory of scientific creativity can come only from a properly constituted view of what is being created. As in most issues in the philosophy of science, all will depend upon how far one regards the analysis of theories to be primarily a matter of laying bare their logical form. This article is written from very much the view that little of interest to the understanding of science and its modes of thought can be found by a search for logical form. Scientific thought cannot be understood in terms of the content-free principles of formal logic, be they deductive or inductive, if indeed there are any content-free principles of the latter sort. So if we regard theories, primarily, to be considered as formally ordered structures of propositions, we shall look only for the sources and means of creation of those structures. We have already seen how this leads to a stultifying psychologism.

In my view, a theory must be considered as it conforms to certain principles of content, and it must be analyzed for philosophical purposes, so as to bring out the various sorts of propositions it involves, classified by reference to the kind of thing they assert about the world. The logical form of such propositions and the logical structure of the discourse within which they appear is not, of course, irrelevant to our understanding of them, but, I hold, is far from exhaustively determining all that a philosopher might want to say about them.[5] Thus, for example, a causal proposition cannot be identified by its form alone, say that of a conditional, but is only truly causal if it explicitly or implicitly refers to an existing natural agent potent to bring about the causation when unconstrained and suitably activated. Thus, 'ignition of petrol causes combustion' is intelligible as a causal proposition on two counts, neither of which can be dispensed with: it has the form 'If *i* then *c*,' and it refers to 'petrol' an inflammable liquid. Our understanding of the proposition as causal depends upon our understanding of petrol as inflammable, that is, as something which naturally tends to burn in natural conditions when lighted.

Let us first ask in the most general way, but with more care than is usually applied to these matters: What is the content of a theory? We shall avoid, for the moment, the few very general, very atypical theories, that one finds in fundamental physics, be it classical or modern, and stay with the kind of theory that is typical of chemistry, or medicine, or physiology, or social psychology (of the reformed, ethogenic, sort). Commonly then, in addressing a theory, we confront a discourse which seems to be describing some arrangement of things with certain definite properties, the modulations and changes of which are responsible for the phenomena we are theorizing about. It might be that the distribution and form of animals and plants, both geographically and geologically, requires explanation. Charles Darwin and Alfred Russel Wallace produced theoretical discourses describing a process, which, repeated billions of times, was responsible for the phenomena, as they saw them, in the light of the theory.

Already much has emerged. Notice first how readily one slips into speaking as much of an explanation as a theory in this sort of example. I shall return to this point. Notice too that the way the observations of naturalists present themselves to the great biologists, the form of order they saw in them (such as spotting the gradation of the size and form of the beaks of Galapagos finches) was a product of holding the theory. This is not just a psychological observation, and we must pause to

---

[5] Rom Harré, "Surrogates for Necessity," *Mind* 82 (1973): 358–380.

examine it further, for here a crucial moment of creativity occurs, one liable to be overlooked in our awe in the face of the invention of the grand design.

Recall, if you will, the discussion of the inductivist view of science and the narrow margin of creativity it allowed, doing science simply being the generalization of regularly recurring observational correlations. Mill, the hero of the inductivist view, describes this process as generalizing over similar cases. The important point to notice here is that he takes similarity for granted. The development, skeleton by skeleton, from eohippus to horse, is similar, for evolutionists, to the development, beak by beak, of one species of finch into another. But why should they be regarded as similar? And in what respects? Their similarity for evolutionists is problematic, and needs to be explained. Taking it for granted, Mill sees scientific method as imposing only a purely formal concept, generality, upon our scientific knowledge.

We must turn to the hero of neo-Kantian realism, William Whewell, for a resolution of what is problematic in the inductivist view.[6] For Whewell, scientific method is creative not only as to logical form, generality, but also as to content. A science, he holds, is produced by the existence of an 'idea,' an organizing conception, which is brought to the phenomena, and creates both the possibility of perceiving similarities, which bring the phenomena into the same class, and supplies the generalities, all at once. In controversy with John Stuart Mill, he cited Johannes Kepler's discovery of the orbit of Mars, involving the ellipse, not as a generalization of the known positions of the planet in the star charts, but as a prior idea which provided organization to those positions (in some cases this may be sufficiently sensory to be called a gestalt) under which they became moments in the career of a planet along an elliptical orbit. So the gradation of the beaks of finches is both a product of, and evidence for, the idea of continuous evolution of species one from another.

But the Darwin-Wallace theory was not just the idea of gradual but accumulated change, the idea of organic evolution, which had been held in other forms prior to their development of it. Their theory purported to describe a process occurring over and over again in nature. But neither had observed this process; indeed, it has scarcely been observed today, outside the glass walls of drosophila boxes. (Ford's

---

[6] See W. Whewell, *The Philosophy of the Inductive Sciences*, new ed. (London: Cass, 1967).

butterflies and industrial melanism are recent exceptions.) How could Darwin and Wallace describe the process of evolution in such detail if they had never, and given the time span of the process never could, observe it? What were they describing? What stood between them and the almost untold aeons of minute changes in millions of species on millions of hectares of the earth's surface that they reduced to order? Clearly they shared an imaginative conception of the organic history of the earth and the natural forces and processes that shaped it. I am not interested, for the moment, in the question of from whence they derived that conception, but in the role of the conception itself.

It is this conception which stands between their limited experience of organic biology, and the utterly out-of-reach organic history of the earth. This again is not just a psychological observation about the personal thought forms of a couple of Victorian giants. By looking very carefully at the form such conceptions commonly take, we shall see how the necessary intermediary between ignorance and the unexperienceable is created, and so how theories can come to have content beyond the description of experienced phenomena. The conception which lies between ignorance and reality I shall call an *icon* of that reality. It is not a delineation since that reality is usually not known, though it may come to be known. In general, a theory describes an icon as a representative and surrogate for that reality. I choose the word 'icon' in preference to the more commonly used 'model,' since the latter has long ceased to be univocal. I also want to draw attention to the frequent sensory or imaginative character of the bearers of conceptions of unexperienced reality, though as we shall see, these develop away from the sensory into abstract forms. Darwin and Wallace 'formed a picture' of the organic process, a picture which by their description of an icon of the organic process they convey to us. Of course, psychological idiosyncrasy is such that no psychological generalizations about how their conception of nature was present to their minds or ours, their readers, is intended. In particular, I do not intend to suggest that they or we must literally visualize the icon of reality at the heart of a theory. But by keeping a sensory connection, by the use of this word, I want to emphasize that nature must be conceived as a process in time, and a structure in space, of individual organisms, geographical and meteorological forms, ecological interrelation, and the like. Darwin and Wallace attempted to conceive of the reality and to convey their conception to us, though neither they nor we can experience that reality.

What then of the supporting evidence that these great men cite in their works? What relation does it bear to the conception of unexperienced processes responsible for all the phenomena of organic change? We know from the arguments of the Humean tradition that it can provide no logical support for the generalization of the theory or for the claim of the theory to universality within its domain. To understand the role of evidence in science we need to take a radically different view of it, more radical than Popper's fallibilism. I shall try to show by examples that a great scientist cites supporting evidence, not as premises or even as evidence in the legal sense, but as anecdotes, illustrative of the power of the theory to make certain widely-selected phenomena intelligible. Conceiving of the citation of evidence as anecdote brings the explanatory power of the theory to the fore, and raises the philosophical problem of what it is to make the phenomenon intelligible. So Darwin's account of the gradations of beak shape among finches from different islands in the Galapagos group appears not as a premise from which his theory might be inferred, together with all the other available evidence, but rather as an anecdote illustrative of the power of the icon to make the phenomena intelligible.

This can be shown in other cases in just as striking a fashion. In a currently influential work, *Asylums*, Erving Goffman sets out a theory of institutions, based upon the idea that an institution should be conceived both as a device for fulfilling its official functions, that is, as a hospital is a place where the staff cure people, and as a setting for the staging of dramas of character, where personas are created and defended, so that a hospital is a place where people perfect dramatic performances as 'surgeon,' 'nurse,' and, of course, 'patient,' learning to conform to and excel in these dramaturgically conceived 'roles.'[7] In his discussion of those closed institutions he calls 'asylums,' Goffman cites instance after instance of people doing things that become intelligible only if conceived on his dramaturgical model, his icon of the nunnery or the barracks or the hospital as a theatre. Each citation is an anecdote, in which the power of the dramaturgical theory to make phenomena intelligible is illustrated. At the same time, it becomes plain that certain structures and textures of life in such places become visible,

---

[7] Erving Goffman, *Asylums: Essays on the Social Situation of Mental Patients and Other Inmates* (Garden City, N.Y.: Anchor Books, 1961).

stand out from other phenomena, only if that life is examined by someone with that icon of the institution in mind.

I can sum up this theory of science in the phrase 'icon and anecdote,' bound into a single discourse by the explanatory power of the icon, its power to make our experience of the world intelligible, since above all our scientific icons are depictions of the productive processes which bring the patterns of phenomena into being. We must also keep in mind that our experience is only wholly what it is when we conceive of the world that way. Thus, understanding its genesis makes the ordering of experience in classificatory systems intelligible. In science, for every phenotype we find convenient to extract from experience, we must conceive a genotype, for every nominal essence we use in practice to select and identify things and samples of materials, we must conceive a real essence. I was pleased to read in Claude Lévi-Strauss the following elegant statement of the icon and anecdote theory:

> Social science is no more founded on the basis of events than physics is founded on sense data: the object is to construct a model and study its property and its different reactions in laboratory conditions in order later to apply the observations to the interpretation of empirical happenings which may be far removed from what has been forecast.[8]

Creativity, then, must be at its most seminal in the origin of conceptions of the unexperienced, icons of the reality beyond but productive of our experience.

But why not just study the discourse, and never mind about the icon? First, it is *assumed* that a discourse can contain all that is in the object of the discourse, so that all relations relevant to the internal structure of the discourse are supposed to be somehow present within it. But there may be relations in the discourse, relations which we know and use, say between predicates, where two predicates permeate each other's sense, or relations of analogy between predicates deployed in an argument, which are dependent on prior icon relations, appearing in the icon as coexisting properties, or likeness and unlikeness between things. Thus, the co-presence of a pair of properties in an icon becomes the source, in a diachronic process of meaning assimilation, of synchronic internal relations between two predicates, relations which may be quite crucial to understanding how the discourse is structured and how its development would be justified. Such relations can never be

---

[8] C. Lévi-Strauss, *Triste Tropiques*, trans. J. and D. Weightman (London: Cape, 1974).

reached by the analysis of a discourse into its logical form, since *a fortiori* logical form extracts from all material relations between predicates, and yet it may be just those relations upon which the coherence of the discourse as a scientific theory rests.

IV   *Two Epistemological Regions*

'Beyond our experience,' you say. 'But surely traditional epistemology teaches us that we have no knowledge of what is beyond our experience.' There are two epistemological barriers, which scientists regularly overleap in their practice. The one is that erected by positivists between actual and possible experience, the other by the critical philosophy between all actual and possible experience and the realm beyond all possible experience. I shall try to show that our powers and techniques of creativity are such that we can, at first tentatively and cautiously, and finally boldly, trust ourselves to pass beyond them, and dwell in thought, in worlds accessible only to our creative imagination.

The realm of actual experience is limited in two ways. We are confined to the senses we actually possess, and invariants we can express between them, so hand, eye, and ear conspire to provide our experience of *a* bell. But without conception, perception is blind. And what we can actually identify within and across our sensory fields depends upon the sort of concepts with which we are mentally prepared for the world. As Kant had it and contemporary psychology confirms, our experience is a product of schematic ordering and supplementing our sensations, the schemata being of conceptual and perhaps even of a linguistic origin.[9] All this is commonplace. But it is not difficult to imagine things, and structures and processes and properties, that are too far, too small, too fast, or too slow, or even too big to be experienced by us as we are presently constituted, though the Gibsonian invariants in the objecthood of these entities are just the same invariants as in the objects of ordinary experience. Locke talks of what we might see with microscopic eyes, or hear with a more acute sense of hearing, and Peter Geach has speculated on the colors we would see were our eyes sensitive to a broader spectrum of electromagnetic radiation. In this way we can

---

[9] See J. J. Gibson, *The Senses Considered as Perceptual Systems* (London: George Allen and Unwin, 1968).

conceive of a realm of possible experiences, and populate it in our imagination with objects undergoing processes which we do not, but might, experience.

But theories describe icons of structures and processes which would be experienced within that very realm. Kepler conceived of a fine structure for the snowflake which would be a natural form of packing for minute ice particles (water molecules, if neat little spheres) and which would, if much repeated, yield the universal hexagon. August Kekulé conceived of a structure in space in which the carbon atoms of benzene would form a stable ring, and William Harvey completed his sanguinary plumbing with minute imagined vessels, closing the hydraulic circuit, while Jan Baptist Van Helmont conceived of disease as the invasion of the body by an army of invisible minute organisms. These men populated a world of possible experience with fabulous creatures of their imagination just as Mohammedans filled the air with djinni, Descartes ignited a furnace in the heart, and Immanuel Velikovsky supposed a radically different history for the earth. So entering a realm of possible experience in the imagination is fraught with hazard, for the imagination is as capable of fantasy as of sober speculation. I shall return to examine the discipline to which it is subjected in science and from which we shall extract the fragments of a creative criterion. It is because of the existence and acknowledgment, and ultimate justifiability, of this discipline that we can override the extremes of positivism, which would have us conceive of science as no more than the 'mnemonic reproduction of facts in thought.' Let us call the activity of thought in populating the realm of possible experience the work of the reproductive imagination.

But the scientific imagination does not confine itself to the same realm of creation as is continuous with the realm of perception. It attempts to conceive of the structure of the world beyond all possible experience. Scientific thinkers are driven to attempt this ultimate barrier to knowledge by two factors. The first is simple. Our ordinary experience is full of instances of phenomena whose effects are inexplicable by any work of the reproductive imagination. Electric and magnetic phenomena are the most striking examples. We are simply not equipped with sense organs sensitive to the magnetic influence.

First attempts to solve the problem of the mechanism of the magnetic influence involved the work of the imagination at its reproductive stage, leading to a proliferation of magnetic fluids, particles and the like, clearly denizens of the realm of possible experience. Norman Gilbert went further. Gilbert's imagination leapt the barrier of all possible experience, leading him to postulate the *orbis virtutis*, a shaped, structured field of potentials or directive powers. A structured field of *powers* was something, though spatially extended and temporally enduring, that was clearly not, as such, an object of possible experience, given our lack of magnetic sensibility. Eventually Michael Faraday offered to the visual sense a picturable icon in the lines of force technique for representing the field.

Not only is the perception of the magnetic influence beyond the range of any of our sensory fields, but magnetism, like electricity and gravity, forces the creative imagination to the transcendental stage, since there is a conceptual, not just a contingent, difficulty about the perception of fields. A field is a distribution of potentials, and though we speak of the energy of the field at a point, that energy is not manifested in any kind of action. Thus a field is *a fortiori* imperceptible, its existence known only from its manifestations, and from the presence of field generators, like conductors carrying a current, iron atoms, lumps of matter, and the like, the laws of structure of whose produced fields we have discovered by examining the manifestations of the field on other similar occasions. The icons which represent fields, like rotating tubes of moving, elastic fluids, are not representative of objects or processes in the realm of possible experience, and to suppose them to be so would be a major epistemological error.

But the matter is more complicated. The transcendental imagination is required to generate not only distributed potentials, but to conceive an intermediary between potential and action, not as far beyond possible experience as the potential, but in its realm. At some definite point in the room there is a gravitational potential. But at this moment no test body is at that point. Suppose we now bring a test body to that point, say an alabaster egg, and support it there on a platform. There is still no action, but since action is now possible if the platform is removed, we are obliged to postulate another entity—the tendency to fall acquired by the alabaster egg from the gravitational field. We know that the egg acquires the tendency from the field, since on the moon, for example, we have good reason to think that the egg's tendency to fall will be much diminished, so the tendency is not an intrinsic property of the egg. And we can easily check whether the egg has indeed acquired the tendency by removing the platform and seeing if, indeed, the egg does fall. If we replace the platform by a hand under the egg we might claim to be experiencing the tendency of the egg to fall, but we could hardly claim that it is an experience of the potential of the field, since that potential will be there when the egg is removed, and then we feel no tendency for downward fall. The tendency, then, is not so far from the edge of the boundary of all possible experience as is the potential, and may indeed be held to within the realm of possible experience if the experience of weight and pressure to which we apply our powers of resistance, frustrating action, is accepted as the experience of a tendency, and I cannot think of any argument that would oblige us to deny this.

Contemplating the egg has led us to a complex icon of the whole situation, and in supposing it to be a delineation of the real, the subsequent fall of the egg becomes intelligible, as does the dent it makes in the velvet cushion upon which it usually rests. There are two material things, the earth and the egg, and two immaterial things, the gravitational field, our conception of which is certainly a product of the imagination in its transcendental phase, and the tendency caused in the egg by the power of the field, a thing arguably on the border of the realm of possible experience.

V   *Two Acts of Creative Imagination*

I shall try to show that though the creative imagination of scientists is, in a certain sense, free, and indeed we shall come to see in exactly what sense, nevertheless, analytical schemata can be constructed to represent the dynamics of concept-construction, in an idealized form, and from which canons, exemplified in rules, can be abstracted. The essential point to be grasped, in considering the acts of the imagination in its reproductive phase, is that in producing an icon of a possible reality, the imagination is not modeling something known, but something which is in its inner nature unknown. We know how the mysterious structures and things behave, since they have produced the patterns of phenomena we wish to make intelligible, so at least our icon must depict a possible being which behaves analogously to the unknown real being.

But simply to conceive possible realities in terms of their behavior is no advance on positivism, since we already know the behavior patterns of things and express these in the laws of nature. The task of the reproductive imagination is deeper, for it must enable us to generate a conception of the nature of the objects which behave exactly like, or in various degrees analogously to, the real things actually in the world. The forms of thought involved in this act of the reproductive imagination can be idealized and schematized by distinguishing between the subject of the conception, what the icon is a model *of*, and the source of the conception, what the icon is modeled *on*. Since the nature of the subject is unknown in the sense of beyond all actual experience, the relation between subject and icon can be mediated only by likeness of behavior: a swarm of molecules behaves like a real gas behaves, a person in a shop behaves like an actor playing 'person in a shop,' the evolutionary process produces results like a plant breeder produces. But the creative act of the reproductive imagination is to produce an icon of the unknown nature of the real world, and this icon must be at least capable of being recognized and understood as a plausible depiction of a possible generating mechanism for the patterns of behavior whose explanation is our problem. So if we imagine an evolutionary process as consisting of minute variations in form and function generation by generation, and certain of these variations leading to greater reproductive rates in their possessors, we have conceived a mechanism (or at least the rough outlines of a mechanism) which would generate the pattern we call 'the evolution of species,' which is itself a product of an act of structuring upon the individual bits of knowledge about form and structures of individual organic specimens.

But the natures of things imagined and the generative mechanisms they severally constitute must be plausible, both as generators of the observed patterns and as possible real existents. Thus, not any sources will do. Sources of models, as icons of reality, must conform to two criteria:

(1) They must be the kinds of things, structures, processes, and properties the current world picture regards as admissible existents—gases rather than imponderable fluids (1800), material atoms rather than atmospheres of heat (1850), electric charges rather than solid atoms (1920), neural networks rather than mental substance (1960), and so on. The metaphysics of science consists in the discussion of the coherence and plausibility of the world pictures, literally conceptions of structures, that occupy space and endure for a time, and any possible systems they may form, which serve as general sources for conceptions of possible realities, though, in one of the examples I have cited, that of elementary electric charges, we are on the borders of possible experience.

(2) Having thus conceived proper kinds of things, we need to be able to imagine plausible laws for their behavior. And we find such laws, or closely analogous laws, in existing science. Electrons obey, *for us*, Coulomb's law, the law obeyed by the charges on suspended pith balls. Gas molecules obey Isaac Newton's laws of motion, the blood in Harvey's imagined tubules obeys the ordinary laws of circulating fluids. It is thus that the disciplined imagination works in reproducing a version of experienced reality in the realm of possible experience. This kind of representation may, in certain cases, turn out to be not just a representation to fill a gap but a depiction of reality itself.

But what about the human imagination in its transcendental employment, its transcendental phase so to speak? The first point to notice is that the behavioral constraint is the same in both phases. The world as conceived beyond all possible experience must behave just as the real world behaves, or in a very similar manner. So the dispositions we assign to reality in our imagination must be closely analogous to the dispositions we find the real world to have. But if these dispositions are to be grounded, that is, to be powers and liabilities, dispositions grounded in the nature of things, must we not try to conceive of natures of things the details of which *must* lie beyond the boundary of all possible experience, and if that nature is beyond all possible experience, how are we to conceive it? Yet it is my contention that physicists, cosmologists, and psychologists both can and do achieve creative acts of the imagination in the transcendental phase of activity, and that we can follow them. How is this possible?

The first point to notice is that the world beyond all possible experience can share one kind of attribute with the objects of the world of possible experience, namely structure. It is this attribute that makes for the possibility of intelligibility of conceptions of that world, and of course for its mathematical description. Objects in the experienceable world must have both sensory qualities, or considered in themselves, at least the power to manifest themselves sensorily, and they must have structure (structure which need not be, though it often is, spatial), while processes in that world, to rise above the dead level of imperceptible uniformity, must have both powers of sensory manifestation within thresholds that allow us to say they have structure in time. (Compare the difficulty that was once experienced in knowing whether the Australian aborigines had melody, when the multi-toned structure of their

tunes is within a semi-tone, our normal unit of melodic differentiation.)
In the world beyond all possible experience, there are, *a fortiori*, no
powers of sensory manifestation, though two connections must remain
with the world of experience. In the one there must be an actual causal
connection, in that the objects in that world must have powers to affect
objects in such a way as to change or stimulate or release their powers
to manifest themselves or changes in themselves to us. And secondly,
more germane to the issue of conceivability, both synchronic and diachronic structure may be attributable. For example, in Medieval chemistry, the four principles which had the power to manifest themselves
in warmth, coldness, wetness and dryness, though not perceptible
themselves as such, nevertheless were imagined to be present in things
and materials in definite proportions (non-spatial synchronic structure)
which might be changed, and so change the nature of the substance,
a process, if intelligible, having diachronic structure.

The role of icons in conceiving quality-less structure thus becomes
both clear and shows itself to be equivocal: for icons, if based upon
the reproductive power of the imagination, but passing into the transcendental phase, will constrain conceived structure to the structures
of possible experience. The imagination, in its transcendental phase,
must proceed to acts of abstraction and generalization to pass beyond
this constraint, and of course the acts of the imagination in this phase
are identical with abstract mathematical creation. In the very last
analysis, icons of the world beyond all possible experience *may* be
required to have the character of abstract mathematical structures. But
of what?

We have already noticed how, in science, dispositions are grounded
in hypotheses about the natures of the individuals which manifest these
dispositions. If the individual is a source of action such as a material
thing as the ultimate source of the gravitational field, or an acid, relative to chemical analysis at the molecular level, then the grounded
disposition is a power. But if, as we move into the transcendental phase,
we have left behind all properties other than structural with which we
might ground dispositions, then those structures in which all secondary
dispositions are grounded must be of primary or pure dispositions, that
is, of ultimate powers, that is, in the elements of the most fundamental conceivable structures, powers, and dispositions must coincide. In
natural science, fields are the best example of structures of pure
powers. Icons, such as Maxwell's tubes of fluid, may be required for

conceiving structures of potentials, but here at least they are but dispensable models of our abstract conceptions of reality. They are, at best, a system of metaphors for holding onto the sense of the abstract objects, and it is to this role that another aspect of the sense of the notion icon is directed. An icon as a religious painting is not just a picture of some worthy person, but is a bearer of meaning, generally abstract with respect to that which it depicts. In their transcendental employment the models generated by this phase of the imagination are truly icons.

VI *Disciplining the Fantasy*

Common sense would have it, no doubt, that the test of the imagination in conceiving objects in the realm of possible experience is whether, when our senses are extended by the development of some device, such as the stethoscope or the microscope, the hypothetical object or process appears, that is, it is a matter of whether and to what extent reality, when it is revealed in experience, matches the icon. But common sense needs defense. There is a tradition in philosophy of casting doubt upon the authenticity of what is perceived, by insisting that only the existence of and properties of the immediate elements of various sensory fields involved are known for certain. Happily, as far as stethoscopes, probes, microscopes, telescopes, and slow motion film are concerned, one can establish a gradual transition from the objects and processes of unaided perception, to the sounds, shapes, colors, motions, and so on, brought into our experience with the help of instruments. One can hear the same sound with or without the stethoscope, but one can also hear clearly sounds heard only faintly or not at all without it. Thus, we establish a continuity of the existence of percepts. By this achievement, the world of possible experience penetrated by instrumental aids is made one with the world of actual experience, so the extended world is no more nor less dubious or inauthentic than the world of unaided perception, the ordinary world. And this is all we need for the control of creativity at the reproductive phase of the work of the imagination. Philosophers may continue to argue about the epistemological and metaphysical status of material objects, but their disputes and distinctions cannot detach bacteria from bodies, nor galaxies from ganglia.

But discipline in the world imagined to lie beyond all possible experience cannot be based wholly upon instruments. However, there is a
kind of penumbral region, wherein structure is simply spatial, where
structures whose elements are beyond all possible experience may
nevertheless be displayed. I have in mind the photographs of molecular structure obtained by field ion microscopes, or the tracks of 'particles' observed in cloud chambers. While the phenomenal properties
of the structure are linked to its elements only by long and sometimes
ill-understood causal chains, the structure so projected is at worst iso-
morphic with the structure of the thing or process being examined, at
best that very structure itself. However, if we consider cases deeper into
the inexperienceable, only reason can come to the aid of the creative
imagination, and that only *a posteriori*. At the deepest level, the best that
we can do is show by argument that the structure of elementary powers we have imagined as the ultimate structure of the world fulfills
certain necessary conditions for the possibility of our having the kind
of experience we do have, and there may be a still more general form
of argument which would link certain structures (and certain powers)
to the possibility of any experience at all. In fulfilling these conditions,
the world as we experience it is made intelligible.

A process or structured object becomes intelligible if the following
conditions are met:

(1) From the imagined fundamental world structure the form of the
process or object can be deduced, that is, from the tetrahedral
distribution of the valences of the carbon atoms the observed form
of the diamond can be deduced with the help of certain ancillary
hypotheses, that is, the structure of the valences provides a reason,
relative to accepted physics, why diamond has the form it has. Form, as
we may say, is inherited from form. The intelligibility of the form
of diamond comes not just from the fact that the proposition
expressing this stands in a certain logical relation with some other
propositions, but that among those other propositions are some
descriptives of some underlying and fundamental form, that is a
structure of units or elements that are, for that case, not further
decomposable. Thus, to cite structure is to make intelligible, and
by linking structure via the deductive link, which has the effect of
preserving content, that intelligibility which derives naturally from
citation of structure alone, is transferred to the form of the diamond.
But sensory qualities, like color or timbre, cannot be so made intel-

ligible, only their associated forms, wavelength, or harmonic structure, can be referred to more fundamental forms and so acquire intelligibility. It is a prime rule of science that qualitative difference should be explained in terms of structural difference, and in so doing, the only final form that an explanation could take is achieved. In short, only form or structure is intelligible in itself. Philosophical argument for this proposition could do no more than take the form of the analysis of all satisfactory explanatory forms and the exhibition that their satisfaction derives from that feature.

(2) In the nodes of the imagined world structure, there are agents, that is the structure is a structure of sources of activity, as for example a complex formed from repressed traces of disagreeable experiences, a concept which represents a state of the world beyond all possible experience, is a structure of agents, its elements having power to effect changes in behavior, so that the complex itself becomes a structured agent, the source of the pattern of neurotic or compulsive behavior, making it intelligible by showing that the form of the behavior is a direct transformation and manifestation of the form of the complex.

VII *Society as Created Icon*

But when we create icons in the pursuit of the social sciences, we cannot take it for granted that there is a real structure, some independent world, of which that icon, however imperfectly, is a representation. Indeed, both the existential status of society and the significance of societal concepts is highly problematic and cannot be taken for granted. We speak of the nation, the army, the middle class, as we were speaking of the island, the Thames valley, and so on. Our power to create societal concepts is, as we shall see, a creativity of another kind.

I shall approach this difficult problem through two examples, illustrating different facets of the role of societal concepts, and their associated icons in our lives. Both examples will illustrate how we are unprepared to live in an unintelligible environment, that is, an environment which does not either exhibit structure or clearly manifest an underlying structure. Imagine a large complex of buildings unified by a boundary wall, and a common calligraphy in the labels displayed at various entrances (that a hole in a wall is an 'entrance' is also a social, not a physical, fact, so in this analysis an underlying and unexamined ethnomethodology is being taken for granted, but at least by me, know-ingly). People move in and out, some prone on stretchers, others arrive with every mark of respect in Rolls Royces. Inside, uniforms are much in evidence. Many people are in bed, and even some of those who are walking around are wearing pajamas and dressing gowns. What on earth is this strange place and what is going on? The innumerable momentary interactions and sayings of individuals, or rather some part of them, are made immediately intelligible by the hypothesis that this is a *hospital*, that is, the whole begins to exhibit structure. The introduc-tion of this concept is strictly comparable to, though much more complex than, the introduction of the concept 'galaxy' which made the appearance of the night sky intelligible by referring its observed form to an underlying and aesthetically pleasing structure, the spiral form of the stars in the galactic plane. As ethnomethodologists have insisted, there is *always* an everyday problem of intelligibility, which it behooves sociologists to contemplate, since it is nearly always solved by those involved. Sometimes the continuous everyday solution needs supplementation by a stroke of scientific genius, as when Irving Goff-man made us realize that many flurries of activity, unintelligible within the official theory which glosses 'hospital' as 'cure-house,' become intel-ligible within a single supplementary theory in which the institution is glossed as a setting for dramas of character. Each theory generates a rhetoric, a unified theory of explanatory concepts, with an associated grammar (in which rhetoric do we put the socio-grammatical rule that the superintendent can refer to the hospital as 'my hospital,' and to whom?). Rhetorics are drawn on in accounting sessions, in which in the course of talk the momentarily mysterious is made intelligible by allowing itself to be so described as to find a place in a structure, this time of meaningful activities within semantic fields recognized as legitimate in the rhetoric. Finally, one should notice that the official theory may find expression in what is literally an icon or icons, diagrams on suitable walls, in which structure, as officially conceived, is laid out. Nowhere on such charts appears such power and influence structures as that of the janitor in a school, where the boiler-room society over which he provides is the apex of the counter-hierarchy, and in which such officially-defined figures as the headmaster carry very little weight.

The position implicit in the example above, which it should be clear is not at all the same as the old theory of methodological individualism, can claim at least one systematic exposition in the past, namely, that of Leo Tolstoy in the sociological chapters in *War and Peace*. As a mark of my admiration for his formulation of the theory, I have called it the 'Borodino Theory,' since he broaches it explicitly in his analysis of that battle and in his recurring theme of the contrast between the manner of generalship of Napoleon and of Mikhail Larionovich Golenishchev-Katusov. As Tolstoy sees it, the Battle of Borodino is a middle-scale social event within an inexplicable, very diffuse, and very-large scale human movement, the periodic movement of very large numbers of people from West to East and East to West. This migratory oscillation has no name, and is not mentioned in historians' accounts of the affair. They are concerned with nations, armies, generals, governments, and the like. And their role, according to Tolstoy, is to impose order and intelligibility upon meaningless eddies in the groundswell, such eddies as the Battle of Borodino. The battle becomes, in *War and Peace*, both an instance of Tolstoy's theory, an anecdote showing its power to make phenomena intelligible, and a kind of model for the analysis for all middle-scale human events.

The battle is joined by accident in conditions which prevent either commander getting a clear view of the battlefield and its changing dispositions. Both commanders are surrounded by eager staff officers and constantly receive messages from the officers on the field. But by the time the message, usually in garbled form, has reached the commander, the situation it described has changed. Napoleon nevertheless issues detailed orders throughout the day based on the 'information' he receives—but these orders rarely reach their destination, and even more rarely are intelligible to the commander they are intended for, and even more rarely still enjoin courses of action still possible by the time they arrive. But on the French side, a great flurry of command goes on. Katusov, on the other hand, does nothing, he believes no messages, he issues no orders. He waits for the issue to be decided. But as a final irony, no issue is resolved, at least in the final dispositions of that battle, though as Tolstoy points out the French losses that day turned out to be fatally weakening to their army.

But, asks Tolstoy, what do historians make of that battle? They *impose* order upon it. They represent the haphazard movements on the battlefield, enjoined by the exigencies and impulses of the moment as splendid tactical moves, flowing from the genius of the commanders, and brought about by their orders. 'The Battle' as a structured, ordered, hierarchical social entity, is a product of retrospective commentary; in the technical language of the new sociology, it is an account. A series of flurries, intelligible as the mutual actions of individual men at the microlevel, become elements in a larger structure, by an act of the creative imagination. In terms of this, commentaries upon and explanations of actions are contrived for happenings which are no longer conceived as closed entities, but as elements in a larger structure having relations with other elements of that structure, for example, with the thoughts and orders of the commanders. But that larger structure has its being only in the imagination of those who share the theory, a theory, of course, which any member can hardly fail to share. Only one who follows at least one step on the phenomenological path, one who, like the ethnomethodologists, wishes to subject the natural attitude and its products, battles, to scrutiny, can come to this. Ironically, it is in the social sciences that the positivist theory of theoretical concepts has its only plausible application, since in the social sciences, the Borodino Theory would counsel us to treat societal concepts as serving only the interests of an imposed intelligibility, and not being referential terms pointing outside the theory to real existents.

The creative imagination of the social scientist is the most potent of all, for he can create an icon whose close simulacrum of a real world is so potent that people will live their lives within its framework, hardly ever suspecting that the framework is no more than a theory for making the messy, unordered flurry of day-to-day life intelligible, and so meaningful and bearable.

VIII   *Evolutionary Epistemology*

But sciences and societies have a history. And the question as to why a particular form *appears*, makes itself visible in various manifestations, at a particular time and in particular circumstances, must be tackled. To get clear on the basis for a diachronic analysis, one must distinguish the productive process of a 'next stage' from the sequence of those stages. Only by clearly separating them can the problem of their several intelligibilities be solved. In general, I would wish to claim that just as in the sequential stages of plant and animal life there is no pattern from which a law of those stages can be inferred, that is, they have no intelligibility as a progression, so there is no pattern in the sequence of stages of sciences or societies. Patterns *are* discerned and described, but I would wish to argue that these reflect current ethnographies and current obsessions—God's will working itself out in history, economic determinism, and the like—the projection of which on the sequence of stages is the source of historicism. But that does not mean to say that the process of historical change cannot be understood, and that it cannot be made intelligible. I follow Stephen Toulmin in his claim that the *general form of all historical explanations* was invented by Darwin and Wallace, a form which allows for the intelligibility of a historical sequence without falling prey to historicism.

The form of our understanding of the diachrony of social and scientific creativity will be evolutionary in the natural selection mode. Thus the origin of new forms, be it animal, vegetable, or structures in thought, will be taken to be (relatively) random, with respect to the environment in which those forms will be tested. Thus, in the moment of inception, all novel forms will have the character of random mutations, and thought forms, fantasies, will be taken to be innumerable. We shall return in a moment to the important issue of how far the inception of thought forms is disconnected from their environment, and we shall find that it is not quite so clearly free as organic mutation.

But by what sort of environment are they selected? We must acknowledge the complexity of that environment. New ideas are contemplated, deliberated upon by people, and in the course of these deliberations are accepted or rejected, or sometimes merely forgotten, or abandoned because of the appearance of a novelty more in fashion. Sometimes they are tested, as to what further intelligibility they lend to what we think goes on, and sometimes even as to what they lead us to think there is. Sometimes ideas are rejected out of hand, as silly, threatening, 'unintelligible,' 'obscene,' and so on. How is some order to be brought to this multiplicity?

The credit for the introduction of the basic idea of evolutionary epistemology must go to Popper, and hindsight, I feel sure, will regard this as his great contribution to philosophy. Effectively, Popper proposed to bring order to the selecting environment by the use of a principle of formal logic.[10] The instrument of natural selection upon ideas whose appearance is serendipitous with respect to that environment, and of only psychological interest, is the principle of *modus tollens*, that a proposition which has false consequences is false. By itself, 'falsification' is just a logical principle, but in Popper's works it is uncritically coupled with an epistemological principle—'rejection'—that is, whatever is

---

[10] K. R. Popper, *Objective Knowledge, an Evolutionary Approach* (Oxford: The Clarendon Press, 1972).

falsified must be rejected as knowledge. Popper's particular version of the evolutionary natural selection theory comes to grief on that coupling, since it cannot be taken for granted and it turns out to rest on two levels of theory, one metaphysical and the other scientific.

In order to pass from falsification to rejection, one must suppose that the falsified principle, hypothesis, or theory is not worthy to be accepted as knowledge. This requires recourse to an assumption about the stability of the universe, a metaphysical assumption that the universe will not so change in the future as to behave in such a way that the falsified principle is then true. But this is a principle to which Popper cannot have recourse, since it is a form of the general inductive principle of the uniformity of nature, the negation of which leads to an evolutionary epistemology for science in the first place.

But even if the passage from falsification to rejection be granted, say, as a principle, itself a mutation surviving in a hostile environment by virtue of its power to make scientific method intelligible, the application of the principle depends upon assuming some embracing scientific theory as true. In general, falsification is itself an interpretation of a yet more fundamental relation, namely contradiction. The product of a 'testing' is a contradiction. 'All A is B' is in contradiction with 'This A is not B.' To assign 'false' to the principle, to make this *its* test, requires that we assign 'true' to 'This A is not B,' that is, the assignment of a truth-value to the general proposition depends upon a prior assignment of a truth-value to the particular. That is what makes this a *test* of the general proposition. But it is notorious that the result of any experiment is very far from being a 'brute fact,' and we might as easily have assigned the truth-value the other way. In practice, 'This A is not B' gets true or false in priority because it is embedded in a more embracing or otherwise more attractive theory than 'All A is B,' which is, for the purpose of the test, detached or isolated in some way. Thus the passage from contradiction to falsification is not unequivocal. (Popper did, of course, attempt a 'basic statements' theory to anchor truth somewhere, but has been forced to relativize it, which is to give it up.) It seems that Popper's own attempt to give body to the general theory of which he was the originator is too much dependent on logicist assumptions as to what is rational, and on the uncritical acceptance of the transitions contradiction to falsification, and falsification to rejection.

Toulmin, by contrast, is prepared to include a much wider range of items in the selection mechanism, and furthermore, makes an important and interesting concession to a mild teleology, unthinkable in the Popperian theory.[11] The appearance of a mutant idea, for Toulmin, is not wholly detached from what has gone before in the realm of ideas, not unconnected with the tests and trials to come. As we get the idea of the kind of tests an innovation is to face, we censor what one might call 'first fantasy,' so that only plausible ideas are offered for the community to test. And synchronic creativity, as I have described its structure in Part I, involves a disciplinary feature in the very process of creation itself, which 'close-couples' the new creation to the old. Mutation occurs, then, within a very narrow range.

What of the selection mechanism itself? Institutional and social factors become prominent once we move away from a simple logicism. Clearly, an idea will have a better chance of discussion and consideration if it is proposed by someone in a certain place in the institution, be it the society of scientists or the board of a company or the general meeting of a commune. And greater effort will be made to make the world conform to the idea before it is rejected. This latter feature is very prominent in the natural history of political ideas, where the 'world' in which the idea will run its course is a human construction which can, within certain limits, still unknown, be reconstructed so as to preserve the idea unrefuted.

Toulmin's particularization of the theory is not without difficulties as well. He chooses to discuss the problem, not in the propositional ontology of Popper, but with concepts as his individuals. However, this leads to considerable difficulties and unclarities in his statement of the theory, occasioned by the problem of individuation of concepts. The problem is central, since he treats 'population of concepts' as strictly analogous to 'population of organisms.' But what is the 'individual' concept? Is it the concept of an individual person, so that my concept of the atom is a different concept from yours, even though our concepts may match throughout their semantic fields? This would seem to be the natural interpretation, so that a concept would reproduce itself by being more and more replicated in the minds of others. But he also speaks sometimes as if it was the concept we shared, which is the individual which is naturally selected, and its progeny, not as its replicas in other people's minds, but the further logical and conceptual descendents that it spawns. It seems clear that this second interpretation must surely be a mistake, and that one must stick to the individuation

---

[11] S. E. Toulmin, *Human Understanding*, vol. 1 (Oxford: The Clarendon Press, 1972).

of a concept as my concept, and apply the species notion to link, under the same phenotype, my concept and yours when they are, as concepts go, alike.

I hope I have said enough to indicate that both the diachrony of theories and societies can be understood in a general way by the strict application of the evolutionary analogy and the idea of selection, but that the final account of the balance between rational, societal, and other factors in the selective environment has yet to be struck.

CHAPTER SIXTEEN

CREATIVE INTERPRETATION OF LITERARY TEXTS

Thomas Leddy

I *Introduction*

The question I wish to consider is the nature of creativity in literary interpretation. The issue comes from thinking about the debate surrounding constructivism.[1] Some authors have held that literary works are, in a sense, constructed not simply by the writer, but also by the interpreter. This view has been much attacked, for instance, in two recent introductions to aesthetics.[2] The issue, of course, is a deep one and cannot be easily resolved or dismissed. It goes to the great debates of our time between realists and anti-realists and between objectivists and relativists.

Constructivism presents two obvious problems. First, if constructivists believe that interpretations actually change the meanings of works of art, then works of art created at one time could be transformed by an action at a much later time; this seems counterintuitive.[3] Second, if

---

[1] One critique of constructivism is Robert Stecker, "The Constructivist's Dilemma," *Journal of Aesthetics and Art Criticism* 55, no. 1 (1997): 43–51. Stecker elaborates his ideas further in *Interpretation and Construction: Art, Speech and the Law* (Malden, Mass.: Blackwell, 2003). A central text is Michael Krausz, ed., *Is There a Single Right Interpretation?* (University Park: Pennsylvania State University Press, 2002). A nice recent version of constructivism is found there in Jitendranath Mohanty's, "Intentionality, Meaning, and Open-Endedness of Interpretation," 63–75, where he says, "A reason why in these cases [for example, poetry] there is no final interpretation is that while the text as printed matter…is a work complete in itself, as an aesthetic object it is constituted by the printed text and the responses of the reader.…The total aesthetic object, growing as it does through time and history, demands ever new interpretations" 75.

[2] Robert Stecker, *Aesthetics and the Philosophy of Art* (Lanham, Md.: Rowman, and Littlefield, 2005); Stephen Davies, *The Philosophy of Art* (Malden, Mass.: Blackwell, 2006).

[3] Opponents do not consider that this happens in everyday discourse, for example when I say "I meant by X so-and-so." Peirce, saw this when he said, "Every utterance naturally leaves the right of further exposition in the utterer; and therefore, insofar as a sign is indeterminate, it is vague, unless it is expressly or by a well understood convention rendered general." Charles Sanders Peirce, "Issues of Pragmaticism," in *Pragmatism and Classical American Philosophy*, 2nd ed., ed. John J. Stuhr (New York: Oxford University Press, 2000), 119.

what is meant is that each interpreter constructs its own text, which then is the one that is interpreted, then there is no basis for disagreement since they are talking about different texts. These are serious problems. Still, the idea of constructivism intrigues, not least because it includes a dynamic element lacking in competing theories. Most non-constructivist theories see interpretation as involving the production of an accurate representation of a meaning which has always existed, unchangingly (since the work's creation), whether in the text, in the mind of the author, or within the cultural context of original reception. This leaves out the possibility of creative interpretation, except in the shallow sense that one could be creative in coming up with a way to *find* or *describe* the pre-existent meaning.

My thought is that creative interpretation is not only possible but also better than interpretation that is not creative. I am speaking of the kind of interpretation that creates as it interprets, and thus that constitutes an understanding of the text in a novel and valuable way. There is a strong distinction between an interpretation that is merely 'correct' and one that brings the text alive through connecting it with lived experience while still remaining consistent with the text. The second sort is better in general, although the first might serve some purposes. Interpretations are only going to be live if they achieve a higher level of creativity, one that is both discovery and invention.[4] Interpretations of literary texts are more or less creative in this sense. More creative interpretations bring out the evolving meaning of the work in its interaction with the surrounding environment.

To accomplish my task, we need to avoid four possible misinterpretations concerning the term 'creative': (1) Creative is not understood here to simply mean conducive to more aesthetic pleasure. (2) Although we sometimes use the term creative in a negative way, I use it here only in the positive sense. (3) Although people sometimes understand the most creative interpretations to be the ones that make the most unusual connections, this approach to defining creative is problematic in that it emphasizes the element of novelty in creativity over that of value.[5] (4) To conclude that either an interpretation is creative or it is

---

[4] This emphasis on discovery and invention is consistent with what Michael Krausz has called constructive realism; see his "Constructive Realism: An Ontological Byway" in *Interpretation and Transformation: Explorations in Art and the Self* (New York: Rodopi, 2007), chap. 7.

[5] Annette Barnes, *On Interpretation: A Critical Analysis* (Cambridge: Basil Blackwell, 1988), 99.

correct is a false dichotomy. A condition for an interpretation to be creative, on my view, is that it be true, although true in a deeper sense than merely being correct.

Some constructivists and pluralists prefer not to use the term 'true' for literary interpretations. I have a broad notion of truth that makes me comfortable with calling some literary interpretations true, or truer than others are. To argue this here is beyond the scope of this chapter, but just so that the reader understands where I am coming from, by truth I mean: truth is a triune concept, all sides in constant, necessary, often fruitful, and sometimes harmful conflict. One side expresses one-to-one fit of elements between the candidate for truth (proposition, picture, etc.) and that to which it is said to be true. The second is best expressed by William James' idea that truth is that which is good in the way of believing. The third is the quality of heightened reality we experience when we believe we have captured the essence of something (for example, conceptually or through art). None of these is reducible to any of the others. They are equally important sides of truth. Exclusive focus on one side of truth neglects its rich and full character and leads to difficulties.

My view is somewhat different from other forms of constructivism in that I hold that each interpretation actualizes a potential presented by the text, the potential changing over time. Actualization is a kind of construction since each interpretation is itself constructed. As Dewey said, "there is a difference between the art product (statue, painting or whatever) and the work of art. The first is physical and potential; the latter is active and experienced. It is what the product does, its working."[6] By 'text,' I mean the sequence of words on paper (or the equivalent) plus the dictionary or dictionary-like meaning the words had at the time of creation.[7] Text does *not* mean the sequence of words plus the meaning of those terms as expressed in interpretations of the text. The name for that entity is 'work.' Competing interpretations are of the same text. The text remains relatively unchanged over time, its most notable change being revision by the author. However, the *meaning* of the text changes over time. Thus, the meaning of the text is not

---

[6] John Dewey. *Art and Experience* (New York: Capricorn Books, 1934), 162. As Michael Krausz says, "Dewey defines a work of art as a complex, co-created by the experiencing viewer and the art product." *Limits of Rightness* (Lanham: Rowman and Littlefield, 2000), 30.

[7] See Stephen Davies, *The Philosophy of Art*, for a discussion of this distinction. Davies, however, uses "text" to refer simply to the sequence of words.

equivalent to the sequence of dictionary meanings of the sequence of words in the text.

All interpretations are creative to some degree, but the term 'creative interpretation': should be limited to the *more* creative of these. Creative interpretation, as creative anything, is not only novel but valuable: a merely novel interpretation would not deserve the term creative. Also, a creative interpretation must be true to the text. One can creatively talk about a text and not be true to the text but that is not creative interpretation of the text.

Some think that creative interpretations of texts are not as good as less creative interpretations. For instance, it might be argued that there could be a creative interpretation of *Animal Farm*[8] that said that it is *not* about totalitarianism. On this view, although such an interpretation would certainly be novel, it would not, and indeed *could* not, be preferable. I think that although such an interpretation would be hard to construct and defend, it would still be preferable to a less creative one *if* it still accurately and comprehensively drew on the text. That it is preferable is not due to its providing greater aesthetic satisfaction but to ways in which it more deeply engages in human issues. Such interpretations, I will argue in what follows, emerge typically from dialogical encounters in which apparent incompatibility of interpretation is in some way resolved in a more dynamic way than mere defeat, subsumption, or conjunction.

One final preliminary note: The view I am proposing is opposed to a strict distinction between significance and meaning.[9] It is often thought that the significance of a work is simply its importance, and that whereas a work's significance can change over time, its meaning cannot. Significance, however, is not just value or importance: it is also meaning. When we say that something has a certain significance we are not just saying that it has a certain importance, but that it has a certain important meaning. Works of art have significance because they can be related in fundamental ways to our lives: they are not just historical documents that we appreciate from an objective distance.

---

[8] George Orwell, *Animal Farm* (New York: Harcourt, Brace, 1946).

[9] It is instructive that even Davies, who holds to this distinction, uses the term "significance" in its broader meaning when he says in the first line of his chapter on interpretation "When the significance of something is not apparent on its face, interpretation is involved in seeking to explain and understand it." *The Philosophy of Art*, 108.

II *The Book Group*

For the last twenty-two years, I have belonged to a book group, which discusses literary works on a monthly basis. Some things seem evident to me based on this experience. My experiences with this group will be my guide for what I will say in this paper. In this, I depart from typical discussions of literary interpretation which seem to be almost exclusively derived from observing the activities of literary critics or of people who are simply reading in private. I choose the book-group over literary critics and private readers as my exemplar, first because I believe a dialogical element to understanding literary works, fairly obvious in the context of a book-group discussion, may be only implicit in the life and work of a literary critic. Second, literary critics and the aestheticians who focus on them often fail to see the forest for the trees, tending to focus on little things while missing the big picture. Third, I believe aesthetics should not ignore everyday life situations of which my book-group activity is an example.

It is understood within my book-group that each of us has our personal interpretation of the work. One's basic interpretation is what one understands the work to mean, one's 'take' on the work, one's 'reading.' It can be expressed, in different ways: (1) as a series of answers to questions like 'How do you understand this passage?' or 'How do you explain this?'; (2) as a series of reactions, positive or negative, to the interpretations of others; as something that follows after a phrase like 'I think the author was trying to say that…' or 'The main point of the book seems to be…'; or (3) as recommendations or suggestions to others on how to read the work. One can also produce a second-level interpretation, which takes the form of an essay, and this in turn can be called 'one's interpretation of the work.'[10]

One thing I take from this is that one's interpretation of the text should not, as some philosophers assume, be strongly distinguished from one's understanding of it. Interpretation, for example, should not be limited to something we do when we feel particularly puzzled or confused.[11] For, even when we do not feel confused, and would insist

---

[10] This would take us beyond the book-group, but not too far, for sometimes book-group members end up posting written accounts of the work to the group.

[11] David Novitz, "Against Critical Pluralism," in *Is There a Single Right Interpretation?* Krausz, ed., 101–121, is an example. I criticized an early view of Novitz's in my "Robust Realism Rejected," *Journal of Aesthetics and Art Criticism* 42, no. 3 (1984): 317–319.

that we are merely describing what is there, someone else might legitimately see what we are doing as interpretation. Also, although the word 'interpretation' does sometimes refer to resolving ambiguous terms and other linguistic puzzles, this is not what we generally mean by 'interpretation of the text.'[12] Instead, such interpretation is the cognitive side of experiencing a literary work when that experience is understood as extending beyond the initial reading to further thought and talk concerning the text's meaning.

Equally problematic is a rigid distinction between interpretation and evaluation. Admittedly, my book-group distinguishes between the time in which we are discussing the text (giving our interpretations of it and our thoughts about the subject matters covered by it) and the time in which we give our final evaluations. Yet, one cannot really say whether any particular statement made by a group member is purely interpretive or purely evaluative. Terms we use in interpreting the text often have evaluative connotations, and our interpretations are often offered in support of our evaluations (sometimes *after* giving evaluations, but sometimes *in anticipation*). That there are different evaluations of the text is often associated with the fact that there are different interpretations. In short, the classical distinction between interpretation and evaluation softens a great deal on closer inspection and in the context of actual discussion of a literary text.

The distinction between interpretation and description is also subject to such softening. Sometimes philosophers talk about the importance of identifying the work—under a description.[13] This is often motivated by the thought that the descriptive level is objective and provides a basis for evaluating interpretations. I do not think that there is a clearly descriptive level of a text independent of interpretation. At best, there are inferences to which all members of the group can agree. Alan Goldman says that descriptions can be known to be true. He offers as an example that we know that Jean Brodie is manipulative.[14] But I have actually attended a discussion of *The Prime of Miss Jean Brodie*, during which even that claim was contested. Someone could argue that the

---

[12] John Gibson, "Interpreting Words, Interpreting Worlds," *Journal of Aesthetics and Art Criticism* 64, no. 2 (2006): 439–450.

[13] Davies, *The Philosophy of Art*, is one example.

[14] "Interpreting Art and Literature," *Journal of Aesthetics and Art Criticism* 48, no. 3 (1990). Brodie is the lead character in Muriel Spark, *The Prime of Miss Jean Brodie* (New York: Harper, 1999).

term 'manipulative' is, although understandable, not quite right, or has misleading connotations.

Contra many aestheticians, I do not believe that identification of the work is usually much of an issue. In our book-group, it is widely understood that we have all read the same work. On rare occasions, the members might come into the room with different editions or translations, and in these cases we sometimes feel as if we are talking about different works. For instance, we recently discussed Henry James' *Daisy Miller*,[15] some of us having read one or the other of his two authorized editions, and this caused some confusion. But that kind of problem is easily resolved, for example, by switching back and forth. (The case of different translations is more problematic since the translator's choice of words already presupposes an interpretation of the original.) We also understand that the words need to be read with the meaning they would have had during the time of writing: for example, that we may not interpret the term 'plastic' in an eighteenth century text to mean the same as plastic today. We also recognize that much of a word's meaning, as it appears in a particular sentence in a literary work, is based on how it has been modified by the context of surrounding words in that work.

Even when we have read a shared text, we almost always disagree about the meaning and evaluation of the work as the discussion develops. Sometimes we support our respective positions by referring to specific passages. However, we also often disagree about the meaning of those passages. Thus, although one *could* speak of a level of description as distinct from a level of interpretation, this is relative. That is, the level of description is simply whatever everyone in the group considers to be fact. The same material or type of material that is considered by the group to be fact might be considered interpretation by a new member. When such a person comes into the group, what *was* considered fact *becomes* interpretation relative to the new situation. Also, what was once considered to be fact might shift to being considered interpretation during the course of our debate. In general, description is never independent of interpretation since it is never independent of worldview. For something to be description, and not mere transcription, different words from those found in the text must be used, and this

---

[15] *Henry James: Daisy Miller, Washington Square, Portrait of a Lady, The Bostonians, The Aspern Papers* (Chapelle Designers, 2004).

requires choice. Such choice is inevitably determined by various larger contexts, whether cultural or personal.

Over the years, the members of our group have come to know that each of us has a point-of-view, a typical set of concerns, and a typical way of reading and evaluating a text. We are quite familiar with the points-of-views expressed previously by members of the group. One member, for example, has been strongly influenced by Buddhism. Although his way of seeing things is more complicated than that, let us say, for simplicity's sake, that he takes a Buddhist point-of-view in reading and evaluating any literary work. For example, when we read *The Schopenhauer Cure* by Irvin Yalom,[16] he read the passage in which the character Pam spends some time in an ashram in India as central to understanding the text as a whole, even though this only took up a few pages and seemed relatively unimportant to others. When we read George Bernard Shaw's *A Black Girl in Search of God*,[17] commonly seen as an indictment of religion in general, he interpreted the ending as providing a Buddhist-like message. And in our discussion of Walter Mosley's *The Man in My Basement* he stressed the lead character's special contemplative attunement to nature, a point missed by many other group members.[18] Moreover, if he interprets the work to be making a Buddhist point, he tends to evaluate it more highly as long as it also meets certain formal criteria.[19]

Each of the other members has its point-of-view, although it is not always so easy to specify. There will always be disagreements between readers based on point-of-view. Indeed, we can assume generally that, given any two readers of a text, there will be at least two interpretations based on different points-of-views. Note that this is not just a matter of different readers holding to different literary theories or standards. Theorists who focus exclusively on academic interpretation tend to assume that this is the only relevant issue. However, differing interpretations may have to do more with general attitudes or even with competing philosophies of life. My overall claim is that to truly understand

---

[16] Irvin D. Yalom, *The Schopenhauer Cure* (New York: HarperCollins, 2004).

[17] George Bernard Shaw, *The Adventures of the Black Girl in Her Search for God* (New York: Capricorn Books, 1959 © 1933).

[18] Walter Mosley, *The Man in My Basement: A Novel* (Boston: Little, Brown, 2004).

[19] Michael Krausz has observed that Buddhists might well have different aims in interpretation than tracking truth, for example, creation of a more caring world (*Limits of Rightness*, 115–116). This view would be consistent with what I say here, especially given my definition of truth and my comments at the end of this paper.

the nature of interpretation, we need to deepen our understanding of the relationship between readers who have such broadly different points-of-view, as is the case with my Buddhist friend and me.

A typical example of a claim that ignores the actual social dynamic of interpretive debate is Novitz: "to accept as jointly admissible two conflicting interpretations that attribute different and exclusive properties to one and the same object is effectively to concede that one does not properly understand."[20] It is not at all clear what is supposed to be happening here. Who is doing the accepting? What does 'accepting' mean in this instance? What does 'admissible' mean? Is one accepting someone else's interpretation that conflicts with one's own, or is one just coming upon two incompatible interpretations not one's own, for example, offered by two other competing members of the book group, and trying to accept both at once? If the first is true, can one accept a conflicting interpretation and still believe it incompatible with one's own? And, if so, how does one know that there is here an issue of p and $-p$, or does one just *interpret* one interpretation as a $-p$ to the p of the other?

I do not accept the view that my interpretations and that of my Buddhist friend are incommensurable. Some social conventions, including our shared language and the authority given to text itself, provide a basis for discussion. (I take the text to be *relatively* interpretation-independent. Except when one it talking about ancient fragments, say of Sappho, there is practically no debate over what words actually appear on the page. However, there is room for debate over which of several dictionary meanings from the time is relevant. Such a choice often does depend on one's interpretive stance.) This is so even though our differences may not be finally resolved. Although each of us has our own conceptual scheme, our own way of seeing things, communication is still possible. It happens by way of each person's interpretation of what the other is saying.

Most philosophers commonly believe that literary pluralism must hold, and paradoxically, that incompatible interpretations must be true, thus violating the principle of non-contradiction.[21] This does not analyze the problem in the right way. We should view it in terms of what

---

[20] Novitz, "Against Critical Pluralism," 117.
[21] With Robert Stecker, I hold that to say two interpretations are incompatible is to say that they contradict each other. See his "Incompatible Interpretations," *The Journal of Aesthetics and Art Criticism* 50, no. 4 (1992): 291–298.

actually happens in the process of two or more people reading the same text with each successively offering an interpretation of it in mutual response. Part of what happens here is that the two are also interpreting each other.

We could pursue various strategies. I might try to understand as much of what my friend says as possible as actually true, charitably reading his interpretation of the text.[22] This could be a good thing. However, such a reading may be, from another perspective, a distortion. We can resolve this issue by insisting that charitable reading is not *always* good and that it should be evaluated in terms of whether it increases understanding. In a charitable reading, what gives meaning to my interlocutor's pronouncements is what gives significance to the text for me.

Although no two ways of seeing a text are ultimately incommensurable (as it is possible to reach agreement, or at least mutual understanding, through an on-going exchange, with the text as the standard) two or more competing interpretations may be *incompatible* for a time. Most discussions about incompatibility are vague because they fail to note that true incompatibility usually requires someone in a debate to interpret someone else's claim to be stating the exact opposite belief: $-p$ to p. This kind of strict disagreement does sometimes happen in the book-group.

For example, I sometimes believe that my Buddhist friend's interpretation of a particular passage is false, and I sometimes even believe (when in an uncharitable mood) that his entire way of seeing the text, or even things in general, is false. If I say, for example, that his interpretation of a sentence or some larger unit of the text is false, then at that time, and on that point, our interpretations *are* incompatible: we have a case of p and $-p$. However,—this may appear to be a surprising thing to say—*this is not very friendly*. It is not an accident that the term 'incompatibility' does not just refer to contradiction but also to the inability of two individuals to get along. The role of friendliness and unfriendliness in interpretive debate is under-appreciated in theory of interpretation. This is not to say, however, that one should never interpret in an unfriendly way.

---

[22] Readers may think of Donald Davidson here. A nice discussion of implications of Davidson's theory is to be found in Reed Way Dasenbrock, "Do We Write the Text We Read?" in *Falling into Theory: Conflicting Views on Reading Literature*, ed. David H. Richter (Boston: Bedford Books, 1994), 237–248.

Reading one's 'interpretations as false is not the only possible approach. Benefits may be gained from taking their interpretations as true, or at least in a more positive way. One might learn something in the process. So, although we might speak of tension between opposing interpretations, it is a bit extreme simply to speak of this tension in terms of incompatibility, as though whether two interpretations actually contradict each other is something written in stone. To put it another way, incompatibility is a move in the language-game of interpretive discussion. One *constitutes* another's interpretation as incompatible with one's own. Interpreting someone's claim as a *-p* to one's *p* is a *decision*.[23] (So too is taking two interpretations neither of which is one's own as incompatible with each other.) Of course, incompatibility is not always one's *own* decision: others may understand their position as a *-p* to *your p*!

One difference between debates in literary journals and debates in book-groups, or even in a seminar room, is that the first *is* written in something very much like stone. If someone claims in a published writing that another person's interpretation is false, that claim will remain on the record for as long as the record persists. But in a verbal discussion, anyone who makes such a claim is always free to modify it in the course of discussion, and is even free to claim that actually *contradicting* the other theory was never intended—this reversal is typically accepted. That is, history is more fluid within the context of verbal than written discussion.[24]

I do not *have to* assume that most of my friend's statements are true. Sometimes it is useful to assume, in a dramatically different kind of move, that many or even most of his statements are *false*. For example, I might bear in mind that all of my friend's statements contain words that have meanings that are holistically affected by every other statement my friend makes and by my friend's overall position. For example, I might say that Buddhism colors all of my friend's statements and positions. I might reject his interpretation of the text because I reject the whole perspective from which it comes. This more negative approach

---

[23] Christy Mag Uidhir, in commenting on an earlier version of this chapter, has said that this implies that no incompatible interpretations *simpliciter* are possible. My position might be better stated as that the notion of incompatible interpretations *simpliciter* is incoherent. "*Simpliciter*" refers to something unconditional or ultimately simple: but nothing in human experience falls into this category.

[24] Peirce's point in "Issues of Pragmaticism" is relevant here.

is sometimes useful because it forces one to sharpen one's arguments, look for new evidence, and clarify one's position.

Some philosophers have argued that although there is nothing wrong with interpreting texts according to an ideology if there are aspects of the text that could not have been influenced by that ideology. It would be wrong to understand, for example, Western texts written prior to any influence of Buddhism in terms of Buddhism.[25] I do not think this is helpful. Buddhists simply have their own way of looking at things, and they tend to focus on certain aspects of the text as they construct their understanding and evaluation of it from that point of view. Am I any different from a Buddhist in this respect? No, although my own perspective may be less clearly or easily labeled. We all interpret things by our own lights.

Interpretations change over time; ideally, they improve in the process. Of course, once an interpretation is written down and presented to the public, it is frozen in time, although, even here, we can speak of it as evolving if the writer produces a revised version later, or if the interpretation itself is subject to a history of interpretation. My interpretation of a text is constantly evolving ('changing for the better,' 'expanding,' 'deepening') not only while reading it but also during the group's discussion. This does not mean, however, that the interpretation is coming any closer to the 'one correct meaning.' Part of this evolution is the result, as I have suggested, of interaction between my interpretation and my understanding of the interpretations of others. Sometimes this happens through my taking the interpretations of others as being incompatible with my own and thus as providing a challenge to my own interpretation, which I must then defend. Sometimes it happens through my interpreting other interpretations as compatible with mine, or even as enhancing mine. I might, for instance, want to incorporate some aspects of my Buddhist friend's interpretation into my understanding, recognizing that in doing so, I am probably not being faithful to his interpretation as I do not accept his perspective. When I take my interpretation and another's as incompatible, so that, taken together, there is a p and $-p$ situation, then I naturally seek resolution of the conflict, and this, in a way, distances me from my own interpretation. I may then resolve the conflict by rejecting or modifying my own interpretation.

---

[25] For example, Davies, *The Philosophy of Art*. For an earlier discussion, see my "Against Surface Interpretation," *The Journal of Aesthetics and Art Criticism* 57, no. 4 (1999): 459–465.

By using imagination, we respond positively to another's interpretation. We might act, for instance, *as if* the other person's interpretation is true by *our* lights. I might do this by taking one of my friend's terms as a metaphor for something else. Or I might systematically substitute in my mind one of my terms for one of his. Done crudely, this will seem like a distortion. But done with delicacy, it may be seen as a friendly accommodation. It might, alternatively, be seen as capitulation. Yet, however it is seen by *others*, it may nonetheless help to deepen and expand my position. Another imaginative approach is to stand back and say something like 'although inconsistent with each other, both interpretations can legitimately apply to the work.'

Members of our book-group operate under two assumptions that *appear* contradictory: one, that there is an ideally correct interpretation (singularism in Michael Krausz's terminology), and the other, that there may be multiple good interpretations of the text that compete with each other (multiplism). Krausz distinguishes multiplism from critical pluralism, where pluralism holds that two or more interpretations are equally preferable amongst admissible interpretations. If pluralism is defined this way, multiplism, I believe, is the better theory.[26] We can still hold that although there are competing good interpretations, and there is no one final interpretation, some good interpretations are better than others are. But this, in itself, does not resolve the apparent contradiction between the two assumptions.

Although singularism and multiplism *appear* to conflict, they do not *have* to. They do not have to *if* we take singularism as only metaphorically true. Once this move is made, not only do they not conflict in any deep way, *they actually work together*. It could even be argued that they are *both* required for the group discussion to work as an interpretation-enriching mechanism. Although they cannot work together when operating at the same time (this would just give a contradiction), one can (and, arguably, should) alternate between stances.

The notion of an ideal correct interpretation might even be necessary for interpretive discussion. Without it, one could not have disagreement about the meaning of the text, and such disagreement is needed for advancement in understanding. One also needs to have such a notion if one is to be willing to give up or to revise some aspect of

---

[26] Michael Krausz, "Interpretation and Its Objects: A Synoptic View," in *Interpretation and Its Objects: Studies in the Philosophy of Michael Krausz*, ed. Andreea Ritivoi (Amsterdam, Rodopi, 2003), 13.

one's own interpretation. Moreover, we expect all good interpretations to be consistent with the facts of the text, although, as I said earlier, what constitutes fact depends on group agreement, unless we are just talking about the actual sequence of words. We also think that the best interpretations are the ones that resolve the most interpretive difficulties or the most important ones while doing this.

But the singularist ideal should not be taken too literally. The ideal interpretation is a myth, a fiction, or, to put it in a more pleasantly, an abstract entity with no real content. No one has ever described one. How would we even know if we got its description right? There is no definitive experiment that could reveal its nature. Belief in such an entity (as something real and describable) is based on nothing but faith. There has never been agreement concerning the one final interpretation of a text. There has never been more than partial and temporary agreement on interpretations of *parts* of texts. When philosophers give examples of interpretations they think everyone will agree to, and which they believe to be patently objectively right, I always think, let him join my book group! Nor has any agreement ever precluded future disagreements. The ideal interpretation is regulative, not actual. (I am using the term 'regulative ideal' differently from David Novitz in "Against Critical Pluralism," who seems to believe that such a thing must really exist in the way, for example, a Platonic Form exists.)

Why do so many philosophers believe otherwise? I think because they do not focus on interpretations of entire texts. It is often assumed that interpretation theory should be modeled after interpretation of individual words or sentences. The idea is probably that novels, for example, are made up out of sentences, so if you understand how to resolve an interpretive dispute about a sentence in a novel, you will understand how to interpret a novel as a whole. But interpretive disputes about sentences are really very different. Annette Barnes is one philosopher who fails to see this. She speaks of debates by scholars over whether there is a contradiction in John Milton's "Millions that stand in arms could not at the same time sit ling'ring" since one cannot both stand and sit at the same time.[27] Yet, to base one's theory of literary interpretation on such an example seems to miss the forest for the trees. Although I am willing to grant that, at the level of individual words and short sentences, theories of interpretation of this sort would be

---

[27] Barnes, *On Interpretation*, 120.

appropriate, I do not see how this must also be so at the macro-level of the paragraph, novel, opus, or genre. There may be two reasons why Barnes takes this position: (1) analytic philosophy in general, of which her work is representative, tends to take sentences as primary; (2) most of her examples are from poetry, which tends to thrive on ambiguity and hence interpretive possibilities generated by single words and short phrases.

Here is an example of how focusing on the micro-level of individual sentences can mislead. Barnes favors the intentionalist theory of literary interpretation. This theory would, she believes, have us interpret Dante's phrase, 'blaze of light,' as it appears in his *Inferno*, in terms of the Catholic theology of the time.[28] This is fine. However, this does not resolve the dispute over whether the overall interpretation of this passage should be ultimately in Catholic, Marxist, or some other terms. It might be fine to give Catholicism primacy in interpreting blaze of light but equally fine to give Marxism primacy in interpreting the work as a whole. Following this approach, Marxist critics would interpret blaze of light in terms of their understanding of the appropriate Catholic construal of the individual passage.

III   *Ontological Implications and Creativity Theory*

How much difference will it make in interpretive practice whether one believes in the meaning as real or as ideal? Those who believe in it as something more than merely regulative might benefit from a sense of certainty, but will be harmed by a tendency to assume that their interpretation is an accurate representation of the ideal. This assumption will tend to hinder growth.

Theorists are coming to recognize that resolution of the difficulties surrounding singularism versus multiplism, and realism versus relativism, can only occur at the level of ontology. My strategy has been to use the ideas of possibility, potentiality, and actualization borrowed from Aristotle. Unlike Aristotle, I do not think that potentiality is only realizable in one proper actualization. A text has potentiality that changes over time. The many interpretations of a text are all actualizations of possibilities directed toward the regulative ideal. This handles

---

[28] Ibid., 53.

the realist objection to pluralism that "there is just one set of properties that a work of art has at one time."[29] The set of properties is a set of potentialities that is generally actualized pluralistically. These properties are generated by the text in its interaction with the world via its interpretations by readers. Each reading of a text is a construction insofar as it creates an understanding of it.

My view should not be confused with what Sondra Bacharach has called 'epistemic historicism,'[30] which holds that all of the properties that emerge later were already there latently in the work. Arthur Danto for instance holds that a work has all of the style properties from the start, and that these only become apparent with further art-historical development. Against epistemic historicism, my position is what Bacharach calls 'metaphysical historicism,' in which the properties change historically, although the relevant properties are not ordinary properties but potentialities. A nice aspect of metaphysical historicism is that it does not require backwards causation.

However, Bacharach offers her thesis as an alternative to relativism, whereas I accept relativism. Also, Bacharach appears to believe that the properties are really there in a time-indexed way, whereas I view them as potentialities. Possibilities, on my view, are not latent properties that are always there. Instead, they are to be found in a gestalt that includes not only the text but background factors that change with time relative to the reader and the act of reading.

In all of this, I do not think it much matters whether one is trying to interpret the actual intentions of the author, the intentions of a hypothetical author, or the meaning of the text as something that is in some sense independent of the author or the time. All of these are legitimate goals; the only problem with their respective associated theories is that they insist that the goals of the other theories are not legitimate. Better interpretations, I think, come through utilizing a good mix of these strategies, perhaps by alternating them.

Proponents of these theories often argue that only with *their* theory can the one definitive interpretation be established. However, each method *by itself* generates competing interpretations based on competing points of view. If actual intentionalism won out over all the other theories, this would not lessen the number of interpretations of texts.

---

[29] Novitz, "Against Critical Pluralism," 115.
[30] Sondra Bacharach, "Towards a Metaphysical Historicism," *The Journal of Aesthetics and Art Criticism* 63, no. 2 (2005): 165–173.

The intended meaning of the author is just another abstract ideal which exists as potential and can be actualized in a variety of ways in our interpretations of it. It is just that the game, in this case, allows that we delve into the writer's biography and notes, while this is not allowed if we operate by the rules of, for instance, hypothetical intentionalism.

It is said by some, and the idea is associated with constructivism, that the properties of the literary work change. To what extent is this true? Properties change in the sense that the range of possibility for interpretation changes. The text itself does not change, nor do the circumstances of its creation. The range of possibilities changes partly because of the history of interpretation of the text. But the importance of this history may be overrated since only academic readers pay much attention to it. More important is just cultural history, which includes, among other things, the history of theories of interpretation. As new styles of interpretation, but more importantly, as new styles of thinking arise, new ranges of interpretation are possible, and others fall out. We approach a text with radically different assumptions based on the kind of world in which we exist.

I view creativity as a process that is continuous from the initiation of the work by the writer (or other artist) through the so-called completion of the work, and then on into the interpretive activity of its readers and critics.[31] Although the term creative interpretation is often associated with those who believe that the reader, or a certain kind of reader, is in some sense the true creator, this is not my position. I have no problem with the reader approaching the text in a way that utilizes the writer's words in ways definitely not intended by that writer. But I have no sympathy with the idea that readers can simply intend the work in their own way. The reader does not replace the writer as the creative artist. But neither is the reader to be excluded from the creative process. Instead, readers *continue* the creative process begun by the writer through their interpretation of the work.

Many singularists are willing to admit that there is some sort of legitimate process in which readers add material to the text, filling in the gaps left by the author, to create something of their own. For example, if the author does not mention the color of the hero's hair, the creative or 'elaborative' reader will, singularists suggest, imagine

---

[31] For elaboration, see my "A Pragmatist Theory of Artistic Creativity," *The Journal of Value Inquiry* 28 (1994): 169–180.

the hero's hair color. Sometimes it is thought that such readers are actually just using the text as a jumping off point for something of theirs, as a collage artist might use works of art produced by others in its new work of art.[32] The strategy depends on a false dichotomy because it assumes that the only legitimate alternative form of reading is just a form of puzzle-solving.

Another dimension of creativity is the creativity of the culture. The culture is creative through the writer and the reader. In particular, I believe that the reader and the writer share in what I have called in an earlier paper 'the Socratic quest.'[33] They search out (discovering and creating simultaneously) the evolving essences of things. The debates over interpretations are actually, indirectly (often not even that indirectly), debates over essences, which themselves change as the debate moves on. This is why debates over interpretation are important: they help us shape and reshape our world. That is why we often name the competing interpretations after major worldviews: Marxism, Freudianism, Buddhism, and so forth. In interpreting a literary work we are interpreting ourselves and our worlds.[34] To understand creativity in the arts we must understand it in terms of these layers of dialectical confrontation, between interpreters, between artist and writer, and between all of these and various forces within the culture. This is why interpretation of literary works can never work on the same model as interpretation of natural phenomena.[35]

The subject matter explored in a text has its own development, its own history. The key concepts of the text exert their own power. They may exemplify changing perspectives in a history of changing perspectives. This dimension cannot be neglected. A novel that raises the question of suicide encourages discussion of suicide. Everyone knows this, but aestheticians do not often view the discussion of suicide gen-

---

[32] Novitz, "Against Critical Pluralism."

[33] Thomas Leddy, "The Socratic Quest in Art and Philosophy," *The Journal of Aesthetics and Art Criticism* 51, no. 3 (1993): 399–410. See also my "Metaphor and Metaphysics," *Metaphor and Symbolic Activity* (Special Issue on Metaphor and Philosophy) 10, no. 3 (1995): 205–222; and my "Metaphor and The Philosophy of Art: Dynamic Organicism," *Theoria et Historia Scientiarum, International Journal for Interdisciplinary Studies*: special issue Metaphor, ed. Tomasz Komendzinski, 6 (2002/1): 43–64 for further discussion.

[34] See Charles Guignon, "Truth in Interpretation: A Hermeneutic Approach," in *Is There a Single Right Interpretation?* ed. Krausz, 264–284, for a similar view that draws from Heidegger and Gadamer.

[35] This point is in accord with Joseph Margolis', "'One and Only One Correct Interpretation'" ibid., 26–44.

erated by a novel as part of literary interpretation. Debates in a book group can be intense because at issue is not just the meaning of the text in a very narrow sense but more importantly its meaning in rela- tion to the meaning of readers' lives—its significance for them. Inter- pretations do not just get us to appreciate items within the world of the work, instead, they get us to engage in debates about our shared world. The world of the work is always a metaphor for the world itself, and understanding the work is a way to understand the world. Put another way, interpretations are not just about the text: they are about the world and about our lives in that world. What is really at issue in a literary debate sometimes is whether or not one should be a Buddhist.[36]

[36] Thanks to Dave Cellers, Stephen Davies, Karen Haas, Michael Krausz, Christy Mag Uidhir, and Richard Whittaker, for comments on earlier drafts of this chapter.

CHAPTER SEVENTEEN

CREATIVITY IN PHILOSOPHY AND THE ARTS

John M. Carvalho

Perhaps no other human capacity is so highly prized by us as creativity. Can there be no other explanation for this above average esteem than that creativity approaches and trades on the power of being God? It is certainly not superficial to claim that those who exercise their creative capacities and those who witness the execution of those capacities elevate themselves or feel themselves elevated above their mundanely human existence. In the presence or the thrall of creativity, we are understandably tempted to say that humans are inspired either to emulate the divine model—"How could there be gods," Friedrich Nietzsche asked, "and I not want to be one?"—or to fill the void left by the God Nietzsche said was dead with their own sense of a divine purpose. Romanticism and the cult of the genius formed a movement from this becoming present and absent of God in art. (Are they not all romantics who believe that divine omniscience, omnipotence and grace can be replaced with the genius of poetry, technique and style?) Even those we would not call romantics commonly claim nothing less for creativity than an elevation of the human spirit to divine or quasi-divine standards. The creative talent of Mozart and the elevated feeling one can have while listening to Mozart's music are the stock (if trite) evidence adduced in support of this claim, but have we no other way of accounting for what we give and what we get from creativity?

In an entry for the recently published *Oxford Handbook of Aesthetics*, Philip Alperson tries to distance this common view of human creativity from the classical conception of God divinely making something out of nothing, *ex nihilo*. He associates creativity on a human scale, instead, with making out of something, *ex non nihil*, something else that is exceptional, original, and rare. We call works of art creative, he says, if "they add something of interest to the world. That is a chief part of what distinguishes the creative from the routine, the pedestrian, the derivative, and the merely novel."[1] Creativity, Alperson tells us, adds something to the world that is not only new but meaningful, but also, he says, the realization of a distinctly human power that is the possession of distinguished human beings. What exactly this power is, he concludes, what distinguishes it from all the other distinctly human powers and traits, and how it comes to distinguish certain human beings from others, has not been satisfactorily decided. Could that be because there is still something extra-human about the power that distinguishes creative human beings from the rest of us clinging to Alperson's account? Can we not advance on this common and still romantic view that finds creativity only in what adds to our world by exceeding the routine and derivative? Can we find something creative, instead, in what subtracts the mundane and pedestrian from our experience of the world? Can we press this alternative further by considering creativity in fields other than art, fields like science, or even philosophy?

Though the subject of his handbook entry is creativity in art, some of what Alperson attributes to creativity there appears to be applicable to the conceptual and theoretical processes that characterize philosophy. The idea, for example, that creativity in art begins with the awareness of a problem, and that it proceeds through deliberation and inspiration to a concretely elaborated result, compares favorably with the way philosophers work. A philosopher might identify a problem, ruminate on some of the received wisdom on the subject, and finally elaborate, in an essay or a book, some intuition that provided its inspiration.[2] Alperson points out, however, that this general account of creativity does not appear to be equipped to capture the significant degree of originality, profundity, and insight we ordinarily associate with it. Neither does it account for the important "social, historical, and cultural context of artistic creativity."[3] For this reason, Alperson concludes his essay by worrying that a general description of creativity in art may not be forthcoming. Still, something remains to be learned from the

---

[1] Philip Alperson, "Creativity in Art," in *The Oxford Handbook of Aesthetics*, ed. Jerrold Levinson (Oxford: Oxford University Press, 2003), 245–257; quote from 246.

[2] The outline for such a view could be drawn from the work of Graham Wallas, *The Art of Thought* (London: Jonathan Cape, 1926); Catherine Patrick, "Creative Thought in Artists," *Journal of Psychology* 4 (1937): 35–73; Vincent Götz, "On Defining Creativity," *Journal of Aesthetics and Art Criticism* 39 (1981): 297–301, as interpreted by Alperson's reading of Monroe Beardsley, "On the Creation of Art," *Journal of Aesthetics and Art Criticism* 25 (1966): 159–165).

[3] Alperson, "Creativity in Art," 251.

comparison with philosophy Alperson's analysis invites. Is it possible that philosophy, by bringing to clarity an otherwise inchoate intuition, might exhibit creativity in a way that *is* sensitive to its social, historical, and cultural context even as it gratifies our desire for aesthetic delectation? Might an account of creativity in philosophy along these lines lead us back to a patently non-romantic, 'ungodly' understanding of human creativity in art?

In the following, I will explore what might make philosophy creative, and how philosophy might, with a sensitivity to its context, gratify our aesthetic sensitivity to pleasure, not by adding or isolating something rare and exceptional, but by tearing away what covers up or obscures something irregular and an exception. Comments Gilles Deleuze makes comparing creativity in philosophy and art will guide my exploration. Deleuze introduces exactly these terms—subtraction, the irregular, the exception—in the short essay, "On the Creative Act," and in his last collaborative work with Félix Guattari, *What is Philosophy?*[4] In these texts, Deleuze argues that artists think as much as they create, and philosophers create inasmuch as they think. Artists, great artists, he says, think with the images they create, while philosophers worthy of the name create concepts when they think. What it means for art to think in this way, I explore elsewhere. What it means for philosophy to create on these terms we can begin to glean from a consideration of Deleuze's claim that we create more by removing or subtracting something from our experience of the world than, as Alperson argues, by adding something of interest and lasting value to it? Is one or the other of these general accounts suited to describing creativity in both philosophy and the arts? By the end of these remarks, I hope to reconcile these apparently competing senses of creativity and arrive at a sense that fits philosophy and the arts and improves on the extant literature by clarifying what appears at first as an exotic interpretation of it.

To think of philosophy as *essentially* and not just occasionally creative is certainly exotic. If philosophy begins with wonder, as Aristotle famously says, it is generally thought to be a wondering about nature and the nature of experience. The purpose of this wondering is to learn what there is to know about nature and human nature, the truth

---

[4] Gilles Deleuze, "What is the Creative Act?" in *French Theory in America*, eds. Sylvère Lotringer and Sande Cohen (New York: Routledge, 2001), 99–107; Gilles Deleuze and Félix Guattari, *What Is Philosophy?* trans. Hugh Tomlinson and Graham Burchell (New York: Columbia University Press, 1994).

perhaps which, when philosophy does its job, we do not create or invent, but discover—because it is there in nature to be found. The conditions for the possibility of knowledge in Immanuel Kant are pure concepts of the understanding, not created by the understanding, but given there and which, by giving sense to the syntheses of the imagination, are the source of the judgments we make about nature. Yet, where would Kant be without the concept *of* an understanding that negotiates the demands of pure, *a priori* concepts and the syntheses in the imagination of the perception of a phenomenal world? Where would Kant be without a host of concepts created to make his transcendental philosophy make sense? Where would Kant be without the concept—rare, exceptional and original with Plato—of the truth of a thing embodied in a Form external to its material reality and a Form of the Good which, though it could not be known, gave the power of being known to the Forms and everything informed by Forms? Where would we be without the concept of the dialectic created by Georg Wilhelm Friedrich Hegel to show how Kant's synthetic *a priori* judgments sustain the Cartesian intuition about the *ego cogito* against the skepticism of Hume? This short inventory (which we could expand easily) suggests that philosophy at its best is creative—so far—because it adds something of lasting value to our experience and understanding of the world. Whether there is a subtractive dimension to this creativity remains to be seen.

Deleuze makes the case for the creation of concepts as the sine qua non of philosophy in an essay, a lecture really, transcribed, collected, and translated for a handbook called *French Theory in America*, where he declares:

> Philosophy is not made for reflection; it is not made to think about other things.... If philosophy exists it is because it has its own content. If we ask ourselves what the content of philosophy is it is very simple. Philosophy is a discipline equally as creative, equally as inventive as all the other disciplines. Philosophy is a discipline that consists of creating or inventing concepts. Concepts do not just exist.... Concepts must be fabricated.[5]

Deleuze, here, reprises and abbreviates the themes he articulated with Guattari in *What is Philosophy?* For Deleuze and Guattari, stupidity not ignorance is the default state of human reason. The ignorant man knows he does not know and so has already started to think, but the stupid man—perhaps also the 'wise' man—believes he knows, because

---

[5] Deleuze, *French Theory in America*, 99.

he can recite the litanies of received opinion or 'wisdom,' and so refuses to think. Truly great thinkers, Deleuze says, do not think or reflect about things. Instead, they create concepts to save themselves from slavishly repeating those litanies, that wisdom that 'everybody knows.' They invite us or inspire us to create concepts ourselves. Creativity in thought, on this way of thinking about it, is synonymous with philosophy. Creative philosophy inspires what Deleuze would like most of all to call 'thinking.'

What are we to make, then, of what Deleuze creatively tells us he thinks and inspires us to think about Hume, Kant, Spinoza, Bergson, Nietzsche, Foucault, Proust, Kafka, Carroll, and Francis Bacon (the subjects of book length studies), or about Samuel Beckett, Herman Melville, D. H. Lawrence, Pierre Klossowski, John Cage, Jean Luc Godard, and others (the subjects of 'minor' studies)? An obvious conclusion is that Deleuze finds the work of all these 'thinkers' to be creative. We can say that Deleuze finds in their work a power he describes as at once a vitalism and an opening, what he calls a 'line of flight.' This line of flight operates as a principle of selection guided by no unabashed 'yes saying' but by a discriminating subtraction and 'no saying' to everything that threatens the creative life of thought. The principle of selection subtracts everything that threatens the flight of thought into the Whole developing alongside it without which there would only be partial samples of thinking but which—because this whole is the Open—never supersedes or supplants these partial effects.[6] Deleuze insists that this openness keeps thinking (in philosophy and art) from becoming generalized, reified, or elevated (though he often speaks of philosophy and art conceptually as if they were intrinsic forces or powers realized or waiting to be realized by one or another 'conceptual persona').[7]

But what—apart from the colorful account of Deleuze's taking them from behind[8]—is especially subtractive or creative about his thinking

---

[6] For this use of the concept of the Open see Henri Bergson, *Matter and Memory*, trans. N. M. Paul and W. S. Palmer (New York: Zone Books, 1988), chap. 4; Gilles Deleuze, *Cinema 1: The Movement-Image*, trans. Hugh Tomlinson and Barbara Habberjam (Minneapolis: University of Minnesota Press, 1986), chap. 1; Gilles Deleuze, *Bergsonism*, trans. High Tomlinson and Barbara Habberjam (New York: Zone Books, 1988).

[7] For the concept conceptual persona, see Deleuze and Guattari, *What is Philosophy?* 61–84.

[8] For the concept of philosophical buggery see Gilles Deleuze, *Negotiations 1972–1990*, trans. Martin Joughin (New York: Columbia University Press, 1995), 6.

about the writers and artists he has singled out for exception in his own work? Well, following that naughty 'image of thought,'[9] we might say that he invents concepts for these writers and artists that draw out of them images or ideas we might not see or conceive otherwise. This is significant because the thinkers and artists he singles out for close scrutiny and appreciation are all especially difficult. They are difficult, on the one hand, because they cannot be easily explicated or understood. One cannot easily see or conceive what Nietzsche, Beckett, Bacon, or Godard are up to in their work. We might be tempted to think that this is just because the concept that would explicate their philosophy or art is lacking or has yet to be created. Just as soon as the concept is grasped, we suppose, their work and the creativity in it will become clear. On the other hand, these thinkers and artists are difficult in the way a child can be difficult: unruly, temperamental, with a mind of its own. Viewed this way, the philosophy or art in question defies any final conceptualization, poses problems for which there are no final solutions, and demands a full appreciation of what has been created. It also demands the creation of ever-new concepts by those who would dare to explore its implications. It dares us to 'complicate the thing' (as Marcel Duchamp said about his strategy for naming readymades) precisely to prolong and promote the life of the thought (or the thing), the art, and the creativity in it. The philosophers and artists Deleuze appreciated most all share this quality of creativity: they cannot be solved. Instead, creativity in their work poses problems that, for a philosopher like Deleuze, are just so many invitations to create concepts that preserve the life of the problems posed.

The principle of selection is one such concept created at one time to respond to the problems posed by Nietzsche's concept of the will to power. The main problem posed by the will to power is, roughly, this: how do we make sense of what Nietzsche says recurs eternally in all forms of life without making it a discreet entity of the sort that would demand a distinct ontology and without giving it a status generalizable across (if not universally present in) all the forms of life in which it eternally recurs? In *Nietzsche and Philosophy*,[10] Deleuze proposes that the

---

[9] For the concept of the image of thought see Gilles Deleuze, *Proust and Signs: The Complete Text*, trans. Richard Howard (Minneapolis: University of Minnesota Press, 2000), 94–102; Gilles Deleuze, *Difference and Repetition*, trans. Paul Patton (New York: Columbia University Press, 1994), 129–167.

[10] Gilles Deleuze, *Nietzsche and Philosophy*, trans. Hugh Tomlinson (New York: Columbia University Press, 1983).

will to power is the one force among the many disparate forces populating and competing to drive the destiny of an individual that commands those forces. The will to power commands not because it is different from those forces. The will to power commands because it *selectively shapes or plasticizes itself* to the multiple, particular condensations and displacements of energies presently cathected in consciousness. It, thereby, gives the individual direction, a selective disposition, a 'will' if you will. For the thousand and one goals of Nietzsche's *Zarathustra*,[11] the will to power is a yoke, not because it is an external force imposed on the otherwise unruly drives, but because it is the force that has selected a form for itself that gives consistency to the forces condensed and displaced around it. This will has attracted a quantum of force to itself that results in a qualitative shift in power.

This concept, the principle of selection—created to prolong the problems posed by Nietzsche with the will to power—already anticipates the concept of creativity as subtractive filtering or analogical reduction created by Deleuze to prolong and vitalize the problems posed by art. The will to power is not something new added to the life of an organism. The will to power results from a selective filtering out, a subtraction of those forces that at any moment do not contribute to the creative potential, the destiny realizable by a constellation of other forces. The concept of a principle of selection is Deleuze's creative contribution to the will to power as conceived by Nietzsche. From all of what might be made of the will to power, the principle of selection subtracts everything that might foreclose on the problems posed by it.

To account for creativity in art, Deleuze adapts and remodels this same subtractive concept. Here, the default state called stupidity in his concept of thinking is identified as cliché in his concept of the arts. Cliché in art can be described most generally as the compulsive iteration of narratives, images, sounds, and scenes we have been told, subject to, or shown repeatedly to keep us from reading, hearing, seeing, feeling, or thinking anything other than what we already read, hear, see, feel and think. Creativity in the arts gives value to painting, photography, filmmaking, composition, writing, and design by giving us something else to see, feel and think. Creativity in the arts, in this way, makes our lives worth living, while the eternal return of cliché in art threatens to take our lives away. When Nietzsche exhorted us to

---

[11] See Friedrich Nietzsche, "On the Thousand and One Goals," in *Thus Spoke Zarathustra*, trans. Walter Kaufmann (New York: Vintage, 1966), pt. 1, sec. 15.

love our fate, *amor fati*, presumably he did not also exhort us to love stupidity and cliché Perhaps we should consider that more carefully at another time.

At this time, I want to focus on painting to elaborate the significance of cliché in art, taking advantage of some things Bacon inspired Deleuze to say about creativity in the art of painting.[12] Deleuze argues that when a painter stands before a canvas for the first time, it is not empty but full, full of all the images and things that have ever been applied to canvas by the variety of institutionalized practices and techniques artists have employed and, predictably, resisted in the history of painting. Rosalind Krauss says something similar when she claims that the structural features of the canvas invariably re-inscribe the history of art in every however avant-garde painting.[13] But Deleuze's point is different. For Deleuze, the challenge the artist faces is not how to add something new and of interest and value to the canvas, the compulsion that plagued the avant-garde, but how to subtract from the canvas what does not fit its creative impulse, openness to the Whole, line of flight. The question is how the artist is to leave behind on the canvas something that is at once recognizable but not reducible to what has already gone before it—a cliché.

We see this nearly literalized in an example from Paul Cézanne, a painter Deleuze holds in high regard and to whom he favorably compares Bacon. It concerns Cézanne's *Large Bathers*, three different paintings with the same title on which he worked simultaneously from 1900 until his death in 1906. One is in London (1900–1906) and two are in Philadelphia (at the Philadelphia Museum of Art [1904–1906] and at the Barnes Foundation [1900–1906]). When Cézanne set out to paint these bathers in 1900, how many bathers were there already standing and sitting and wading and stretching and striding on those large canvases?[14] Every other painting of bathers—and the very idea of bathing—from those clothed in Georges Serat's *Bathing at Asnières*

---

[12] Gilles Deleuze, *Francis Bacon: The Logic of Sensation*, trans. Daniel W. Smith (Minneapolis: University of Minnesota Press, 2003).

[13] Rosalind Krauss, "The Originality of the Avant-Garde," in *The Originality of the Avant-Garde and Other Modernist Myths* (Cambridge, Mass.: MIT Press, 1985), 151–170. Krauss argues there that the weave of the canvas and the crossed stretcher bars that support it sign the perspective system that sustains the whole history of painting so that painting only ever repeats its history however far it tries to deviate from it.

[14] The dimensions of these paintings vary from 52" × 81" in the Barnes painting to 68" × 77", and in the London bathers, to 82" × 99" in the large bathers in the Philadelphia Museum of Art.

(1883–1884, retouched in 1887), to those half-dressed and ethereal in Claude Monet's *Dejeuner sur l'herbe* (1863), to those isolated or grouped disconsolately or distracted in Cézanne's *Bather with Outstretched Arms* (1880–1885), *Bathers at Rest* (1875–1877), *Bathers* (1890–1894), and *The Bather* (1885–1887) were all set out before him competing for his attention. What could not be taken out of this plenum if it were to remain a painting of bathers? What must be taken out to avoid repeating or trivializing what he or others had already done? How to battle the figurative and probabilistic givens that occupied and preoccupied those canvases?

In the three *Bathers* from this period, painted in relative spatial and temporal proximity to one another, constituting a definite experiment, Cézanne arrives at what Deleuze would call an analogical reduction and subtractive filtering of the bathing scene, endowing each of these three canvases with a motif and material sensibility that gives each different painting a unique clarity and duration. This process of subtraction and reduction is most visible in the Barnes Foundation *Bathers*. We see it already in the economic rendering of the physical forms, the abstraction in the limbs, the torsos, the gestures and the facial features—there are no articulated fingers or toes, eyes or mouths, the arrangement of the figures is a piece of artifice and not the rendering of their natural physical disposition—but we especially see what Deleuze calls subtraction in the distinctive outlining of the different figures in this painting. A photograph of Cézanne seated in front of the painting in 1904, so at some time before it was completed, shows how the dark lines separating the figures from one another became more pronounced in the final version, paring the figures down, removing from them everything not specific to the vision of bathers Cézanne is seeking to leave on the canvas.[15] This is taken to such an extreme in the striding figure at the far left that she is barely distinguishable as a human form. Her head is reduced to a suggestively phallic phase, and her feet are truncated by or planted in the landscape that she would otherwise be represented as traversing.

Following Deleuze, we would see in this figure (and in this painting generally) Cézanne extending himself to the point of preserving his painting from collapsing into the compulsive figuration and narrative

---

[15] The photograph is reproduced by T. J. Clark in *Farewell to an Idea: Episodes from a History of Modernism* (New Haven: Yale University Press, 1999), 148.

predictability that had caught up every other representation of bathers in a cycle of cliché. This is, perhaps, not so satisfactorily realized in the London *Bathers,* though it is still there in the abstracted and artificially arranged figures. In the *Large Bathers* in the Philadelphia Museum, however, the same effect is present in the relative absence of pigment, the unfinished effect on the surface of the bodies where the ground of the canvas shows through the flesh giving a material sensibility to those bodies whose motif is figured singly on this large canvas and generally across the three paintings taken together. Deleuze would presumably count as creativity here exactly the preservation and clarification of sensation on the canvas achieved by a subtractive technique that, at the same time, analogically extends a unity to the array of bodies filling out the scene. In his analysis of Bacon, Deleuze will call this arrangement the 'diagram.' In the language of *What is Philosophy?* this arrangement or motif is called the 'plane of consistency,' which intersects the plane of composition of a work of art to lend the work value and a sense, a meaning characterized as a line of flight toward the Open which makes the work a whole without subordinating the parts to that whole. On this view, creativity shows up in the motif Cézanne lends to the bodies in these *Bathers*, in these scenes of haute bourgeois indulgence they occupy, and in the ambiguities of painting and modern life they represent.

Bacon's paintings, it is well known, are exercised mightily by the human form. Their canvases are densely populated with bodies either isolated or working in tandem with other, otherwise isolated, bodies. Others depict bodies working together to struggle against, or hold their shape against, the competing demands of gravity, on the one hand, or what Deleuze calls a framing element on the other. Still others have a field that composes the ground against which these shapes figure without ever becoming narrative or figural. In his book on Bacon, Deleuze analyzes the specifically subtractive procedures Bacon deploys to battle the compulsive figurations that constitute the occupying force and unavoidable preoccupation of the bodies in these paintings. The specific procedures are the 'round form' corresponding to the framing element, 'meat' or what I will call 'boned flesh' corresponding to gravity and 'color' corresponding to the field. Taken together, these devices constitute a strategy that allows an image to figure on the canvas in spite of the figural demands of cliché. They sign Bacon's special creativity, a creativity Deleuze will describe as 'Egyptian' and which Deleuze will say Bacon shares with J. M. W. Turner, Monet, Vincent van Gogh and Cézanne.

The round area is the concept Deleuze creates to draw our attention to, and extend the problem addressed by, a particular framing device in Bacon's paintings. It shows up most dramatically in *Figure at a Washbasin* (1976). In this painting, the round area is defined by a parallelpiped outline that surrounds the figure as an echo of the oval of the washbasin and the circular drain into which the figure in the painting appears to be emptying his viscera. In this image, the figure becomes Figure, not a figure of anyone or anything but Figure itself, a stand-in for the figure in every image, but without becoming figural, the subject of a clichéd narrative iterated to make sense of this image. Who is this figure? Is he sick? Is she bulimic? The contortions of the body make it appear as if something more is going on here than some simple ritual of oral hygiene. But what can it be? It is precisely the isolating function of the round area that it subtracts the context in relation to which this figure might become compulsively figural, might make narrative sense. So isolated, the figure becomes a fact, an image that does not and cannot illustrate or explain his sickness or distress, her exaggerated hygienic techniques or even his isolation from any other detail either inside or outside the painting that might explain him. An extension of the modernist impulse, this figure simply is.

Boned flesh is my way of rendering the concept of meat that Deleuze deploys to account for themes literalized in Bacon's art, as in *Painting* (1946) or *Figure with Meat* (1955), and extended to the bodies of the figures that populated Bacon's canvases, as in *Painting* (1978) or the central panel of the triptych *Crucifixion* (1965). Bacon's figures have no spine, no supporting armature or structure. Instead, in Bacon's figures, Deleuze tells us "flesh and bone confront each other locally."[16] The incidental weight of the one is not dependent on the overall structure of the other. Instead, flesh hangs on bones, and the spirit that might animate the body or give it meaning has taken a bodily form, become "a corporeal and vital breath, an animal spirit."[17] This is especially evident in Bacon's portraits—of *M. Leiris* (1978), for example, or of Bacon himself in *Self-Portrait* (1976)—which image heads but not faces, meat on a bone and not fleshed out visages. Faces tell a story, illustrate an internal world constituted by the anonymous, floating narratives that penetrate everyone of us, reducing what can be reflected in that

---

[16] Deleuze, *Francis Bacon: The Logic of Sensation*, 21.
[17] Ibid., 19.

face to "one cliché among others in a world that surrounds us."[18] Bacon's portraits "dismantle the face to discover the head,"[19] the local form on which the flesh hangs.

Here, Bacon subtracts, as a butcher might, the skeleton of what would make the image an illustration of the kind of life we have heard about time and again. Bacon gives us a modulation of the human form that is, Deleuze says, decidedly analogous: a human being becomes an animal to suffer, to scream, as in Bacon's series of portraits after Diego Velázquez's *Portrait of Innocent X* (1650) such as *Head VI* (1949) and *Study after Velázquez's Portrait of Pope Innocent X* (1953). In these portraits, and in his series of *Studies from the Human Body*, Bacon images a body without organs, a deterritorialization of the body (a pope becomes a man, becomes an animal, to feel) that is the condition for its reterritorialization in a form (a scream) that cannot be narratively trivialized, a form that is, again and again, condemned to break down. This is, Deleuze thinks, an unqualified and uniquely creative achievement of Bacon's art, one that Deleuze highlights and complicates for us with a concept, meat or, as I would have it, 'boned flesh.'

There is, however, a third subtractive gesture that Deleuze will say signals the distinct triumph of Bacon's art: the logic of sensation constituted by Bacon's use of color. According to Deleuze, Bacon achieves an immediate subtractive effect in the specific tonal quality of his colors. Flat, saturated, making up a distinctly artificial palette, these are not colors that appear in nature. The yellows (*Study from the Human Body* [1986]), oranges and teal greens (*Study from the Human Body* [1970], and the reds (*Blood on the Floor* [1986]), when used to define the field for one or more figure, have a patently plastic appearance and sensibility. There is nothing to connect them to one another or to the figure apart from the equally artificial relations that can be established between them by what Deleuze calls (borrowing the term from Charles Sanders Peirce) the diagram; Bacon himself called it an armature or a graph. As Deleuze applies this concept, the diagram operates on and in the act of painting to connect and trouble the random marks, lines and traits, scrubbed and wiped local zones of color, thrown paint and framing devices that fill these canvases. The diagram is at once the operative set of these marks, zones of color and thrown paint and the frame that

---

[18] Dan Smith, "Translators Introduction," ibid., xxiii.
[19] Ibid., 19.

sets them into operation with one another. In setting these features of the act of painting together, the diagram tends toward chaos and catastrophe, but in this operation it also sustains, Deleuze says, the germ of an order or a of rhythm beat out between the diagram and its collapse. "Of all the arts," Deleuze declares, "painting is undoubtedly the only one that necessarily, 'hysterically,' integrates its own catastrophe and consequently is constituted as flight in advance." It would no doubt be more careful and correct to say (I see no way of saving Deleuze's point here) that Bacon's paintings share this tendency to integrate catastrophe with certain accomplishments in music (by John Coltrane, for example), dance (by Merce Cunningham), photography (by Mike and Doug Starn), and theater (by Beckett).

Continuing with the concept of the diagram, Deleuze says it can fail to be creative in two crucial ways, failures Bacon's art ostensibly avoids. It can fail when it becomes an optical preoccupation in the act of painting—an obsession with setting up catastrophes that consistently dissolve in satisfying, abstract rhythms (the example he gives is Piet Mondrian). It can also fail when it so overloads the surface manually as to botch the diagram and make it inoperative (the example he gives is Jackson Pollock). In the first case, Deleuze objects to the over-coding of the field of the painting, to the digital opticality of the rules governing works of this sort. Besides Mondrian, Deleuze mentions Auguste Herbin. Presumably Sol Lewitt would also fit in this category, along with others. In the second case, Deleuze objects to the subordination of the eye to the hand as in 'action painting' (retaining this quaint nomenclature) where there is a reduction to all-over sensation undeterred by any code (including the code of the easel). "Michaux" Deleuze writes, referring to the Belgian artist, journalist and poet Henri Michaux, "went further than Pollock because he remained a master of the diagram."[20] Presumably he means by this that recognizable figuration in Michaux's canvases keep them from devolving fatally into an all-over effect. We are finally, perhaps, at a point where we can discern somewhat more precisely what Deleuze counts as creativity in art.

For Deleuze, Bacon exemplifies creativity in art by refusing the lure of cliché without repressing or rejecting it. Mondrian, Wassily Kandinski, or Mark Rothko, as Deleuze would have it, repress cliché and substitute for it a hyperbolic visual or spiritual code that deprives their

---

[20] Ibid., 89.

canvases from opening onto a Whole by way of an *involuntary diagram*. Pollock, on the other hand, rejects cliché by painting all over it a diagram so proliferated that it misses the reserved, unifying impulse of consistency operating on the plane of composition of the work. The creativity in Bacon's art can be found most precisely, Deleuze says, in a haptic sensibility, a coincidence of the visual and the tactile that Alois Riegel attributed to Egyptian bas-relief sculpture where figure and ground occupy the same space or plane. According to Deleuze, Bacon accomplishes this by deploying the diagram analogically, drawing line and color into the kinds of relations, scrutable only on close inspection, which bring into relief the expressive movement and paralinguistic signs of sighs or screams. Deleuze gives the name 'aesthetic analogy' to relations established in the absence of a code that nonetheless create resemblances through non-resembling means. "A sensible resemblance is produced," Deleuze says, "but instead of being produced symbolically, through the detour of the code, it is produced 'sensually' through sensation."[21]

To return to where we started, then, if creativity in art adds something of interest to our world, it cannot, on Deleuze's account, accomplish this by merely repeating or modifying what is already a part of that world or by introducing something new that is recognizably valuable and of interest. As Deleuze would have it, we find creativity when we fabricate the conditions for a law (a diagram) to involuntarily take over a subject or a medium to such an extent that something of lasting value and meaning appears in it precisely because the impulse in that subject or medium to figuration and narrative or figural simplicity has been subtracted from it. We accomplish this without either imposing on a subject an alternative code or by stripping codes from it altogether. Creativity, on this model, sets in motion a law that takes flight involuntarily toward an openness whose horizon is a plane of consistency. In what Deleuze calls the plane of composition of the work, namely, the space and collection of materials brought together to make a work of art possible, a plane of consistency, an impulse for unity, is drawn in it and out of it by the operation of a diagram that takes over the composition and makes it whole because it opens the composition to unknown possibilities already present in it.

---

[21] Ibid., 94.

This may sound, finally and ironically, like a very modernist view of creativity in art, an echo of the romanticism, about which we warned at the start, achieved by very different means. From out of the raw materials of canvas and paint, and by an involuntary process, what Deleuze calls the diagram, art is made to appear. However, neither a valorization of the kind of novelty that modernity or romanticism prizes, nor talk of a genius, exists in this account. Moreover, nothing redeeming exists in a god who would populate the planet with creatures from the world of Bacon's paintings or Cézanne's baths. Neither can we easily imagine ourselves aspiring to emulate such divinity. The tension present in such figures does not capture the presence and absence of God but the decidedly human potential to create and to think not *ex nihilo* but from out of the materials produced and left behind by artistic, technological and ecological acts that were not themselves divinely inspired.

On this description, creativity in the arts does not add anything obviously new or interesting to the world. Instead, it strips away all the distracting, reductive, mundane, and compulsively iterated elements populating the Whole to draw the flow of art, involuntarily, toward a creation, which stands out in its singularity, in its irregularity, in its difference. While this singularity may appear new and original in our experience, it was always there but overlooked until everything that distracted us from noticing it could be subtracted from its field. We might expect that fields and flows like this exist for all the arts. More likely, though, Deleuze would have said that a flow for art exists in general and techniques specific to the different arts for extracting creatively what we call painting, literature, film and so on, are always contextualized by precisely the social, historical, and cultural circumstances of their production to which Alperson would alert us.

Having followed this Deleuzean concept of creativity this far, perhaps we can start to point in the direction of a response to some of Alperson's cautions and concerns on this score. The question of how to account for the social, historical, and cultural context of creativity would be restated or repositioned as the problem of how to subtract or filter out enough of that context to find an exception, something irregular in it that does not collapse into the everyday, into cliché. What needs to be explained is not a distinctively human power to make something meaningful and new from the available raw materials, but how and where this or that otherwise undistinguished individual connects with these and not those materials in ways that draw out something unnoticed but not unfamiliar. What we prize so highly about creativity is not the more or less divine capacity to add (whether *ex nihilo* or *ex non nihil*) something meaningful to our world but the not all-too-human connection to things that singles out of the world something rarified but not unique, something we recognize because it was already there. To the question why, if this view is correct, some creativity goes unrecognized by so many for so long, the answer would be that the things singled out in these creative acts are not yet part of what so many recognize as the world.

The same conclusions would guide an account of creativity in philosophy. For Deleuze, there is what he calls, somewhat obscurely, a 'universal thought flow,' a field or plane that carries in it everything that is being or has been philosophically or mundanely thought.[22] The idea is that, like the canvas filled with images, the space of what there is to think is already replete with everything that is being and has been thought. So long as it remains undifferentiated, so long as it lacks a direction or a sense, this flow of thought, whether "philosophical" or not, Deleuze says, is the domain of stupidity. This rather unforgiving evaluation sounds less harsh if one considers that Deleuze is attempting to specify a quality that distinguishes those figures in the history of philosophy we esteem from those we hardly notice. What is truly philosophical, what Deleuze calls thinking in philosophy, is the creation of concepts. The thinker who deserves the title 'philosopher' is the one who extracts a concept from this universal thought flow by subtracting from it everything distracting, idle, doxic, and common. The philosopher subtracts the noise, the babble, the ordinary nonsense that occupies and preoccupies this flow and draws it, toward a concept that opens onto what is locally singular, irregular and different in that flow. Wittgenstein might call such a concept patent nonsense. Deleuze would say it gives the flow a direction, a sense, a line of flight into the Open of thought. The concept so described is to philosophy what the diagram is to art.

Finally, we might ask whether creativity in philosophy so described is bound to suffer the same fate as art, condemned to create, if it wants to be thoughtful, concepts that are monsters involuntarily directed to a unifying motif that will never capture them so long as they continue

---

[22] Gilles Deleuze, "*Sur Leibniz: Cours Vincennes* 15/04/1980," in *Les Cours de Gilles Deleuze*, retrieved 22 May 2008 from http://www.webdeleuze.com.

to create. Certainly not. In the first place, the creatures in the paintings discussed above, that might be described as sired from behind, suffer only in those narratives that keep them from being born. On the canvases of Bacon and Cézanne, they thrive and exude life, as the progeny Deleuze 'fathers' enliven the thought of the figures he subjects to 'philosophical buggery.' Still, if philosophy exists only where we find creativity, and we do not force creativity on thought the way Deleuze says Mondrian and Pollock forced the diagram on art, then we will not find creative philosophy in the hermeneutic or analytic re-codification of philosophy's perennial themes. Neither will we find it in an absolute rejection or deconstruction of philosophy's abiding ideas and codes. We will find it, instead, in the playful abandon and irreverent transgressions that leave philosophy's limits intact as a measure of the creative modulations they have made in the code. The aim of creative philosophy would be to introduce not the rare but the irregular, not the unique but the singular. The lasting value of this philosophical creativity will be to become fruit forever more creative thought. "Whether you like them, these fruits of ours?" Nietzsche once asked. "But what is that to the trees! What is that to us, to us philosophers!"[23]

---

[23] Friedrich Nietzsche, *On the Genealogy of Morals*, trans. Walter Kaufmann (New York: Random House, 1967), Preface.

INDEX

Philosophy of History and Culture

ISSN 0922-6001

1. HERTZBERG, L. and J. PIETARINEN (eds.). *Perspectives on Human Conduct.* 1988. ISBN 90 04 08937 3

2. DRAY, W.H. *On History and Philosophers of History.* 1989.
ISBN 90 04 09000 2

3. ROTENSTREICH, N. *Alienation.* The Concept and its Reception. 1989. ISBN 90 04 09001 0

4. ORUKA, H.O. *Sage Philosophy.* Indigenous Thinkers and Modern Debate on African Philosophy. 1990. ISBN 90 04 09283 8

5. MERCER, R. *Deep Words.* Miura Baien's System of Natural Philosophy. 1991. ISBN 90 04 09351 6

6. Van der DUSSEN, W.J. and L. RUBINOFF (eds.). *Objectivity, Method and Point of View.* 1991. ISBN 90 04 09411 3

7. DASCAL, M. (ed.). *Cultural Relativism and Philosophy.* North and Latin American Perspectives. 1991. ISBN 90 04 09433 4

8. WHITE, F.C. *On Schopenhauer's* Fourfold Root of the Principle of SuYcient Reason. 1992. ISBN 90 04 09543 8

9. ZEMACH, E.M. *Types.* Essays in Metaphysics. 1992.
ISBN 90 04 09500 4

10. FLEISCHACKER, S. *Integrity and Moral Relativism.* 1992.
ISBN 90 04 09526 8

11. Von WRIGHT, G.H. *The Tree of Knowledge and Other Essays.* 1993.
ISBN 90 04 09764 3

12. WU, Kuang-ming. *On Chinese Body Thinking.* A Cultural Hermeneutic. 1997. ISBN 90 04 10150 0

13. ANDERSSON, G. *Criticism and the History of Science.* Kuhn's, Lakatos's and Feyerabend's Criticisms of Critical Rationalism. 1994.
ISBN 90 04 10050 4

14. VADEN HOUSE, D. *Without God or His Doubles.* Realism, Relativism and Rorty. 1994. ISBN 90 04 10062 8

15. GOLDSTEIN, L.J. *The What and the Why of History.* Philosophical Essays. 1996. ISBN 90 04 10308 2

16. BARRY, D.K. *Forms of Life and Following Rules.* A Wittgensteinian Defence of Relativism. 1996. ISBN 90 04 10540 9

17. Van DAMME, W. *Beauty in Context.* Towards an Anthropological Approach to Aesthetics. 1996. ISBN 90 04 10608 1

18. CHATTOPADHYAYA, D.P. *Sociology, Ideology and Utopia.* Socio-Political Philosophy of East and West. 1997. ISBN 90 04 10807 6
19. GUPTA, C. and D.P. CHATTOPADHYAYA (eds.). *Cultural Otherness and Beyond.* 1998. ISBN 90 04 10026 1
20. WU, Kuang-ming. *On the "Logic" of Togetherness.* A Cultural Hermeneutic. 1998. ISBN 90 04 11000 3
21. DESJARDINS, Rosemary. *Plato and the Good.* Illuminating the Darkling Vision. 2004. ISBN 90 04 13573 1
22. MOFFITT, John F. *"Inspiration": Bacchus and the Cultural History of a Creation Myth.* 2004. ISBN 90 04 14279 7
23. MOU, B. *Davidson's Philosophy and Chinese Philosophy.* Constructive Engagement. 2005. ISBN 90 04 15048 X
24. BOULTING, N.E. *On Interpretative Activity.* A Peircian Approach to the Interpretation of Science, Technology and the Arts. 2006. ISBN 978 90 04 15409 4
25. STRAYER, J. *Subjects and Objects.* Art, Essentialism, and Abstraction. 2007. ISBN 978 90 04 15714 9
26. VANHESTE, J. *Guardians of the Humanist Legacy.* The Classicism of T.S. Eliot's Criterion Network and its Relevance to our Postmodern World. 2007. ISBN 978 90 04 16160 3
27. MOU, B. (ed.). *Searle's Philosophy and Chinese Philosophy.* Constructive Engagement. 2008. ISBN 978 90 04 16809 1
28. KRAUSZ, M. and D. DUTTON and K. BARDSLEY (eds.). *The Idea of Creativity.* 2009. ISBN 978 90 04 17444 3
29. GUPTA, S. *Notions of Nationhood in Bengal.* Perspectives on Samaj, c. 1867-1905. 2009. ISBN 978 90 04 17614 0

Brill — P.O. Box 9000 — 2300 PA Leiden — The Netherlands